VICTORY OVER LIFE'S CHALLENGES

VICTORY OVER LIFE'S CHALLENGES

Winning the War Within
How to Handle Adversity
The Gift of Forgiveness

Charles Stanley

Inspirational Press • New York

Scripture Quotations

First Inspirational Press edition published in 1995.

Inspirational Press
A division of Budget Book Service, Inc.
386 Park Avenue South
New York, NY 10016

Inspirational Press is a registered trademark of Budget Book Service, Inc.

Published by arrangement with Thomas Nelson, Inc., Publishers.
Library of Congress Catalog Card Number: 94-74481
ISBN: 0-88486-113-9
Text designed by Hannah Lerner.

Printed in the United States of America.

CONTENTS

Book One

WINNING THE WAR WITHIN

*This book is dedicated
to all those who knew they shouldn't
but went ahead anyway.*

CONTENTS

Part I

Defining The Problem

Chapter 1

THE PROBLEM AT HAND

THE TERM *TEMPTATION* brings to mind different things for each of us. For some, this word conjures up a delicious hot fudge sundae with whipped cream and nuts dripping off the sides. For others, it's the man or woman who has become the focus of secret fantasies at the office. For the businessman who works under unrelenting pressure, it may be the corner bar. For the woman who long ago lost her zeal for being a wife and mother, it may be the corner drugstore where she knows she can get that prescription filled one more time. For the traveling salesman, temptation may mean the R-rated cable movies so readily available in hotels and motels today.

For the teenager, the term *temptation* may bring to mind a can of beer or a pack of cigarettes or a member of the opposite sex who has been declared off-limits by parents. It may be the uncontrollable urge to rid oneself of a meal by forced vomiting, thereby controlling calorie intake. Maybe temptation has something to do with the magazine rack at the local convenience store or the video rental library down the street.

Think for just a moment. When you hear the term *temptation*, what flashes into your mind? What pictures and emotions does it conjure up in your thinking? This is an important question as we begin our study together. In a sense, whatever comes to mind is what this book is all about. It is about you and your particular temptation(s). For some, this book is about drug addiction. For others, this book will seem to speak almost exclusively to the area of sexual temptation. What area of temptation would you like to find covered in this book? What is your greatest temptation?

I want you to choose one temptation or one area of temptation to which you can apply the principles of this book throughout our discussion. As you begin to see God giving you victory in one area, you will be motivated to apply these principles to every area in which you find yourself tempted. But for the purpose of measuring your progress, choose just one area for now.

I've Tried That!

The prospects of overcoming your greatest temptation may seem rather slim to you right now. "I've tried and failed so many times before," you might say. "Why frustrate myself all over again?"

There are several reasons why you must take up the struggle once again. First of all, a defeating habit in your life will rob you of your confidence in the power of God to give people victory over sin. Consequently, you will be hesitant to offer Christ as the answer to others who are controlled by sin. A sinful habit in your life will destroy your incentive to share your faith. You will feel like a hypocrite. And on those occasions when you do muster enough conviction to say something, you will not have the confidence you could have if you were free.

One of the immediate results of being set free from a controlling habit is the desire to share with others the power of God that has been experienced. Satan loves to keep us in bondage to sin because it greatly diminishes our potential for the kingdom of God. It diminishes our potential because we *feel* like hypocrites and we may also *look* like hypocrites if others know about our sin.

I've known several Christians who were never seriously motivated to quit smoking until they committed themselves to making an impact on their world for the Lord. One fellow commented: "Nobody will take me seriously as long as I smoke. People look at me as if to say, 'If God is so powerful, why doesn't He help you quit smoking?'" That's a valid question.

Another reason you must once again take seriously those areas of your life you have allowed to slip is that choosing not to deal with sin ultimately leads to what Scripture calls a hard heart. A hard heart develops when people hear the truth, believe the truth, but refuse to apply the truth. Developing a hard heart is a process that takes time. But each time Christians recognize sin in their lives, feel convicted, and yet do nothing about it, they become less and less sensitive to the promptings of the Holy Spirit. Finally, they reach the point where they feel no conviction at all over particular sins. They become callous, and they quench the Spirit in their lives (1 Thess. 5:19), which is a dangerous thing to do.

The Bible warns that if this process is allowed to continue, God will eventually turn people over to their sin. That is, He will in a sense say, "You want to live your way? Fine, do so, and without any interference from Me." At that point believers lose all moral and ethical direction insofar as the Holy Spirit is concerned. They are on their own. I believe this is what happened to the man described in 1 Corinthians 5 who was carrying on an incestuous relationship with seemingly no remorse whatsoever. I think the man failed to heed the instruction of the Holy Spirit, and Paul said he had been turned over to Satan. Such is the risk one runs if sin is not dealt with.

One Thing Leads to Another

Along these same lines, a third reason you must once again take up the battle against the sinful elements of your lifestyle is that one sin always leads to another. Sin is like a cancer in that it spreads. One undealt-with area opens up other areas as well. Once you become accustomed to a particular sin, once it becomes entrenched in your lifestyle, it is only a matter of time until other areas become problems. It seems like most of the counseling sessions I am involved in begin with a story about some small sin that was allowed to go undealt with. This one area opened the door for other things that soon blossomed into major problems.

I know of a teenage girl whose involvement with soap operas developed an inordinate amount of sexual curiosity in her. After numerous one-night stands and a short marriage that ended in catastrophe, she found her way to our church and told one of our pastors her story. It was unthinkable that someone with her background could ever live the way she found herself living; she was a model teenager at home, church, and school. Yet by her own admission, the afternoon soaps led her into sin that she never imagined possible.

A fine Christian man began stopping at a local bar after work to spend some time with his buddies. He had never had any desire to drink, but he figured one beer wouldn't hurt anything. He even convinced himself that by drinking one beer he would be able to relate to his friends better and maybe get an opportunity to share Christ with them. Before long, one beer became two, then three. Soon he was going home drunk, and eventually he lost his wife and kids. As he told his story to me, he said, "In my heart I knew it was wrong, but I figured every man has his vice." Did he wish he could go back and deal with his drinking problem when it was just one beer every once in a while? You bet he did. But it was too late; the damage had been done.

Sin and Death

One final reason you must take seriously even the smallest of sins is that sin always results in death of some kind. James put it this way:

But each one is tempted when he is carried away and enticed by his own lust. Then when lust has conceived, it gives birth

to sin; *and when sin is accomplished, it brings forth death.*
Do not be deceived, my beloved brethren.
—James 1:14–16, emphasis added

James gives us an equation:

Temptation + Sin = Death

Whenever there is sin, there is always death of some kind. The most obvious example would be physical death as the result of an alcohol-related automobile accident or suicide. Other sins result in physical death after a prolonged period of time. Examples would include smoking, excessive alcohol or drug consumption, and various eating disorders.

Sin results in death on another level, however, and often the problems on this level lead to destructive habits like the ones cited above. Sin brings death to relationships. Sin causes relationships to deteriorate. When a man is insensitive to his wife, he causes her to withdraw emotionally for a time. If he continues to emotionally abuse his wife in this way, he will eventually destroy every bit of affection she ever had for him. In essence, their relationship will be dead.

If a young couple in the dating stage of the relationship allows physical involvement to take priority over verbal communication, it will be only a matter of time before there is no relationship at all; it will be dead. If an employer neglects his employees, treats them unfairly, and shows no sensitivity to their needs and family responsibilities, in time he will destroy their loyalty to him and his company. If parents neglect children, that relationship will gradually disintegrate until it no longer exists. If a man fills his mind with pornographic material, he will eventually destroy any potential for intimacy between him and his wife. A father who continually ignores the traffic laws with his kids in the car destroys their respect for the law. By example they are taught, "As long as I don't get caught, there is nothing wrong with breaking the law." The teenager who takes just one drink at the prompting of his friends destroys his potential to influence them in the right direction. Sin always results in death of some sort. Something is always destroyed, whether it is respect, loyalty, or life itself.

Excuses, Excuses, Excuses

Think for just a moment. Are you allowing sin to destroy what is most important to you? Are your vices, or "weaknesses" as we sometimes call them, slowly sapping the life out of your relationships with people you love? Do you find yourself lacking the confidence you need to share your faith because of the sin in your life? Have you fallen into the habit of making excuses for sin in your life? Are you ready to allow God to change all that?

Be Realistic!

If you are like many people, you may not have taken temptation any more seriously than you have because somewhere along the way you adopted some erroneous thinking about God's attitude toward temptation. One of the most common statements people make to excuse failure in the area of temptation is this: "I'm just human, and besides, nobody's perfect." Let's take a look at that for just a minute.

There is some truth to this statement. Only God is perfect. The problem is that this statement confuses present character with potential behavior. Let me explain. When people say, "I am not perfect," they are referring to their personhood or character. They are basically saying, "Since I am not perfect internally, don't expect perfect behavior externally." But in a discussion of temptation, character is not really the issue. The issue is whether or not at a given moment in time people (in this case, believers) have the potential to *do the right thing*. God says they do. Paul wrote,

No temptation has overtaken you but such as is common to man; and God is faithful, who will not allow you to be tempted beyond what you are able, but with the temptation will provide the way of escape also, that you may be able to endure it.

—1 Corinthians 10:13

We will look at this passage later in more detail, but suffice it to say that *all* believers have the potential to say no to temptation, regardless of whether or not we are *perfect*. Pointing to character as an excuse for giving in to temptation holds no weight with God. We are all in the process of developing character, but where we are in that process has no bearing on our potential to overcome temptation. It may affect our *desire* to overcome temptation, but not our *ability*.

Are you willing to exercise your potential as a believer and say no to temptation? I hope that you started to read this book because you are willing and you want to know how to proceed.

No Relief in Sight!

Another excuse often voiced in opposition to taking temptation so seriously has to do with the nature of the struggle. It has no end. We will always be tempted, so why should we adopt a lifestyle of continual struggle? Why not just accept certain things as a part of life and not worry about them? The first part of this chapter addresses this excuse to some degree, but this question is important because it brings to light the issues of time and tension. To rephrase the question, since temptation will continue to harass us regardless of how many times we successfully combat it, is it really worth the continual struggle? Absolutely!

Oftentimes we forget that in the process of struggling with sin—in both our victories and our defeats—God is at work. Through the trials of temptation He develops in us patience, endurance, sensitivity to others, and most of all a sense of moment by moment trust in the sufficiency of Christ. On this subject James wrote,

Consider it all joy, my brethren, when you encounter various trials, knowing that the testing of your faith produces endurance. And let endurance have its perfect result, that you may be perfect, lacking in nothing.

—James 1:2–4

The apostle Paul understood the value of unrelenting trials in regard to developing dependence on Christ's strength in him. He wrote,

And He [Christ] has said to me, "My grace is sufficient for you, for power is perfected in weakness." Most gladly, therefore, I will rather boast about my weaknesses, that the power of Christ may dwell in me. Therefore I am well content with weaknesses, with insults, with distresses, with persecutions, with difficulties, for Christ's sake; for when I am weak, then I am strong.

—2 Corinthians 12:9–10

The awful, never-ending process of combating temptation is God's means of maturing us and conforming us to the image of Christ. To throw our hands up in defeat is to abandon the process and to miss out on life's most important lessons. To grow is to be tempted. We can't have one without the other.

In the mountains of northern Georgia there is a white water river called the Chattooga. People travel from all over the Southeast to paddle down this river. The last two sections are especially treacherous, and many people have drowned as their canoes broke up on the rocks and they were sucked helplessly under by the powerful current. I want you to imagine a skilled paddler in his kayak making his way through the rocks and hydraulics of the Chattooga River. As he maneuvers himself along, something is taking place that onlookers may not be aware of. The potentially destructive force of the river is actually helping the paddler develop his balance, coordination, strength, and concentration.

But imagine that as the paddler approaches the next set of rapids, he thinks to himself, *I'm tired of paddling. This is getting old. My arms hurt. My legs hurt. I'm tired of concentrating.* With that he tosses his paddle into the water and lets the river take control. You can guess what will happen. But here's the point. The force that at one point was aiding in the development of his skill and strength has the potential to destroy him once he refuses to struggle against it.

So it is with the power of sin. As long as we take a stand against temptation, even if we fall momentarily, God will use the struggle to make us into the men and women He wants us to be. But once we throw in the paddle, once we give up and allow the forces of sin to dictate our behavior, it will be only a matter of time until we are swept away and our lives destroyed.

You may be thinking, *That sounds so extreme. My particular problem is not nearly as serious as the ones you must be alluding to.* You may be right. And you are wise to take what seems like a little temptation and deal with it instead of allowing it to take root in your life. But I speak in what may seem like extreme terms because week after week I sit in my office and hear stories of how "little" habits turned into bigger ones. I hear stories of how lives, marriages, businesses, and homes were destroyed because somebody decided that a particular temptation was really not that big a deal and was certainly no cause for alarm. Remember, every *big* habit had a *small* beginning. We don't know the damaging potential of even the smallest sin. And if we wait until things get really bad to deal with them, oftentimes we lose our desire to deal with them at all.

Starting Over

Are you ready to get back on the cutting edge? Are you ready to experience the power of God in your life once again? Then you must be willing to get involved again in the process of working with God to gain consistent victory over temptation. It will not necessarily be easy or instant. There are no magic prayers to say or buttons to push. There is, however, a loving, powerful, heavenly Father who has provided the "way of escape" if you are ready to take advantage of it. It is my prayer that you are ready indeed.

Chapter 2

A TALE
OF TWO KINGDOMS

IN THE FIELD of education the "law of integrality" states that learning tends to be more effective when what we learn is related to other areas of our experience. In other words, it is easier to learn something that is clearly related to the world around us than something that seems to exist in isolation from the things touching our lives. I believe that this law kept me from learning geometry. Somehow geometry never related to anything outside the four walls of the classroom. Consequently, my motivation level remained very low—as did my grades!

As we begin a study on temptation, the law of integrality demands that we have a clear understanding of how our individual struggles with temptation relate to the broader scheme of things. It may come as a surprise to you that there is a broader context. When temptation comes, if you are like me, you probably feel very much alone and abandoned. With those feelings comes the feeling that it really doesn't matter what you do anyway; nobody will know, and nobody will care. In fact, what you do always matters. Second, you never struggle alone. Our heavenly Father takes very seriously every victory or defeat in the life of a believer. As we will see in this chapter, every battle, every defeat, and every victory is part of a broader struggle that began long before you or

I came on the scene and will continue long after we are gone—
should Jesus tarry.

Creation from Chaos

> In the beginning God created the heavens and the earth. *And*
> *the earth was formless and void, and darkness was over the*
> *surface of the deep;* and the Spirit of God was moving over
> the surface of the waters. Then God said, "Let there be light."
> —Genesis 1:1–3, *emphasis added*

The creation account as we have it in Genesis is a description
of God's bringing order out of disorder, creation from chaos. Some
people see a time gap between verses 1 and 2 and argue that Satan
was cast from heaven during that time, thus bringing the world
into a state of chaos. Now I don't want to get involved in that
argument here. Regardless of whether or not there was a gap, one
thing is for sure. The earth "was" formless, and God gave it form;
the world "was" in darkness, and God brought forth light. This
pattern follows throughout the creation narrative. He brought
order to the water resulting in a separation between the oceans
and the sky. He brought order to the oceans and created dry land.

He then brought order to the land by creating plants, each yielding seeds and bearing fruit after its own kind. Then God brought
order to the heavens by separating the night from the day. This
brought about the seasons and thus a tool for measuring time.

Next God created the different animals. They were perfectly
suited for the environment in which they were placed: the fish
for the sea, the birds for the air, and the mammals for the land.
Like the plants, each brought forth its own kind.

God completed His order by creating man. Unlike the rest of
the creation, man had a special role to fulfill. He was to rule over
all God had created.

> Then God said, "Let Us make man in Our image, according
> to Our likeness; and let them rule over the fish of the sea
> and over the birds of the sky and over the cattle and over all

the earth, and over every creeping thing that creeps on the earth."

—Genesis 1:26

God told man to

"rule over the fish of the sea and over the birds of the sky and over every living thing that moves on the earth." Then God said, "Behold, I have given you every plant yielding seed that is on the surface of all the earth, and every tree which has fruit yielding seed; it shall be food for you; and to every beast of the earth and to every bird of the sky and to every thing that moves on the earth which has life, I have given every green plant for food"; and it was so.

—Genesis 1:28–30

Man was to be God's representative on the earth. In a sense, God had delegated the responsibility of the whole earth to man; he was to rule over God's creation. This was all a part of God's ordering process.

To ensure that man was equipped for the job, God gave man some special qualities. These are summed up in the declaration: "Then God said, 'Let Us make man *in Our image, according to Our likeness.*'" Much has been written on what it means to be created in God's image. Some things, however, stand out as particularly important when we think about the awesome responsibility of ruling the whole earth. First of all, the image of God implies personality. That is, man, unlike any other part of creation, shares with God an intellect, a will, and emotions. Thus, he has the ability to reason and make decisions—a necessary quality for ruling. This ability also means that man can love, obey, and even disobey.

A Unique Relationship

Second, man's being created in the image of God means that he had a unique relationship with God. Man was and is God's prize creation. Man has the greatest potential of all creation to reflect the nature and character of the Creator. That man was God's favorite is clearly seen in God's special provision for man. God provided a special garden (Gen. 2:8–9). When He saw man was lonely, He created a special counterpart (2:18). He desired man's loyalty and obedience (2:16–17). He desired to communicate with man (3:8). All these things point toward the unique relationship man had with God. It was different from God's relationship with any of His other creations.

Man's Godlike personality and his special relationship with his Creator equipped man to fulfill his role as ruler and representative on the earth. Thus, God's original plan was to rule the earth through man and his helpmate as they exercised their free wills in obedience to and dependence upon Him. This was God's way of maintaining order on the earth.

Back to Chaos

As you know, things did not continue as God had originally planned—humanly speaking that is. Sin entered the world through Adam and Eve, and the whole creation was sent into a tailspin, both morally and physically. You may be wondering at this point what any of this has to do with temptation. The answer to that is found in the answers to some questions you may never have thought about: Why did Satan go to the trouble to tempt Adam and Eve to begin with? What was the point? What did he have to gain?

The prophets Isaiah and Ezekiel give us brief descriptions of a cosmic war that took place sometime before the ordering of the world. According to their accounts, Satan at one time held a very high position in the kingdom of heaven. Ezekiel writes of him,

> You were the anointed cherub who covers,
> And I placed you there.
> You were on the holy mountain of God.
> —Ezekiel 28:14

Satan became filled with pride, however, and decided he should be God. Isaiah writes,

> But you said in your heart,
> "I will ascend to heaven;
> I will raise my throne above the stars of God,
> And I will sit on the mount of assembly
> In the recesses of the north.
> I will ascend above the heights of the clouds;
> I will make myself like the Most High."
> —Isaiah 14:13–14

What ensued was a battle resulting in Satan's being cast out of heaven along with those angels that chose to side with him. Ezekiel writes,

> By the abundance of your trade
> You were internally filled with violence,
> And you sinned;
> Therefore I have cast you as profane
> From the mountain of God.
> And I have destroyed you, O covering cherub,
> From the midst of the stones of fire. . . .
> I cast you to the ground
> —Ezekiel 28:16–17

Satan's rather swift exit from heaven was a sign of ultimate defeat and humiliation for him. He had been defeated, and he knew once and for all that a direct attack against almighty God was a futile attempt. Think for a moment. If Satan could not defeat God, what would be the next best thing?

Satan went right to the top of God's order of authority—man. To defeat man would be to defeat all of God's creation on this earth, for it had been put under man's authority. Satan's attack on mankind was simply his way of striking back at God. His intent was to reverse God's process and return the world to a state of disorder and chaos. History is in one sense a record of how successful Satan has been. Man has suffered and so has everything under his authority. God cursed the ground (Gen. 3:17), and since that day, all of creation has suffered. Paul said,

> For the anxious longing of the creation waits eagerly for the revealing of the sons of God. For the creation was subjected to futility, not of its own will, but because of Him who subjected it, in hope that the creation itself also will be set free from its slavery to corruption into the freedom of the glory of the children of God. For we know that the whole creation groans and suffers the pains of childbirth together until now.
> —Romans 8:19–22

The Agent of Decay

Sin is an agent of decay. Once sin is introduced into anything—a relationship, a community, or an individual—order and productivity begin to diminish. The term *decay* means "to pass gradually from a sound or perfect state to one of unsoundness and imperfection." Such is the nature of sin. Satan's goal was to undo what God had done. The introduction of sin or evil accomplished just that. Man's first sin was all it took to begin a chain reaction that sent shock waves throughout creation.

Evil is not a thing; it is a lack in a thing. Evil is a lack of perfection. God's creation was perfect. Thus, He was able to say about it: "And it was good." Evil was and is Satan's tool to chip away at God's order and perfection. Evil reverses everything God set out to accomplish.

The Moral Avalanche

An in-depth historical survey of the worldwide consequences of sin is certainly beyond the scope of this book. What I want you to see, however, is how the introduction of sin caused God's order to crumble. First God's order of authority was broken down. No longer could He trust man to submit to His leadership. Man had made himself a god, and he sought to control his own destiny. Along the same lines, the order of family authority changed. Now the man would rule over the woman (Gen. 3:16). The tone of this verse seems to indicate that such an arrangement was not in God's original plan for men and women. But God knew that sin would result in conflict between men and women, and some provision had to be made to cope with that problem. So He made one the head over the other.

As time has passed, we have seen numerous illustrations of the perpetual slide from order to disorder, from creation, as God meant it, to chaos. Everything from the extinction of certain animals to the abuse of the land and its resources speaks of this downward spiral. The escalation of the occurrence of abortion is another illustration of Satan's attempts to reverse God's plan. Whereas God told Noah and his family to populate the earth (Gen. 9: 1), abortionists seek to do just the opposite.

The acceptance of homosexuality and the increasing incidence of people caught up in the homosexual lifestyle are also examples of how Satan is seeking to reverse God's order and return things to a chaotic state. A homosexual lifestyle is the exact opposite of what God prescribed in the Garden of Eden (Gen. 2:24). The feminist movement seeks to reverse the roles of men and women in the home. Now feminists are advocating having children out of wedlock. That way they can fulfill their maternal instincts without sacrificing their independence. One feminist said on the news recently, "Women need to be freed from the constraints of family life while at the same time given the opportunity for motherhood. Society has held us captive too long with its narrow interpretation of what motherhood is all about." So they find a friend who agrees to make no claim on the baby, and they go to bed together.

Every day the news is filled with illustrations of how the world is seeking to undo all God designed for both society and family. Behind all of this is Satan. In setting this world on a collision course with disaster, he strikes back the best he can at almighty God.

God's Reaction

Fortunately, God has not just been sitting back watching what's been happening. After Adam and Eve ruined things, God decided to wipe everything out and start over.

> Then the LORD saw that the wickedness of man was great on the earth, and that every intent of the thoughts of his heart was only evil continually. . . . And the LORD said, "I will blot out man whom I have created from the face of the land, from man to animals to creeping things and to birds of the sky; for I am sorry that I have made them."
>
> —Genesis 6:5–7

But the next verse explains why God did not destroy the whole earth and why He had to come up with another plan.

> But Noah found favor in the eyes of the LORD.
>
> —Genesis 6:8

God decided to spare the human race. He was determined, however, not to leave things in the chaotic state they were in. His ultimate goal was to restore man and his world to its original state. But there was still the problem of sin and the curse it brought upon all creation. What resulted was a two-part plan by which sin and its consequences could be dealt with once and for all.

Brand-New People

First of all, God tackled the problem of His relationship with man. Sin had put a barrier between man and God. Until it was removed, the two could never come together as they had in Eden. In sending Christ to die for man's sin, God dealt with the problem of personal sin. Through Christ, men and women have the opportunity to deal with both the penalty and the power of sin in their lives. Before individuals put their trust in Christ, a constant decaying process is taking place; after they trust Christ, a new process goes into effect. The cycle of sin is broken, and a renewing process begins. God reverses the chaotic cycle of sin. Paul was speaking of this reversal when he said,

> Therefore we do not lose heart, but though our outer man is decaying, yet our inner man is being renewed day by day.
> —2 Corinthians 4:16

God has re-created us on the inside. We become brand-new creatures when we are saved. Although our physical bodies continue to decay, our inner man—our eternal aspect—is getting stronger and more sensitive to God. That is why we use the term *born again.* This renewal process makes it possible for you and me to rise above our circumstances and live godly lives in the midst of this ungodly society. This inner renewal enables us to overcome even the strongest temptations—as we shall see later on. When we put our trust in Christ, God won a decisive victory over Satan, for He permanently reclaimed us as His own and He restored order to disordered and chaotic lives.

A Brand-New Place

Making men new was only the beginning. Remember that all creation suffered when Adam fell. In order to gain final victory over Satan, God had to redeem nature as well. By nature, I am referring to the physical world. This part of His plan has not been accomplished. The world as we see it today is still in a state of decay. Tornadoes still rip through trailer parks, and people still catch diseases and die. God's victory is not complete until all kinds of evil in the world are vanquished.

In the book of Revelation the apostle John describes what part two of God's plan will be like. The book of Revelation is God's promise to men that He will complete what He has begun in Christ. One day the world will be restored, and evil will be banished completely from the scene. Order will be restored. Creation will be as it was intended to be. John writes,

> And I saw a new heaven and a new earth; for the first heaven and the first earth passed away, and there is no longer any sea. And I saw the holy city, new Jerusalem, coming down out of heaven from God, made ready as a bride adorned for her husband. And I heard a loud voice from the throne, saying, "Behold, the tabernacle of God is among men, and He shall dwell among them, and they shall be His people, and God Himself shall be among them, and He shall wipe away every tear from their eyes; and there shall no longer be any death; there shall no longer be any mourning, or crying, or pain; the first things have passed away." And He who sits on the throne said, "Behold, I am making all things new." And He said, "Write, for these words are faithful and true."
> —Revelation 21:1–5

In the Meantime

By this time you may be thinking that this is really a Bible survey. Not so! I've taken you through this seemingly long discussion to make a simple point. A point that serves as the context for the rest of the book—and the rest of your life, I might add.

Simply put, the point is that *you do not struggle with temptation in a vacuum.* Every temptation you encounter is Satan's way of striking out against God. By attempting to introduce into your life disorder and chaos, Satan continues his work of undoing all God sought to accomplish in the beginning. On the other hand, every victory you experience is a testimony to both Satan and the world that God is at work restoring things to their original state, a state in which Satan has no place or power.

As a Christian, you are called to be God's delegate to a lost world. Your message is that God is in the world reconciling men to Himself and that one day He will return to rule and reign forever. This is the last thing Satan wants anyone to hear. Therefore, your Christianity sets you up to be a primary candidate for attack. Satan knows that if he can get you caught up in some sin—however small it may be—you are sidelined as far as the kingdom of God is concerned. Not only that, you become a feather in his hat, so to speak. Every victory Satan has over you is a victory over the advancement of God's kingdom.

Another reason I felt compelled to begin our discussion of temptation in this way is that it establishes a whole new perspective on spiritual warfare. I will be the first to admit that I have a great deal to learn about this somewhat mystical subject. But one thing I do know is that every temptation is part of a larger struggle. Another thing I know for sure is that I have a difficult time remembering this fact.

When I am being tempted with the little things that pop up every day, I tend to think that it is just my little problem and that no one else will be affected. I forget that I am an ambassador for Christ and that every victory—no matter how small—is a sign to the "spiritual forces" that Jesus is alive and working. Each victory reminds Satan that the same power that gives me victory over sin will one day give our King victory over all His enemies!

Paul could not have been any more clear about this than when he wrote,

> For our struggle is not against flesh and blood, but against the rulers, against the powers, against the world forces of this darkness, against the spiritual forces of wickedness in the heavenly places.
>
> —Ephesians 6:12

He did not qualify which struggles. He did not distinguish between the big ones and the little ones; the struggles of the mind versus the struggles within relationships; the struggles of the well-knowns versus the struggles of the unknowns. All our struggles are spiritual in nature. Each one is a part of an ongoing struggle between the kingdom of God and the kingdom of Satan. As we begin to look at the specifics of temptation, it is imperative that we keep this simple truth in mind: we do not struggle in a vacuum; every temptation is a small part of a universal struggle between the kingdom of darkness and the kingdom of the living God.

Chapter 3

WHO'S TO BLAME?

T HE OTHER DAY I saw a bumper sticker that read,

> LEAD ME NOT INTO TEMPTATION,
> I CAN FIND IT MYSELF.

Initially we would all shake our heads in agreement. Temptation seems to be lurking everywhere; we certainly don't have to look for it. Implied in this humorous statement, however, is the idea that we are ultimately responsible for the things with which we are tempted. That is, we don't need any assistance when it comes to being tempted. Interpreting the statement in that light, we may find ourselves thinking twice about its accuracy. We don't like to take complete responsibility for our temptations. It is much easier to blame someone or something else. Yet this tendency keeps many of us from dealing successfully with the besetting sins in our lives.

Alcoholics are classic examples. People with drinking problems have well-rehearsed stories about why they have problems with alcohol. Stories range from family problems to difficulties at work to broken relationships. Regardless of the particulars of the stories, the conclusion is that their problems are really somebody else's fault; if certain people or circumstances would change, then they could straighten up, but not until then. The sad result is that by blaming somebody else for their problems, they never get themselves in a position to change. They short-circuit the whole process.

So What's New?

Passing the buck in regard to temptation is certainly nothing new. It started with the line:

> The woman whom Thou gavest to be with me, she gave me from the tree, and I ate.
>
> —Genesis 3:12

The very first time man was confronted by God about his sin, he blamed it on someone else—his wife! Apparently this tendency ran in the first family because Eve responded the same way when she was confronted:

> The serpent deceived me, and I ate.
>
> —Genesis 3:13

But blaming someone or something else did not work in the beginning, and it will not work now! Even though it was true that the woman did give the fruit to Adam and the serpent did deceive Eve, God held them accountable for their actions and threw them out of the garden.

> Therefore the LORD God sent him out from the garden of Eden, to cultivate the ground from which he was taken. So He drove the man out.
>
> —Genesis 3:23–24

Blaming someone or something else for your particular weaknesses and temptations appears to take the responsibility off your shoulders. But by mentally removing yourself from a position of responsibility, you also remove yourself from a position wherein you could correct the situation. *Until you are willing to take responsibility for your failures, you will be unwilling and therefore unable to do anything about them.* That being the case, if you do not deal with this issue now, the rest of this book—or any book dealing with temptation for that matter—will be a waste of time. In this chapter we will take a close look at what I find to be the most common ways people try to shift the responsibility of temptation.

But That's Just the Way I Am

Many people blame their personality for their inability to deal successfully with particular temptations. They say, "That's just the way I am," or "I've always been this way." I hear this a good deal from men who have a problem controlling their temper: "Ever since I was a kid I've had a hot temper." The implication is that "I have always been this way, and I always will be. There is no use in my trying to change." Often accompanying this way of thinking is a plea to "accept me the way I am."

But the distraught wife and kids have tried accepting him the way he is, and somehow they still find themselves running for cover when Dad gets upset. Accepting him the way he is does not soothe their hurt feelings when they catch the brunt of his caustic language. Not only that, God considers slander, wrath, malice, and abusive speech to be sin (Col. 3:8). God does not excuse his behavior, and no one else should have to, either.

Another unacceptable behavior that often gets excused as part of someone's personality is the habit of closing up and refusing to talk when there is tension or conflict. You may say, "What has that got to do with temptation?" Simply this, becoming non-communicative under pressure is an inappropriate outward response to one's feelings. It is the same as lying when one *feels* threatened or cursing when one *feels* angry. We don't usually associate closing up with giving in to temptation, but that is exactly what it is. It is a bad habit. And as with many such habits, it is usually defended as part of one's personality: "That's the way I always handle pressure."

Although such behavior may appear to be deeply ingrained into one's personality, it must be changed. I talk to adults all the time who trace the root of their problems back to a parent who would not communicate. The rebellion of a great many teenagers is simply a ploy to gain their father's attention, to force him out of his shell. A noncommunicative parent has the potential to destroy the self-esteem of kids. Therefore, the behavior is a sin and must be corrected. To correct it, however, a person must stop using personality as an excuse.

I'm dealing right now with a teenager who has an extremely difficult time communicating. He has a high IQ and is very talented, both musically and athletically. He and I have concluded that most of his problem stems from his inability to communicate with his dad—the one person he desires most to communicate with. His dad's response to all this is, "I don't like to talk much; that's how I was raised; that's just the way I am." I believe God will eventually deliver this teenager from his difficulty with communication. He will overcome his problem in spite of his father's unwillingness to deal with his own sin. "Sin?" you say. "You mean not communicating is sin?" If it keeps a person from fulfilling a God-given responsibility as a parent or an employee, it certainly is. The great thing is that once someone sees it for what it is and quits excusing it, God can set the individual free!

Can you remember hearing yourself say, "That's just the way I am"? Do you expect people to accept and adjust to your peculiarities? Have you been using your personality as an excuse for the way you are rather than trying to change? If you have, it is time to quit making excuses and begin making progress. To do otherwise is to rob yourself and others of the joy that comes with the freedom of putting bad habits behind you.

It's Everywhere

Another excuse people use is that of circumstances or environment. "If it wasn't for the people I work with, I wouldn't have this problem." "If I didn't have all the pressure at home, I am sure I could change." "It's not my fault. My friends make me do it."

More and more singles are using their singleness as an excuse for engaging in premarital sex. "I'm thirty, and it's not natural for someone my age to be celibate. If I had a spouse, I wouldn't have this problem." And so like many people, they use their circumstances as an excuse. "If only my circumstances were different."

BART

I was talking to a single man in our church about smoking. For illustration's sake, I'll call him Bart. He believed smoking was a sin. He knew it was ruining his testimony as well as his health. He even quit for a short time. In our conversation he admitted, however, that he had given up hope of ever quitting because all his friends smoke. "I can't quit unless they do," he said, "and I know they aren't about to give it up."

Without really saying it, Bart was blaming his smoking habit on his friends. He put his destiny in their hands insofar as smoking was concerned. In essence he was saying, "Until my surroundings change, don't expect me to change." Granted smoking carries with it other considerations when it comes to temptation, but Bart never even got far enough to deal with those. He was content to blame his habit on his friends.

You may respond to Bart's situation by saying, "He just needs some new friends." Though that may be true, Bart needed more than new friends. Like many people, he needed to quit blaming his problems on his associates. Bart's problem wasn't really his friends; it was his unwillingness to take responsibility for his problem. Until a person is willing to do that, he can change friends, jobs, or families and still end up being molded and controlled by his environment.

To put the blame for your habits on your circumstances is to allow someone or something to control your destiny in that particular area. You have handed the direction of your life over to an entity you cannot change and thus cannot control. Certainly, there comes a time to change jobs or friends or whatever is contributing to your problem. But first you must come to grips with the fact that *you* are responsible for your behavior.

All in the Family

A third excuse people are tempted to use is the family. "If you knew the kind of family I grew up in, you would understand why I'm this way." "If you had known my mom, you would know why I act the way I do." "My dad always told me that a real man never . . . and so l cannot . . . to this day."

It seems that I am running into more and more Christians who have been to a counselor or have read books on counseling and now have some understanding of the impact parents make on children and how that can affect them as adults. Consequently, an increasing number of believers have good insight into why they act and react the way they do in given circumstances and relationships. Gaining this insight into the past can be a positive step in correcting problem behavior when it is acted upon. Unfortunately, it seems that some people use this insight as an excuse rather than a tool to aid in the process of change. They shift the responsibility for their sins from themselves to their parents. "If my parents hadn't treated me the way they did, I wouldn't have these problems."

TINA THE TALKER

Tina was just that sort of girl. She knew as much or more about counseling than I did. When she came to see me, she gave me a detailed description of her childhood; she followed that with an amazing analysis of how her childhood had affected her as an adult. She was able to relate every single thing she was dealing with at that time back to an event or series of events from her childhood and adolescence. I can remember thinking, *We need to hire this girl.* As she talked, I began wondering why she had even made an appointment for counseling. She seemed to understand everything going on inside and around her.

Then I questioned her about what positive steps she had taken to correct her problem. She would evade my questions and explain all over again scenes from her childhood and how they had scarred her as an adult. Soon I realized that Tina did not want help; she just wanted to talk. She had grown somewhat comfortable with her sin. When it really started to bother her, she would find someone to talk to, and that helped to ease the guilt for a time.

I met with Tina several times before explaining to her that her problem was not her parents. It was her unwillingness to take responsibility for her own actions. As I sit here writing tonight, Tina is still bouncing around from counselor to counselor, friend to friend, telling the story she has told so many times— a story that I have discovered is true and could very well be the root of her problems. Yet the story has become an alibi and thus an excuse to allow in Tina's life a habit that will ultimately destroy her.

LET IT GO

Having been raised in a family situation that was far from ideal, I know the weaknesses and propensity for sin that can be woven into the fabric of a personality from childhood. I understand the temptation to look to the past as an excuse to allow sin to go undealt with. After what I had been through, it did not seem fair to expect me to change.

But I also know the pain and frustration that such irresponsibility causes to one's family. So there came a time in my own life when I had to leave the past behind and deal with things as they were. It was difficult. Yet it was only after I took responsibility for my actions that I was able to change them. Until that time any effort to improve was only a halfhearted attempt; *really* changing seemed like an unrealistic goal. By the grace of God, however, things did change.

My friend, things can change for you, too. But you must let go of the past. You must be willing to see sin for what it is and then prepare to deal with it. As long as you hold on to your well-rehearsed excuses, things will stay the same. Your parents may have intentionally or unintentionally set you up for the problems you are facing today. However, *you* are the one responsible before God to deal with the things in your life that need to change.

The Devil Made Me Do It

It may have been Flip Wilson who most recently popularized the phrase "the devil made me do it," but this excuse has been around since the beginning. Since we know Satan has something to do with the temptation process, it makes sense that he would be the one to blame. But we need to be aware that the devil cannot *make* us do anything. The Bible says Satan is a deceiver (Gen. 3: 13; 2 Cor. 11:3; Rev. 18:23). Jesus called him the "father of lies" (John 8:44). Satan's only power over people is through manipulation and deceit. If he could actually *make* us do things, he wouldn't need to go to all the trouble of deceiving us. When he dangles the right bait in front of us at the right time, we become so tuned in to our fleshly desires that we feel as if something is drawing us toward sin; but it is not a power that literally controls us. In each case we choose to disobey. If Satan could make us sin, the temptation process would be unnecessary.

Think of it this way. Imagine yourself standing at the edge of a cliff that drops off into a deep rocky gorge. Now suppose I walked up to you and said, "We have kidnapped a member of your family. If you refuse to jump, your relative will be brutally beaten and then killed." Have I made you jump? If you believed my story and you believed by jumping you could save your family member, I may have made you *willing* to jump or even *anxious* to jump. But I have not *made* you jump. Even if you jumped and you found out on the way to the bottom that I had lied about the whole thing, I still did not *make* you jump. I simply tricked you into jumping. On the other hand, if I walked up behind you and pushed you off, then I made you do something contrary to what you wanted to do, felt like doing, or even thought about doing.

Now think about the last time you were tempted to sin. Did you suddenly discover that you were sinning or had sinned? Were you in the process before you ever thought about it? Or did it begin with a thought; then a feeling; then maybe a little struggle; then the actual sin? Nobody held Eve down and forced the fruit down her throat; and no one holds you down and forces you to sin, either. Later on we will deal more fully with the devil's role in the temptation process. For now, suffice it to say that he cannot *make* you do anything.

"Lord, How Could You?"

Many believers, some intentionally and some unintentionally, blame God for temptations. In actuality, you are ultimately blaming God when you blame anything or anybody for your weakness in a particular area. God allowed you to be born into your family. He allowed you to meet the group that keeps getting you into trouble. He allowed you to meet that individual you finally became involved with. He knew what kind of personality you would have. If you thought about your sin long enough, you could find a way to pin the blame on God.

But Scripture is clear that God is not the cause of your temptation. James writes,

Let no one say when he is tempted, "I am being tempted by God"; for God cannot be tempted by evil, and He Himself does not tempt anyone.

—James 1:13

Although James states that God does not tempt anyone, he does not clear up the mystery of why a good God would allow things that lead to our being tempted when He certainly has the power to stop them. This question leads to the whole issue of God and evil. Without getting off onto a completely different discussion, suffice it to say that our good God originally created a perfectly good world. In that perfectly good world were human beings who were given the wonderful gift of choice, and they used that gift as we discussed earlier.

When Adam and Eve made a wrong choice, they made evil a reality. It was always a possibility since they were able to make choices for themselves, but they made it real insofar as human beings are concerned. God is working toward reestablishing a perfect creation once again. In the meantime we live in an imperfect world surrounded by people who continue to abuse the gift of choice. God is not to blame; man is. So each of us is to blame for our own unwillingness and at times inability to withstand temptation.

They Had Every Excuse in the World

The Bible offers two major arguments against our being able to pass the buck in regard to temptation. The first is by illustration. Adam and Eve tried to blame their failures on someone else. Each of them had what appeared to be a legitimate excuse. The serpent really did trick Eve, and Eve really did give the fruit to Adam. How was Eve supposed to know the serpent was lying? She had never heard a lie before. How was Adam supposed to know he could not trust Eve? She had never proved untrustworthy in the past. Besides that, if God had not allowed the serpent to tempt Eve in the first place, she never would have sinned. Maybe it was God's fault after all. Adam seemed to think so. He said, "The woman *whom Thou gavest* to be with me, she gave me from the tree, and I ate" (Gen. 3:12). It's as if he was saying, "God, if You hadn't given me this 'helpmate,' I wouldn't be in this predicament!"

I can remember reading this story and thinking, *Come on, God. Give them one more chance.* I mean, it hardly seems fair that two people who did not know the first thing about deceit or sin or death should be held accountable for such a seemingly small thing. Yet God did hold them accountable, and He threw them out of the garden.

No Place to Run

A second argument for each of us being personally accountable for our inability to resist temptation is found in biblical passages dealing with the judgment. The apostle Paul wrote,

> Therefore also we have as our ambition, whether at home or absent, to be pleasing to Him. For we must all appear before the judgment seat of Christ, that each one may be recompensed for his deeds in the body, according to what he has done, whether good or bad.
>
> —2 Corinthians 5:9–10

According to this passage, Paul's motivation for pleasing God was the knowledge that he would eventually have to stand before Him and give an account of his life. Notice what he said he would have to give an account for: "His *deeds* in the body, according to what he has *done*." Each of us will be "recompensed" or paid back by God for what we *do* in this life. This is not simply a matter of being rewarded for the good things we do. Paul was clear that in the judgment God will give attention to the bad things as well: "According to what he has done, whether *good* or *bad*."

I wouldn't be honest if I told you I completely understand all that Paul was saying in those verses. What is unavoidably clear, however, is that God is going to hold us accountable for what we do—both right and wrong. Paul wasn't counting on being able to excuse his shortcomings because of his tough childhood, his various persecutions, his long nights alone at sea, or his tireless work for God's kingdom. He was expecting to meet God head-on with no place to run and no alibis to try to absolve himself. You and I can expect the same. The Bible makes that very plain.

Who's to Blame?

Have you fallen into the habit of making excuses for the recurring sins in your life? Have you begun to believe your own story so much that you don't feel convicted anymore over sin that used to drive you to your knees in confession and repentance? Have you convinced yourself that God understands your particular situation and surely He will not hold you accountable? Have you found a person or a group of people on whom you can blame your failures?

If you answered yes to any of the above questions, you must make a decision. The decision you make will determine whether or not you will ever experience consistent victory over sin in your life; it will also determine whether or not you should even finish reading this book. The first step in overcoming temptation is to stop deceiving yourself into thinking that someone or something else is responsible for your actions. God didn't accept Adam and Eve's attempts to shift the blame. He doesn't accept yours, either. Who is to blame for your failure to deal successfully with temptation? You are. To face up to this simple fact is to take a giant step toward overcoming temptation.

Chapter 4

THE ROOTS OF
EVIL

ALL OF US have had the frustrating experience of feeling convicted over a particular sin, confessing it, and then turning right
around and committing it again. In fact, that may be the very cycle
of events that has led you to read this book. Every week people
come down the aisle of our church confessing the same sins they
have confessed a thousand times. Every summer thousands of
teenagers leave church camps all over the country having rededicated their lives in the same areas they rededicated them the previous summer. I know there have been times in my life that I
wanted to tell God, "God, if I am destined the rest of my life to
fall into temptation, could we at least change the category every
once in a while so I will not get completely frustrated?"

To effectively deal with the recurring temptations that plague
our lives, we must get to the root of the problem. We find ourselves dealing with the same things again and again because we
usually never get to the thing causing us to be so susceptible;
we never discover what is setting us up to be tempted the way
we are. We deal with sin like my kids used to deal with weeds in
the flower bed. Instead of taking the time to pull them up by the
roots, they would simply cut them off at ground level. The flower

bed looked good for a while, but in a matter of days the weeds were back, making it just as unsightly as before.

The principle we are going to look at in this chapter has the potential to set you free once and for all from things you may have been beset with for years. When I discovered this simple truth, it revolutionized my relationship with my wife and kids. For years I had struggled with something that drove a wedge between my family and me. I would confess it over and over and over, and yet I could not whip this temptation. It was during one of my down times that God, through some friends, revealed this principle to me.

Simply put, whatever we view as our source of security or significance will ultimately determine our actions. Our behavior, for the most part, is determined by the thing or person we believe makes us somebody worth knowing. My son, Andy, rephrased the principle this way, "What we view as our source will determine our course."

For Example

Imagine for a moment two graduate students studying for exams. Student A is not really all that concerned about grades. He believes a person should do his best and trust God with the outcome. Student B, however, has a tendency to equate his worth and potential as a businessman with his grade point average. He knows companies take a student's grades seriously, and because of that, he can't stand the thought of making anything less than an *A*.

That night as they study, they both receive a visitor who somehow managed to get a copy of the exam. Both students are Christians. Both believe cheating is wrong. Which one will have the most difficult time overcoming the temptation to cheat? Do you see how Student B's confusion about his self-worth and security sets him up for this temptation? In the same way many of us have set ourselves up to be tempted. Anytime our sense of self-worth or security becomes attached to something or somebody, we set ourselves up to be controlled by that thing or person.

This principle explains why a businessman who knows he should spend more time at home and less time at work just can't seem to change. Why? As long as his sense of significance and security is wrapped up in his business, he will be controlled by it. This principle explains why a single Christian woman, who knows and believes what the Bible says about being unequally yoked, will turn right around, date, and eventually marry a non-believer. Why? Because somewhere in the past she began equating success and fulfillment in life with marriage. Not God's choice of a partner necessarily, just marriage in general.

I see this principle illustrated in the lives of young men in two ways. Some buy into the mind-set that says, "He who has the prettiest girlfriend is the coolest." So they set out to find the "prettiest girl." All the time they know that God's priorities are different, yet they are driven by the desire to be viewed with admiration by their peers. Other guys become convinced that being a great athlete is the way to find significance and an inner sense of security. So they go after it with all their energy and dedication. Soon they begin to live for sports. They know they should be involved at church, but they just don't have enough time. They know they should keep a core of Christian friends, but they would rather be with other athletes. They know they should have daily devotions, but they are always too tired at the end of the day. Before long, football, basketball, or some other sport controls their lives.

I know evangelists whose sense of significance is defined in their minds by the number of people who make decisions at their crusades. Soon that is all they talk about. When things don't go well, they begin to stretch the truth about their results. It isn't that they believe lying is right; they are just too insecure to tell the whole truth.

I have seen couples in our church get so caught up in the social life of Atlanta that soon they are too busy to go to church.

Having their kids involved in the "right" clubs becomes more important than attending Sunday school. When they are confronted, they jokingly make excuses and finally say something like, "You're right, pastor. We'll see what we can do." And they usually do nothing. Why? Because what they view as their source of significance and security controls how they spend their time.

A Tragic Illustration

Some of the most tragic examples of how this principle works itself out come from the kids of broken homes. Often a girl who grows up with little or no affection from her father is set up to be tempted to a greater degree sexually than a girl who receives the right kinds of male affection at home. A girl who did not get the love she needed at home may seek it somewhere else. With no conscious decision on her part, male affection may come to mean security to her. The initial feelings she experiences—even in a bad relationship—are so much better than the emptiness she felt before that she gives in over and over again to the sexual invitations of men she knows she should not associate with.

Telling a girl like this that premarital sex is wrong is like cutting off weeds at ground level. It may alter her behavior for a while, but when those feelings of emptiness and insecurity begin to surface again, she will be drawn to get her needs met the way she always has.

Anyone who was brought up in a home where there was a deficiency of parental love will experience a stronger pull toward certain sins than a person who enjoyed a warm, loving home life. The majority of homosexual men who come to our counseling offices are from homes where there was no strong father figure. These men grew up without the male affection everybody needs. Thus, they were vulnerable to the offer of male affection available in a homosexual relationship. As I stated in chapter 3 these unfortunate circumstances in no way relieve people of the guilt or responsibility of their behavior. But if they can understand the connection between their childhood experiences and their present struggles, it is my hope that they will be able to deal with the root of their particular temptations.

As long as men and women seek to gain their sense of significance and self-worth from anything other than God, they will be set up for temptation. Certain people, places, or things will always have an inordinate ability to lure them into sin. Until they change their definition of significance and until they transfer their security to Someone who can give them real security, they will never experience lasting victory in their lives.

Where It All Began

So how did all of this begin? When did man become so insecure that he felt he must attach himself to something or someone else in order to feel successful and worthwhile? Once again we find ourselves looking at the opening chapters of Genesis.

Man, before the Fall, found his significance through his creature/Creator relationship with God. Man was God's representative on the earth (Gen. 1:26–30). By serving and obeying God, man had a reason to live and a great deal of security. It was really a simple system. Man served God, and God took care of man. Man was important because he served and had a close relationship with the God of the universe. What could be more significant than that?

When Satan tempted Adam and Eve, the temptation he offered was really to establish for themselves an identity apart from God. Think about the implication of Satan's words to Eve:

> And the serpent said to the woman, "You surely shall not die! For God knows that in the day you eat from it your eyes shall be opened, and you will be like God, knowing good and evil." When the woman saw that the tree was good for food, and that it was a delight to the eyes, and that the tree was desirable to make one wise, she took from its fruit and ate; and she gave also to her husband with her, and he ate.
>
> —Genesis 3:4–6

Satan was in effect saying to Eve, "Eve, God has lied to you. You cannot always trust Him to do what is best for you. You need to begin looking out for yourself. It is time to make some decisions on your own; be your own person. You can be like God. Why serve Him when you can be like Him? Why take care of His stuff when you can have stuff of your own? You don't need Him to take care of you. You can take care of yourself!"

Adam and Eve were tempted to abandon the security and place of significance offered by God. They were tempted to establish an identity of their own apart from Him; and they fell for it. The Scripture says, "When the woman saw . . . that the tree was desirable to make one wise"(3:6). To Eve, the wisdom offered by the tree represented independence. It was wisdom beyond what God had offered. It was wisdom that would allow her to function as God's equal. She would no longer be at His mercy in terms of what she could know. She could know on her own. So she ate.

Paradise Lost

The verse following the exchange between Eve and Satan would be comical if it weren't so tragic. In verses 7 through 13 we find the first decisions of these independent self-made human beings as they strike out on their own for the first time.

> Then the eyes of both of them were opened, and they knew that they were naked; and they sewed fig leaves together and made themselves loin coverings.
>
> —Genesis 3:7

The first feeling these "independent, free-thinking" creatures had was shame—certainly not an improvement over what they had felt under the authority of God. Consequently, the first thing that they did was to cover up. They weren't off to a very good start, were they?

And they heard the sound of the L ORD God walking in the garden in the cool of the day, and the man and his wife hid themselves from the presence of the L ORD God among the trees of the garden.

—Genesis 3:8

The next thing our liberated ancestors did was to run and hide. Now that is no way for individuals who are equal to God to be acting! What happened to their new sense of security and confidence? Where was all the "wisdom" they were promised?

Then the L ORD God called to the man, and said to him, "Where are you?" And he said, "I heard the sound of Thee in the garden, and I was afraid because I was naked; so I hid myself." And He said, "Who told you that you were naked? Have you eaten from the tree of which I commanded you not to eat?"

—Genesis 3:9–11

Adam and Eve's new independence resulted in shame, and they experienced fear for the first time as well. Fear drove them to the irrational behavior of attempting to hide from God. How foolish! But so it is with men and women who strike out on their own.

And the man said, "The woman whom Thou gavest to be with me, she gave me from the tree, and I ate." Then the L ORD God said to the woman, "What is this you have done?" And the woman said, "The serpent deceived me, and I ate."

—Genesis 3:12–13

Now that's a *real* picture of confidence. As soon as God questioned Adam and Eve about their sin, they immediately blamed someone else.

Search for Security

Adam and Eve quickly learned a lesson that takes some people a lifetime to learn. Simply put, man has no significance or security apart from his relationship with God. The creature finds his total value in the context of his relationship with the Creator. Apart from that, there is nothing. As soon as Adam and Eve unplugged (as it were) from God, everything fell apart—both inside and out.

Imagine for a moment that you have been in a terrible traffic accident. When you regain consciousness, you are in the hospital. Soon the doctor walks in and says to you, "Well, we have some good news and some bad news. The bad news is that your arm was severed from your body during the accident." With a great deal of anxiety in your voice you ask, "What's the good news?" He responds, "The good news is that we were able to save your arm." At that point a nurse walks in holding a rectangular box. As she lowers it to eye level, you gasp in horror to find they have saved your arm all right, but they saved it in a box!

In an instant what was supposed to be good news becomes a nightmare. Why? Because your arm is absolutely worthless when it is separated from your body. What was once a great significance to you has become horrible to even look at.

In the same way, apart from a living relationship with the Creator, the creature will experience a sense of purposelessness and worthlessness. There will always be something missing, something that cannot be replaced by possessions, money, or relationships.

Plugged in, But Turned Off

You may be thinking, *But I have a relationship with my Creator. Why do I still find it so hard to resist temptation?* The answer is that Satan is still in the business of deceit. Through his demonic cohorts, he is constantly working to convince us that to really be somebody, to really be secure, we must accomplish certain goals, we must have certain things, we must be seen with certain people, and we must be a part of the "right" organizations. Just as he lured Adam and Eve away from their relationship with God, he lures us away mentally and emotionally so that we look elsewhere for our self-worth and security. We try to meet God-given needs through the ingenuity of our minds rather than the way God intended.

What results is exactly what we saw take place in the Garden of Eden. We live with unnecessary shame. What if someone sees where I live? What if my business associates don't like my car? My son didn't make the first-string football team. I don't have anything new to wear. I didn't make the dean's list. What if people find out what my dad does for a living? I hope nobody asks me where we went on vacation.

Like Adam and Eve, we create for ourselves a world of fear. What if I don't have enough? What if my spouse divorces me? What if I don't win? What if I don't get the raise? What if I don't get the loan? What if I have to go to a community college? What if people find out we had to move? What if I lose my job? What if I don't make an *A*? What will happen if I have to sit home this weekend?

Then we hide. We do our best to appear to be something we are not. If necessary, we lie in order to maintain an image. It's not that we think lying is right. It's just something we find ourselves doing to cover for what we feel are our failures or inadequacies.

The Cover-Up

A good friend told me about his battle with lying. Every time someone would ask him about his involvement in athletics as a high-school student, he would say, "I played soccer and ran track." It was true that while he was in high school, he did play the game of soccer as well as run around the track a few times. But he never actually played on the school teams as he led people to believe.

He felt terrible each time he repeated the lie. He would pray and ask God's forgiveness and promise never to lie again. But as soon as he was questioned the next time, he found himself telling the same old story. Finally, one day as he was driving home from a friend's house, the Lord revealed to him the root of his problem.

When he was in the eighth grade, he had tried out for basketball. It was very important to him to make the team. Being an athlete meant instant popularity and lots of attention from the girls. As it turned out, he didn't make the team. The circumstances that led to his being cut were so traumatic that he never again tried out for anything. Although he didn't make the team, his value system remained the same—athletes are cool and deserve attention. This value system stuck with him right through college and into graduate school. Whenever someone asked him about his involvement in athletics, he felt like a failure, so much so that he lied about it.

He was looking to athletic accomplishment to mark him as somebody worth knowing and admiring. In his way of thinking, athletic accomplishments were a sign of a person's worth. Since he had none, he felt compelled to lie. As he described it, it was not really a premeditated sin; he just caught himself doing it. It was an emotional response to a deep feeling of insecurity when the subject of athletics was brought up.

As he was driving home that evening, the truth of his situation dawned on him. Immediately he began renewing his mind to the truth: athletic ability doesn't determine a person's worth. A person's true worth is wrapped up in the creature/Creator relationship with God. That was the end of his lying. He is now free to tell the truth and to laugh at his own inability in the area of athletics.

Making the Switch

Not every temptation you face will be the direct result of a misplaced sense of security and significance. Those that are, however, can be dealt with by simply transferring your value system from the world's standard to God's. By using the term *simply*, I don't mean to imply that it will necessarily be easy. How quickly you are free depends to some extent on how deeply your present value system is entrenched. Perhaps a childhood experience or a series of experiences in your past has set you up for the temptations you have been experiencing. If that is true, you may need a longer period of time to experience total emotional freedom.

Making the switch from your present set of values to God's involves two steps. First of all, you must identify the things and people from which you draw your identity. I call this step of the process *reviewing your life*. It involves answering a series of questions:

1. What do you fear the most?
2. Who has the potential to hurt you?
3. Who hurts you frequently?
4. What areas of your life do you tend to overemphasize?
5. What circumstances make you feel really uncomfortable?
6. In what or whom have you put all your hopes and dreams for the future?

When you prayerfully answer these questions, God will begin showing you the things and/or people around which you are consciously or subconsciously building your security and self-worth. What you are looking for in the answers to these questions is an *inordinate* amount of dependency on any one thing, person, or activity. Great athletes are to be admired as well as successful people in any area. There will always be some emotional dependency on a boyfriend, girlfriend, or spouse. It only becomes negative when your ultimate sense of security or significance becomes wrapped up in anything other than your relationship with God. When your behavior is controlled or at least highly influenced by forces other than God's standard of behavior, things have gone too far.

A second step in making this switch involves *renewing your mind to the truth*. To renew your mind, you must remove the old ways of thinking and replace them with the truth. We are going to deal with this subject in a later chapter on a broader basis. But at this point in our discussion the truth that you need to focus on has to do with the areas of security and significance. The truth is that all of your security and significance is wrapped up in your relationship with God through Jesus Christ. Think through these questions:

1. Who created you?
2. Who chose you to live with Him forever?
3. Who holds the power of life in His hands?
4. Who is ultimately in control of all that goes on in the world today?
5. Who sent His Son to die for you?
6. Who promised He would never leave you?
7. Who promised to be available at any time?
8. Who has the power to bring about in your life all He has promised?
9. Who has promised to structure your circumstances so that you will be brought to maturity?
10. Who has given you an eternal identity based upon His work?
11. With whom, then, does your true security rest?
12. What relationship is the true test of your significance?

God created you, and He controls when your life on this earth ends. Along with that, His Son has promised to never leave you. That being true, your relationship with God provides you with more security than any other relationship could possibly offer.

In regard to significance and self-worth, God loves you enough to apply His Son's death on the cross to your sins. He accepts you just as you are. What you own, wear, drive, live in, or have in the bank holds no weight with Him. You are significant because He created you.

Begin Now

These are some of the truths on which you must focus if you are to break the power of sin in your life. What you view as your source *will* determine your course. There is no way around this principle. You can confess and promise and rededicate all you want. But until you are willing to transfer your sense of security and significance to your relationship with God, you, like the world, will spend the rest of your life trying to regain what was originally lost in the Garden of Eden. You will be a driven person, always looking for that thing or person to fill a void in your life that your Creator was meant to fill.

Begin today reviewing your life, asking God to show you the things and/or people you have allowed to replace Him. Think through the questions I have listed. Write down the things that come to mind. Then renew your mind to the truth about you and your relationship with God. In time even your emotions will change, and you will experience the freedom God originally meant for you to experience.

Chapter 5

THE APPEAL

ONE OF THE most frightening passages of Scripture to me is found in Ephesians 6:11: "Put on the full armor of God, that you may be able to stand firm against the schemes of the devil." Satan is not haphazardly wandering around tossing temptations here and there. He has a plan, a plan he has tested and perfected. His schemes worked against men like David, Samson, Peter, Abraham, Jacob, and on and on we could go.

This passage is frightening because the implication is that he is out to destroy every believer. That means me, my wife, my daughter, and my son. He is scheming to destroy you as well. If that is true, it is of utmost importance that we understand how he plans to go about doing that so we can be ready to resist him.

Have I Got a Deal for You!

Probably the closest parallel to Satan's strategy to be found in our contemporary society is used by the advertising business. A good advertiser can manipulate your thoughts and emotions from just about any state you could possibly be in right up to the point of believing you must have his product *now!* Think about it.

There you are, watching some sort of athletic competition on television. The last thing on your mind is purchasing a new car. Then a car advertisement comes on. The next thing you know, you are sitting there coming up with reasons why it would be advantageous to trade in your old car for a new one! Before you can finish your list, the next advertisement begins, and you find yourself feeling thirsty. Before you can make it to the refrigerator, the next commercial has you dreaming about an exotic vacation. By the time the game resumes, just about every emotion and desire in your body has been stimulated. And you never left the room!

In this chapter we are going to analyze Satan's appeal. Understanding his strategy and learning to recognize his handiwork are important parts of learning to overcome temptation. The temptation process usually begins long before we are aware that anything is going on. Consequently, by the time we catch on to what is happening to us, it is almost too late. I say *almost* because at no point in the temptation process do we lose our ability to say, "No!"

A Paradigm for Temptation

Anytime we try to equate the temptation process with some sort of mathematical formula or series of steps, there will be a tendency to oversimplify the matter. Although I don't wish to paint anything less than a real picture of what is happening, I know from experience that not every temptation falls into a neat, well-defined category. What I am attempting to do in this chapter is to give you the general blueprint Satan uses. Every temptation has its own set of circumstances and actors. There are, however, certain ingredients that appear in every situation. It is these basic ingredients that we are going to discuss.

A good example of what I am saying is found in language study. If you have ever learned a foreign language, you probably learned to conjugate one particular verb as a pattern for all the other verbs. This verb was called a paradigm. As you continued your study, you found that not every verb followed the exact pattern of the original verb. There was enough similarity, though, to aid you in recognizing the form of each new verb. In this chapter we are going to look at a paradigm for temptation.

One Strike Against Us

Another thing we must keep in mind as we study Satan's appeal is that we are not neutral targets. When Adam and Eve sinned in the garden, the whole human race was polluted by their sin. Adam's decision to disobey God and to strike out on his own became interwoven into the fabric of humanity. Everybody is born with a propensity to sin. Theologians call this the "depravity of man."

This is why you do not have to teach your kids to sin. They are able to figure that out all by themselves. This built-in sin mechanism resides in what the Bible calls the "flesh" (Rom. 7:18). When we become believers, the power of sin is broken, but the presence of sin remains. That means that believers do not have to give in to sinful desires, but we will still have those desires from time to time. We will discuss all of this in greater detail later. Suffice it to say, when we are tempted, we already have one strike against us, the presence of sin.

Satan's Aim

Satan's short-range goal in the temptation process is to get us to satisfy God-given needs and desires in ways that are outside the boundaries God has set up. All of our basic desires are ultimately from God. Most of them reflect the image of God in us. For example, the desires for love, acceptance, respect, and success mirror desires we find in God throughout the Scriptures. Only when these are distorted do they become negative characteristics. And so Satan sets out to turn our desire to be loved into lust, our desire to be accepted and respected into pride, and our desire for success into greed.

God gave us other desires and needs in order to demonstrate our dependence on Him and to enhance our relationships with one another. Our need for food and desire for sex are two examples. There is nothing wrong with eating (obviously). But here again, Satan takes this natural, God-given need and distorts it. As a result, some people destroy their bodies by overeating or eating the wrong things; others starve themselves for fear of being overweight.

Of all the gifts God gave humanity, sex is probably the one Satan distorts and abuses the most. Sex was given to mankind to make possible a unique relationship between a man and a woman. The desire is from God. The philosophy concerning sex today is from Satan. God says, "One man for one woman for life." Satan says, "Any man for any woman until you are ready for someone else." God says, "Sex is to be a part of the marriage relationship." Satan says, "Sex *is* the relationship." God is not against sex any more than He is against food, love, or success. But He is against the gratification of that desire, or any desire, outside the confines He has lovingly and skillfully designed.

"The Things in the World"

The apostle John in his first epistle grouped all of Satan's distortions into three categories. He wrote,

> Do not love the world, nor the things in the world. If anyone loves the world, the love of the Father is not in him. For all that is in the world, the *lust of the flesh* and the *lust of the eyes* and the *boastful pride of life*, is not from the Father, but is from the world.
>
> —1 John 2:15–16, *emphasis added*

Every single time we are tempted, we are tempted through one of those three avenues. The lust of the flesh represents our appetites, our cravings, our desires, and our hungers. The lust of the eyes includes those things we see that spark our different desires and appetites. The boastful pride of life refers to anything that promotes or elevates a sense of independence from God—anything that causes us to think we can do our own thing, live our own kind of life, have it our way. In all three cases we can see how these are simply distortions of some of God's most precious gifts to us.

Now let's go back to Genesis 3 and watch how Satan used those three avenues to deceive Eve. Keep in mind that we are looking for Satan's strategy: the methods he uses to get people to meet their God-given needs in ways that are outside the boundaries God has set up.

The Temptation of Eve

The account of Eve's temptation begins with Satan causing Eve to doubt God (Gen. 3:1–4). Oftentimes this is a major part of the temptation process. For now, however, I want to skip over this particular aspect of temptation and get right to Satan's attempt to distort Eve's God-given needs and desires.

> And the serpent said to the woman, "You surely shall not die! For God knows that in the day you eat from it your eyes will be opened, and you will be like God, knowing good and evil." When the woman saw that the tree was good for food, and that it was a delight to the eyes, and that the tree was desirable to make one wise, she took from its fruit and ate.
> —Genesis 3:4–6

First Satan chose to appeal to Eve's pride. Notice his first offer: ". . . your eyes will be opened." Satan offered insight, knowledge, and understanding. "Certainly there cannot be anything wrong with any of those things," Eve may have said to herself. "Why, the Lord God is always teaching us new things. How could He blame us for wanting to find out a few things on our own?"

Next Satan offered power and authority: ". . . and you will be like God." "Well, there is certainly nothing wrong with this,"

Eve could have rationalized. "God wants us to have authority. He put this whole garden under our care." Once again she would have been right. But once again Satan was pushing a God-given desire beyond God's parameters.

There was nothing wrong with wanting to increase in knowledge and understanding. That very desire has driven engineers and scientists for decades. Man's insatiable curiosity and desire for knowledge brought about the computer I use to write as well as the paper upon which this book is printed. In the same vein, there was nothing wrong with Eve's desire for authority and power. That, too, is God-given. This is clear because God promises both as rewards to those who are faithful to Him in this life (Matt. 20:23–28; Rev. 20:4). But when these are exercised apart from God's direction, they become destructive and unjust.

"Good for Food"

After appealing to Eve through her pride, Satan used her appetite, her "lust of the flesh" as John put it: "The woman saw that the tree was good for *food*." Once again we can hear Eve arguing, "Well, if God didn't really want me to eat it, He shouldn't have made it edible! Why give me an appetite for food and then create food I can't eat?" Sounds pretty good to me. And it must have sounded pretty good to her.

Next he used the "lust of the eyes": "The woman saw that the tree was good for food, and that it was a *delight to the eyes*." We don't really know what kind of fruit it was. We usually think of an apple when we hear this story. But that is purely conjecture. Whatever it was it must have been unique to this particular tree and extremely appetizing to look at. The very sight of it made Eve want to eat.

We may be tempted to ask, "Is that a sin? Didn't God put in Eve's body the mechanisms to send a 'pick it and eat' signal to her brain when she saw appetizing food?" Of course He did. We have all seen food or even pictures of food that made us feel hungry. There is nothing wrong with that. The problem was not Eve's appetite; it was the manner in which she chose to satisfy her appetite.

"But Why Would I Feel This Way If God . . ."

It seems like every week someone comes into my office with a story that ends, "If God doesn't want me to _____, then why do I feel the way I do?" or "Why would God give me such a strong desire to _____ if He didn't want me to fulfill it?" These arguments sound convincing. Think about it. What kind of God gives His creatures desires they are not allowed to fulfill? But these people are asking the wrong questions. It is not, *"Why* won't God let me fulfill my desires?" It should be, *"When* in God's perfect timing can I fulfill my desires?" Or *"How* would God prefer me to fulfill my desires?"

A couple came into my office several years ago for premarital counseling. As we began talking, I got the impression there was something they were not telling me. I turned to the young man and said, "Have the two of you been sleeping together?" He glanced quickly at her and then back at me. That told me all I needed to know. Before he could answer, his bride-to-be blurted out, "We love each other."

As we continued to talk, they both defended their actions by explaining how strong their attraction was for each other. "God understands. He allowed us to feel this way." Then I asked a question that left them both speechless. I turned to the young man and said, "What are you going to do when you meet a woman at work to whom you feel a strong physical attraction? Are you going to use the same rationale? 'If God didn't want me to meet this need, He wouldn't have let me feel this way?'"

We forget that although God gave us the potential to feel and desire certain things, Satan has the ability to manipulate and misdirect those feelings and desires. That is the essence of temptation. Satan's appeal to you and me is to meet God-given needs and fulfill God-given desires the easiest, quickest, and least painful way.

Taking the Easy Way Out

An old friend of mine burst into my office one afternoon and said, "Charles, I've got to talk to you." I told my secretary to hold my calls, pushed what I was working on out of the way, and began to listen. He said, "Pastor, you know my business has been rocking along at a steady pace of growth. Nothing to write home about, but it is growing slowly." Jim had started his own printing company a few years back. Actually he had done quite well. He had been a faithful contributor to the church and to other ministries as well.

"Well, last week a man came by to see me and offered to buy me out. He offered me almost twice what my business is worth. If I sell, he will keep me on as president and increase my pay. That means I can stay in the work I love without the headaches of owning my own business."

"What's the problem?" I asked.

"If I sell out," he said, "I won't have total control over what is printed anymore. Not only that, I will not be able to give off the gross income of the business. In fact, my giving will be cut to a percentage of my personal salary."

As we talked, I began to see Jim's struggle a little clearer. As it would for most men, the lure of more money had a strong appeal. That along with the prospects of less pressure and responsibility made it seem ridiculous to think about turning down the man's offer. Besides, there is nothing wrong with making more money; and there is certainly nothing wrong with easing the pressure at work.

As we talked, however, Jim realized that what he would give up by selling his company was far greater than what he would gain. He knew in his heart that God led him to start his company and that God had guided him every step of the way. "This would be the easy thing to do," he said, "but not the right thing." He was convinced that he needed to do something about the pressure he was under. But this was not God's plan for meeting that need. He decided to keep his company and wait for God to provide another solution to the pressure problem.

In the following months Jim was able to restructure his company so that almost all the day-to-day pressure was shifted to his employees. He began to enjoy what he was doing more than ever. Since that time, his business has almost doubled.

It's Really All the Same

Whether it is a long, drawn-out situation like Jim's or simply an opportunity to walk away from a cash register with too much change, every temptation is simply an alternative to meeting God-given needs God's way. Here is how it works. Satan uses your circumstances to stimulate some desire, whether it's a desire for money, sex, or acceptance. Then he starts working on your emotions. Once your emotions have convinced you that you just have to have whatever it is, your mind kicks in. Soon you find yourself working on a plan to meet the need with as few consequences as possible. Then, WHAM! You go for it.

It doesn't matter if you have a problem with gossip, jealousy, anger, gambling, lying, or lust; it's really all the same pattern. Satan hasn't changed his strategy since he tempted Adam and Eve in Eden. He has no need to. If it worked on two perfect people in a perfect environment with a perfect relationship with God, think how much more effective it will be on us—especially if we are unaware of what is going on and have made no provision to stop him.

Stop and think for just a minute. What temptation do you struggle with the most? What is the one that came to mind when I asked this question in the first chapter? Can you see how in one way or another your experience fits this pattern? Let's take it a step further. What God-given need or needs are you being tempted to meet outside of God's parameters? Is it a desire to be loved? A desire to be held? A desire to be accepted? What is it? Before you can go any further, you must know the answer to this question.

Time and time again I have talked to people who were struggling with some area of temptation, but they had no idea why
they did the things they did. They felt driven. They knew that
their sin brought no long-lasting relief or satisfaction, yet they
continued. One good illustration of this is a man I knew who was
extremely greedy. To put it another way, every time there was
an opportunity to give, he was tempted not to give! He would
make all sorts of excuses, none of which were very convincing.

As we talked, it became clear to us that what he really wanted
was financial security. He had been raised with nothing and lived
with an inordinate fear of poverty. For years he had been greedy
and did not even know why. But when he realized that this was
his problem and that the Scripture clearly teaches that what we
hold on to diminishes and what we let go of multiplies, his attitude began to change.

Anxious for Nothing?

*God does not intend for you to live a life full of frustration and
anxiety.* On the contrary, Satan is the one who wants your life
to be filled with anxiety. That is why he is always so quick to
offer a substitute for God's best. He knows his offer will not satisfy. He also knows that if he can get you hooked on his alternative, many times you will completely miss God's best.

When I think about the multitude of teenage girls who have
compromised their morals in order to be "held," it breaks my
heart. They did not need someone just to hold them. They needed
someone to love them unconditionally. Many will never know
that kind of love simply because they cannot or will not break
away from the substitutes Satan has thrown in their path.

Thousands of men and teenage boys in this country are addicted
to pornography. For most of them, it all began by accepting Satan's
substitute. Now the relationship they really need is beyond their
grasp in most cases. Day by day their ability to think about sex
and women in the way God intended diminishes.

The alcoholics and drug addicts that fill our streets and occupy positions of prominence are another testimony to the human unwillingness to wait for God's best. For whatever reason, these men and women chose to cope with life's pressures by running. It seemed a quick and easy way to cope. Yet it never solves any of life's problems. It simply postpones the solution. And for many, the pressures that drove them to their vice were the same pressures God was trying to use to drive them to Himself. But they chose the easy way, the quick way, the way of least resistance, the way of destruction.

You see, God does not want you to live a life of frustration and anxiety. If He did, He never could have inspired the apostle Paul to write these words:

Be anxious for nothing, but in everything by prayer and supplication with thanksgiving let your requests be made known to God. And the peace of God, which surpasses all comprehension, shall guard your hearts and minds in Christ Jesus.
—Philippians 4:6–7

The interesting thing about this passage is that God does not promise to give you what you ask for; He does not promise to meet your need immediately. What He promises is "the peace of God," that is, the inner strength to endure until your desires and needs are fulfilled. It will surpass "all comprehension" because the world will look at you and say, "How can you go without _____? How do you make it without _____?" From the world's perspective, it won't make any sense.

My son was thirty before he married. His lost friends used to ask him, "Andy, what do you do about sex?" He would respond, "I wait!" That was amazing from their frame of reference. They could not imagine being "that old" and not being sexually active. The ironic thing was that he was far less frustrated than they were. And so it will always be for those who wait on God to meet their needs His way.

God does not promise to meet your need immediately. But He does promise the inner strength you need to keep going in the meantime. By opting for His peace rather than Satan's substitute, you can be assured that when the time comes for God to meet your particular need, you will be ready.

This principle applies to everything from meeting the right marriage partner to finding the money you need to pay the rent. God knows your needs; He knows your desires. Jesus said,

If you then, being evil, know how to give good gifts to your children, how much more shall your Father who is in heaven give what is good to those who ask Him!

—Matthew 7:11

What an incredible promise! What an incredible God!

Peace at a Price

In all my years as a pastor I have never met one person who waited on God and was sorry. Yet the majority of people who come to my office for counseling or to the counseling offices of our church have problems stemming from a point in their lives where they settled for Satan's substitute. The story is always the same. Things were fine for a while, but before long, they grew restless. Many have made peace with God. Some are still out there bouncing around between jobs, marriages, lovers, and bars. Yet they know in their hearts that they will never find what they are ultimately looking for until they surrender to the One who holds it all in His hands.

What do you really need? What has Satan fooled you into thinking you need? Are you willing to wait and trust God to meet your needs His way? If so, you too can experience the peace that surpasses comprehension.

The remaining chapters of this book are designed to help you deal with Satan's attempts to pull you back into the sin that you have struggled to overcome. You may find some more helpful than others. Depending on the nature of your particular sin, you may need to read certain sections more than once. Whatever the case, do not give up. Peace can be yours if only you will continually take your struggle to God. Ask Him to lift your burden and flood your heart with the peace He has promised.

Part II

*Developing
a Self-defense*

Chapter 6

OUR GREAT DEFENDER

A WISE INDIVIDUAL prepares for those things that are inevitable in life. Temptation is one of those inevitable things. A plaque I saw not long ago summed it up this way:

> OPPORTUNITY ONLY KNOCKS ONCE,
> TEMPTATION LEANS ON THE DOORBELL.

Whoever came up with that saying certainly could see the big picture. In this life we will always be within arm's reach of temptation. As we have seen, the Scriptures teach that temptation is common to all men and women everywhere. That being the case, we should do all we can to be prepared.

A general whose task is to defend a city against attack doesn't wait until the city is being besieged to plan his defense. A wise general plans his defense strategy long before the threat of attack even presents itself. "How will the enemy attack? From which direction will they approach? Where are our weak spots?" These are some of the questions a general should ask when preparing his defenses. Likewise believers should sit down ahead of time and plan their defense against temptation.

In these next chapters we are going to take an in-depth look at how to develop a self-defense. Step by step I'm going to explain what God would have us do to prepare to combat temptation. This chapter and the next one will focus primarily on God's part, that is, the provision He has made available to us for dealing with temptation. The other chapters in this section will focus on our role. Every stage of this defense strategy is crucial. You may need to read some of these chapters several times, but keep in mind that simply reading this book will not help you in your struggle against temptation. You must apply these principles to make a difference in your life.

God, Our Defender

As we have seen in previous chapters, God has not abandoned us here on earth to struggle through life on our own, nor does He expect us to bear the burden of temptation alone. One of the most exciting truths that surfaces in a study of temptation is that God is intimately involved in the life of every single believer. This will become even more apparent as we focus on the part He plays in our defense against temptation.

When he wrote the Corinthian church, the apostle Paul gave the believers there a warning and a promise concerning temptation. In his promise there are two principles that give us some insight into God's involvement in our defense against temptation. He said,

> Therefore let him who thinks he stands take heed lest he fall. No temptation has overtaken you but such as is common to man; and God is faithful, who will not allow you to be tempted beyond what you are able, but with the temptation will provide the way of escape also, that you may be able to endure it.
>
> —1 Corinthians 10:12–13

Loving Limitations

The first principle that surfaces in this passage is this: *God has set a limit on the intensity of every temptation.* God knows you perfectly, inside and out. In accordance with His perfect knowledge He has set a limit on the intensity of the temptations you will face. He knows how much you can handle; He knows your breaking point. Regardless of the nature of your temptation—be it in the area of finances, sex, anger, or gossip—God knows your limitations. He promises to keep a watchful eye on the pressures Satan brings against you.

Scripture presents several examples of this. One of the most dramatic is found in Luke when the disciples were gathered with Christ for His last Passover meal. At one point in the dialogue Jesus turned to Peter and said,

> Simon, Simon, behold, Satan has demanded permission to sift you like wheat; but I prayed for you, that your faith may not fail; and you, when once you have turned again, strengthen your brothers.
>
> —Luke 22:31–32

A significant point in this passage is that Satan had to get "permission" to tempt Peter, and he had to demand it. This, however, in no way negates the fact that God determined whether or not Satan would have the chance to tempt Peter the way he did. Before Satan could go after Peter, he first had to check it out with God.

In the same way, God determines how far Satan can go with us. We are not at his mercy. Satan, like all creatures, is ultimately under God's authority. We usually don't think of him in that way. When it comes to temptation, we oftentimes equate God and Satan. We view them as two giant powers battling it out for possession of the universe. The war for the universe, however, ended long ago. Now the battle is for the possession and corruption of men's souls.

The fact that God has put limitations on our temptation assures us of three things. First, we will never be tempted more than we can bear—never! Not in our weakest moments; not even when we are tempted in our weakest areas. Second, God is involved in our struggle against temptation. He isn't watching from a distance. He is right here functioning as referee to the whole situation. Third, God is faithful; He can be trusted. Even in our darkest hour of temptation, God has not turned His back on us. No matter how we respond, God remains faithful. In both our victories and defeats, He continues to keep the enemy in check.

In order to build an effective defense system, you must accept this simple premise. To reject it or simply forget it is to open the door for all kinds of excuses: "I can't help it." "The devil made me do it." "There was no way I could say no." As long as you believe you are at the mercy of the devil when it comes to temptation, you will never know victory because you will never make more than a halfhearted attempt. After all, why try if the temptation is unbearable to begin with?

Imagine a city whose citizens were convinced that no matter what measures they took, their enemies would eventually overrun their walls. What defensive measures do you think they would take? Probably very few or none at all. Why waste their time? They would probably just surrender without a fight.

Satan has many believers convinced that it is a waste of time to try to resist temptation. They believe it is only a matter of time and they will fall. Why go through the frustration of trying if failure is unavoidable? So they surrender without a fight.

That attitude can develop if you do not accept the fact that *God puts a limit on the intensity of your temptation.* Despite your past experience, you must accept by faith that God will not allow you to be tempted beyond what you are able to bear. Think about it. Since you have been a Christian, every temptation you have faced thus far could have been overcome. The same is true for the temptations you face from now on. No matter how difficult this may be to comprehend, you must accept this premise if you are to build an effective defense against the enemy.

The Way Out

The second principle that you must accept if you are going to develop an effective defense against temptation is this: *alongside every temptation, God has designed a way out.* Although the situation may seem hopeless at the time, there is a way to avoid falling. Paul wrote,

> God is faithful, who will not allow you to be tempted beyond what you are able, but with the temptation *will provide the way of escape also,* that you may be able to endure it.
> —1 Corinthians 10:13, *emphasis added*

Someone may say, "I already know of a temptation I am going to face tomorrow!" If that is the case, then you can rest assured that God has already provided a way of escape. Notice the way Paul parallels his ideas: ". . . *with* the temptation will provide the way of escape." Every temptation has an accompanying escape hatch. There is always an alternative action.

Many people live or work in situations where they are constantly being tempted to sin. Oftentimes there is no place or opportunity for them to run. God is faithful even in those situations. He will always provide a way out.

A girl in our fellowship grew up in such an environment. I'll call her Michele. The nature of her family was such that she and her sister were constantly tempted to rebel in the worst way. Her parents were warned several times by both friends and neighbors that they were driving their girls away.

Eventually Michele's sister ran away and got married. Her decision to marry was more an effort to escape than it was an act of love. Michele, on the other hand, stuck it out all the way through high school and college. I must admit that even I was amazed at her ability to cope with the situation at home. Eventually she fell in love with a fine Christian young man, and I had the opportunity to marry them.

During one of our premarital counseling sessions, the subject of her home life surfaced. In a very tactful way I expressed my respect for her ability to have handled things as well as she did. She smiled and said, "Sometimes you just have to do what you are told and then look for alternatives when you can't." I asked her if she ever felt like rebelling. She said, "All the time. There were days when I just didn't think I could stand it one more minute. I learned that if I would stop, take a deep breath, and think for just a minute, there was always another way to handle the situation other than blowing up." Michele learned that *even when we cannot escape a situation, God always provides a way to escape temptation.*

Our problem may be that we don't bother to look for His way out. We assume the situation is hopeless and just go along with what our flesh is directing us to do. And if we are honest, sometimes we don't look for God's way of escape because we don't really want to escape. If that is your problem, you need to go back and reread the first three chapters of this book. You still don't have the big picture as far as the sin is concerned.

On the other hand, if you sincerely want to escape temptation and you know you are going to face a particular temptation, go ahead and ask God to reveal to you the way out. Remember, a good general doesn't wait until the battle has begun to plan his strategy. He thinks ahead.

I know a pastor in another city who had problems with a woman in his church. She was obviously interested in more than a pastor-parishioner relationship. I'll call her Doris. The pastor did everything he could to avoid her advances. The only situation he could not seem to find a way to deal with occurred after each Sunday morning service. Doris would stand in line with the other church members to greet him, and she would always give him a lingering full frontal hug. Week after week he knew what was coming, and yet he couldn't find a way to avoid her without making a scene. Then one morning he had an idea. Just as it was Doris's turn in line, he reached down and picked up a small child. Holding the child in front of him, he greeted Doris with a handshake from his free hand. From then on when the pastor would see her coming, the Lord was faithful to provide a "way out." There was always a child nearby. After a few weeks, Doris got the message and no longer bothered him in that way.

God will be faithful to provide a way of escape, but we must be faithful to look for it. And having identified it, we must take advantage of it

"Deliver Us From Evil"

Before we move on, I want to point out what 1 Corinthians 10:13 does *not* say. It does not say that God will remove the temptation. God will not provide a way to escape being tempted. (We may wish that He would, but that's just not the way things are.) The point of this verse is that He will provide an alternative course of action. God's ultimate desire for us is not that we should be delivered from being tempted, but that we should be delivered through temptation. Notice how this verse ends:

> But with the temptation will provide the way of escape also, *that you may be able to endure it.*

God's desire for us is that we should be able to endure, or bear, temptation.

When Jesus was praying in the Garden of Gethsemane before His arrest, He prayed,

> I have given them Thy word; and the world has hated them, because they are not of the world, even as I am not of the world. I do not ask Thee to take them out of the world, but to keep them from the evil one.
>
> —John 17:14–15

Jesus specifically mentioned that it was not His desire for the disciples to be taken out of the world and therefore avoid all temptation. His desire for them was that they remain in the world, but at the same time be protected from Satan, the evil one. In other words, "Give them the power to overcome the onslaught of the devil." Part of God's answer to His Son's prayer is "the way of escape."

I stress this point in view of our tendency to feel as if God has somehow let us down when we are tempted. "God, if You really love me, if You really care for me, why are You allowing me to be tempted this way?" But nowhere does God promise to structure our lives so that we can avoid all temptation. He does, however, limit our temptations and provide us a way out.

Promises, Promises

In this chapter we have focused on the first part of God's provision for our defense against temptation. God stands guard over Satan when he tempts us. He will not allow us to be tempted beyond what we can bear. Second, with every temptation God provides a way of escape. It is our responsibility to look for it and take advantage of it.

The awesome implication of both principles is that God is intimately involved in our lives. He is aware of every temptation we face. Before you read any further, stop and answer these two questions for yourself:

1. Do I really believe God only allows me to be tempted within the confines of what He knows I can bear?
2. Do I really believe God provides a way of escape through every temptation?

If you have trouble accepting these two premises, please take some time to meditate on 1 Corinthians 10:13. Ask God to make this verse real to you. Think through the experiences you have had that make this verse so unbelievable. Ask God to help you reinterpret your experiences from His perspective. In the next chapter we will take a look at two other ways in which God has involved Himself in helping us develop a defense against temptation.

Chapter 7

THE POWER
OF HIS MIGHT

THERE IS A third aspect to God's involvement in our temptations. He limits our temptations and provides a way to escape, and *He also provides us with the power to overcome.* Of all the concepts discussed in this book, this one is the most difficult to explain. The very term *power* introduces an intangible into our discussion. Power is not something that can be seen. Power is something that is applied. After properly applying power to a situation, one can see the results of power, yet the power itself remains as illusive as ever.

Wind is a good example of this. You cannot see wind. Yet you can readily see the results of wind. If you have ever driven through an area immediately following a hurricane or tornado, you know firsthand what I'm talking about. A tornado passed through the neighborhood of a family in our church several years ago. Their roof was torn completely off, and all the windows were shattered. Right next to their house was a huge magnolia tree. It must have been twenty feet high. The power of the tornado was of such great magnitude that it ripped up the magnolia tree by the roots and carried it away. They never found a trace of the tree! Every time

I see the place where that tree once stood I can't help wondering where it eventually landed. Such is the nature of power. Rarely seen, always felt.

We need to keep in mind three things about power. I'll refer to these as the "laws of power." First, *power determines potential.* The potential weight a bodybuilder can lift is limited by his strength or power. Certainly his attitude is important, but even a good attitude does not compensate for a lack of power. Our potential to accomplish any particular task, whether it is moving something heavy or saying no to temptation, is determined by the power we possess or to which we have access. Power determines potential.

Second, *power must be harnessed and applied toward a specific goal before it serves any purpose.* Power in and of itself is useless. Its value lies in its application. The Colorado River has a great deal of potential power. It is not until the force of the river comes into contact with the turbines underneath the Hoover Dam, however, that the power of the Colorado River serves any useful function. Power must be applied. Setting a chain saw down by a tree accomplishes nothing. There may be no doubt in anyone's mind that the potential for cutting down the tree is there. Nothing will be accomplished, however, until someone comes along and applies the power of the saw to the tree. Power must be harnessed to be useful.

Third, *power, when harnessed and focused, can greatly extend the potential of the one in whose hands the power rests.* When individuals have access to a source of power beyond what they possess themselves, there is a sense in which that power becomes theirs. Yet at the same time there remains a distinction. The potential of the one to whom control has been given is greatly enhanced. If you were to ask a man holding a chain saw, "Can you cut down this tree in ten minutes?" he would probably reply, "Sure!" He knows that with the power the chain saw affords him, he can cut down the tree. He does not mean that he can cut down the tree with his bare hands. Power becomes an extension of the one who controls and directs it.

The Promise of Power

Keeping all this in mind, think about the implications of this passage:

> Finally, be strong in the LORD, and in the strength of His might. Put on the full armor of God, that you may be able to stand firm against the schemes of the devil.
>
> —Ephesians 6:10–11

Those verses made two very important points to the Ephesians—and they still pertain to us. First, a power was available to the Ephesian believers that was not of them. Paul exhorted the Ephesians to be strong in the strength, or power, of "His" might. Second, when the power was properly harnessed and focused, the Ephesian believers would be able to stand firmly against any of the devil's schemes.

Paul made the same point in Romans when he wrote,

> So then, brethren, we are under obligation, not to the flesh, to live according to the flesh.
>
> —Romans 8:12

To state it another way, "Brethren, you have the *power* to say no to your fleshly desires." In the same book he said,

> For sin shall not be master over you, for you are not under law, but under grace.
>
> —Romans 6:14

In those verses Paul was teaching something really amazing, especially in light of the way believers often live. The truth Paul was getting at can be stated this way: *believers have a power greater than that of the devil, the flesh, or sin.* Believers have the potential to say no to the devil, no to the flesh, and no to sin! And not once did Paul qualify his statements; there are no exceptions.

Probably the most important role God plays when we are tempted is that of *empowerer*. God has made available to us the power, His power, to say no to sin and yes to Him. Regardless of the intensity of our temptation, the frequency of our temptation, or even our failure in the past to successfully deal with it, God has made available the power to resist.

Seeing Is Believing

Someone may respond, "Well, if God has given me all this power, why do I keep giving in to the same temptations over and over? I pray and ask God to help me, but nothing changes!" It was in anticipation of this very response that I took the time to describe the three laws of power earlier. The second law stated that *power must be harnessed and applied toward a specific goal before it serves any purpose.* Remember, power in and of itself is useless. Its value is in its application. *Having* the power of God available and *using* that power are two entirely different things. A believer who is unable to say no to sin is like a man who owns a chain saw but is attempting to chop down trees with his bare hands. He has the potential through the chain saw, but he is not using it. Owning a chain saw with the potential power to cut down trees is not the same thing as sawing down trees. Having the power of God at your disposal is not equivalent to overcoming temptation.

This is exactly what James is talking about when he writes,

> What use is it, my brethren, if a man says he has faith, but he has no works? Can that faith save him?
> —James 2:14

And then a few verses later he writes,

> But are you willing to recognize, you foolish fellow, that faith, without works is useless?
> —James 2:20

James's point is that faith apart from the application of that faith is useless; it accomplishes nothing; it might as well not even be there! The application of faith or power makes things happen. Practically speaking, there is really no value at all in having the power of God residing in you if you are not putting it to use. It's like owning a car and keeping it parked in the garage all the time. What use is it? A believer's inability to cope with a particular temptation is in no way a reflection on the power of God; only the individual's inability or unwillingness to apply that power becomes evident.

I was in the ministry for years before I began to understand my relationship to the power of God. I knew that God had made His power available, but for a long time I did not know how to make it a reality in my own life. Most of the Christians that I counsel have the same problem. They believe victory is possible, but not very probable. The remaining portion of this book is dedicated to explaining how to make the power of God a reality, how to get God's power working for you.

A Change for the Better

Before we get to that, however, let's examine a fourth aspect of God's involvement in our temptations. This one has to do with the *changes that took place in our relationship to sin and our relationship with God the moment we trusted Him as our Savior.* The realization of these two things really paved the way for me to begin experiencing consistent victory in my life. As a child, I had been taught some things that were incorrect; they were so deeply ingrained in my thinking that without knowing it, I read them back into the Scripture. When the truth finally broke through, however, and my perspective was brought into line with God's, I found it far easier to apply the power of God to my particular temptations.

Dead to Sin

The Bible says that each of us is born under the dominion of sin (Rom. 5:17–19). Through the desires of the flesh, the power of sin directs a man's or woman's actions and attitudes. The power of sin functions much like an internal dictator. Its commands flow from a desire to fulfill every desire and meet every immediate need in whatever fashion it deems appropriate. The power of sin knows no rules, for it functions as a law unto itself. Therefore, it eventually comes into conflict with any standard of behavior, whether it is social, legal, or biblical.

The power of sin is that innate desire within each of us to assert ourselves against our Creator or authority in general. The power of sin causes us to resent being asked to go out of our way for someone else. No doubt at some point in your life you have been told to do something and immediately felt something spring up inside that made you want to lash out at the one giving the command. That is the power of sin. It tends to make itself heard in statements like these: "I don't want to!" "Do it yourself!" "Give it to me!" "I did the work, not him!" "I don't care what you think!" "Don't tell me what to do!" This is the way sin responds to authority—God's, the government's, or your employer's.

The power of sin oftentimes drives us to sin. It is the force we battle when we are tempted. It is that extra entity within that seems to always push us in the opposite direction from which we know God would have us go. The power of sin is so real that biblical authors personified it. When he was describing Cain's anger toward his brother Abel, Moses wrote,

> Then the LORD said to Cain, "Why are you angry? And why has your countenance fallen? If you do well, will not your countenance be lifted up? And if you do not do well, *sin is crouching at the door*; and its desire is for you, but you must master it."
>
> —Genesis 4:6–7

The power of sin is described here as a wild beast waiting to devour its prey. That is exactly how the power of sin operates. It waits for just the right opportunity to leap out and destroy our relationships, homes, thoughts, and self-esteem. The power of sin expresses itself in most cases as an attitude of rebellion. It can be as extreme as the declaration: "I don't care what is the right thing to do; I'm going to _____." Or it can be expressed in more subtle ways: "I know I should _____, but I don't want to." Or "I know I should _____, but I just can't." Usually "I can't" really means "I won't." In each case the power of sin has won out over what is right.

The apostle Paul described his battle with sin in these terms:

For we know that the Law is spiritual; but I am of flesh, sold into bondage to sin. For that which I am doing, I do not understand; for I am not practicing what I would like to do, but I am doing the very thing I hate. But if I do the very thing I do not wish to do, I agree with the Law, confessing that it is good. So now, no longer am I the one doing it, but sin which indwells me. . . . I find then the principle that evil is present in me, the one who wishes to do good.

—Romans 7:14–17, 21

All of us have experienced a similar struggle. We know what we should do; at times we even want to do it; but we cannot find it within ourselves to do what is right. Nonbelievers do not have the power to consistently overcome the power of sin in their lives. For them, it is a futile struggle. For believers, however, it is a different story.

Do You Not Know?

Now here comes the part that took me years to really understand. The Scripture teaches that believers are "dead" to the power of sin. Paul wrote,

What shall we say then? Are we to continue in sin that grace might increase? May it never be! How shall we who *died to sin* still live in it? Or do you not know that all of us who have been baptized into Christ Jesus have been baptized into His death?

—Romans 6:1–3, emphasis added

Then a few verses later:

Even so consider yourselves to be dead to sin, but alive to God in Christ Jesus.

—Romans 6:11

When Paul used the term *dead* in relationship to sin, he meant that sin no longer has the power to force us to do or think anything. But he did not mean that the power of sin no longer exists as an influence. The power of sin has *access* to us but no *authority* over us. Unfortunately, it is difficult sometimes to distinguish between the two. This is especially true for those who become believers later in life.

Several years ago a friend of the family gave us a schnauzer puppy. We named him Rommel. While Rommel was still a puppy, my son, Andy, put a collar around his neck and proceeded to teach him how to sit down, lie down, and shake hands. The way he did this was by saying, "Sit, Rommel!" Then he pushed the puppy's rear down while yanking his collar up to force Rommel into the appropriate position. Once this process was complete, Andy would reward Rommel with something to eat. This went on for days. Then he went through similar steps with the other commands. Finally, all Andy had to do was walk up to Rommel and say, "Sit," and Rommel would sit. "Lie down," and he would lie down. "Shake hands," and he would shake hands. There was no yanking on his collar or even a reward for his performance. Yet for the rest of his life, Rommel responded immediately to those three commands.

There is a sense in which Satan has a collar around the neck of each unbeliever. That collar is called the power of sin. When Satan says, "Lie," the power of sin yanks the unbeliever toward lying. When the unbeliever has an impure thought, the power of sin fastens his attention on that thought. When an unbeliever is given an order, the power of sin focuses her attention on her right to do whatever she pleases. An unbeliever can resist the power of sin, but eventually he will give in.

When a person becomes a Christian, God removes the collar. That is what it means to be dead to sin. Satan can still give commands. And impure thoughts may still flash through one's mind. Thoughts of independence may still surface on occasion. The difference is that the believer is free to choose against these things. The power of sin has been broken. Satan and the flesh still have access to the mind, but they have no authority over the will. The believer is free to choose. The believer is free to say no.

The problem may be that, like Rommel, you are so used to responding a certain way that you give in without a fight. You think, *What's the use? I've done it a thousand times. There is no use struggling; this is just the way I am.* Wrong! That is not the way you *are;* that is the way you have *chosen* to be. Regardless of how you feel, regardless of what you have done in the past, God says that once you have trusted Christ as your Savior, you are free from the power of sin.

After we took the collar off Rommel, he never *had* to obey us again. From then on, he freely *chose* to obey. Once the power of sin has been broken in your life, you never have to obey the desires of the flesh, the commands of the devil, or the call of the world. You are free to choose. The problem oftentimes is that your past experience has conditioned you. You expect to fall to certain temptations. By applying the principles outlined in this book, however, you can recondition yourself. The Bible calls this renewing your mind. We will deal with that in more detail in a later chapter. For now, you must accept the truth that the power of sin has been broken. What you do is a matter of choice.

Alive to God

Dying to sin is only half the story. The other half is that believers are alive to God. Paul wrote,

> For the death that He [Christ] died, He died to sin, once for all; but the life that He lives, He lives to God. Even so consider yourselves to be dead to sin, but alive to God in Christ Jesus.
>
> —Romans 6:10–11

Not only did our relationship to sin change, but our relationship with God changed as well. Now this may seem elementary at first. We know our relationship with God changed when we trusted Christ, but we may not know how it changed and to what extent it changed. And if we do not have this knowledge, the power of sin will continue to have an influence.

Paul knew this to be the case. In fact, his whole discussion of the believer's relationship to sin and with God is introduced with a question: "Or do you not know . . . ?" (Rom. 6:3). He knew that believers who were still living under the influence of the power of sin had not yet come to grips with the unique changes in their relationship with God. So at the risk of insulting their intelligence or covering old territory, he explained it again:

> Or do you not know that all of us who have been baptized into Christ Jesus have been baptized into His death? Therefore we have been buried with Him through baptism into death, in order that as Christ was raised from the dead through the glory of the Father, so we too might walk in newness of life. For if we have become united with Him in the likeness of His death, certainly we shall be also in the likeness of His resurrection, knowing this, that our old self was crucified with Him, that our body of sin might be done away with, that we should no longer be slaves to sin; for he who died is freed from sin.
>
> —Romans 6:3–7

When you trusted Christ as your Savior, the Bible says you were "baptized into Christ." In our culture that phrase communicates little or nothing, but in Paul's day it meant a great deal. The term *baptize* literally means "to immerse something into something else." In Bible days they would *baptize* a piece of cloth into dye in order to change its color. We would say "dip."

The term *baptize* had a figurative meaning as well. A study of first-century literature reveals that this figurative meaning of the term was used more often than the literal meaning. The figurative meaning of the term *baptize* had to do with the concept of identification. For instance, if Gentiles (non-Jews) wanted to join the Jewish faith, they would go through a series of rituals that would culminate with their baptism. The custom was for them to dip themselves under water. This signified a transformation from whatever form of religion they had embraced to Judaism. The act of baptism represented death to the old way of life and resurrection to a new way of life. The baptism was an outward expression of an inward decision to identify with the Jewish race and religion. Now, practically, all that was true of a Jew would be true of them. The Jewish God would be their God. Enemies of the Jews would now be their enemies. They would assume Jewish customs, dress, and eating habits. For all practical purposes, they had become Jewish.

A Family Affair

When Paul speaks of believers as having been baptized into Christ, he means we have been identified with Christ to the degree that what is true of Him becomes true of us. The legal ramifications of adoption in our culture closely parallel this concept. Imagine for a moment a married couple who for medical reasons is unable to have children. Several years into their marriage they win $10 million in a lottery. The following year they adopt a son. The papers are drawn up in such a fashion as to give him all the rights of a natural son. Thus, he is the heir to all his parents own. Now think about this situation.

QUESTION: How much is the son worth?
ANSWER: As much as the parents.
QUESTION: Was the adopted son *actually* there when they won the money?
ANSWER: No!
QUESTION: Is it *actually*, legally his?
ANSWER: Yes.
QUESTION: When did it become his?
ANSWER: When he was legally placed into the family.

The truth Paul wants you to understand is that when you became a Christian, you were placed into God's family through adoption. God baptized or identified or adopted (however you want to look at it) you into Christ. Therefore, what is true of Christ, in respect to what has happened to Him in the past, is true of you!

What happened to Christ? He was put to death. Since we are in Christ now, we have all the benefits of a Person who was put to death. Thus, Paul wrote that we "have been baptized into His death" (Rom. 6:3). In the same vein he continued,

> Therefore we have been buried with Him through baptism into death, in order that as Christ was raised from the dead through the glory of the Father, so we too might walk in newness of life.
>
> —Romans 6:4

Were we *actually* there when Christ was put to death and raised from the dead? No. Do we *actually* have the benefits of One who was put to death and raised from the dead? Yes! And what is the benefit of being identified with Christ's death and resurrection?

> For the death that He died, He died to sin, once for all; but the life that He lives, He lives to God.
>
> —Romans 6:10

Christ died to sin. Since we have been identified with Christ, we too are actually dead to sin. So Paul continued,

Even so consider yourselves to be dead to sin, but alive to God in Christ Jesus.

—Romans 6:11

We have the same relationship to sin that Christ had. What is even better, we have the same rights of relationship with God that Christ has. We are alive to God!

Making it Work

This truth may sound utterly ridiculous in light of your experience. You might ask, "How can I be 'dead' to sin and alive to God and act the way I do?" Simple. Remember the second law of power: *power must be harnessed and applied toward a specific goal before it serves any purpose.* Until you apply these truths to your specific situation, you will continue to respond like a dog on a leash. Every time you feel those old feelings creeping in you will reach for whatever you have been conditioned to reach for in order to temporarily quench that desire. You must accept that God has set the stage for you to experience victory over the temptations plaguing your life. He has placed you into Christ. You are a brand-new person. You have the benefits of actually having died to the power of sin. You are tapped in to the life and power of God. It is time you began putting that power to work.

The following chapters focus on making this simple principle a reality. However, until you are able to accept this final premise as reality, you will probably find very little lasting help from this book. The starting point for lasting victory over sin is accepting the fact that you are dead to the power of sin. Satan, the flesh, and the world may stand on the sidelines and scream for your attention, but they cannot force you to do anything. That power has been broken. Christ's death on the cross broke once and for all the power of sin. The collar has been removed.

Second, you are alive to God. His power resides in you. The power that raised Christ from the dead is available to you every day. This is the same power that moved Christ through this life without His once giving in to temptation. If you will put it to use, you too can move through your days and nights in victory.

A Simple Suggestion

As you continue through the principles outlined in the following chapters, let me encourage you to begin doing one thing. Meditate on this simple statement: "I am dead to sin and alive to God." Repeat it over and over under your breath as you go about your daily activities. When you are tempted, say it out loud. Sing it out loud as you drive. Write it down on an index card and place it where you can see it every day. Scribble it on your notepad during meetings. Use every opportunity during the day to get this simple yet life-changing principle ingrained into your mind. When you feel those old feelings creeping in, speak it out loud, "I may feel the way I used to feel, but the truth is that I am dead to sin and alive to God."

I'll never forget what a professor of mine once told a new convert, "You cannot live the way you used to live, for you are not the person you used to be." That is the truth. It is my prayer in closing this chapter that the truth of that statement will become a reality in your experience.

Chapter 8

AVOIDING
THE DANGER ZONES

CHUCK WAS A successful young attorney. Along with his wife and new baby, he rarely missed a church service. He had been raised in a fine Christian home, and for the most part he had walked with God throughout both college and law school. But one afternoon Chuck made a decision that eventually cost him his family and his job.

Chuck's firm needed another paralegal secretary, and he was assigned the responsibility of interviewing the applicants and hiring one of them. The second woman he interviewed seemed like the perfect choice. She had several years of experience as well as a pleasant personality. Chuck was so impressed he considered cancelling the other interviews. But he realized that would be somewhat unfair to the women who had already made appointments, so he chose to continue with the interviews.

Chuck was in a great mood as he got out of his car Thursday morning and began walking toward his office. That morning he would conduct his last interview and then get on with his "real" job. As he reached for the door, he noticed in the reflection on the glass that a woman was walking up behind him. Politely, he opened the door and waited for her to enter first. He couldn't help noticing that she was a very attractive young lady. Without thinking about it he watched her walk ahead of him to the elevator. He followed her into the elevator, thinking, *There is certainly nothing wrong with riding in the elevator with a beautiful woman. Besides, it's the only one available.*

"Four, please," she said. Chuck quickly pushed the button for the fourth floor. He grinned. That was his floor. Then the thought occurred to him, *Is this the woman who is interviewing?* And of course she was.

The interview went well, considering the fact that Chuck had a difficult time keeping his mind on what she was saying rather than on how she looked. Something inside kept saying, "There is no way you can hire her." At the same time his well-trained, analytical mind kept responding, "But it will enhance the image of the office to have an attractive young lady around. Besides, the fact that she has very little experience will make it easier for us to train her to our way of doing things. There is nothing wrong with hiring her." In the end his reason reigned, and Joyce became the firm's new paralegal.

As time passed Chuck began paying more and more attention to Joyce. For the first time in his career he actually looked forward to Secretary's Day. He spent over an hour looking for just the right card to give her. The whole time a little warning kept popping up in his conscience, "Chuck, back off." But he would always have a good reason for everything he did, "She has worked hard. I need to show her my appreciation." Soon other people in the office began to notice the extra attention Chuck paid to her. Every once in a while someone would say something about it. Chuck would smile and say, "There is nothing wrong with . . . ," and excuse whatever it was that had been brought up.

Lunch became a regular thing for Chuck and Joyce. Then it was dinner after work. The gifts continued and began to increase in size and value. All the while Chuck told himself, "There is nothing wrong with showing my apprecition. There is nothing wrong with eating out with my secretary."

It wasn't long before Joyce's professional admiration for her boss became a romantic attraction. One thing led to another, as it almost always does, and what ensued was an adulterous relationship that neither Chuck nor Joyce anticipated.

What Happened?

Chuck's story is one that has been repeated thousands of times with different people in different circumstances. In fact, as you read his story I'm sure you anticipated the ending; it came as no surprise. As common and predictable as this story may be, I want us to analyze it because it carries with it all the ingredients that make for disaster in all of our lives.

Like many of us, Chuck followed this line of reasoning about sin: "There are right things, and there are wrong things. My goal as a Christian is to always stay on the right side of things. As long as I do that, everything will be fine. As long as something is not clearly wrong, it is permissible." So every time he felt a little hesitant about his relationship with Joyce he could dismiss it by saying, "But I'm not doing anything wrong." And by his way of looking at things, he was exactly right.

We all have a tendency to think this way. We have a line drawn in our minds that separates right from wrong. As long as we are on the right side of things, we feel as if everything is all right. And should someone try to warn us about something, we may become defensive and say, "I'm not doing anything wrong! The Bible doesn't say anything about this."

Along with this way of thinking comes another tendency. That is to move as close to the line of sin as we can without actually sinning. For instance, when we see a policeman somewhere in the traffic behind us and we are in a 55-mile-per-hour speed zone, what speed do we slow down to? Usually right down to the line, 55. That is the way we think.

High-school students often express the same way of thinking with this question, "How far can my steady and I go?" What they are really asking in most cases is, "Exactly where is the line between what is permissible and what is not? After you tell us, we are going to camp out right on the line!" We want to go as far as we can; we want to know how close we can get to sin without actually sinning. This question is constantly being asked of relationships, tax deductions, speed limits, expense accounts, rock music, dancing, and anything else where there is a margin of vagueness.

Unfortunately there will never be an agreed-upon biblical answer for these "grey areas." The Bible doesn't address itself to the question of how far a person can go toward sin without actually sinning. That was never a concern of the biblical authors as they wrote. Moved by the Holy Spirit, they were addressing an entirely different question, "How can I become more Christlike in my character? How can I be used to encourage those around me to become more like Christ?" Those were the concerns of the biblical writers.

The problem with wanting to know how close to sin we can get without sinning is that the motivation behind the question is such that once we find a satisfactory answer we immediately position ourselves on the edge of moral or ethical disaster. We develop lifestyles so close to the edge that Satan has to do very little to push us over into sin.

The Calorie-Conscious Counselor

Imagine for a moment that a friend of yours complained to you about his inability to stay on his diet. Being a concerned friend, you ask him when he finds it most difficult. What would you think if he replied, "I do pretty good until I go into the ice-cream shop, order a hot fudge sundae, and put a big spoonful right in front of my mouth. Every time I do that I just can't resist the temptation"? Not very bright, huh?

Let's take it one step further. Without losing your cool you share with him that if he is really serious about staying on his diet, he needs to stay out of the ice-cream shop. How would you feel if he responded, "There's nothing wrong with going into the ice-cream shop! People do it all the time. I even saw the pastor and his wife in the ice-cream shop. You are so legalistic"?

Well, he has a point. There is nothing wrong with going into an ice-cream shop. But he is missing another point, isn't he? He is missing the point that many Christians miss when it comes to successfully dealing with temptation. When we are faced with decisions about opportunities, invitations, vacations, gifts, movies, music, books, magazines, videos, dates, or anything else that pertains to our daily lives, we shouldn't be asking, "What's wrong with this?" Instead we should be asking, "What is the wise thing to do?"

Walking Wisely

When he wrote to the believers in Ephesus, Paul concluded a lengthy discussion concerning issues of right and wrong with this admonition:

> Therefore be careful how you walk, not as unwise men, but as wise.
>
> —Ephesians 5:15

The relationship between Paul's exhortation here and the verses that preceded it cannot be overemphasized. The term *therefore* communicates the idea of, "Now if you're serious about following through with what I have just said . . ." Paul had just described how believers are to respond to those whose lives could be described as immoral, greedy, impure, covetous, or crude. He instructed them not to "participate" with them. He even encouraged them to go so far as to "expose" what those people were up to. At that point he shifted his discussion to the issue of wisdom. His point is clear. If we are to stay untainted by the sinful people we rub shoulders with every day, we must learn to walk wisely.

Scope It Out!

As Paul used the phrase here, *be careful* meant to "examine carefully." He was saying that in all of life we must scope out each opportunity and situation carefully; we must weigh the pros and the cons. We must get in the habit of testing each opportunity in light of our past experience, present weaknesses, and future plans. My experience as a pastor tells me that people rarely plan to get into trouble. Their problem is that they fail to plan to stay out of trouble.

In terms of one's past experience, wisdom asks, "What happened the last time I was involved with this group?" "What usually happens when I go to this place?" Wisdom does not rationalize, "There's nothing wrong with those people." That is not the issue. The issue concerns the wisdom of your going out with them.

Like most pastors, I have seen countless young people and single adults go down the drain morally. For many couples I could see it coming a mile off. Time and time again I have warned people or had members of my staff warn them. And over and over again we get the same routine. A young man or woman will defend the relationship based on the partner's overall character or background while ignoring the fact that the relationship is outside God's parameters and that past experience indicates it will stay that way as long as they are together.

They say things like, "But you don't understand. He is a great guy. He is so polite and sensitive." Or "She is the finest girl I've ever dated. Sure we have our problems, but she has so much going for her. I would be a fool to drop her." And so they continue outside God's will, promising over and over again that things will change until the bottom drops out. These relationships are usually short-lived. Finally, one of the two will lose interest in the other. Or the girl may get pregnant. Either way, there is a great deal of hurt. They always wish they had listened.

What About Now?

Wisdom makes decisions in light of the past, and it is also sensitive to present weaknesses. By present weaknesses, I am referring to the fact that we are more susceptible to certain temptations at some times than at others. For instance, right after teenagers have a big argument with their parents, they are usually more prone to do things they would normally not do. I have talked to kids who took their first drink right after a big blowup at home. They were not sure why they did it. They just felt "extra rebellious" as one boy put it.

A businessman who has just landed a big deal that he has worked for weeks or months to put together may be more vulnerable than normal to certain temptations. When a man experiences a great deal of success, he sometimes feels as if he owes it to himself to take some extra liberties. Sometimes he feels above the law.

People who are committed to walking wisely stay in touch with their feelings and frustrations. They realize that what may have been safe last weekend could possibly lead to disaster this weekend; that what was easy to resist last night may be more difficult to say no to tonight. They approach every opportunity, invitation, and relationship in light of their present state of mind and feelings.

Planning Ahead

The third area wisdom always considers is the future, which includes plans, goals, and dreams. Just about every sin we are tempted to commit has a direct or an indirect effect on our future. Whether it is cheating, lying, stealing, gossiping, or some sort of sexual sin, it touches our future. If we are wise, we will look beyond the immediate pleasure of sin to its ultimate effect on our plans for the future. Therefore, the clearer our goals are, the easier it becomes to say no to temptation. Why? Because one of the lies of Satan is, "This won't hurt a bit!" As we have seen, however, every sin hurts; nobody gets by with sin. Goal-oriented people are more apt to view present decisions in light of future consequences.

A young girl who has purposed in her heart to keep herself morally pure for the man she will eventually marry will have more resolve when tempted to compromise than the girl who has never really given much thought to what kind of woman she wants to be someday. A father who desires to keep his kids on his team once they become teenagers will resist the temptation to constantly busy himself with his own pursuits while his children are young. The wife who has purposed in her heart to keep her marriage exciting will resist the temptation to slack off in her efforts to look pleasing to her husband. The wise person always measures each thought, opportunity, and relationship by its effect on future plans and dreams.

Christians don't wake up one morning and just out of the blue decide to go out and have an affair. Businessmen don't begin their careers with the intent of being dishonest. Singles don't plan dating relationships that will result in an unwanted pregnancy. Families don't plan to go into debt up to their ears. Married couples do not start out planning somewhere down the road to get divorced. I have never met a Christian teenager who planned to drink the first beer. Neither have I met a Christian young lady who set out ahead of time to lose her virginity. Yet all of these things happen every day. Why? Because we don't plan well enough for these things not to happen.

It Is an Evil Day

We live in an age in which everything is working against the things we hold dear. Think about it. What force in our society is working to help you remain faithful to your partner? None that I can think of. The message of our world is just the opposite. What force in our society is working to help your kids remain true to principles the Bible sets forth in regard to sexual purity, honesty, loyalty, and the priority of character development? None! The message our kids are bombarded with is, "Acquire all you can and do whatever feels good." We don't live in a neutral world that beckons us to choose between right and wrong. The world we face every day is one in which right has become wrong.

Believers cannot afford to go out into the world without taking major precautions. Paul lists two things believers should do if they are serious about surviving morally and ethically. The first one is found immediately following the verse we just looked at:

Therefore be careful how you walk, not as unwise men, but as wise, *making the most of your time*, because the days are evil.

—Ephesians 5:15–16, *emphasis added*

Apparently the Ephesian society was not much better off than ours. In fact, in some respects it was worse. In our society immorality is associated with godlessness, but in Ephesus immorality played a central role in the religion of that culture. In their worship of the goddess Artemis, the Ephesians participated in sensual fertility rituals that included orgiastic rites as well as prostitution. Imagine living in a society where religious convictions were demonstrated through immoral conduct!

In addressing the believers of this city, Paul advised them to make the most of their time. That is, they should use their time carefully. Paul realized that it required absolutely no effort on their part to become like the world. They did not have to study or set goals or even make any plans to become worldly. All they had to do was get out in the world and live. If they took no precautions, it would be just a matter of time before they looked, acted, and thought just like the world. And that applies to us, too.

That being the case, Paul warned the Ephesian believers to take every available moment and work toward reversing this process. To keep from becoming like the world takes a conscious effort, and that means time. It is so easy to become lazy with "extra" time. Yet to do so is really a step toward failure.

The wise father, for instance, does not walk into the house, throw down his briefcase, and plop down in front of the television or pick up the newspaper. He thinks, *I have thirty minutes until dinner. I haven't seen my kids all day. I haven't talked to my wife all day. I'll take this time and invest it in those relation-*

ships instead of watching the tube. Is that to say there is something wrong with watching television after work? Not at all. That is just the point. The question is not one of wrong versus right. It is a matter of choosing the wise thing. Our world crowds out family time. So those who are serious about overcoming the pressures of this world system must take advantage of every spare minute to do so.

The wise housewife does not turn on the television to keep her company while she is cleaning. She thinks instead, *Ah! An hour to choose what I must listen to. What is the wisest thing to fill my mind with? Television? Not hardly.* So she reaches for some Christian music or tapes of sermons or something that will be edifying. Is that to say a housewife must never watch television while she is at home alone? Of course not. But the wise housewife realizes that these are evil days in which we live. She must, therefore, use every spare minute to safeguard against becoming like the world that is working so hard to destroy everything she holds dear.

Wise teenagers or college students do not jump into the car and immediately turn up the radio. As they shut the door, they think, *Silence! For the next few minutes I can control what goes into my head. I can't control it in class. I can't control what I hear in the locker room. I don't even have too much control at home. But for now I can decide.* Instead of pumping in more error from the radio, wise students use that time to fill their minds with something good for a change. And again, the issue is not whether Christians should listen to the radio! The issue has to do with the wisest way to use precious spare time.

You may be thinking, *What has all of this got to do with temptation?* Simply this. One of Satan's tricks is to keep our minds off the truth for extended periods of time. During this time he slowly leads our thinking and our emotions further and further away from the truth. Then when we are least expecting it, WHAM! We fall. That is why we are so vulnerable during vacation. We get out of our routine. We let the spiritual disciplines go for a while. We go for hours and even days without any direct reminders of what is true and right. Our emotions grow more sensitive to the things of the world rather than the things of God. And then we wonder how we slip so easily into sin, sin we would never have considered at home.

In this evil day in which we live we need constant reminders of the truth. If we are not careful with our time, we will allow others to fill it up for us. There will be no time for God. Consequently, we will be set up to fall. Wise men and women are careful with their time. They use their extra time to draw close to God; to check themselves out; to make sure they are not creeping ever so slowly toward that illusive line dividing things that are of God from things that are of the world.

Face the Music

According to Paul, this is the second thing believers should do:

So then do not be foolish, but understand what the will of the Lord is.

—Ephesians 5:17

Upon first reading this, we may think it makes no sense. How can he command us to understand the Lord's will? Isn't that what we are always trying to figure out anyway?

What Paul means is this: "Don't go on willfully ignoring what you know in your heart God would have you do. Face up to it!" Paul is calling us to quit playing games; to quit excusing those things in our lives that may not be "wrong" but lead us into sin time and time again. "Quit rationalizing away those relationships that keep causing you to stumble. Only a fool continues to play games with himself!" he admonishes.

If doing business with certain individuals or groups puts you in a position that causes you to violate your convictions time and time again, quit doing business with them. If watching certain television shows causes you to lust, don't excuse them because of their entertainment value. Just quit watching them. If being with a particular group of people causes you to stumble, don't rationalize by saying, "But they are my friends." Get some new friends!

In every area of life, face up to what God would have you do. As long as you play games, as long as you ignore what you know in your heart God would have you do, you set yourself up to fail. You *camp out*, so to speak, right on the line between what is right and what is wrong. It is only a matter of time, and Satan will push you over. If you aren't willing to deal with the areas of your life that lead you into temptation, you are really not serious about dealing with temptation itself. Consistency in the Christian life demands wisdom; and wisdom demands that you face up to those things that set you up to fail.

Our Heavenly Guide

It is interesting that immediately following this passage, Paul writes,

> And do not get drunk with wine, for that is dissipation, but be filled with the Spirit.
>
> —Ephesians 5:18

The Holy Spirit plays a very important role when it comes to wisdom. If you will think back to the story of Chuck and the paralegal, you will remember that throughout the entire episode something kept warning Chuck about hiring Joyce. Chuck did not recognize it at the time, but that was the Holy Spirit working through his conscience. I call it a check in my spirit. It is hard to explain, but if you're a believer, you know exactly what I'm talking about. It's that feeling of hesitation located somewhere between your throat and your stomach. It defies logic at times. And it is usually not overbearing. It is perceived as a feeling, but it is more than a feeling.

In regard to temptation, the Holy Spirit functions much like a tour guide. Imagine that you are visiting the Grand Canyon, and you and your family sign up for a tour. What would you think if your tour guide led your entire group right up to the rail over-looking a sheer cliff and then climbed up on the narrow rail? Now imagine that as he stood there teetering back and forth, he in-structed all of you to climb up for a better view!

More than likely your first response would be to call the man-agement and have that guy locked up! Beyond that, however, your reply to his request would sound something like this, "That is quite all right. We can see just fine from back here," as you stepped back from the edge.

Do you know what the Holy Spirit wants to do for you? He wants to hold out His arms several stages away from sin and say, "This is close enough. You can see fine from here." When you ignore those warnings and move ahead, you set yourself up for disaster. You see, there is nothing harmful about balancing on the security rail overlooking the Grand Canyon. But only a fool would do such a thing. In the same respect, only a fool would continually ignore the warnings of the Holy Spirit.

A Few Steps Back

If you are serious about dealing with the temptations that ha-rass you day after day, you may need to take a few steps back— a few wise steps toward safety and away from temptation. A friend of mine in another city had to take a few steps back in the area of lust. One afternoon we pulled up in front of a convenience store to get a paper. As I was about to get out of the car, he said, "Don't go. I'll send Sarah." Sarah was his eight-year-old daughter. He gave her some change and off she went, barely able to open the door by herself.

I made a humorous comment about his being too lazy to get the paper himself. His reply, however, explained why he sent his daughter and why he was the godly man I knew him to be. "You see," he said, "I used to go in all the time. But just inside the door to the left is a magazine rack. It is full of trashy magazines. Every time I would go in I would battle the temptation to pick one up and flip through it. I decided the wisest thing to do would be to send Sarah. That way I could avoid the temptation altogether."

Now that's taking a few steps back. Does my friend think it is wrong to go into convenience stores? No. That is not the question at all. The question is, what is the wisest thing to do?

I have another close friend who battled with changing the television channel once something of inferior quality came on. He would sit for hours, late into the night, watching whatever was on. He had to take a few steps back. He made it a rule never to turn on the television and just flip through the channels to see what was on. He always checks first to see if there is anything on worth watching. He learned that it is easier to walk away from the programming guide than from an actual show.

As we close, let me share my conviction concerning this principle. I believe this principle alone could eliminate some of the most difficult temptations confronting you. You say, "But you don't even know me." That may be true. But the people with whom I have shared this principle, and who have taken it seriously, always see a dramatic decrease in the power of the temptations with which they struggle.

Leaving the Danger Zones

Let me warn you. It may be a simple principle, but it is not always an easy one to apply. People will not understand why you can no longer go with them to the places you used to go. Even some of your Christian friends will not understand. They will think you are being legalistic or "holier than thou." Your lost friends certainly will not understand. Their comments may sting. "He can't go. He's a Christian." You may find yourself sitting at home more often.

But let me ask you again, are you really serious about gaining victory over temptation? If you are, are you willing to take a few steps back? Are you ready to step back away from the edge as if to say, "That's OK. I can see fine from here"? Are you willing to evaluate every opportunity in light of your past experiences, your present state of mind, and your future goals, plans, and dreams? Are you willing to question every invitation and decision in light of what is the "wisest" thing to do?

Are you willing to use your spare time carefully? Not always reaching for the radio or the television or the newspaper. And are you willing to face up to what you know in your heart God wants from your life? If you are, why don't you take a few minutes right now and think through those areas in which you feel you need to take a step or two back. Write them down. Perhaps you'll want to take an index card and record some of the key points of this chapter and put it in a prominent place so that you'll see it often. Then pray and ask God to forgive you for ignoring the promptings of the Holy Spirit. Ask Him to increase your sensitivity to His Spirit as He leads you down the path of wisdom and away from the danger zones.

Chapter 9

DRESSING
FOR THE BATTLE

IN RECENT YEARS Americans have become more and more fashion conscious. People spend outlandish sums of money updating their wardrobes every season. Advertisers are focusing on smaller segments of the population and designing the right "look" for every age group. You can even buy designer clothes for babies, and I'm sure the babies appreciate it!

The Bible, however, speaks of a different kind of wardrobe, one that is usually overlooked by most believers. Yet it is far more important than the current style. Paul described this spiritual outfit:

> Therefore, take up the full armor of God, that you may be able to resist in the evil day, and having done everything, to stand firm. Stand firm therefore, having girded your loins with truth, and having put on the breastplate of righteousness, and having shod your feet with the preparation of the gospel of peace; in addition to all, taking up the shield of faith with which you will be able to extinguish all the flaming missiles of the evil one. And take the helmet of salvation, and the sword of the Spirit, which is the word of God.
>
> —Ephesians 6:13–17

No doubt you have heard sermons on the armor of God before. This is a very popular passage among preachers. But as familiar as most Christians are with the content of this passage, I find very few who take seriously Paul's application of these verses. Paul did not say, "Understand the full armor of God." Neither did he say, "Research each piece of Roman armor alluded to in these verses." Paul said, "PUT IT ON!"

Dressed for Success

Of all the people in the world, American believers should be the first to understand the force of this passage. We have different clothes for every occasion, and we are careful to wear just the right thing at the appropriate time. We have clothes to work in. Clothes to relax in. Clothes to go out on the town in. Clothes to exercise in. Clothes for weddings, formals, parties, dates, bridge clubs, pool parties, hiking, swimming, and on and on it goes. Chances are you will never catch a banker at work in his bathing suit. Or a welder at work in a tux. Neither would you find the mother of a bride wearing hiking boots at her daughter's wedding. We are careful about what we wear and where we wear it.

There is one occasion, however, that we rarely think to dress for—*war*, the spiritual war in which each of us as a believer is involved. Think about it. Would a soldier go into battle without first getting dressed for it? Not a soldier with any sense who wanted to survive. Yet every day of our lives we who profess the Lord Jesus as our Savior enter a battle. And unfortunately, most of us do not take the time to dress appropriately. Then we get to the end of the day and wonder why we don't have any willpower or discipline or resistance.

In chapter 2 we focused on the context for the temptations we experience. We saw how each temptation is a small part of an ongoing struggle between God and His enemy, the devil. We talked about how easy it is to forget that we are in a war; we are lulled into thinking that we struggle in a vacuum. And we saw how that was not the case at all. Yet even since you read that chapter, I imagine the truth about the war in which we are involved has faded from your thinking. Not intentionally, I might add. We are just not used to thinking in those terms.

Home Sweet Home

Imagine a soldier who falls asleep one night and dreams that the war is over and he is back in the States. His dream is so real that when he wakes up, he really believes he is back home and the war is over. How do you think he would dress? Like he was going into battle? I doubt it. Worse yet, what would happen to him if his squad was attacked?

Most believers do not take seriously Paul's commands in this familiar passage because we do not live conscious of the fact that we are in a war! Until we accept this simple truth, we will never develop the habit of preparing ourselves properly. Ephesians 6 is not the only passage that refers to believers being involved in a war. Paul reminded Timothy of the same truth when he said,

> Suffer hardship with me, as a good soldier of Christ Jesus. No soldier in active service entangles himself in the affairs of everyday life, so that he may please the one who enlisted him as a soldier.
>
> —2 Timothy 2:3–4

The Scriptures are clear. When we trust Christ as our Savior, we enter a war. And just like an unprepared soldier can expect to suffer in a physical war, an unprepared soldier will suffer in a spiritual war as well.

Perhaps one reason you cannot overcome temptation in your life is that you are going into battle unprepared for what you will face. Once the enemy has begun his attack, it is usually too late to start getting ready. Yet, more often than not, that is exactly when you find yourself scrambling around, looking for verses, praying meaningless prayers, and wondering why you never get anywhere.

Meet Your Opponent

Before we get into how we are to prepare for battle, we need to deal with one other matter. One of the enemy's most effective tricks is to divert the focus of our attention away from him and onto someone or something else. He wants us to see someone else as the enemy, not him. He wants husbands to see their wives as the enemy; kids to see their parents as the enemy; pastors to see their deacons or elders as the enemy.

Paul says, however, that this war is not against flesh and blood. We are not struggling with one another. Our enemy is spiritual in nature.

> For our struggle is not against flesh and blood, but against the rulers, against the powers, against the world forces of this darkness, against the spiritual forces of wickedness in the heavenly places.
>
> —Ephesians 6:12

One reason we struggle so in our earthly relationships is that we forget oftentimes where the real problem lies. That is why couples who pray together generally stay together. Prayer is the best reminder of who the enemy really is or is not! I have found in my own experience, for example, that the more our deacons pray together, the less time we spend in meetings.

Our enemy is invisible, but he is very real. He is not omniscient; he does not know everything. But he has been around long enough to have figured out our every move. He does not announce his presence with a trumpet fanfare; he is subtle. He does not attack us like the British in the Revolutionary War, wearing bright colors and making himself known. He attacks more like the colonists. He blends in well with the surroundings and waits for just the right moment.

Last of all, our enemy does not fight alone. He has under his authority scores of demonic hosts that are loose and active in the world today. There was a time when people laughed at the idea of demons and demonic possession. But more and more the truth is coming out into the open. This is especially true in countries where black magic is practiced openly. But even in our country the authorities are continually uncovering evidence of spirit worship and witchcraft.

The point is, our enemy is not alone. For the most part, overt demonic activity, such as spells and possessions, is not our concern. I do believe, however, that we struggle with demonic influence. I am no expert in the area of demons and how they work. The Scripture does not give us much insight here. But the Scripture is clear about how to deal with these hellish hosts:

Put on the full armor of God, that you may be able to stand firm against the schemes of the devil.

—Ephesians 6:11

Take a Chance

Before you read any further, I want you to make yourself a promise. Promise yourself that you will at least try what I am about to suggest. And not just for one day, but for seven days, one whole week. Wait! Don't keep reading until you make yourself that promise. Why? Because this is going to sound silly to some of you, especially those of you who are the more "serious" type. You know who you are. Anyway, if you will give this a try, I guarantee you won't be sorry. And if you think this is a ridiculous idea, I challenge you to study this passage on your own and figure out what you think Paul is talking about when he says, "Put on the full armor of God." I would be happy to hear from you and get your opinion.

A Closer Look

Now, at the risk of sounding contradictory, I want to take a quick look at the actual Roman armor Paul had in mind and its relationship to the spiritual armor we are to wear. The first piece he mentions is the belt: ". . . having girded your loins with truth." The Roman soldier had a girdle to put around himself. It was more like an apron than a belt. It was made of thick leather and covered his abdominal region. It also supported his sword.

The truth about God and about us as His children serves as the foundation for everything else we do as believers. That is why Paul associated the girdle with truth. The power of God is greater than the power of sin or Satan. This is the truth that gives us hope when we face temptation. The truth about us, as we have seen, is that we have been baptized into Christ. Therefore, we have been identified with His death and are dead to sin. These truths serve as the foundation for the rest of our spiritual armor.

Next Paul mentions the breastplate: ". . . and having put on the breastplate of righteousness." The breastplate was usually made of leather, although some of them were covered with metal. The breastplate protected the chest region and, thus, all the vital organs.

In ancient days, men believed the emotions resided somewhere in a person's chest. This belief probably arose from the fact that so much of what we feel emotionally is felt in that area of the body. The breastplate is associated with righteousness because what is right often conflicts with the way we feel. The breastplate of righteousness is to guard us from making decisions based on what we feel rather than what we know to be right. So often temptation begins with our emotions. We must keep our emotions in check. Not that there is anything wrong with being emotional. On the contrary, our emotions are just as much a gift of God as any part of our makeup. They were never intended, however, to be our guide.

Paul moves on to the foot covering: ". . . and having shod your feet with the preparation of the gospel of peace." The foot covering of the Roman soldier was a thick leather sandal. It wrapped around both the foot and the ankle. Sometimes the bottom was covered with spikes or nails to allow him to keep his footing in hand-to-hand combat.

The shoe is associated with peace because that is what we are to leave everywhere we go, much like a footprint. Wherever we go, we should be sharing the good news of how men and women can have peace with God.

The focus shifts here from actual clothing to a defensive weapon, the shield: ". . . in addition to all, taking up the shield of faith with which you will be able to extinguish all the flaming missiles of the evil one." The shield Paul is referring to here is not the little round shield like you see on television; it was much larger. The word translated "shield" comes from the word that meant "door." In fact, some of these shields were almost as big as doors.

They had an iron frame with thick leather stretched over it, and some of them had metal on the front. A soldier could kneel down behind such a shield and be completely protected in the front. On occasion, the Romans would soak their shields in water so that when the enemy shot flaming arrows, they were extinguished on impact.

Faith is associated with the shield because God may ask us to go places or say things that leave us open to criticism or possible failure. In and of ourselves we would be fools to even try. When we choose to obey, we walk by faith. We move out expecting God to come through for us in the areas we know we are incapable of handling. Faith, then, is our defense against fear, insecurity, anxiety, and anything else that would keep us from moving out in obedience to God.

Next Paul refers to the helmet: "And take the helmet of salvation." The helmet was the most costly and most ornate piece of the soldier's armor. It was designed to protect the entire head.

I think two ideas are implied here. First, the helmet was the piece of armor that attracted the most attention because of its elaborate design. In the same way our eternal salvation is the thing about us that should get people's attention. It is the thing for which we are to be most grateful. Jesus made that clear in Luke 10:20 ("Nevertheless do not rejoice in this, that the spirits are subject to you, but rejoice that your names are recorded in heaven").

A second idea implied in this parallel has to do with the mind. The mind is where most of our battles are won or lost. That is where the ultimate decision is made as to whether or not we will obey. We are saved from temptation when we choose with our minds to be obedient. Just as the helmet protected the head of the soldier, so our salvation gives us the potential to say yes to God and no to sin. In so doing, we are saved in a temporal sense from the act and consequences of sin.

Last of all, Paul refers to the primary offensive weapon of the Roman soldier, the sword: ". . . and the sword of the Spirit, which is the word of God." The Roman sword was designed for close combat. It was actually more of a dagger than what we normally think about when we think about a sword.

The Word of God is viewed as a sword because of its power to overcome the onslaught of the enemy. In the next chapter we will discuss exactly how this works. Suffice it to say that the Word of God sends Satan and his hosts running for cover.

A Roman soldier would not dream of going into battle without every piece of equipment secured and ready for action. To have done so would have meant certain death. Paul, understanding the day in which he lived, knew that the Ephesian believers dared not enter into the spiritual war they were involved in every day without being equally prepared.

Preparing for War

Now here is the part you may be "tempted" to skip. I have made it a habit of putting on the armor of God every morning before I get out of bed. Right over my pajamas! Remember, this is spiritual armor. Therefore, it must be put on by faith. Paul understood that spiritual warfare was somewhat of a difficult concept to grasp. So he gave us an illustration through his description of the Roman soldier. Using that mental image as a guide, we can properly prepare ourselves for the battle. But it is done by faith, not by sight.

The best way to explain this is to simply walk you through the routine I follow every morning. You do not have to do it just like I do. Paul did not leave us directions as to how to put it on by faith. There is no right or wrong way. He simply said, "Put it on."

Each morning when I first awaken I say something like this,

Good morning, Lord. Thank You for assuring me of victory today if I will but follow Your battle plan. So by faith I claim victory over _____ (I normally list some things I know I will be faced with that day).

To prepare myself for the battle ahead, by faith I put on the belt of truth. The truth about You, Lord—that You are a sovereign God who knows everything about me, both my strengths and my weaknesses. Lord, You know my breaking point and have promised not to allow me to be tempted beyond what I am able to bear. The truth about me, Lord, is that I am a new creature in Christ and have been set free from the power of sin. I am indwelt with the Holy Spirit who will guide me and warn me when danger is near. I am Your child, and nothing can separate me from Your love. The truth is that You have a purpose for me this day—someone to encourage, someone to share with, someone to love.

Next, Lord, I want to, by faith, put on the breastplate of righteousness. Through this I guard my heart and my emotions. I will not allow my heart to attach itself to anything that is impure. I will not allow my emotions to rule in my decisions. I will set them on what is right and good and just. I will live today by what is true, not by what I feel.

Lord, this morning I put on the sandals of the gospel of peace. I am available to You, Lord. Send me where You will. Guide me to those who need encouragement or physical help of some kind. Use me to solve conflicts wherever they may arise. Make me a calming presence in every circumstance in which You place me. I will not be hurried or rushed, for my schedule is in Your hands. I will not leave a trail of tension and apprehension. I will leave tracks of peace and stability everywhere I go.

I now take up the shield of faith, Lord. My faith is in You and You alone. Apart from You, I can do nothing. With you, I can do all things. No temptation that comes my way can penetrate Your protecting hand. I will not be afraid, for You are going with me throughout this day. When I am tempted, I will claim my victory out loud ahead of time, for You have promised victory to those who walk in obedience to Your Word. So by faith I claim victory even now because I know there are fiery darts headed my way even as I pray. Lord, You already know what they are and have already provided the way of escape.

Lord, by faith I am putting on the helmet of salvation. You know how Satan bombards my mind day and night with evil thoughts, doubt, and fear. I put on this helmet that will protect my mind. I may feel the impact of his attacks, but nothing can penetrate this helmet. I choose to stop every impure and negative thought at the door of my mind. And with the helmet of salvation those thoughts will get no further. I elect to take every thought captive; I will dwell on nothing but what is good and right and pleasing to You.

Last, I take up the sword of the Spirit, which is Your Word. Thank You for the precious gift of Your Word. It is strong and powerful and able to defeat even the strongest of Satan's onslaughts. Your Word says that I am not under obligation to the flesh to obey its lusts. Your Word says that I am free from the power of sin. Your Word says that He that is in me is greater than he that is in the world. So by faith I take up the strong and powerful sword of the Spirit, which is able to defend me in time of attack, comfort me in time of sorrow, teach me in time of meditation, and prevail against the power of the enemy on behalf of others who need the truth to set them free.

So, Lord, I go now rejoicing that You have chosen me to represent You to this lost and dying world. May others see

Jesus in me, and may Satan and his hosts shudder as Your power is made manifest in me. In Jesus' name I pray—AMEN.

Now, let me ask you a question. Can you think of any better way to start your day? Some might respond, "You're just psyching yourself up." To which I say, "Exactly." But I am not psyching myself up by telling myself a bunch of lies so I will like myself more or have more self-confidence. It is not self-confidence we are after; it is Christ confidence, confidence in Christ and His power through us. Sure, it sounds like a one-person pep rally, but it's all true! And we are to set our minds and emotions on what is true.

My way may not be for everybody. I even debated on whether or not to include this chapter in the book. But I want you to be victorious in your life. And apart from putting on the entire armor of God, you don't have a chance. None of us do.

Faith is being able to visualize ahead of time what God is going to do. By lying there in bed, putting on the armor piece by piece and thinking through the significance of each piece, I am exercising faith. Biblical faith. Faith in what God has done as well as what He promised to do.

First Things First

Sunday is such a busy day for me that I often stay at church all day. When I plan to do so, I always carry clothes for the service that night. More times than I care to remember I have forgotten something, either socks, a tie, or a fresh shirt. Fortunately, I have a wonderful wife who always comes to my rescue. I'll call her up, and she'll arrive a little early to guarantee that I have what I need.

I can't imagine going out to preach without having my socks on. Neither could I imagine preaching without wearing a shirt or shoes. Yet I have learned that I can get by much better without certain physical garments than I can the spiritual ones God has made available.

Paul did not suggest that we put on the whole armor of God. He *commanded* that we do so. Think for just a moment. Have you ever thought through the armor in the way I have just explained it? Have you ever taken this command seriously? Or has it always been simply an interesting passage to study and hear sermons about?

A recurring plot in war novels as well as recent science fiction movies has been that of the supposedly impregnable military complex or battleship. As the story moves toward its climax, someone discovers the Achilles' heel, the one weak spot in the defense system of the base or ship. Everyone then goes to work on a plan to capitalize on the weakness.

That was the plot of *Star Wars*, the first film in the popular trilogy about the conflict between a group of young heroes and the evil Empire. No one who has seen that movie will forget those last few scenes of the fighters shooting their way down the channel leading to the one spot where a well-placed rocket could destroy the entire base. Remember the panic on the inside of the Empire's ship when they discovered that they were vulnerable? By then, it was too late for them to do anything to save themselves.

Satan is scheming against each of us. Part of that scheme is to discover our area of least resistance. That area in which we have let down our guard. The one spot that if attacked at just the right time will put us into a spiritual tailspin. Can we really afford to move out in the mornings without first suiting up? Are we not fools to think that we are so together that we can handle Satan and his host without putting on all that armor?

I know what you are thinking. *That will take all morning.* No, it won't. You'll be surprised at how quickly it goes by. You may think, *Well, I have my quiet time at night.* I am not talking about your quiet time. Besides, whoever heard of putting on armor after the battle? Your battles begin the moment you wake up each morning. That is when you need to put on the armor.

Once again, are you willing to try this for seven days? When I first challenged my congregation with this concept, I had no idea how many of them would take me seriously. Almost immediately I received reports about the difference it made. I still get letters from people who heard that message on tape and have started suiting up for battle every morning before they start their day. If you are serious about gaining lasting victory over temptation in your life, "Put on the full armor of God, that you may be able to stand firm against the schemes of the devil." It worked for Paul. It has worked for me. I am confident it will make a difference in your life as well.

Chapter 10

WIELDING
THE SWORD

MY FAVORITE HOBBY is photography. An ideal vacation to me is loading up all my camera equipment and taking off for a couple of weeks on a photographic safari. I have had the joy of taking photographs all over the United States and in many foreign countries. In my endeavor to increase my skill as a photographer I have learned some important lessons. One of them is that there are no problems unique to me. Regardless of the questions I have or the predicaments I find myself in, some other photographer has already wrestled with the same dilemma and usually has discovered a solution. Until I realized this, I would let the simplest things hold me up for weeks and sometimes months.

I will never forget my first attempts at developing color film. What a disaster! I went through boxes of paper with very little to show for my hours of labor; and even at that, nothing I could be proud of. Then I met a guy who had been working in a color lab for years. He came over, showed me what I was doing wrong, and in a couple of hours we were turning out some nice pictures.

From that point on, I began to research my questions to discover how the pros dealt with them. Doing so saved me hours of headaches and freed me to do what I like best—taking photographs.

What Did Jesus Do?

Now, let's apply that same kind of thinking to this matter of temptation. First of all, let's state the problem: How do we resist temptation? Second, who has struggled with the same problem and dealt with it successfully as well as consistently? The writer of Hebrews answers that question for us,

> For we do not have a high priest who cannot sympathize with our weaknesses, but One who has been tempted in all things as we are, yet without sin.
>
> —Hebrews 4:15

If Jesus is "the pro," then we would do well to study His strategy for dealing with temptation. Strangely enough, Jesus' approach is so straightforward and simple that many believers tend to overlook it entirely. Others, after hearing it, make the most ridiculous excuses as to why they cannot follow His example. In doing so, however, they resign themselves to a life of defeat.

Unfortunately, we have only one clear passage of Scripture describing Christ's encounter with temptation. We know from the Hebrews passage cited above that He was tempted more often than this, but the Holy Spirit chose not to include these in the Gospels.

The Ultimate Temptation

Matthew sets the stage for us in the first two verses of this narrative,

> Then Jesus was led up by the Spirit into the wilderness to be tempted by the devil. And after He had fasted forty days and forty nights, He then became hungry.
>
> —Matthew 4:1–2

This last phrase may be the greatest understatement of all time: "He then became hungry." I think starving would be more like it! The text seems to indicate that Christ was unaware of His physical needs during this time. G. Campbell Morgan made this comment about this period in Christ's life,

> Notice carefully that it was after the lapse of forty days that Jesus was hungry. It would seem as though during their passing, He was unconscious of His physical need. His thoughts had been of things within the spiritual realm, and the demands of the physical had been unrecognized. At the close of the forty days the sense of need swept over Him. He was hungry.
> —*The Crisis of the Christ*, p. 165

Now before we go rushing into the rest of the story, let's pause for a moment and think. Forty days without food. One month and ten days. It is difficult for some of us to go one hour and ten minutes. No doubt the reason for choosing to include this particular temptation scenario in the Scripture is that there was probably no other time in Christ's earthly life when He was more susceptible to temptation. He was weak physically from not having eaten. He was probably drained emotionally from His prolonged time of prayer. If there was ever a time to tempt the Lord Jesus, that was it; and Satan knew it. At the same time, if there is a way to have victory when tempted in circumstances such as these, we need to know about it. It is doubtful that we will ever find ourselves in a more vulnerable position.

"And the Tempter Came"

Matthew continues,

> And the tempter came and said to Him, "If You are the Son of God, command that these stones become bread." But He answered and said, "It is written, 'Man shall not live on bread alone, but on every word that proceeds out of the mouth of God.'"
> —Matthew 4:3–4

Thus ended round one. But the devil didn't give up.

> Then the devil took Him into the holy city; and he had Him
> stand on the pinnacle of the temple, and said to Him, "If You
> are the Son of God throw Yourself down; for it is written,
> 'He will give His angels charge concerning You'; and 'On
> their hands they will bear You up, lest You strike Your foot
> against a stone.'" Jesus said to him, "On the other hand, it is
> written, 'You shall not put the LORD your God to the test.'"
> —Matthew 4:5–7

And so ended round two.

> Again, the devil took Him to a very high mountain, and
> showed Him all the kingdoms of the world, and their glory;
> and he said to Him, "All these things will I give You, if You
> fall down and worship me." Then Jesus said to him, "Begone,
> Satan! For it is written, 'You shall worship the LORD your
> God, and serve Him only.'" Then the devil left Him; and
> behold, angels came and began to minister to Him.
> —Matthew 4:8–11

This is hard for me to comprehend. The Son of God—the One
who knows all things and has the power to do all things, the One
whose words we study, memorize, and meditate on—never made
an original comment during the entire interaction.

He did not say, "What do you mean *if* I am the Son of God? Of
course I am." He never drew on His own wit. He never even relied on His own power. He simply responded with the truth of
His Father's Word. That was all it took. Nothing creative. Nothing fancy. Just the plain truth directed at the deception behind
each of Satan's requests.

The lesson is unmistakably clear. If the only One who ever lived
a sinless life combated temptation with God's Word, how do we
hope to survive without it? I am so glad He did outsmart Satan
in a battle of the minds. I have tried that and failed miserably. I

am glad He did not discuss the temptation with Satan and resist him that way. Eve tried that, and she got nowhere. I am glad Jesus did not use raw willpower, though I imagine He could have. My willpower is pretty useless when Satan really turns on the steam. Jesus verbally confronted Satan with the truth; and eventually Satan gave up and left.

The Power of the Word

There are four primary reasons that a well-chosen passage or verse of Scripture is so effective against temptation. First of all, God's Word exposes the sinfulness of whatever you are being tempted to do. This is extremely important because one of Satan's subtle snares is to convince you that what you are being tempted to do is really not so bad after all. What is wrong with turning a stone into bread if you are hungry and have the power to do so? There is no law against that. What is wrong with a little sex? You love her, don't you? There is nothing wrong with leaving that income off your tax form; the government takes too much of your money as it is.

Satan has such a smooth way of rationalizing sin. Once you bring a temptation under the scrutiny of God's Word, you expose it for what it is—a lie. The lie behind Satan's first request of Jesus was, "Jesus, You have the right to meet Your God-given needs when You deem appropriate. You're hungry now, so eat!" Satan was tempting Jesus to take things into His own hands on the basis of His personal needs. Jesus' response brought to light the motive behind Satan's request. In essence He said, "My ultimate responsibility is not simply to satisfy My physical needs, but to obey My Father in heaven." The truth of His Father's Word showed the sinfulness of Satan's request.

So often the things you are tempted with seem so harmless. It is not until you shine the truth of God's Word on those temptations that you see what is really at stake. God's Word takes you right to the heart of the matter. It allows you to see things for what they really are.

Divine Perspective

A second reason the Word of God is so effective against temptation is that you gain God's viewpoint through it. The Scripture provides you with a divine perspective on the temptation you are facing as well as your relationship to it.

Since many temptations carry a strong emotional punch, you tend to get caught up in your feelings. You perceive the temptation as something that is a part of you rather than something happening to you. Once you identify with the feelings temptation evokes, it becomes increasingly difficult to respond correctly. The truth of Scripture allows you to be more objective about the temptations you face. God's Word enables you to see temptation for what it is. It allows you to separate yourself just far enough mentally so that you can deal with it successfully.

The Displacement Principle

Another reason for turning to God's Word in times of temptation is what one pastor calls the principle of displacement (Bud Palmberg, "Private Sins of Public Ministry," *Leadership* magazine [Winter 1988]: 23). This principle is based on the premise that it is impossible *not* to think of something. For example, stop reading for a moment and try your best not to think about pink elephants. It is impossible. You cannot avoid thinking about something. What you must do is focus your attention somewhere else when your thoughts are dominated by a seductive topic.

It is clear that the sinful thoughts accompanying temptation must be redirected, and when you turn your attention to the Word of God during temptation, you do just that. No doubt Paul had this in mind when he wrote,

Finally, brethren, whatever is true, whatever is honorable, whatever is right, whatever is pure, whatever is lovely, whatever is of good repute, if there is any excellence and if anything worthy of praise, let your mind dwell on these things.
—Philippians 4:8

He echoed the same idea in Colossians when he said,

> Set your mind on the things above, not on the things that are on earth.
>
> —Colossians 3:2

If you don't shift your attention away from the temptation, you may begin some form of mental dialogue: *I really shouldn't. But I haven't done this in a long time. I am really going to hate myself later. Why not? I've already blown it anyway. I'll do it just this once, and tomorrow I'll start over.* When you allow these little discussions to begin, you are sunk. The longer you talk, the more time the temptation has to settle into your emotions and will.

You are to use the Word of God to head temptation off at the pass. As soon as the thought enters your mind, you are to turn your thoughts in the direction of God's Word. Eve's biggest mistake was talking things over with Satan. She should have repeated back to him verbatim what God had commanded her to do and then just walked away. Instead she got into a discussion.

Faith

The fourth reason the Word of God is so effective against temptation is that you are expressing faith when you turn your attention to His Word. You are saying, "I believe God is able to get me through this; I believe He is mightier than the power of sin, my flesh, and Satan himself." Nothing moves God like the active faith of His people.

Building an Arsenal

Most believers would find the above discussion very convincing—and probably not very original. The account of Jesus' temptation is convincing in itself without any commentary. So why, then, do so many Christians continue to complain about their inability to deal with temptation and at the same time excuse their ignorance of God's Word? "I don't understand it. I can't memorize Scripture. I don't have time."

There are no good excuses. It really comes down to one thing: laziness. We are just too lazy to fill the arsenal of our minds with those truths we need to combat the lies of the enemy. And consequently, when he attacks, we get wiped out.

So many books, seminars, and study courses are available on how to understand the Bible that it would take a lifetime to get through them all. And yet most believers refuse to take the time to remedy their ignorance.

My son, Andy, works with the young people of our church. Every year he goes through a course designed to teach the teenagers how to have an effective quiet time. Part of that training covers Scripture memorization and meditation. Every year he hears the same excuse, "I can't understand the Bible." Here is how he answers that excuse:

Imagine that tomorrow the best-looking girl in your school (or a guy if he's talking to girls) walks up to you and says, "Hey, I've been watching you, and I think you're cute. I would love for you to come over to my house for dinner tomorrow night. Here is a map. I'll see you around 7:00." As she walks away, you can't believe it. It's too good to be true. You race over to your locker and open the map to see where she lives. It's the messiest thing you've ever seen in your life. You can't tell which way is up. How many of you guys would say, "Too bad, I can't understand the map. I guess I won't go"? How many of you would do whatever you had to in order to figure out what the map meant?

At that point all the hands in the group usually go up.

Why would we go to great lengths to figure out a map to a girl's house, but when it comes to the Word of God, we read a few verses and give up the moment we don't understand something?

The point of his illustration is simple. We do what we want to do. After we have been convinced of the importance of a task, we can usually figure out a way to get it done. Our problem with learning about the Word of God is not time, knowledge, or education; it is a problem with priorities.

I know Christians who spend hours figuring out crossword puzzles, but they declare they don't have time to study the Word of God. Let's get real practical. If you spend two hours a day watching television and ten minutes each day reading God's Word, which do you think is going to have a greater overall impact on your life?

Jesus had the truth He needed fresh in His mind. It was only one thought away. He didn't struggle to dig up some long-forgotten memory verse from primaries. "Now hold on a minute. I memorized a verse about that one time. Let's see, it went something like . . ." Sound familiar?

To effectively combat the onslaughts of the enemy, you need an arsenal of verses on the tip of your tongue. Verses that are so familiar that they come to your mind without any conscious effort on your part. If you have to dig them up from the caverns of your memory, they will do you no good. There isn't time for that in the midst of temptation.

Truths for Lies

The process of Scripture memorization is never easy, but most things in life worth having cost something. A few pointers will make it easier for you, though. First of all, select verses that focus on the areas in which you are most tempted. At the end of this chapter I have listed some categories of temptation along with some corresponding passages of Scripture.

Every man, for instance, should have several verses on the tip of his tongue that have to do with lust or immorality. We are bombarded at every turn with the promise of pleasure through illicit sex. What a lie! Yet all of us have the potential to buy into that way of thinking and thus fall.

All of us should have a verse on hand for gossip. It's so easy to participate in pointless chatter about other people. As soon as you hear someone begin or as soon as a juicy tidbit comes to your mind concerning someone else, you should be reminded that "if anyone thinks himself to be religious, and yet does not bridle his tongue but deceives his own heart, this man's [or woman's] religion is worthless" (James 1:26). It should be that natural.

We all need a verse to remind us of our Christian duty to obey the laws set forth by our government. When we are tempted to break them, we need to be reminded that it is God's will for us to "submit [yourselves] for the Lord's sake to every human institution. . . . For such is the will of God that by doing right [we] may silence the ignorance of foolish men" (1 Pet. 2:13–15).

Do you know why God wants us to obey the law? It's not because they are all good laws. We are to keep the law for testimony's sake. To do otherwise is to be hypocritical. Once again, the truth of God's Word exposes the lie of Satan. He says, "Go ahead and break the law. Everybody else does. It's a dumb law anyway. Besides, doesn't the Bible say something about being free from the Law?" But Satan's arguments collapse under the scrutiny of God's Word.

Keep It Simple

Another thing to keep in mind when memorizing Scripture is to keep it simple. Set small goals at first. One verse a week is enough to begin with. Often after reading a book on Scripture memorization or hearing someone's testimony concerning it, we set out with the intention of memorizing the entire New Testament. After about four verses, we become discouraged and give up altogether.

Remember the purpose in all of this. Memorizing Scripture isn't the ultimate goal. It is just a means to an end. The reason to memorize Scripture is to provide you with an arsenal to use the next time Satan attacks.

Howard Hendricks tells a humorous story about a kid in his church who had memorized the entire New Testament. He could quote the text and he knew the references as well. Hendricks says you could say to this kid, "Ephesians 4:9," and he would start right there and keep right on going.

During the course of time, someone began noticing that money was missing from the offering collected in the junior boys' class. Sure enough, the adults discovered that this same kid who knew half the Bible was stealing money from the plate. Dr. Hendricks was given the responsibility of confronting him.

In a sincere attempt to handle things in a biblical manner, he sat down with the boy and said, "You know the Bible says . . . ," and he quoted a verse on stealing. Quickly, the boy looked up at Dr. Hendricks and informed him he had misquoted the verse! As the conversation ensued, it became apparent that the youngster was oblivious to the connection between what the Scripture said and his action of taking money from the offering plate. All that is to say, memorizing Scripture isn't enough. It is simply one in a series of stages. The ultimate goal is to have the truth ready at a moment's notice.

Review, Review, Review

The only way to keep something fresh and to guarantee that it has become part of your long-term memory is to review it. The simplest way I know to develop a review system is to use index cards. That way you can keep all your verses together. When you have a few minutes between appointments or tasks, you can pull them out and review them.

Several companies sell Scripture memorization programs. Some of these have a review system built in. What you will find, however, is that the verses corresponding with the temptations you face will stick most readily in your mind. I have claimed some verses so many times that I can quote them without even concentrating. These are the ones I rely on every day. For the verses that you don't use as often, you need a review system.

Think about it this way. If you memorize one verse a week for a year, and even skip two weeks for vacation, that is fifty verses. That is more verses than many Christians learn in a lifetime. Just think about how far along you would be if you had started last year at this time. If you don't begin now, next year you will look back and wish you had.

A Personal Matter

Another thing I would suggest is to personalize the Scripture you memorize. The first time I heard about this idea was at a Basic Youth Conflicts Seminar. Bill Gothard shared a personal testimony about the difference this made in his spiritual life. That was over fifteen years ago, and I've been doing it ever since then.

Personalizing Scripture makes it come alive. Substitute your name or a personal pronoun for pronouns such as *you* and *we*. "Thank You, Lord, that I am not under obligation to my flesh to obey the lust thereof." "Lord, I choose to set my mind on the things above and not on the things on earth, for I have died and my life is hidden with Christ in God." "Lord, I am casting all my cares on You, for I know You care for me."

"Call Upon the Name of the Lord"

One last suggestion is to get in the habit of quoting these verses audibly when you are tempted. This may seem a little strange at first, but there are good reasons to do this. First, I do not believe Satan and his host can read our minds. He can put thoughts there, but the Scripture does not indicate that he can read them.

If that is true, simply thinking through a verse poses the enemy no threat. It may help you refocus your attention and therefore relieve the pressure for a time. But in terms of really challenging the devil and putting him in his place, I am not convinced that mentally reviewing Scripture does much good.

The second reason speaking the truth aloud is important is that it shifts the point of tension from an internal conflict to an external one. Throughout this book, I have referred to our tendency to emotionally latch on to temptation and own it as part of our being, to mistakenly think, *This is the way I am. Otherwise why would I feel this way?*

When you speak the truth out loud, you are reminded that *you* are not your enemy. And He that is within you is not your enemy. Your enemy is the devil. He roams around like a lion looking for someone to devour (1 Pet. 5:8). Satan hates to be recognized. He would much rather have you internalize the battle so that he can remain anonymous.

There are times when we are our own worst enemy. This is certainly the case when we ignore the principle outlined in chapter 8 and make unwise decisions. But even in those cases, I have found it extremely helpful to speak the truth aloud.

Now I'm not talking about shouting it at the top of your lungs. There are times when you will simply have to whisper it. At other times you can speak in a normal tone of voice. You may feel silly the first time you do this, but you will notice an immediate difference when you do.

When you speak the truth out loud, it is as if you have taken a stand with God against the enemy. When I begin speaking the truth aloud, I often feel a sense of courage and conviction sweeping over me. Usually this turns into joy, and what started out as a bad thing becomes a time of praise and rejoicing. If you don't believe me, just try it.

The last reason I think it is a good idea to speak aloud when tempted is that Jesus did it. Need I say more?

Conformed or Transformed?

When you get involved in building up an arsenal of verses, you will be in the process of doing something else as well—renewing your mind. To renew something is a two-stage process. It involves removing the old and putting on the new. When you fill your mind with the truth of God's Word so that you can root out the error that keeps you from being victorious, you are renewing your mind.

The importance of this process cannot be overemphasized. It guards you against falling prey to temptation and it protects you from being brainwashed by the world. This is what Paul was talking about when he wrote,

And do not be conformed to this world, but be transformed by the renewing of your mind, that you may prove what the will of God is, that which is good and acceptable and perfect.
—Romans 12:2

The "how to" of defending ourselves against becoming like the world is to renew our minds. Everywhere we turn we find ourselves being asked to adopt a way of thinking that is contrary to what Christ and His church stand for. Unless you and I make some effort to combat this onslaught of propaganda, we will fall victim to its debilitating poison.

Get Started!

I hope you will not wait until you have finished reading this book to start developing your arsenal. That is what Satan would have you do. Why? He wants you to forget. I have listed several categories of things most of us struggle with, and I have included a few verses to get you started. Begin with the area that troubles you the most. Then work on other areas. Don't start too fast. Don't give up if you miss a couple of weeks. And above all, remember, if the perfect, sinless, sovereign Son of God relied on Scripture to pull Him through, what hope do you have without it?

Truth for Lies

Any temptation that seems to be unbearable.—1 Corinthians 10:13.

The temptation to gossip—James 1:26.

The temptation to lust—Psalm 119:9; Proverbs 6:24–33; Galatians 6:7–8; Colossians 3:2–3.

The temptation to fear—Psalm 56:3; John 14:1.

The temptation to think you are getting away with sin—2 Corinthians 5:10; Galatians 6:7–8.

Troubled by circumstances—John 16:33.

The temptation to get involved with debatable things—2 Corinthians 5:9.

The temptation not to do the wise thing—Ephesians 5:15–16.

The temptation not to obey your parents—Ephesians 6:1–3.

The temptation to disobey the law—1 Peter 2:13–15.

The temptation to demand your own way—1 Corinthians 6:19–20.

The temptation to do things that will harm your body—1 Corinthians 6:19–20.

Chapter 11

NO LONE RANGERS

ONE OF THE great truths of the Christian faith is that each believer has the opportunity to develop a personal relationship with God through Jesus Christ. This is one of the most significant differences between Christianity and other established religions of the world. This truth, however, like any other truth, has negative potential as well when it is stressed to the point of being out of balance with the rest of God's Word.

It is true that each of us can approach God independently. He hears and answers our prayers. It is true that He can empower us to deal with the difficulties in this life and that His grace is always sufficient. But God never intended for any of us to function as spiritual lone rangers. At no point does the intimacy of our walk with God relieve us of our responsibility and accountability to the whole body of Christ. Such independence does not work in a physical body; neither will it work in the church of the Lord Jesus Christ.

The Final Stage

The final stage in developing a self-defense against temptation is *accountability*. Generally speaking, accountability is a willingness to provide an explanation of one's activities, conduct, and fulfillment of assigned responsibilities. All of us are accountable to someone in some way. On the job, you are accountable to your employer or to a board of some kind. You are expected to accomplish certain tasks in an allotted amount of time. Since your employer hired you and is paying you for your work, he has the right to hold you accountable. If he doesn't feel you are working up to par, your employer has every right in the world to confront you and demand an explanation.

Accountability of that sort is something we can all relate to in one way or another. Most of us began to learn that lesson when we started our first job. But moral and ethical accountability is something most people have thought very little about. It seems appropriate to save this particular area of defense for last, not because it is the least important, but because it is the most overlooked. And no wonder. Who wants to admit secret sins to someone? Who wants to appear weak? Who wants to invite criticism? The whole idea of providing someone with an explanation of my moral conduct seems a little strange. "That is nobody's business! That is between me and the Lord." But is it really?

We have mistakenly come to believe that since we have a personal relationship with the God who promises to help us when we are tempted, we should omit any mention of that aspect of our lives from the rest of our relationships. After all, temptation is a private thing. *Temptation may be a private thing, but sin rarely is.* Sin eventually reaches out beyond the confines of a single life and touches the lives of all those around it. Ask any woman whose husband has left her for someone else. His private temptation eventually became public knowledge. Ask the husband whose wife's private struggle with alcohol eventually became a source of embarrassment to the whole family. Ask the parents of the teenager whose private struggle with failure eventually led to suicide. And what about the countless families who lose everything because of the father's private struggle with drugs or gambling? Sure, temptation is a private matter; but sin never is.

The real question is, who is going to find out and when? "But my temptation is so small, there is no way it is going to turn into a public scandal." Just remember, every single person whose sin became public knowledge said the same thing. No one ever anticipates the harm that can come to others. Satan does everything possible to keep that thought from ever entering the mind.

Working It Out

Specifically, what we are talking about here is a relationship with a person or a small group of people in which you can share anything: your hurts, your fears, your temptations, your victories, and even your defeats. It must be a relationship committed to honesty, openness and, above all, privacy. Later in this chapter we will focus on the "how to's" of an accountability relationship, but at this point I want to explain why the concept of accountability is so effective against temptation.

Recurring temptations carry with them a great deal of emotional stress. This results from both the internal struggle and the guilt once we give in. An accountability relationship provides an outlet for those feelings and frustrations that otherwise have no other outlet. In fact, part of the deceptiveness of sin is that we feel the only way we can deal with the internal pressure we are experiencing is to go ahead and sin. Sin, however, only compounds the problem. Then we have to cope with guilt *and* the possibility of others finding out. Before long, the inner frustration builds up again anyway.

Having someone to whom we can spill our guts provides us with a temporary substitute for the frustration we feel as well as the sin we are tempted to commit. I say "temporary" because until we deal with the root issues of a problem, the pressure and frustration will eventually return. In this respect, an accountability relationship serves as a kind of halfway house.

Many times in my life I have been so frustrated with the way things were going at church or at home that I just wanted to run.

In those times I have turned not only to the Lord, but to my friends as well. I tell them everything I am feeling; what I would like to do; where I would like to go. Usually by the time I am finished, I am all right again. I don't really need for them to say anything. Just knowing that they will listen with open minds and hearts is enough. Most of the time there are some things that need to be dealt with in the areas that cause me frustration. But after I pour out my heart, they seem much more manageable than before.

I believe most extramarital affairs have little or nothing to do with sex. Pressures at home and work build, and men and women feel like running away from all responsibility and accountability. At the same time everybody has a desire for intimacy. And since nothing kills intimacy like tension, the first inclination is to look for intimacy somewhere new, somewhere free of tension.

Everybody needs someone to run to, someone who will listen, pray, and offer wise counsel when appropriate. Individuals who have someone like that will find it much easier to deal with temptation, for they have an alternative.

Never the First

There is a second reason why an accountability relationship aids in the struggle with temptation. The apostle Paul hit on it when he wrote,

> No temptation has overtaken you but such as is common to man.
>
> —1 Corinthians 10:13

Regardless of what you are struggling with, you are not the first. Others have walked this road before you. And they probably wrote a book about it! The point is, your struggles are not unique. Time after time I have poured out my heart to other men expecting them to look surprised. Instead, they just smile and say, "You, too?" Knowing you are not alone relieves some of the pressure.

Couples who come to me for premarital counseling often share the struggle they are having in the area of physical intimacy. Often the guilt they feel for even having the struggle clouds their ability to deal with the problem rationally. I have learned that one of the most helpful things to do is to pair them up with a couple who have just recently been married. I encourage them to talk about the engagement period, and eventually the subject of physical intimacy surfaces. Once the newly married couple share the struggle they had in that area, the engaged couple often feel some sense of relief. Not that this gives them license to sin. It does, however, remove the false guilt they were experiencing for being tempted in the first place.

Often the experience of others can provide us with great insight into how to approach the temptations we are facing. Sometimes simply talking through a problem leads to the discovery of a solution. Anyone in a management position knows the value of brainstorming. Pooling the wisdom and creativity of a concerned group always gives birth to new ideas and solutions. When we discuss our spiritual struggles with others, the same thing occurs. Our accountability partners have the advantage of objectivity and fresh insight. They are able to bring their experience and the experience of others they know to bear on our situation.

Stubborn Love

There is one other way in which an accountability relationship can help during times of temptation. The following story illustrates it perfectly. A member of our church who was away at school at the time told me about it. I'll call him Al. It was the Thursday night of exam week, and both he and a friend of his, Randy, had taken their last exam that afternoon. They were ready to paint the town that evening. Since they were both believers, painting the town amounted to going out to eat and driving around town with the sunroof open. On the way to pick up Randy, Al stopped by the apartment next door to see if Stacy would like to go along. Stacy and Al hadn't really ever dated, but being next-door neighbors, they did see each other frequently.

Stacy was not doing anything that evening, so she decided to join the boys for an evening of harmless fun. Al and Randy were pretty wound up from having been cooped up all week studying. As the evening wore on, Randy couldn't help noticing that Stacy and Al were getting pretty cozy with each other. After a while it became obvious to Randy that they were ready to take him home so they could be alone.

As they dropped him off, Randy had an uneasy feeling about Al and Stacy. He knew Al pretty well, well enough to know that he was not acting like himself. Heading upstairs to his apartment, he grew increasingly worried about Al and Stacy. They were both believers, but they had apparently gotten caught up in the excitement of the moment.

Randy went inside and called Al on the phone. It was just as he had expected. He could hear Stacy talking in the background; Al had invited her over. "Al, this is Randy," he said. "I'm coming over to spend the night with you."

Al admitted that he had gotten mad when Randy announced he was coming over. "He didn't even ask me if he could come. He just told me to get ready!" By the time Randy showed up, Stacy was gone. Al had fixed Randy a pallet on the floor by his bed.

As Al related this story to me, he said, "We both lay there in the dark several minutes without saying a word. Finally, I said, 'Thanks.' That was all I had to say. He understood. 'No problem,' he said. 'I know you would have done the same for me.'"

Now that is accountability. Sometimes an accountability partner has to take an active role in the temptation process. We all need a friend like Randy, someone who is willing to risk criticism for the sake of our spiritual growth and moral protection. Solomon put it this way,

> Better is open rebuke
> Than love that is concealed.

> Faithful are the wounds of a friend,
> But deceitful are the kisses of an enemy.
> —Proverbs 27:5–6

Bearing One Another's Burdens

People often object to the idea of accountability because they don't feel that what other people are doing is any of their business. But just the opposite is true. The Bible says within the body of Christ we all have a responsibility to one another. Listen to what the apostle Paul said regarding this subject of accountability:

> Brethren, even if a man is caught in any trespass, you who are spiritual, restore such a one in a spirit of gentleness; each one looking to yourself, lest you too be tempted. Bear one another's burdens, and thus fulfill the law of Christ. For if anyone thinks he is something when he is nothing, he deceives himself.
>
> —Galatians 6:1–3

Paul said that if a believer is caught in sin, the strong members of the church are to help shoulder the responsibility of that person's sin. They are to work with the sinner and help him get back on track. The implication is that our sin is other people's business. And conversely, their sin becomes part of our business or responsibility. Sin is not just the responsibility of the people directly affected. This passage does not even mention those people. Paul said Christians who aren't even involved in what is going on are to come to the rescue of those caught in sin.

If confronting our brothers and sisters in Christ about their sin is being "nosy," Paul never would have written those verses. At the same time, if you and I were expected to work out our problems without the aid of other Christians, Paul never would have written them, either. Nowhere in Scripture are we told that our sin is something just between us and God. The Bible teaches just the opposite.

A woman in our church in Miami was married for only a short time when she found out her husband was a homosexual. Soon after she discovered it, he left her to be with his lover. As I talked with her, she said something I shall never forget. "After I was divorced, several of my friends came to me and said they knew he was gay. When I asked them why they didn't say anything to me, they said, 'We didn't think it was any of our business.'"

Her friends were dead wrong. They violated a scriptural principle. After hearing her story, I made up my mind never to stand by quietly and watch a friend make what I was sure in my heart was a mistake. This resolution has made me very unpopular with people at times. People have left my church over things I have confronted them about. But when I start thinking that maybe I should keep my mouth shut, I always remember what Solomon said,

> He who rebukes a man will
> afterward find more favor
> Than he who flatters with the tongue.
> —Proverbs 28:23

It is amazing how through the years people have come back to me or written letters to apologize for their reaction to my warnings. More often than not, they admit that they should have listened.

Remember this, in an accountability relationship you are not responsible for how the other person responds to your warnings or counsel. You cannot guarantee that the individual will take what you say to heart. But you are responsible to tell the truth and then continue to love that person through the whole process.

You and Your Accountability Partner

The Bible doesn't outline a program for accountability groups. There are no rules that govern when and how often you should meet with your accountability partner or partners. I have seen it work in a variety of ways. My daughter, Becky, gets together with her partner once a month. In between meetings they stay in touch by phone. Andy meets with his accountability partner every week for breakfast. One pastor on our staff meets with his group on Tuesday evenings. Some of our teenagers meet during lunch at school.

Accountability partners don't necessarily have to have a formal meeting. I know two who work out together three mornings a week. They discuss things as they exercise. One fellow in our church meets his partner once a week on the golf course. I go hunting and fishing with mine on a regular basis.

An accountability partner should be someone of the same sex. And you should be naturally attracted to that person; that is, you wouldn't mind developing a lifelong friendship. The more you have in common, the better. You may have the most helpful discussions in the midst of some other activity you are participating in together.

Your accountability partner should be someone you respect spiritually. I don't mean that the person should be a Bible scholar or should have been a Christian since adolescence. Rather, your partner should be someone who is seeking to gain God's perspective on life and really wants to develop personally in keeping with God's desires. Chances are, you already know someone who would make you a good partner. It may just be a matter of discussing it together. Or you may just begin to open up and let things take their natural course.

Striking a Balance

The last thing you want is a relationship with someone who criticizes you every time you get together. But you don't want someone who will let you get by with murder, either. The key here is a balance between encouragement and exhortation or instruction, but not a fifty-fifty balance. The relationship should be about 75 percent encouragement and 25 percent exhortation.

Another way to handle this is to make an agreement to never give unsolicited advice or criticism. If you want your partner's opinion on a decision you are making, ask for it. Remember, you are not there to assume the role of therapist. You are meeting as friends who are committed to love and care for each other.

Most of the accountability partners I know did not begin their relationship with that in mind. They were just good friends who eventually felt comfortable sharing their most personal struggles with each other. The more natural it is, the better.

Why Not?

In general, women have an easier time developing accountability relationships than men do. There are several reasons for this. The biggest hindrance for men, however, is ego. God calls it pride. We want to handle things ourselves. There is no task too difficult, no mountain too high, no temptation too strong . . . , and on and on we go. You know the old saying, "Me and God is a majority." Sounds good, but it doesn't work well in real life.

The bottom line is that we don't like admitting our weaknesses to anyone else (as if those around us did not already know), especially to another man. At least with a woman there is a chance we will get sympathy and possibly a shoulder to cry on. But another guy? We think, *He will see right through me. He may make me face myself as I really am. God forbid, I may look bad!*

So you are left with a choice to make. Are you willing to expose your weaknesses to a hand-picked individual or group now, or would you rather run the risk of having your weaknesses exposed to the whole world later? We all need somebody to talk to. Don't let your pride keep you from finding somebody. The more prominent and successful you become, the more you need accountability. Unfortunately, it will become increasingly difficult to find because people may be intimidated. "Who am I to offer him advice?" they may ask. But don't give up. There may come a time in your life when your accountability partner is all that stands between you and disaster.

Starting Young

Wise parents of teenagers encourage their kids to develop relationships with godly singles or college students, people they can look up to. At that stage in their development kids often do not feel comfortable talking about private matters with their parents. But they need somebody other than their peers with whom to share. As a teenager, my daughter began meeting with a woman who is her accountability partner to this day. I'm so grateful for the people God sent our way to fill the gap for our kids while they were going through those difficult teenage years. Accountability is for everybody. The younger you can begin teaching your children this fact, the better.

No Lone Rangers

Now that I think about it, this chapter may be mistitled. Even the Lone Ranger had Tonto. We all need someone like Tonto. Someone who knows us inside out. Someone we can't deceive. Someone who will accept us as we are, yet who knows how to push us toward Christlikeness. Someone we can depend on. Such a friend is hard to find but is worth more than all the treasures of the earth. Friends of that stature may one day keep us from losing all that is dear to us.

Recently I heard in full the public confession given by one of my brothers in the ministry who had allowed his involvement with pornography to wreck his personal life and ministry. He described the measures he went to in order to be freed of his addiction: fasting, praying, crying out to God. But nothing seemed to work. Then he said something I will never forget. He said, "I realize now that if I had turned to my brothers and sisters in Christ for help, I would have been delivered."

No one is a spiritual island. We need one another. It is my prayer that you will find someone with whom you can develop an accountability relationship. Whatever you are struggling with, you are not alone. Ask God to bring into your life the kind of person Solomon had in mind when he wrote,

> A man of many friends comes to ruin,
> But there is a friend who sticks
> closer than a brother.
> —Proverbs 18:24

Part III

Discovering the Truth

Chapter 12

OUR MISUNDERSTANDINGS

IN CHAPTER 5 we discussed the fact that Satan is scheming against believers. A big part of overcoming temptation is understanding exactly what Satan is up to and how he goes about carrying out his schemes. In this chapter we are going to look at six commonly held theories regarding temptation. As we will see, none of them can be supported biblically. What's worse, these misunderstandings cause many well-meaning believers to live under a burden God never intended them to bear; their expectation level becomes totally unrealistic. Consequently, they become discouraged and unmotivated. I believe Satan is the source of these misunderstandings, for at the bottom of each is a distortion of God's truth.

In Paul's second letter to the Corinthians he pointed out that ignorance of Satan's schemes would allow Satan to take advantage of them (2 Cor. 2:11). A misunderstanding in the area of temptation does just that. It sets a person up to be taken advantage of. It is like the situation of a woman who takes an office job but never receives instruction about exactly what is expected of her. Anyone in this position is set up to be taken advantage of. As people discover her naivete, they will tend to pass off some of their undesirable duties on the "new girl." Soon she will find herself swamped with more work than she could ever finish. As the unfinished work piles up, she becomes discouraged and feels like a failure. But she isn't a failure at all! It just appears that way because she never knew exactly what was expected of her.

Perhaps part of the reason you are so discouraged is that you have heaped upon yourself unrealistic expectations, expectations God never intended for you to live with. Consequently, you are set up to be abused by Satan, maybe even to the point of giving up altogether. As we look at these six misunderstandings, examine your heart to see if either consciously or subconsciously you are operating from the basis of one or more of these falsehoods.

1. To Be Tempted Is to Sin.

Oftentimes when we are tempted, the feelings associated with that temptation are so strong that we associate the evil feelings with our character rather than with the temptation. Then we condemn ourselves for even having such feelings. Without actually giving in to the temptation we feel as if we are already guilty. That is when Satan usually chimes in, "Well, you might as well go ahead now and do it! After all, what kind of person would even come up with such an awful idea? You are already guilty."

We must keep in mind that we are not responsible for what flashes through our minds. Our responsibility is to control the things that dominate our thoughts. Paul clarified this difference to the Corinthian believers when he wrote,

> We are destroying speculations and every lofty thing raised up against the knowledge of God, and we are taking every thought captive to the obedience of Christ.
> —2 Corinthians 10:5

If God expected us to be able to control what came into our minds, why would He move the apostle Paul to instruct believers to take "every thought captive"? He implies that we cannot control what rushes into our minds. What we can and must do, however, is take control of each thought and deal with it. That is, we should dwell on the good and drive out the bad.

Our environment determines to a great extent what comes into our minds. Even the most cautious people will at some point be exposed visually and audibly to things that will summon ungodly thoughts and feelings. We cannot control what other people wear or say. We cannot control what we are invited to participate in (although we can obviously control what we choose to participate in). We cannot control what we accidentally overhear in the office or in the rest room. All of these things are thrust upon us without our consent.

Many of these external messages pack an emotional punch. And when our feelings get involved, things often become confusing. These feelings may raise serious doubts in our minds about our commitment, and for some of us, it can become a question of salvation. "If I was really committed, would I feel this way?" "Would a real Christian want to do that?"

These feelings are usually natural, God-given feelings. The problem is that when we are tempted, our feelings are being focused outside the parameters God has established for us. For example, people who like chocolate will find their taste buds going crazy when a double fudge nut brownie is brought to the table. There is nothing sinful about their physical reaction. God made us react that way to certain foods. Whether or not people are on a diet has nothing to do with how their taste buds react. The brownie serves as an external stimuli that causes an internal reaction. If the brownie is outside the parameters of what people believe God would have them eat at that time, the brownie becomes a temptation. No sin has taken place, however, until a bite is taken.

The same is true for sexual temptation, the temptation to lie, the temptation to gossip, and even the temptation to be lazy. All of these temptations begin with a thought that carries with it some sort of emotional punch. Sometimes it is so strong we are overwhelmed with condemnation. But the thought of doing something evil, even when combined with the desire to do it, is not a sin, only a temptation.

There is another reason we know that being tempted could not possibly be a sin. Jesus was tempted. The writer of Hebrews tells us,

> For we do not have a high priest who cannot sympathize with our weaknesses, but One who has been tempted in all things as we are, yet without sin.
>
> —Hebrews 4:15

This verse makes two important points. First of all, Jesus was tempted just like we are. If our temptation is a sin, so was His; our temptations are just like His. Second, Jesus never sinned. If Jesus was tempted and yet never sinned, then temptation cannot be a sin.

When Jesus was tempted on the mountain as described in Matthew 4, Satan put ideas in His head much like he does ours. One of these ideas certainly conjured up some strong feelings and emotions in our Lord:

> Then Jesus was led up by the Spirit into the wilderness to be tempted by the devil. And after He had fasted forty days and forty nights, He then became hungry. And the tempter came and said to Him, "If you are the Son of God, command that these stones become bread."
>
> —Matthew 4:1–3

This passage makes it clear that Jesus had sinful ideas bombarding His mind and that He had feelings right along with them. The text goes so far as to tell us that "He became hungry." Yet even with all of that, it was not considered sin, for He never ate.

We serve a just and righteous God. He will not hold us responsible for things over which we have no control. He knows Satan is working full time to flood our ears, eyes, and minds with things that will sidetrack us. God will not judge us for those evil thoughts that dart through our minds, not even for those longings and desires that often accompany certain thoughts. On the contrary, He sent His Son to enable us to successfully deal with the onslaught of temptation. Temptation is not a sin; it is simply Satan's attempt to make us fall.

2. Spiritually Mature People Are Not Harassed By Temptation.

I am always amazed at how people respond when I share something I am struggling with in my personal life. Whether it is from the pulpit or in private, their response is usually the same. "I can't imagine *you* being tempted like that!" Behind their amazement stands another misunderstanding concerning temptation: *spiritually mature people are not harassed by temptation.*

All of us will face temptation the rest of our lives. There is no escaping it. When people tell me they are struggling with temptation, I want to say, "So what's new?" Somewhere we have gotten the erroneous idea that our ultimate goal as Christians is to come to a place in our lives where we are never tempted. Ironically, the very opposite is true. The more godly we become, the more of a threat we become to Satan. Thus, the harder he works to bring us down.

Temptation will always be a part of the believer's life. Maturity only causes Satan to increase the pressure. So if you feel the pressure is on like never before, praise the Lord!! That could be an indication that Satan sees you as a threat to his work in this world. Don't be discouraged. In the words of James, "Consider it all joy, my brethren, when you encounter various trials" (James 1:2).

I have heard people say, "If you are truly filled with the Holy Spirit, you will be above temptation." That is not only unbiblical; it is antibiblical. The Bible teaches just the opposite. Jesus was certainly filled with the Holy Spirit. Yet not even He escaped temptation.

This particular misunderstanding is the reason many people

fail to pray on a regular basis for their spiritual leaders. They falsely assume that these spiritual giants have no problems, much less any serious temptation. Your spiritual leaders need your prayers more than anybody else. Satan is probably working over-time to bring them down. He knows that when godly men and women fall, seeds of doubt are planted in the minds of all those who held them in esteem. What's worse, it confirms to the lost world what they already suspected: "The church is full of hypo-crites and liars; there's nothing to religion." Pray for your pastor and church leaders! They struggle with the same temptations you do. Nobody is immune.

As long as you are on this earth in its present condition, you will be faced with temptation. The more "spiritual" you become, the more of a target you become. As your spiritual maturity and responsibility increase, so must your sensitivity to and depen-dence on the Holy Spirit. If the Son of God never reached a point where He was above being tempted, it is highly unlikely you would ever reach such a point in this lifetime, either.

3. Once a Sin or Habit Is Truly Dealt With, Temptation in That Particular Area Will Subside.

This misunderstanding really leaves people confused and dis-couraged. Once again, it is because their expectations are unre-alistic. Often Christians will struggle with a particular sin for a long time—sometimes for years. Then something will happen, and they will be delivered. Usually deliverance comes through a new understanding of their power in Christ over sin.

For a while they will walk in such victory that they will get lulled into thinking that they are above falling back into that particular sin and that they are beyond being tempted by it. Sooner or later, however, a situation will arise, and they will be tempted once again. Many times the fact that they are even "temptable" sends them into such a tailspin that they crash. This one failure may be so discouraging that it catapults them right back into the very sin from which they had been delivered.

This is exactly what happened to a friend of mine who had been delivered from an addiction to pornography. He went for months without even being tempted. He thought the problem was behind him once and for all and then WHAM! He found himself feeling the same way he used to feel and thinking about things he had not thought about for months. The very fact that he could feel that way again almost overwhelmed him. As he tells the story, it was like Satan was whispering in his ear, "Nothing has changed; you are still the same person as before. Why kid yourself? If you had really changed, you wouldn't feel this way or want to do these things." He made the mistake of falling for Satan's lie and gave in to the temptation.

This one incident made such a deep impression that he almost gave up the fight completely. He explained to me how he became very introspective, always looking for some hidden problem that caused his downfall. Through all this searching, he realized what had happened. He admitted that as the weeks and months passed after his deliverance, he had grown lazy in his Bible study and prayer time. He had stopped renewing his mind, and he took pride in the new truths God had revealed to him. He admitted that he really believed he was above being tempted with pornography again.

Today he walks in victory once more. Not because of a one-time event, but because he has come to grips with his own frailty. He knows now that temptation can come at any time and that he must walk in moment by moment dependency upon Christ. If you were to ask him whether or not he has been delivered from his addiction to pornography, he would tell you, "I am being delivered daily." By that he means every day he has the potential to be tempted; but every day God is giving him the victory. I have watched this fellow develop into one of the most godly young men I know. Yet he will never reach the point of being beyond temptation.

God has promised to deliver you from giving in to temptation. Nowhere has He promised to deliver you from *being tempted.* Satan knows your weak points. If he has tripped you up in an area before, you can rest assured he will come at you again from the same angle. He is smart. He knows when to back off for a time. He also knows when your pride has set you up to fall.

When you are tempted time and time again with the same temptation, don't automatically assume that you have some deep, underlying problem. Neither should you assume that you are any more "sinful" than anybody else. Nowhere in Scripture is a person's spirituality judged on the basis of frequency of temptation. Satan propagates this misunderstanding so that you and I will become discouraged and give in to temptation. The truth is that we are all weaker in some areas than in others. Satan will always capitalize on our weaknesses. Therefore, we will experience recurring temptations for the rest of our lives.

4. We Fall into Temptation.

It is not uncommon for someone to say, "You know, I was going along just great when all of a sudden I *fell* into temptation." The notion that people *fall* into temptation points to another misunderstanding. People do not *fall* into temptation. Such phraseology portrays sinners as victims, innocent bystanders who are swept into sin against their will. That is not the case at all.

Someone may object, "But you don't know the pressure I was under. It was unbearable. I couldn't help what happened." That objection is simply an attempt to bypass personal responsibility for sin. It is an attempt to put the blame somewhere else. We do not fall into temptation; we *choose* to sin. In every single temptation there is a point at which we cast a deciding ballot either to sin or not to sin. No one can cast it for us—regardless of the pressure we may be facing.

It is true that we do not choose to be tempted. In that respect it could be said that we fall prey to temptation. But being surprised by temptation is never a cause or an excuse to sin. Temptation in no way impairs our freedom to choose. And as long as we have that freedom, we are always responsible for our actions.

When someone falls into a hole or falls off a bicycle, it is usually not the result of a conscious decision to do so. On the contrary, something overtakes the individual and forces him down against his will. Giving in to temptation is different. Sin, in the context of a temptation, is always the result of a decision.

Regardless of the pressure, we still hold the deciding vote. Never are we forced, kicking and screaming against our will, to give in to temptation. Temptation is not something we *fall* into; it is something we choose to *give* in to. That is why Christ is just in judging men and punishing according to the deeds. If sin was something we fell into, then Christ would have no right to hold us personally accountable.

I've never heard anyone say, "I don't know what came over me, I just found myself doing good things. I couldn't help it. I didn't really want to do all those nice things; I just fell into it." We always take personal responsibility for the good things we do, don't we? It is only the bad we want to pass off as unavoidable. But we are responsible for both. Just as we *choose* to do good, so we *choose* to do evil.

5. God is Disappointed and Displeased When We Are Tempted.

When we are tempted, the feelings of condemnation are often so strong that we are sure God must be disappointed; He must be shaking His head in disgust. Surely He finds it hard to believe that we would even entertain such ideas after all He has done for us.

In one respect we have already dealt with this misunderstanding. Since temptation is not a sin and even the most spiritual people are tempted, God could not possibly be disappointed or displeased when we are tempted. Certainly He was not disappointed in His own Son when He was tempted!

We continue to feel we have disappointed God when we are tempted because there is a tendency to confuse how we feel about ourselves with how God feels about us. When we feel disappointed in ourselves, we assume God is disappointed as well.

Such, however, is not always the case. As we have seen, much of the disappointment we feel toward ourselves in regard to temptation has to do with failing to live up to unrealistic expectations to begin with. As long as we have unrealistic expectations, we will disappoint ourselves.

God, on the other hand, has no expectations. He is omniscient; He already knows about every temptation that will come our way as well as how we will respond. Nothing takes Him by surprise; therefore, He does not even have the potential to be disappointed.

There is another reason we know God is not disappointed when we are tempted. Temptation is one of His primary tools to develop character and faith in believers. James made this clear when he wrote,

> Consider it all joy, my brethren, when you encounter various trials, knowing that the testing of your faith produces endurance. And let endurance have its perfect result, that you may be perfect and complete, lacking in nothing.
> —James 1:2–4

When we are tempted, our faith and character are tested. When we resist successfully, we come out stronger.

If you have ever seen a dog trained, you have seen this principle in action. The trainer at some point in the training process will tell the dog to stay and then put something the dog loves to eat just a few feet away. A well-trained dog will wait until permission is granted before going over to the food. Setting the food before the dog tests the animal's loyalty to his trainer. In the same way, temptation tests our love for Christ. For this reason, James said,

> Blessed is a man who perseveres under trial; for once he has been approved, he will receive the crown of life, which the LORD has promised to those who love Him.
> —James 1:12

God could not possibly be disappointed when we are tempted. James said that God rewards those who are tempted—if they persevere. It is not temptation itself that grieves God; He is displeased when we give in to temptation.

God is not disappointed when you are tempted. He has no reason to be. He knows Satan is out to get you. Remember, God gave you the foundational desires Satan capitalizes upon when you are tempted. He also gave you the power to choose. There is a sense in which God gave you the potential to be tempted in the first place. He is not disappointed.

6. *Temptation Is Overcome By Running.*

Earlier I said that one method of defending ourselves against temptation was to avoid situations that set us up to be tempted. That is, we should flee temptation whenever possible. Now it is true that fleeing certain places and relationships does facilitate our victory at times. However, running doesn't solve the problem of temptation in general. Temptation is not a war waged at a particular geographical location. The battlefield of temptation is the mind. Thus, running does not always guarantee victory nor does it do away with temptation.

I meet people all the time who are changing jobs, churches, and even cities in order to "escape" temptation. Most of the time they end up in a situation just like the one they left. Why? They changed their circumstances but they never changed themselves. They failed to renew their minds, thus allowing God to change their character and heart.

What's going on internally ultimately determines what happens externally. God wants to change your heart. He wants you to grow so that you can stand firm in the midst of temptation. He isn't going to take you out of the world. He has left you here to have an impact on it. That means you are going to face temptation. Spending all your time trying to avoid temptation will ultimately bring you to a point where you will be too isolated from society to have any impact. There is a time to run and a time to stand.

Cutting Through the Confusion

God does not want us to be ignorant about temptation. He wants us to know the truth. Part of Satan's scheme is to confuse the facts concerning this issue of temptation. In this chapter we have examined six commonly held theories regarding temptation. None of them could be supported biblically. In every case the Bible teaches just the opposite. If you have held to one or more of these misunderstandings, you need to begin today to renew your mind to the truth: being tempted is not a sin; spiritual people are tempted, too; victory now does not guarantee victory later; we do not fall into temptation—we choose to sin; God is not disappointed when we are tempted; running is not always the best way to overcome temptation.

At first you may find it difficult to put away these misunderstandings. You may have held to some of these for years. But until you begin to see your temptations the way God sees them, you will feel a weight of responsibility God never intended for you to feel; your expectation level will remain totally unrealistic. Consequently, you will become discouraged and unmotivated. God wants you to be free, and freedom comes through knowing the truth. Now that you have seen the truth, work to make it a part of your experience.

Chapter 13

WHY WE
CONTINUE TO FALL

NOTHING IS MORE frustrating for a counselor than a counselee who appears to be doing everything he or she is told and yet comes back week after week to report, "It didn't work." Having exhausted all the usually effective methods, the counselor will either admit failure or do some further probing into the nature of the counselee's problem. Because this is a book rather than a series of counseling sessions, it is doubtful that you have had time to apply all of the principles outlined in the preceding chapters. For those who have, and yet still continue to fall, here are three suggestions as to why nothing has worked so far. These are a culmination of things I have discovered in my counseling with others as well as in my own passage through the mine field of temptation.

Who, Me?

One reason we continue to fall is that *we deny that we have a problem.* We know we have some things we need to work on. But a "problem"? No way. That sounds too serious. Consequently, we don't pursue a solution with the determination we need to see it through to the end. By suppressing the truth about our situation, we automatically cut ourselves off from getting the help we need.

The real danger is that people tend to ignore the truth until what began as a small thing becomes a major problem. This pattern of behavior is common among alcoholics and drug abusers. Instead of approaching their problem as a full-blown addiction problem, they treat it like it's simply a matter of balance. "I just need to cut back."

Going to the doctor is about my least favorite thing to do. When I start feeling under the weather, my tendency is to say, "This is just a head cold. A couple of aspirin and I'll be fine." Regardless of how I'm really feeling, I convince myself that I'm not really *sick*; I'm just reacting to the change in the weather. If in fact I do have a virus of some kind, treating it like a head cold or the result of changing atmospheric conditions will be worthless. I will continue to be sick until I get an accurate diagnosis of my problem and then follow the prescribed treatment.

The same is true when it comes to dealing with sin. Most of us underestimate the power of sin and overestimate our spirituality. As long as you treat a bona fide problem like it is just part of your personality or the result of pressure at work or anything else besides what it is, you will find no relief. You must face your failure head-on to get serious enough to do anything about it. Perhaps you continue to fall to the same temptation because you have not admitted to yourself that you have a genuine problem.

I Surrender All

Another reason we may continue to fall is that *we have not surrendered to the lordship of Christ. By* that I mean we have not recognized Christ's unconditional right to rule and reign over every area of our lives. As long as we refuse to give up our right to rule in a particular area of our lives, we will never know victory.

Oftentimes we play a power game with God. We want Him to give us the power we need to have victory in our lives. But we aren't willing to surrender that area to His unchallenged rule. We want to use His power for our ends.

I talked to one of our singles recently who wanted me to explain how to deal with peer pressure. His problem was that whenever he spent time with his old college buddies, he was tempted to do the things they all used to do together in college. Over and over he had given in to the temptation to do these things.

I began to explain to him the wisdom principle outlined in chapter 8. I told him that part of God's answer may be for him to find some new friends. As soon as I mentioned that prospect, his body language told me he didn't think that was a good idea at all. "But they are my best friends," he argued. "We've been best friends for years!"

I explained to him that his real problem wasn't the things he had mentioned earlier that were normally associated with his friends. His real problem was lordship. He wasn't willing to allow Jesus Christ to be Lord of all his relationships. I asked him if he was willing to surrender all his relationships to the lordship of Christ, even if it meant breaking off some relationships completely. He was not ready to do that.

His response is characteristic of how we all respond at times to this issue of lordship. We want our lives to go "right." But we want them to go right on *our* terms, by *our* standards. We want God's help, but not to the point that it interferes with our plans and desires.

God is not interested in giving us victory for victory's sake or victory for the sake of making life easier for us. Power over sin is the means by which we are freed to serve Christ more effectively. It is not something God hands out to make life smoother for us.

The Missing Father

A father in our fellowship came to see me about his fourteen-year-old son. He said that they did not communicate anymore and that Jimmy did not respond to authority like he used to. As we continued to talk, it became clear that part of the problem had to do with this man's work schedule. He left early in the morning, before his son was up. And he returned late at night, usually after his son was in bed. On Sunday it wasn't unusual for him to go into the office after church and stay there until early evening. In his profession he could basically set his own hours, but he had convinced himself that the long hours were necessary to provide adequately for his family.

I explained to this man the relationship between his being away from home so much and his son's loss of interest and respect. I made it clear that part of the answer would be for him to change his schedule. Our conversation came to an abrupt halt. You see, he may have been interested in restoring his relationship with his son, but he was interested in doing it on his terms, not God's. He wanted things to be "right," but he was not willing to surrender his work schedule to the lordship of Christ.

The real issue when it comes to lordship is trust. We hold back areas of control because we don't trust God to do it "right." We think He will let a need go unmet. Or that He won't meet it the way we think is best. We are afraid God will wait too long to do something. We just don't trust Him, so we hold back.

It is ironic that we want Him to come rushing into our lives when things get out of our control, when there is a death or an emergency. At those times we are more than willing to admit our inadequacy and our dependence on Him. But as soon as things return to normal, as soon as life gets "easy" again, we are afraid to hand it all over to Him. Think about it. If God can be trusted when we are most vulnerable and helpless, can He not be trusted in the times when things are going smoothly?

God wants control over every area of your life. Not partial control, total control. He wants you to be victorious over temptation. But He wants you to be victorious for His purposes, not yours. You may not have achieved victory over temptation because you are holding to the reins of your life and trying to get God to intervene in the rough spots. That isn't the way God works. He wants all of you. And when He knows you are His, He will do whatever He needs to do to make you into an effective servant for His kingdom.

"Forgetting What Lies Behind"

There is a third reason for our repeated failures. *We continually focus on past failure.* To focus on the past causes us to be problem oriented. We allow our past failures to persuade us that we will never change, that there is no use even trying to do things differently. When we are tempted, we are set up to fall. Mentally, we have already been defeated.

The truth is that God has made available to you the power to change. The sins of the past need not characterize your life in the future. No one is destined to be a certain way throughout a lifetime. Your past sins should simply serve as a reminder of God's grace and forgiveness. But even then, they should not be the focus of your attention.

There is another problem with focusing on our past failures, however. It is easy to allow our past failures to serve as an excuse to sin again. "Well," we reason, "I have already done it once. I might as well do it again." We are easily deceived into thinking that "one more time" will not really hurt anything. The tragedy is that each "one more time" just keeps the sin cycle alive in our lives. A habit is simply a string of individual sins committed on separate occasions.

To commit a sin one more time does matter because each time we sin, it just ingrains that habit a little bit deeper into our emotional being. Sin becomes more and more entrenched. Each time we give in, it becomes that much more difficult to say no the next time.

These are the hazards of focusing on our past failures. We get bogged down or deceived. The apostle Paul certainly had some things in his past that could have slowed him down. However, in reference to his past he wrote,

Brethren, I do not regard myself as having laid hold of it yet;
but one thing I do: *forgetting what lies behind* and reaching
forward to what lies ahead, I press on toward the goal for the
prize of the upward call of God in Christ Jesus.
                    —Philippians 3:13–14, emphasis added

Paul understood that a believer must put the past behind and
move on. Do you have a tendency to focus on the past? Do you
rehearse the sins of your past over and over in your mind? Does
reflection on your past sins cause you to doubt that things will
ever change? If that is the case, then join with the apostle Paul
by turning your focus toward the future, toward the things you
want to see God do in your life. The past is something you can
do nothing about. The future, however, is whatever you allow
God to make it.

Could It Be?

Think for just a moment. Could it be that you have a genuine
problem with sin but are unwilling to deal with it as such? Is Jesus
Christ Lord of every known area in your life? Is He Lord of your
family, friends, jobs, goals, relationships, time, money? Is there
an area you are holding back? Do you have a tendency to focus
on the past? Do you use your past failures as an excuse to sin?
Are you overwhelmed with such a deep sense of failure that you
find no reason to try anymore?

If you answered yes to any of these questions, then you may
have just discovered why you continue to fall. As long as you
refuse to surrender fully to the lordship of Christ, His power will
be cut off. As long as you treat a problem as anything but a problem, it will never go away. And as long as you focus on the past,
you will never find strength to move ahead. Ask God to give you
insight into how you can correct your attitude.

Chapter 14

AFTER WE FAIL,
WHAT THEN?

YOU HAVE BEEN reading an entire book dedicated to helping you overcome temptation, but you went out and blew it anyway. Now what? Do you give up? Do you reconcile yourself to a life of defeat? Do you take the book back for a refund? What do you do?

In this final chapter I want to outline what I call the steps to recovery. These seven steps or stages are necessary if you are to emerge from failure victorious rather than defeated. The idea of coming out of failure victoriously may sound like a contradiction in terms. But God has provided a way by which even your worst failure can be transformed into great gain. And not only for you, but for as many people as you are willing to share it with.

It is important for us to respond properly to failure. Oftentimes our incorrect response to failure sets us up to fall again. The more we fail, the more discouraged we get and the less faith we have in God's ability to make us victorious. In the book of Psalms David records his prayer of remorse after sinning with Bathsheba. This prayer includes the seven steps that I believe are necessary for all of us to follow after we have given in to temptation. Once we complete these steps, we actually emerge from our failure stronger than before. We will be more suitable for God's service, and we will be better prepared for the next time we are tempted.

God has a beautiful way of taking what is negative and turning it around for His glory—if we let Him. Think about it. The greatest tragedy in all of history—the death of the Son of God— turned out to be mankind's greatest blessing—the resurrection of the Son of God. If we will respond properly to our failure, God can use it to bring Himself glory and to better prepare us for His service.

Repent!

The first stage in the recovery process is *repentance.* Two counterfeit forms of repentance are often passed off as the real thing. One of them goes like this, "Lord, I am really sorry I got caught." The other sounds like this, "Lord, I am really sorry I sinned. I certainly hope I can do better next time." Both of these are prompted out of guilt or embarrassment, not a heartfelt sense of remorse over the fact that almighty God has been grieved. People who pray such prayers have no intention of changing. They are simply attempting to get God off their backs.

Genuine repentance involves several things. First of all, confession. Not just, "Lord, I am sorry for my mistake," but, "Lord, I have sinned against You." Confession acknowledges guilt. Second, repentance involves the recognition that the sin was against God. Notice what David said,

> Against Thee, Thee only, I have sinned,
> And done what is evil in Thy sight.
> —Psalm 51:4

Now that does not mean he failed to recognize that he had sinned against Bathsheba and her husband. He was saying that he realized that his sin was primarily against God. Against the backdrop of all the grace and goodness God had showered down upon him, David's sin was primarily against God.

All of us need to recognize that our sin is primarily against God. Other people may be hurt as well, but when we hold our sin up to the unconditional love and grace of God as expressed through the giving of His Son, we see clearly that there is where sin looks its darkest. We see sin for what it is, the most extreme expression of ingratitude. So repentance includes a confession of our guilt, recognition that our sin is against God, and two other things.

Repentance includes taking full responsibility for our sin. David clearly accepted full responsibility for his actions with Bathsheba. He said,

> Wash *me* thoroughly from *my* iniquity,
> And cleanse *me* from *my* sin.
> For I know *my* transgressions,
> And *my* sin is ever before *me*.
> —Psalm 51:2–3, *emphasis added*

Nowhere do we find him saying, "Now, Lord, You know it takes two. I wasn't the only one involved. She should have been more careful than to bathe right underneath my balcony. You know I am only human." David never accused Bathsheba. He never mentioned her name.

Whenever we catch ourselves blaming someone else for our sin, our repentance is incomplete. If we are truly repentant, we will take full responsibility for sin, no matter what happened or who was involved. Regardless of the nature of the temptation, ultimately we are the ones who make the decision to give in.

Last, repentance requires total honesty with God. Repentance is not complete without honesty. Think about this for a moment. Which of the following two qualities are more important when it comes to our fellowship and relationship with God, *honesty* or *holiness*? *You* know, we won't always be holy, but we can always be honest. I believe God is looking for us to be honest about our sin—honest about our weaknesses, our failures, and our frustrations. Honesty promotes fellowship. As long as we continue to be open and honest with God, He can continue to work with us, even after we have committed our most grievous sin.

We get into trouble when we start trying to cover things up. "Now, Lord, I know I have made a mistake. But after all, everybody makes mistakes. Nobody's perfect." Responding like that is simply avoiding the real issue and is therefore dishonest. As long as we approach God in that fashion, there is not much He can do with us.

What Happens Then?

Before we go to the second stage in the recovery process, I want to say something about God's discipline in connection with repentance. The Bible teaches that God disciplines those who are disobedient. The Scripture is full of illustrations of God's discipline. The story of David and Bathsheba is one of the best examples. I believe, however, that when true repentance follows quickly on the heels of sin, the discipline is lessened.

When David committed adultery with Bathsheba, he did not repent immediately. It was some time later when David finally faced up to what he had done. And even then he did not do it of his own accord. God had to send a prophet to confront him (2 Sam. 12). It was only after Nathan told him the story of the man who had the many sheep stealing from the man who had one that David realized the great evil he had done. That was when David repented of his sin. The discipline that followed, however, was very severe in nature, and part of the reason for the severity was David's failure to repent sooner.

It is my personal conviction that if you and I deal with our sin genuinely, openly, and immediately, God will lessen the severity of our discipline. This makes sense in light of the nature of discipline anyway. Discipline is for the purpose of getting us to change, to obey. If God sees that we want to cooperate and that we have purposed in our hearts to obey the next time around, there is no need for discipline, except as a reminder.

When we let our sin go on and on with no intention of stopping until we are finally caught, it is too late to escape the disciplining hand of God. For our own sake, and for the testimony of His kingdom's sake, He cannot let us continue in our sin. The longer we put off repentance in our lives, the greater our discipline will be. Those who are wise will repent quickly.

Accept God's Forgiveness

The second stage in the recovery process is *acceptance of God's forgiveness.* Oftentimes this is difficult because we feel so guilty, especially if it is a sin we have repeatedly committed. Sometimes we just feel plain stupid coming to God with it again, but that is what we must do.

Remember, when Jesus died on the cross two thousand years ago for your sin, He died for all your sins—past, present, and future. Your sin causes you embarrassment because you expect better of yourself. But God doesn't. He already knew about it. Even as you prayed time before last and promised Him you would never do it again, He already knew you would. And He had already made provision for it. So you need not be embarrassed; you need not avoid Him.

Someone always makes the comment at this point, "Well, if all our sin is paid for, past, present, and future, why do we have to repent and confess every time?" For the simple reason that until we face up to what we have done, we are out of fellowship with the Father. What if I steal something that belongs to you and you know about it? You can forgive me in your heart and never think about it again. But when I know that you know, I can never act natural or feel at ease around you until I confess what I have done.

The same is true in our relationship with God. Until we confess our sins—one at a time—we remain out of fellowship with Him. The guilt will remain as far as we are concerned, and we will never experience the peace we are intended to have. We will continue to avoid Him, and we will be set up to fall again. That is why it is so important to keep short accounts with God. Satan would have us avoid confession and repentance as long as possible. That way we are prone to sin because we are running from God. And you remember where that got Jonah, don't you?

Along with accepting God's forgiveness, we must forgive ourselves. We shouldn't make the mistake of holding ourselves more accountable than the God who created us does. If He says our sin is paid for, then it is paid for. We can't try to make it up to Him through good works. That is impossible. If the One we sinned against no longer holds our sin against us what right do we have to do so? In essence we are usurping His authority. We must just accept it by faith and move on. As long as we feel we must punish ourselves or in some way make it up to Him, we will avoid Him. And just like the people who refuse to accept His forgiveness, we will play right into the hands of Satan.

Don't mistake God's discipline as evidence that He has not forgiven you. If He had not forgiven you, He would not be disciplining you; He would have to punish you. When people are punished, they are "paid back" for what they have done. The Bible says that the punishment for any sin is death (Rom. 6:23). If God were going to punish you for your sin, He would have to put you to death physically and then send you to hell eternally. The fact that God is only disciplining you is evidence that you are one of His children and therefore forgiven! (For a more in-depth discussion on the subject, see chapter 9, "Forgiving Ourselves," in *Forgiveness*.)

Restitution

The third stage in the recovery process involves *restitution*. You must make restitution to those against whom you have sinned. Sometimes this is not always easy. If you have stolen something, you can give that back without much trouble—and pay for any damages as well. But how do you make restitution when you have robbed someone of purity or honor or reputation?

You must ask that person to forgive you. By that, I do not mean you simply say that you are sorry. You must ask for forgiveness.

Make it clear that you realize you have sinned against the person and God and that you are willing to do whatever is possible to remedy the situation.

In making restitution, you need to be careful not to involve other people. You are not called on to repent of anyone else's sin, just your own. In the same way, you need to make sure you are confessing your sin to the person you sinned against. You may be tempted to confess your sin to someone who has nothing to do with your sin. This is usually a ploy to relieve yourself of the guilt you are bearing. This is a waste of time and it can be harmful. Anytime you involve a third party, you run the risk of others finding out as well, which could result in embarrassment to you and the one to whom you really owe the apology. The one exception is when you share your burden with an accountability partner beforehand. But even then, there is no need to go into detail about the sin. As a general rule, it is best not to involve someone else.

Accept God's Discipline

The next stage in the recovery process is *acceptance of God's discipline.* Oftentimes we do not recognize the disciplining hand of God. When there are personal consequences resulting from our sin, such as an injury or a financial loss, we can usually recognize those right away. But sometimes God's discipline comes in forms that at first seem to have no relationship to what we have done. In time, however, the truth usually becomes apparent.

When we recognize that we are being disciplined, one indisputable sign that we really mean business for God is that we don't fight it. By willingly accepting His discipline, we are acknowledging our guilt and His sovereign right to exercise authority over us.

When people resist the discipline of God, it is evidence that they have yet to come to grips with their sin and with the nature of sin itself. By resisting God's discipline, they are saying, "I don't deserve this. I deserve better. What I did wasn't really so bad." Their understanding of sin and what it cost God is so deficient that it is unlikely they will do much to guard against repeating the same error again and again.

On the other hand, people who accept the discipline of God realize that His discipline is for their own protection. They do not view it as something negative. They see it as an expression of His love, for that is exactly what it is.

Imagine for a moment a child who has been told repeatedly not to play in the street. But he goes right ahead and does it anyway. His parents, if they are wise, will discipline him. Why? Because they are the parents and he is just a child and how dare he break their rules? No. They know that if he doesn't learn to stay out of the street, he could be killed or crippled. The disciplinary action they choose may seem painful to their child, but a simple spanking is far better than being hit by a car. A lesser evil is used to guard the child from a much greater evil.

So it is when God disciplines us. He is trying to keep us from the greater harm that comes from involvement with sin. We will not fully appreciate the love God has expressed toward us through His discipline until we get to heaven.

Live and Learn

The fifth stage in the recovery process involves *identification of the lesson or lessons* God is attempting to teach us through our failure. The tragedy of skipping this stage is that the whole series of events becomes a waste of time. God is in the process of bringing something good out of the mess we have caused. However, if we don't discover what He is trying to teach us, the whole process is short-circuited.

When it comes to learning from our mistakes, we need to keep in mind humility, purity, and instruction. When we fall, we should pray, "Lord, humble my spirit before You. Purify my sinful heart. And instruct me in Your ways so that this habit can be broken and I can experience the freedom You have made available."

Since pride is always connected with our sin, we should take every available opportunity to allow God to rid our lives of it.

The same is true of impurity, whether it is moral impurity or impure motives. These are two areas we always need work in. Each time we are working back through the stages of recovery, God breaks us little by little of our pride and impurity.

Let me ask you a question. When you blow it, do you ask God to teach you something? Or do you rush through a quick 1 John 1:9 type of prayer and keep moving? The truth is that you should always take the time to learn something from your mistakes. Otherwise you are bound to keep repeating them. Not only that, you rob somebody else of the privilege of learning from your mistakes.

When your attitude is right, you are going to want to learn everything you can. Your first response won't be, "God, get the pressure off. Relieve me of my guilt. Make me feel better. AMEN." I know you don't use those words, but does that reflect your attitude sometimes when you are approching God after you have sinned? If it does, you are not really serious about making any real changes in your life. You do not desire an intimate relationship with God. You basically want to be left alone to do your own thing without any outside interference.

God wants to teach us something through our failures. But as is the case in all of God's lessons, only those who are paying attention are going to learn them. Only those who are seeking Him will find Him. Only those with ears to hear will hear Him. Those who fail and learn nothing have wasted not only an opportunity to learn but have pretty much guaranteed for themselves another trip through the recovery process.

Get Help!

The sixth stage in the recovery process involves *consultation with a qualified counselor*. If you continue to struggle with the same temptation and nothing seems to help, you may need professional help. By professional, I mean someone who can listen and help you gain insight into why you are struggling the way you are. We discussed in chapter 4 the fact that sometimes there are root causes of the temptations we face. You may need help discovering the root of your particular problem. It could be something related to your childhood that you cannot remember. It may be something more recent that you have failed to connect with your present temptations. Whatever it is, you may need a counselor to help you make the discovery that could set you free.

If you are too proud to ask for help, you will be the loser. I have talked to counselors more times than I can remember. All of us run into things in our lives that just don't make any sense. Sometimes one basic insight can unlock doors that have kept us prisoners for years, but it takes someone trained to know how to get to those remote places in our memories and experiences.

Don't ever be too proud to say, "Hey, I need help. I have run up against something that I don't quite know how to handle." All of us need the objective opinion and insight of someone else at some point. That is why God has equipped counselors and made them available to the body of Christ.

Teach Others

The last stage in the recovery process is *readiness to share what we have learned* with others. Consider what David said,

> Create in me a clean heart, O God,
> And renew a steadfast spirit within me.
> Do not cast me away from Thy presence.
> And do not take Thy Holy Spirit from me.
> Restore to me the joy of Thy salvation,
> And sustain me with a willing spirit.
> Then I will teach transgressors Thy ways,
> And sinners will be converted to Thee.
> —Psalm 51:10–13

David wanted God to completely cleanse his heart and restore his relationship. After that process was complete, David wanted God to allow him to teach other sinners the ways of God. And notice his goal: "And sinners will be converted to Thee." David wanted to take what he had learned and teach others.

When you and I have really repented of our sin, faced up to our responsibility and willingly accepted the consequences of what we have done, God will teach us some fabulous lessons. He will grant us deep insight into His Word. The process is not complete, however, until we make ourselves available to teach others what we have learned. By doing this, we demonstrate to God and to ourselves that we are totally given over to His purposes; we are His and His alone.

Don't misunderstand. By teaching others, I don't necessarily mean in a formal sense, although it may come to that. Think of the blessings you have received from those who share their testimony of what God has done in their lives. Regardless of how God chooses to use you, you must be willing to share with others the lessons God has taught you. After all, that is half the reason He taught you to begin with.

When you hit bottom, who would you rather talk to? Somebody who always seems to be doing exceptionally well and appears untouched by sorrow and pain? Or somebody who like you has hit bottom, but is slowly making progress? We all need someone we can identify with. Through your failure and then your proper response to your failure, God is preparing you to be an instrument of encouragement in someone else's life.

Be Careful!

You should use discretion when you share the lessons God has taught you through your failures. Be wise. Don't tell the details of your sin. That is not really important. Avoid making sin sound glamorous. Hollywood does an excellent job of that. The film-makers certainly don't need your help. Too much detail often stirs people's imagination and curiosity to the point of causing them to sin.

Focus on the lessons God has taught you. When you mention your sin, point out the consequences. Include the things that could have happened if God had not rescued you when He did. Oftentimes testimonies leave the impression that we can have our cake and eat it, too. That is, we can enjoy sin for a while, and then when we are good and ready, we can turn our lives over to the Lord. Testimonies should cause people to fear the consequences of sin so that they would never dream of becoming involved in similar sinful situations.

There is a second thing you need to keep in mind when you share with others what God has taught you. Never say, "I have learned. . . ." No one has "learned" anything in the sense of reaching the point of no longer being subject to temptation in a given area. We are all still in the process of learning. A better way to say that is, "God is teaching me . . . ," or "Every day I continue to see . . ."

As soon as you think you have finished learning something or even give that impression to someone, Satan is going to unleash a vicious attack. He loves to publicly embarrass Christians. Mark it down. What you announce publicly, Satan will test you in privately.

We are all still learners. That is what a disciple is—a learner. We are all in the process of becoming what God wants us to be. No one has arrived. No one ever will in this lifetime. So when we share with others what God has taught us through our failures, we need to make sure we communicate it in such a way as to ensure a humble spirit on our part and realistic expectations on theirs.

Complete Recovery

God's plan for you includes several trips through the recovery process outlined in this chapter. We all fail. There is no question about that. The question you have to ask yourself is this: "Now that I have sinned, how will I respond?" You have two options. You can run from God and resist His discipline. Or you can genuinely repent of your sin, submit to His discipline, and learn everything you can in the process.

If you resist Him, you will be the loser. And so will all the people you could have helped if you had only allowed the Lord to teach you a few things. Nothing is sadder to me than believers who got stuck. God wanted to teach them something, and they decided they did not want to learn—so they stopped growing right there. They stagnated spiritually. Usually the issue was some sin they refused to repent of. They ran from God, and now they are stuck. They refuse to let go of their sin, and God refuses to use them.

However, if you will work through these recovery stages, you will watch God take what started as a negative thing and transfer it into some of the most positive experiences of your life. At times it will be painful. But growth always is. The choice is yours. Not just once, but every time you give in to temptation. As you allow God to work you through this process, He will give you insight into why you are so susceptible to certain temptations. Your willingness to respond correctly to failure may provide you with the insight you need to be victorious next time.

Please don't waste your failures. Allow God to use them to mature you into the man or woman He wants you to be. Allow Him to turn your defeats into victories. Let Him take your failures and develop in you a testimony that will make an impact on all those who hear. The choice is yours. It is my prayer that everyone who reads this book will choose not to waste the failures, but will place them in the hands of the One who said,

Come to Me, all who are weary and heavy-laden, and I will give you rest. Take My yoke upon you, and learn from Me, for I am gentle and humble in heart; and you shall find rest for your souls. For My yoke is easy, and My load is light.
—Matthew 11:28–30

Book Two

HOW
TO HANDLE
ADVERSITY

To Mrs. Ralph Sauls
my steadfast inspiration
in a time of great adversity

CONTENTS

Acknowledgments

I want to thank my son, Andy, for his insight and assistance in research and editing.

Chapter 1

ADVERSITY:
WHO IS BEHIND IT ALL?

As JESUS AND His disciples passed through Jerusalem, they came upon a man who had been blind from birth. This surfaced a question in the minds of the disciples that they must have been wrestling with for some time. They asked,

> Who sinned, this man or his parents, that he should be born blind?
>
> —John 9:2

Their dilemma was based upon a wrong assumption they had been taught all their lives, namely, that illness is a sign of God's judgment. There was no question in their minds that someone had sinned. But who?

The disciples were trying from their limited perspective to answer a question we often find ourselves asking. It is the *why* question. *Why* did this happen? *Why* did my son run away? *Why* did my father contract cancer? *Why* did our house burn? *Why* did I lose my job? *Why* was I sued?

The questions are endless. Each of us has a specific list. Sometimes there is so much emotion involved we dare not even allow ourselves to verbalize the frustration we feel because asking for and finding no clear-cut answer threatens the foundation of all we believe about God and His goodness. And yet, the questions still linger.

Like the disciples, we are prone to view adversity narrowly. We turn on ourselves and begin an often fruitless journey into our recent—and sometimes not-so-recent—past. Our purpose is to find the reason for the adversity we face. The thought may arise: *Surely this is God's way of paying me back.* If, however, we are convinced that nothing we have done merits the magnitude of our adversity, we have no choice, it seems, but to question the goodness and faithfulness of God.

In His response to the disciples' question, Jesus revealed yet another error that plagued the theology of the day. But His answer did much more than that. It enlightens us and offers a much broader perspective on suffering than that held by many. His answer brings hope to those who have thus far been afraid to ask *why*. It allows us to look beyond ourselves—and that is always an improvement!

Jesus answered, "It was neither that this man sinned, nor his parents." In others words, "Your thinking is too narrow. You need some new categories." I believe many well-meaning Christians need some new categories when it comes to the subject of adversity. Thinking too narrowly on this subject sets one up for needless guilt. And as in the case of Jesus' disciples, it warps one's perspective on the suffering of others.

Jesus said,

It was neither that this man sinned, nor his parents; but it was in order that the works of God might be displayed in him.
—John 9:3

The implications of that statement are staggering. The phrase "in order that" denotes purpose. There was a purpose to this man's blindness. The disciples saw his blindness as the *result* of something. In fact, they saw all illness in terms of result. Jesus, how-

*Is it
possible that
adversity
can originate
with God?*

ever, let it be known in no uncertain terms that this blindness was not the result of something the man did. This man's blindness was a part of God's *purpose.* In other words, *this man's blindness was from God.* That was a difficult sentence to write—much less believe.

Is it possible that adversity can originate with God? All of us would be more comfortable if Jesus had said, "This man is blind because he sinned, but God is going to use it anyway." That would be a much easier pill to swallow. But Jesus leaves us no escape. Sin was not the direct cause of this man's blindness; God was.

A Case in Point

I am aware that such a statement flies in the face of the prosperity theology so prevalent today. Yet, a statement such as this one in the gospel of John makes it perfectly clear that God is the engineer of some adversity. We cannot let our theological biases (which we all have) interfere with the clear teaching of Scripture. Fortunately for us, this blind man is not the only scriptural example of God's engineering adversity. In 2 Corinthians 12 the apostle Paul describes his struggle with adversity. He clearly identifies God as the engineer behind his suffering:

> And because of the surpassing greatness of the revelations, for this reason, *to keep me from exalting myself*, there was given me a thorn in the flesh, a messenger of Satan to buffet me—*to keep me from exalting myself!*
> —2 Corinthians 12:7, *emphasis mine*

One might argue, "But it says it was a messenger of Satan." Right! But notice the purpose of Paul's adversity: "To keep me from exalting myself." Do you think Satan would engineer a plan to keep Paul from exalting himself? Of course not. Satan's goal is to *cause* us to exalt ourselves. He is certainly not going to work against his own destructive purposes. So how does all this fit together? It would seem that God wanted to cause Paul some pain in order to keep him humble. To accomplish this, God sent a messenger of Satan into Paul's life. What exactly this was, we do not know. One thing is certain, however; the idea originated with God. It was His plan, and He used His resources to carry it out.

As difficult as it may be to grasp, the Bible depicts God as the instigator of some adversity. In the remaining chapters we are going to expand upon the relationship between God and adversity. I realize that for some people I have raised many more questions than I have answered. That is all right, as long as you keep reading!

Our Own Doing

God is not the only source of adversity. Oftentimes adversity comes as a result of our own doing. Jesus' disciples were not completely off base in their approach to discerning the cause behind the man's blindness. Adversity is in many cases the result of sin. In fact, sin always results in adversity of some kind. James writes,

> But each one is tempted when he is carried away and enticed by his own lust. Then when lust has conceived, it gives birth to sin; and when sin is accomplished, it brings forth death.
> —James 1:14–15

Sin always results in some form of death. Sometimes it is physical death, but usually it is more subtle. Sin causes our relationships to die. It causes our self-esteem to die. Certain sins kill ambition and discipline. All of these forms of death result in adversity to some degree.

The classic case would be the story of Adam and Eve. Their lives were free of adversity. There was no sickness, death, decay, or suffering of any kind in the Garden of Eden. There was no tension in their relationship with each other. Neither was there any conflict between them and the environment. They could not have wished for anything more. We are not sure how long Adam and

Eve lived in the Garden of Eden. We are certain, though, about why they had to leave—*sin*.

After they disobeyed God by eating of the forbidden fruit, everything changed. Eve would experience pain in childbirth. There would be the potential for conflict between the man and the woman. There would even be conflict between man and his environment. To top it all off, man would have to experience death and thus live his life under the shadow of that monumental foe. Death brought with it fear, sorrow, doubt, and insecurity. All of these were the result of sin. From that moment on, life for Adam and Eve would be full of adversity—and all because of sin.

The Roots of Evil

This biblical narrative does more than simply illustrate the possible connection between sin and adversity. It serves as the foundation for answering many of life's toughest questions. It is clear from even a cursory reading of these first few chapters that God never intended for man to experience the adversity and sorrow brought about by our forefather's sin. Death was not a part of God's original plan for man. Death is an interruption. It is God's enemy as well as man's. It is the opposite of all He desired to accomplish.

Sickness and pain are certainly no friends of God. There was no sickness in the Garden of Eden. It was not a part of God's original plan for man. The ministry of Christ bears witness to this truth. Everywhere He went He healed the sick. God shares our disdain for disease. Sickness is an intruder. It had no place in God's world in the beginning; it will have no place in His world in the end.

Death, disease, famine, earthquakes, war—these things were not part of God's original plan. Yet they are part of our reality. Why? Did God lose His grip? Has He abandoned us? Is He no longer a good God? No. Our reality has been fashioned by Adam's choice to sin. And sin always results in adversity.

God's goodness and power are not to be measured in the balance of the tragedy and adversity we experience day in and day out. If His goodness is to be questioned, let it be done in light of His original purpose as well as His ultimate plan.

> And I heard a loud voice from the throne, saying, "Behold the tabernacle of God is among men, and He shall dwell among them, and they shall be His people, and God Himself shall be among them, and He shall wipe away every tear from their eyes; and there shall no longer be any death; there shall no longer be any mourning, or crying, or pain; the first things have passed away."
>
> —Revelation 21:3–4

It is God who will wipe away every tear. It is God who will do away with death, crying, pain, and sorrow. Why will He do these things? Because He is a good and faithful God. How can He do such things? By the strength of His might. He is the all-powerful Sovereign of the universe. Nothing is too hard for Him.

A Living Example

The idea that adversity is sometimes the result of sin hardly needs biblical support. Each of us could give testimony to this principle. Every speeding ticket or fine we have ever paid serves as evidence. The last argument you had with your spouse, parent, or child probably stemmed from sin in some form or another. The sorrow and pain caused by a divorce or even separation are always related in some way to sin. Sometimes it is personal sin that brings adversity into our lives. On other occasions the sin of someone else causes us difficulty. Jesus' disciples were not completely wrong; adversity and sin do go hand in hand.

As self-evident as this may seem, it is amazing how we sometimes cannot see, or refuse to see, the relationship. Recently a mother brought her teenage son to see me. The problem, as she

saw it, was her son's involvement with "the wrong crowd." She
went on to explain how her son's interaction with this group had
caused him to develop a bad attitude toward authority. As a result, he had become impossible to live with.

After several meetings, the truth finally surfaced. The situation was one in which the boy's mother had left her husband (the
boy's father), and she was completely unwilling to work toward
reconciling the relationship. The boy wanted to live with his
father, but his mother would not hear of it. I talked with the father on several occasions. He took responsibility for his part in
the conflicts at home. He was willing to do whatever he had to
do to get his family back together. His wife, on the other hand,
would not budge.

When I explained to the woman how a hostile separation usually affects the children involved, she became angry. "I told you
why he is acting the way he is," she said, "It's his friends." Nothing I said made any difference. She could not (or would not) see
any connection between her son's behavior at home and her response to her husband. As far as she was concerned, the problem
was her son's. On several occasions she was willing to publicly
request prayer for herself in regard to the sorrow her son was
causing her. But she never came to grips with the fact that the
conflict she was experiencing with her son was directly related
to her own sin.

It is hard to put a percentage on this, but I would guess that 60
to 70 percent of the people I counsel are suffering from the consequences of their own sin or the sin of another. Some of the most
difficult counseling situations I deal with are those in which an
innocent party is suffering from the disobedience of another. It
always seems so unjust. Yet part of coping with that type of adversity is realizing its source—sin. I admit that this is not a very
satisfying answer in some cases. One reason is that if I am suffering because of someone else's sin, there is really nothing I can
do about it, except suffer! If it is my sin I am suffering from, I can
at least take some consolation in the fact that if I had not erred

in some way, I would not be suffering. But when it is truly some-one else's fault, the situation can be extremely frustrating.

Later on we will discuss how to respond to different types of adversity. The point I am making here is that sometimes there is no explanation for adversity other than the fact that we are feeling the effects of someone's sin.

The Adversary Himself

There is a third source of adversity: Satan. In one sense he is ultimately behind all adversity. He is directly responsible for Adam and Eve's being led astray and, therefore, for the calamity that followed. However, his involvement in adversity extends far beyond his activity in the Garden of Eden. He is alive and active today.

Several biblical accounts illustrate Satan's role in adversity. The clearest example is the story of Job. Those who attribute all adversity to sin of some kind or a lack of faith have a difficult time with this narrative. They attribute Job's problems to his pride or the sin of his children. But the writer puts those theories to rest in the first verse of the book.

> There was a man in the land of Uz, whose name was Job, and that man was *blameless, upright, fearing God, and turning away from evil.*
>
> —Job 1:1, *emphasis mine*

Later in the same chapter God Himself gives His evaluation of Job.

> And the LORD said to Satan, "Have you considered My servant Job? For there is no one like him on the earth, a blameless and upright man, fearing God and turning away from evil."
>
> —Job 1:8

There can be no doubt about it. Job was a righteous man. The adversity he faced was not the result of pride. The ensuing discussion between God and Satan spells out exactly why Job suffered the way he did.

> Then Satan answered the LORD, "Does Job fear God for nothing? Hast Thou not made a hedge about him and his house and all that he has, on every side? Thou hast blessed the work of his hands, and his possessions have increased in the land. But put forth Thy hand now and touch all that he has; he will surely curse Thee to Thy face." Then the LORD said to Satan, "Behold, all that he has is in your power, only do not put forth your hand on him." So Satan departed from the presence of the LORD.
>
> —Job 1:9–12

So Satan sets out to destroy all Job has. Yet Job continues to serve God and walk in His ways. So Satan makes another request of God.

> And Satan answered the LORD and said, "Skin for skin! Yes, all that a man has he will give for his life. However, put forth Thy hand, now, and touch his bone and his flesh; he will curse Thee to Thy face." So the LORD said to Satan, "Behold, he is in your power, only spare his life." Then Satan went out from the presence of the LORD, and smote Job with sore boils from the sole of his foot to the crown of his head.
>
> —Job 2:4–7

Job's adversity was from Satan. The writer makes a clear distinction in this book. Satan dares God to send adversity into Job's life. But God in turn instructs Satan to do the dirty work. Permission came from God. The adversity came from Satan.

Peter tells us that Satan is roaming around like a lion seeking those whom he can destroy through adversity. He writes,

Be of sober spirit, be on the alert. Your adversary, the devil, prowls about like a roaring lion, seeking someone to devour. But resist him, firm in your faith, knowing that the same experiences of suffering are being accomplished by your brethren who are in the world.

—1 Peter 5:8–9

Oftentimes this passage is used to talk about Satan's involvement in our temptations. The real context, however, is that of suffering. Satan roams around looking for ways to bring adversity into our lives. He wants us to suffer, for suffering often destroys one's faith in God. Peter instructs these believers to be on the alert so that in the midst of their suffering they will not lose sight of who is causing it as well as how God is going to use it.

How Do We Know?

In our day-to-day experience it is sometimes difficult to determine the source of our adversity. Adversity related to our personal sin is usually easy to identify. Beyond that, though, things begin to run together. We certainly do not want to rebuke the devil for something God is behind. Neither do we want to just grin and bear it if there is something we can do to put an end to our suffering.

The Bible does not give us three simple steps to aid us in determining the source of our adversity. This used to really bother me. For a long time, when I faced adversity, I would pray and pray for God to give me some indication as to why I was suffering. Then I realized why those kinds of prayers rarely seemed to be answered. There was and is a much more important issue at stake.

Far more important than the *source* of adversity is the *response* to adversity. Why? Because adversity, regardless of the source, is God's most effective tool for deepening your faith and commitment to Him. The areas in which you are experiencing the most adversity are the areas in which God is at work. When someone says, "God is not doing anything in my life," my response is always, "So then, you don't have any problems?" Why? Because the best way to identify God's involvement in your life is to consider your response to adversity. God uses adversity, regardless of the source. But your response to adversity determines whether or not God is able to use it to accomplish His purpose. In fact, adversity can destroy your faith. If you do not respond correctly, adversity can put you into a spiritual tailspin from which you may never recover. It all hinges on your response.

As much as we all want to know the answer to the *why* question, it is really not the most significant question. The real question each of us needs to ask is, "*How* should I respond?" To spend too much time trying to answer the *why* question is to run the risk of missing what God wants to teach us. Ironically enough, concentrating on *why* often hinders us from ever discovering why. If it is in God's sovereign will to reveal to us, this side of eternity, the answer to that question, it will be as we respond correctly.

One of the greatest struggles of my life surrounded my decision to move from Bartow, Florida, to Atlanta. Bartow is a small town in central Florida. Our home was in walking distance of three lakes. The neighborhood was safe. We knew all of our neighbors. Bartow seemed like the perfect environment in which to raise our children. To complicate things even further, we had only lived there about one year when a friend of mine approached me about moving to Atlanta to be the associate pastor at First Baptist Church. I thanked him for his vote of confidence but made it clear that I was not at all interested.

A few weeks later a pulpit committee showed up to hear me preach. Once again, I was polite, but I told them I was not interested. They asked me to pray about it. I told them I would. What else could I say? So one evening my wife, Anna, and I began praying about whether or not it was God's will for us to move to Atlanta. The strangest thing happened. The more we prayed, the more both of us became convinced we should go. When we would talk about it, it did not make any sense at all. Why would God want me to become an associate pastor when I had already been the senior pastor for three churches? Why would God move us after being in Bartow only thirteen months? Why would a good God want me to move my family to a place like Atlanta?

Two months later we moved. And about two years after that, I understood *why*. My point is this: oftentimes, the explanations we are so desperately seeking will become clear as we respond properly to adversity.

Surely the disciples stood at Calvary wondering why such a thing was allowed to take place. Humanly speaking, it made no sense at all. But in a few days all the pieces fit together. Oftentimes we stand like the disciples at Calvary. We watch our hopes and dreams shatter before our eyes. We see our loved ones suffer. We see family members die. And like the disciples, we wonder why.

We must remember that Christ's death, burial, and resurrection serve as the context of all our suffering. God, through those events, took the greatest tragedy in the history of the world and used it to accomplish His greatest triumph—the salvation of man. If the murder of the perfect Son of God can be explained, how much more can we trust that God is accomplishing His purposes through the adversity we face every day?

The source of our adversity is not to be our primary concern. Think about it. What was the source of the adversity Christ faced? Sin, Satan, or God? Actually, all three were involved. Yet Christ's response allowed our heavenly Father to take this tragedy and use it for the greatest good. That is the pattern. That is God's goal for us through all the adversities of life.

Have you been so hung up on trying to figure out *why* adversity has come your way that perhaps you have missed God? Has the adversity in your life strengthened your faith, or has it weakened your faith? Adversity is a reality that none of us can avoid. Therefore, it is in your best interest to begin responding in such a way that the negative can be used to accomplish the will of God in your life. And as you begin responding correctly, perhaps you will begin to understand *why*!

Chapter 2

THE POWER OF PERSPECTIVE

As I WRITE this chapter, one of my good friends is watching his wife die of cancer. The doctors have given up hope. We have prayed and prayed, and yet there seems to be no sign of God's healing hand. Jim sits by his wife's side all day, every day. Anything he can do to make his wife more comfortable, he does gladly. And yet he remains powerless to do the one thing he desires most of all—heal his wife.

I have heard Jim pray. I have seen him hurt. His faith has not been shattered; but it has been dealt a severe blow. He will recover. But the question will always remain: Why did this happen? What was the point? What was accomplished? Why the grief so unfairly imposed upon such a God-fearing family?

Jim and his family are certainly not the first persons to ask such painful and complex questions. And they are well aware of that. In anticipation of questions raised by circumstances such as these, God has given us in the gospel of John a narrative that helps us gain the perspective needed to survive tragedies such as that faced by Jim.

The problem with studying any familiar passage is that we rarely allow ourselves to feel what the characters must have felt.

Why should we? We usually know what happens in the end. Unfortunately, this familiarity with the Scriptures often robs us of their intended results. It is hard to feel the fear David must have felt when he faced Goliath when we know from the outset that he comes out the victor. We miss the sense of isolation Moses must have felt as he fled Egypt for his life. After all, he ends up a hero. So as you approach this familiar narrative in John 11, try to forget the end of the story. Do your best to put yourself in the shoes, or maybe the sandals, of the people involved. If you read what happens but neglect to consider what must have been felt, you lose some of the richest insights of this story.

"He Whom You Love Is Sick"

> Now a certain man was sick, Lazarus of Bethany, the village of Mary and her sister Martha. And it was the Mary who anointed the LORD with ointment, and wiped His feet with her hair, whose brother Lazarus was sick. The sisters therefore sent to Him, saying, "LORD, behold he whom You love is sick."
>
> —John 11:1–3

The household of Mary and Martha is one in which Jesus and His disciples had been given hospitality whenever they had been in the area of Judea. Apparently, Lazarus was a wealthy man, and he used his wealth to support the ministry of Christ. The fact that Mary and Martha sent for Jesus as soon as Lazarus became ill is evidence of their faith in His power. No doubt they thought, *If Jesus is willing to heal total strangers, certainly He will jump at the opportunity to heal one who has been a friend.* But such was not the case.

> But when Jesus heard it, He said, "This sickness is not unto death, but for the glory of God, that the Son of God may be glorified by it." Now Jesus loved Martha, and her sister, and

Lazarus. When therefore He heard that he was sick, He stayed then two days longer in the place where He was.

—John 11:4–6

These verses make absolutely no sense, humanly speaking. That is why I love this story, because most adversity makes about as much sense from our perspective. It is obviously stated that Jesus loves this family; then He makes no move to relieve their suffering. I can relate to that. Whenever the bottom drops out, I go scrambling for the verses in the Bible that remind me of God's love—yet at times it seems God is unwilling to follow through with any action.

We need to pause here because at this point in the narrative we have our greatest struggles. I am referring to that time between the point we ask God for help and the point at which He does something. It is so easy to read, "He stayed then two days longer." But the delay was like an eternity for Mary and Martha. The Scripture informs us that they knew the general area in which Jesus was ministering at the time. They also knew about how long it would take Him to make the trip to Bethany. So they waited. And as the hours dragged on, they watched their brother grow weaker and weaker.

Finally the day arrived when, according to the normal traveling time, Jesus should arrive. No doubt they took turns sitting with Lazarus. That way one of them could go out to the road to look for Jesus. I can imagine Mary or Martha asking all the men and women coming from the direction of Perea if they had seen a group of twelve or so men headed that way. As they would shake their heads no, the sisters' hope burned a little lower. "Why didn't He come? Maybe He never got the message? Maybe He left Perea without sending word back to us? Where is He? After all we have done for Him, it is the least He could do." And yet He failed to come when they expected Him.

Lazarus died. Maybe Mary came in early one morning to check on him and found him dead. Perhaps it was in the afternoon when both Mary and Martha were at his side that he breathed his last breath. Whatever the situation, both women felt that hollow, helpless feeling that always accompanies death. It was over. He was gone. Soon their thoughts turned to Jesus, *Why didn't He come? How could He know what we were going through and yet stay away?*

These, no doubt, are some of the questions you have asked as you have cried out to God in the midst of the adversity in your life. How can a God of love stand back and watch my friend and his wife suffer and not do anything about it? How can He watch from the balcony of heaven as women are physically or sexually abused? How can He watch husbands walk out on their wives and children? Does He know what is going on down here?

Once again, this narrative is helpful. Jesus knew exactly what was going on. He knew what Mary and Martha were going through. He knew his friend's condition was worsening. And He knew the moment Lazarus died.

> And after that He said to them [the disciples]. "Our friend Lazarus has fallen asleep."
>
> —John 11:11

Yet He did nothing! Keep in mind, Lazarus was not some guy off the street. He had invited Jesus into his home. Lazarus had expressed faith in Christ and His ministry. He was a good man. He certainly had more faith than most of the other people Jesus had healed. Some of them did not even know who Christ was (see John 9). But Jesus was nowhere to be found when Lazarus needed Him most.

To add insult to injury, Jesus had the nerve to say to His disciples,

> Lazarus is dead, and *I am glad* for your sakes that I was not there.
>
> —John 11:14–15, *emphasis mine*

Jesus was "glad"? How could He say such a thing? Two of his best friends go through emotional turmoil; another friend dies of an illness; and Jesus says He is glad? What could He have possibly been thinking? What was going through His mind?

My friend, the answer to that question is the key to unlocking the mystery of tragedy in this life. To understand what was going on in the mind of Christ and in the economy of God in a situation like this one is to discover the universal principle that puts together and holds together all of life—both now and for eternity. Christ had a goal in all of this, a goal so important that *it was worth the emotional agony* Mary and Martha had to endure. It was worth risking the destruction of their faith. It was even worth the death of a faithful friend. What Jesus, in conjunction with His heavenly Father, had in mind was so incredible that even through the pain surrounding the whole event Jesus could say, "I am glad this has happened." In other words, "Men, what you are about to see is so fantastic that it is worth the pain and death of my beloved friend." If they were like us, they probably thought, *What could be worth all of this?*

"If You Had Been Here"

Now Bethany was near Jerusalem, about two miles off; and many of the Jews had come to Martha and Mary, to console them concerning their brother. Martha therefore, when she heard that Jesus was coming, went to meet Him; but Mary still sat in the house. Martha therefore said to Jesus, "LORD if You had been here, my brother would not have died." . . .

And when she had said this, she went away, and called Mary her sister, saying secretly, "The Teacher is here, and is calling for you." And when she heard it she arose quickly, and was coming to Him. . . .

Therefore, when Mary came where Jesus was, she saw Him, and fell at His feet, saying to Him, "LORD, if You had been here, my brother would not have died."

—John 11:18–21, 28–29, 32

Mary and Martha, for all their time spent with the Son of God, were still human to the core. They wanted to know one thing: "Jesus, where in the world have You been?" They had no doubt that Jesus could have healed their brother; Martha even indicates that she believes there is still hope (see John 11:22). But the fact that He had seemingly ignored their plight had left them confused and frustrated. Why did He delay?

> When Jesus therefore saw her weeping, and the Jews who came with her, also weeping, He was deeply moved in spirit, and was troubled, and said, "Where have you laid him?" They said to Him, "LORD, come and see." Jesus wept. And so the Jews were saying, "Behold how He loved him!"
>
> —John 11:33–36

At this juncture any doubt about Jesus' love and concern for Lazarus is laid to rest. "Jesus wept." Yet His overt concern about His friend Lazarus adds another layer of mystery to the story. If Jesus was so concerned, why did He not come to Lazarus's aid? Why did He let him die?

Once again we are faced with what appears to be an unsolvable mystery. It becomes apparent that whatever Christ had in mind, whatever He was trying to accomplish, it was worth sacrificing the emotions of the ones He loved as well as His own. Jesus wept when He arrived to find Lazarus dead. Think about it. His knowledge of the future did not keep Him from identifying with the sorrow of those around Him.

Asking the Right Questions

If anything is clear from this story, it is that *some things are so important to God that they are worth interrupting the happiness and health of His children in order to accomplish them.* That is an awesome thought. To some, it may seem like an indictment of the character of God. But this principle will become clearer through the pages and chapters that follow. Whether some persons can fit this idea into their theology or not, the fact remains that the Son of God allowed those He loved to suffer and die for the sake of some higher purpose.

Some individuals may think such a statement implies that we are merely pawns to be moved about and even abused at God's whims. But remember, "Jesus wept." He was moved with emotion at the sight of Mary and Martha's sorrow. He was touched by the love they had for their brother. He was not emotionally isolated from the pain suffered by those whose perspective was different from His own.

When you hurt, God hurts. Regardless of what He may be in the process of accomplishing, regardless of how noble His purposes may be, He is in touch with what you are feeling. He is not like the football coach who sneers at his players when they complain of their pain. He is not like the boxing coach who whispers into his fighter's ear, "No pain, no gain." Neither is he like the parent who laughs and says to a child who has lost a first love, "Don't worry. You'll get over it."

Through all the pain and adversity God may allow us to face, two things are always true. First, He is sensitive to what we are feeling:

For we do not have a high priest who cannot sympathize with our weaknesses.

—Hebrews 4:15

Jesus wept over Lazarus. He weeps over our sorrow as well.

Second, whatever He is in the process of accomplishing through our suffering will always be for our best interest. The degree to which things actually work out for our best interest is determined by our response. As we trust God through our adversity, when all is said and done, we will sincerely believe it was worth it all.

"How?" you might ask. "How could what I am going through at home work out for my best interest? How could God ever use the death of my spouse (or child)? What could possibly be worth the isolation and hurt I am feeling now?"

When I was a little boy, I used to ask some of those same questions. My father died when I was seven months old, so I grew up without a dad. I remember watching my friends with their fathers and wondering why I couldn't have one, too. It didn't make any sense. My mom had to work long, hard hours in a textile mill. By the time I got up in the morning to go to school, she was already at work. I had to learn to fix my own breakfast and dress myself for school by the time I was six years old.

By the grace of God, my response to all of that was different from that of many young men who lose their fathers. Instead of rebelling against God for taking my dad, I decided at a very young age that I would look to Him to be my Father. My dad's death did not cause me to turn away from God; rather, I turned toward Him. I learned early in life about the daily sufficiency of Christ. I learned how to pray. I learned how to walk by faith. The untimely death of my father was actually the catalyst God used to teach me the most important lessons of life—the lessons that have allowed me to survive intense rejection as an adult on both a professional level and a personal level. But at the age of seven or eight I could not see what God was up to. It made no sense at all then. There was nothing to compensate for the loneliness I felt. In fact, it has taken me over forty years to make sense out of the adversity I faced as a child. And the lessons continue.

Not too long ago, my son, Andy, said to me, "You know, Dad, Becky and I probably reaped the real benefits of your not having a father when you grew up."

"What do you mean?" I asked.

"Well," he said, "when it came time to raise your own kids, you didn't have a pattern to follow. You had to be completely dependent upon the Lord for everything."

As I thought about it, he was right. and when I realized how committed they are to the Lord, when I thought about how different they are from many preachers' children, I was even able to thank the Lord for not giving me a father. If that was what it took to prepare me to raise my own children, *it was worth it all*!

A Sickness Not Unto Death

What, then, did Jesus have in mind by delaying His return to Bethany, thus allowing Lazarus to die? What was so important that He was willing to allow His close friends to go through the agony of watching their brother die. The answer to that question gives us a great deal of insight into the character and economy of God. Jesus Himself provided the answer when He was first informed of Lazarus's illness and then again when He stood at the tomb.

> The sisters therefore sent to Him, saying, "LORD, behold, he whom You love is sick." But when Jesus heard it, He said, *"This sickness is not unto death, but for the glory of God, that the Son of God may be glorified by it."* Now Jesus loved Martha, and her sister, and Lazarus.
>
> —John 11:3–5, *emphasis mine*

> And so they removed the stone. And Jesus raised His eyes, and said, "Father, I thank Thee that Thou heardest Me. And I knew that Thou hearest Me always; but because of the people standing around I said it, *that they may believe that Thou didst send Me."*
>
> —John 11:41–42, *emphasis mine*

From the very beginning, Jesus had two specific purposes in mind. His purpose was not to cause Lazarus to die. Neither was it to cause Mary and her sister mental and emotional anguish. On the contrary, His goals in all that happened were to bring glory to God and to cause others to believe in Him. The opportunity to accomplish these two things was worth the pain and suffering Mary, Martha, and Lazarus had to experience. To Christ, this opportunity to publicly display the power of God was worth risking the rejection of some of His closest friends. It was even worth the death of a loved one.

But for the Glory of God

To glorify something is to so arrange things as to focus attention on it or bring it honor. We glorify a picture when we hang it at a focal point in a room. We may further glorify it by shining a light on it. We glorify a singer when we put him or her on a stage and focus our attention on the performance. When we stand and applaud at the end, we are, again, glorifying the performer.

Jesus said that the purpose of this seeming tragedy was the glorification of Him and His Father. Lazarus died so that for a short moment in time the focus of attention might be God and His Son. Jesus was so given over to seeing His heavenly Father glorified that He was "glad" Lazarus died if that was what it took. This was not out of character for our Savior. He spent his whole life in an attempt to focus the attention of man on His Father. He did everything with that purpose in mind. At the end of His earthly ministry He summed up His life's work by saying,

> I have glorified Thee on the earth, having accomplished the work which Thou hast given Me to do.
>
> —John 17:4

As much as Jesus dreaded the cross, He knew that His own death was a part of His Father's plan to draw attention to Himself. Yet knowledge of what He would accomplish through His death and resurrection in no way erased the pain of the cross. Neither did it minimize the emotional anguish of watching His followers abandon Him at the moment He needed them most. When He uttered the words, "Yet not My will, but Thine be done," He in essence said, "Whatever it takes, regardless of the sacrifice, let it be done!" He then went to the cross determined to bring His Father glory, even at the expense of His own life.

Many Believed in Him

The second purpose behind Jesus' delay was that many might put their trust in Him as the Messiah. More important than keeping everybody healthy was moving people to faith. So Christ purposefully waited until it was too late so that He might perform a miracle of such magnitude that many would put their faith in Him. And that is exactly what happened (see John 11:45). Just as He allowed those He loved to suffer for the sake of those who had not believed, so He will allow us to suffer today. Nothing gets the attention of an unbeliever like a saint who is suffering successfully. It is easy to talk about Christ when everything is going fine. Our words take on a great deal more significance when they are spoken from a life filled with pain.

I can hear the skeptic now, "Are you saying that God would allow me—His child—to suffer for the sake of some unsaved person?" That is exactly what I am saying. But keep in mind, it was His Son who prepared the way. If almighty God saw fit to allow His own Son to suffer unjustly that we might be saved, why should we think it below us to suffer so that others might believe?

The late Dr. Barnhouse had an experience during his ministry that illustrates this point perfectly. He was conducting a week of services in a church. The pastor of the church and his wife were expecting their first child. During the week, Dr. Barnhouse would kid with the pastor about his being so uptight.

On the last night of services the pastor did not show up. Dr. Barnhouse assumed he was at the hospital with his wife, so he went ahead with the service. Toward the end of the service he noticed that the pastor slipped in quietly and took a seat on the back pew. When the service was completed, the pastor made his way to the front, dismissed everyone, and asked Dr. Barnhouse if he could see him in his office.

"Certainly," he said and followed him to the back.

As they shut the door behind them, the pastor wheeled around and blurted out, "Dr. Barnhouse, our child has Down syndrome. I haven't told my wife yet. I don't know what I'm going to tell her."

"Friend, this is of the Lord," Dr. Barnhouse said. And then he turned to this passage in the Old Testament:

And the LORD said to him [Moses], "Who has made man's mouth? Or who makes him dumb or deaf, or seeing or blind? Is it not I, the LORD?"

—Exodus 4:11

"Let me see that," the pastor said. He read it again.

As the pastor studied the passage, Dr. Barnhouse said, "My friend, you know the promise in Romans 8. All things work together for good—including this special child—for those who love the Lord."

The pastor closed the Bible. Slowly he walked out of the office and went straight to the hospital room of his wife. When he arrived, she said, "They won't let me see my baby. What's wrong? I've asked to see my baby, and they won't let me."

The young pastor took his wife by the hand and said, "Who has made the dumb or deaf or seeing or blind, is it not I, the Lord? Darling, the Lord has blessed us with a child with Down syndrome."

She cried long and hard. Then as she began to settle down, she said, "Where did you get that?"

"From God's own Word," he said.

"Let me see." Then she read it.

Meanwhile news of the birth swept through the hospital. This information was of special interest to the switchboard operator in the hospital. She was not a Christian. In fact she was a cruel woman who enjoyed seeing Christians crumble. She was convinced that under pressure, there was really no difference between Christians and everybody else. When the pastor's wife called her mother to give her the news, the operator listened in—expecting the young mother to go to pieces.

"Mother, the Lord has blessed us with a child with Down syndrome. We don't know the nature of the blessing, but we do know it is a blessing." There were no tears, no hysteria, no breakdown.

The operator was shocked. But when she absorbed what she heard, she began telling everyone. Soon the entire hospital was buzzing with the story of the pastor and his wife's response. The following Sunday the pastor was back in his pulpit. In the congregation, unknown to him, were the telephone operator and seventy nurses and staff members from the hospital. At the conclusion of the service the pastor offered an invitation.

"If you have never met Jesus Christ, I want to extend to you an invitation to do so."

That morning thirty nurses from the hospital came forward receiving Christ. All because of one special child and the faith of the young pastor and his wife.

Would God allow this child to be born with a handicapping condition for the sake of thirty nurses? Absolutely. Just as He allowed a man to be born blind that His Son might heal him. Just as He would allow one whom He loved to die in order that he might be raised. And just as He allowed His own Son to be murdered in order that many might receive eternal life. God allows suffering so that others might come to faith in His Son.

The Role of Pain

It has been said that where there is no pain, there is no gain. This phrase applies not only in the realm of athletics, but in the spiritual realm as well. The pattern we see in Christ's earthly ministry and in His personal pilgrimage bears this out. Suffering is the means by which God brings glory to Himself and His Son. Although suffering is usually the last thing to be considered useful, it is God's most useful tool. Nothing compares with suffering when it comes to bringing God glory, for nothing else highlights our dependence, weakness, and insecurity like suffering.

But suffering is also the way God brings honor and glory to His children. In his second letter to the Corinthians Paul makes this clear when he writes,

For momentary, light affliction is producing for us an eternal weight of glory far beyond all comparison, while we look not at the things which are seen, but at the things which are not seen; for the things which are seen are temporal, but the things which are not seen are eternal.

—2 Corinthians 4:17–18

Adversity in this life, when handled properly, provides for the
believer glory and honor in the life to come. In this passage Paul
speaks of glory as if it were a tangible thing that could be pro-
gressively added to. It is as if each believer has an eternal account
wherein glory is being applied in relation to personal suffering
on this earth.

He closes this section by giving us the motivation we need to
adopt this perspective. Simply put, our suffering is temporary—
just like the bodies in which we are suffering are temporary. But
the rewards we are accumulating while in these temporary bodies are eternal. What an investment! What a system! God has
allowed us to participate in a system by which the temporal can
be used to gain what is eternal.

This truth is especially important as we focus on the end of
the story of Lazarus. Many may be tempted to say, "Well, it always works out fine for people in the Bible, but my husband was
not raised from the dead." Or "My wife never came back to me."
Or "I have not seen God get any glory out of my situation." To
which God would add one essential word, "YET!" Remember,
eventually, Lazarus died for good. Christ's miracle was in that
sense only temporary. The glory connected with Lazarus's being
alive was short-lived. Any time God bails us out of adversity—
as He often does—the glory connected with that is to some degree temporary. Yet God has established a means by which our
suffering can result in eternal glory, glory that exalts not only
Him, but also those who suffered.

"Remove the Stone"

> Jesus said, "Remove the stone." Martha, the sister of the de-
> ceased, said to Him, "Lord, by this time there will be a
> stench, for he has been dead four days." Jesus said to her, "Did
> I not say to you, if you believe, you will see the glory of God?"
> —John 11:39–40

Had they refused to remove the stone, they would have suffered for nothing. No good would have come from it. Mary and

her sister would have missed the glory of God. I meet people all the time who are dealing with personal tragedy of the worst kind. Sometimes it is their own fault. At other times they are the victims. Oftentimes greater than the tragedy itself is their response. Because they see no immediate good, they assume that there is no good to be found, that God has abandoned them or perhaps was never interested in the first place. They refuse to remove the stone. They will not trust God with what they cannot see.

If God can gain glory for Himself from the unjustified murder of His Son, can we not trust Him to somehow glorify Himself in and through the things we struggle with on a daily basis? If God can find for Himself glory in the death of His Son's close friend, should we not trust Him to do the same through even the major tragedies in our lives? God specializes in taking tragedy and turning it into triumph. The greater the tragedy, the greater the potential for triumph.

There will always be things we cannot explain. In time some answers will become clear, while others will remain a mystery. One thing we do know, God is in the business of glorifying Himself. He wants the world's attention, and oftentimes adversity is His way of getting it. As Christians, we are His representatives. We are extensions of the ministry of Christ on the earth. We, then, are the tools through which God will attract the world's attention. He works through our conversations, our character, our preaching, and our adversity. His success in all of these areas depends in part upon our response.

"If You Believe, You Will See the Glory of God"

Martha trusted Christ and removed the stone. I believe Jim, too, will trust God to gain glory for Himself through the tragedy of his wife's terminal illness. What about you? Are there stones in your life that are blocking the Lord's ability to gain for Himself the glory that is rightfully His? Have you cut your faith off at the point where things quit making sense? Have you attached your faith only to what can be seen? Have you refused to look beyond your loss? Have you allowed your pain to so consume you that you have forgotten that God may have something He wants to accomplish?

You have only two options. You can trust God to glorify Himself through your adversity. Or you can focus on your loss and spend your time searching for answers. In doing so, you may cause the means by which God was going to do something great to become a tragic end in itself.

An old saint contemplating his life summed up the point of this chapter perfectly:

> And I may return in faded armor
> Full of patches bent and aged.
> And I may face the heat of battle,
> To free the damned and free the slaves.
> And I may know both pain and rejection,
> The betrayal of my friends.
> But the glory that awaits me,
> Will make it worth it in the end—in the end.

Friend, regardless of the adversity you are facing, if you trust God, you, too, will one day say, "It was worth it all!"

Chapter 3

WHEN
GOD IS SILENT

ONE OF THE most frustrating things about Christianity is that our God is oftentimes so quiet. When I have finished pouring out my heart to the Lord, I would like a little response. Anything would be fine; and yet He is silent. I'm sure you have felt the same frustration. The strange thing is that I am acutely aware of God's silence when I need Him the most. There have been plenty of times, after weeping over a crisis either in my life or in the life of someone I love, that just a word from the Lord would have been comforting—and yet He was silent.

I can think of counseling situations that have left me dumbfounded. So many situations arising today seem to go beyond the bounds of what the Scriptures address. A word from God would have been so timely, so helpful to those involved—and yet He was silent. There are times I wish He would just send an angel to answer a few basic questions for me. I have faced adversities that seemed at the time to be such a waste: children dying, men leaving their godly wives, a close friend suddenly becoming ill. If only the Lord would have appeared and simply said, "I am still in control." Anything would have helped, but He remained silent.

225

No Comment

To make things even worse, when we read the Bible, it seems as if God was always speaking to the men whose stories fill the pages. When Peter was thrown into prison, an angel appeared to tell him everything was going to be all right. When Abraham got ripped off by Lot, the Lord spoke a word of comfort to him. Paul had some theological questions and was taken up into the third heaven to have a talk with God. It does not seem fair. After all, my faith would be stronger, too, if every time I faced adversity, an angel from God showed up to tell me what to do. But it does not work that way for us. God is incredibly silent sometimes; we receive no comment from Him to help us.

For believers, God's silence makes adversity much more difficult to endure because our worldview includes a loving God who has presented Himself to us as a Father. When tragedy strikes or difficult times overtake us, our worldview comes under attack. The questions reach the surface of our consciousness. We begin to doubt. Then more than ever we need a word from God. Yet, so often, He remains silent.

You may be one of the thousands of singles in this country who is seeking the right spouse. You have done your best to be faithful to your standards. You are committed to waiting for God's best. But nothing is happening. So you have begun to wonder if there is anything to this bit about "waiting on God."

You may have a job or career in which you are very unhappy. You pray and pray and pray, but feel no peace about staying or leaving. You are willing to do the right thing—whatever it is. But God just doesn't seem to be saying anything.

Or maybe you are dealing with the death of a loved one or some other tragedy that has taken you by surprise. You are doing the best you can to make yourself believe that God has a purpose in it, that He has not abandoned you. But in your heart you wonder: *Maybe there is no God*, or *Maybe He is just not interested in me.* Slowly your faith begins to erode. *If only God would say something—anything.*

*God's silence
is in no way
indicative of
His activity
or involvement
in our lives.*

Questions . . . Questions . . . Questions

All of this raises two basic questions. First, *what in the world is God up to when we are hurting and need to hear from Him so desperately?* Second, *what are we to do in the meantime?* The answers to these questions are indispensable if we are to deal successfully with adversity. As long as we are in a fog about God's whereabouts and His response to our situation, there will always, be room for doubt. But reassurance of His involvement alone is not enough. We need direction as well.

The purpose of this chapter is to answer these two questions. By doing so, I pray that God will erase from your heart forever the awful fear that perhaps He is not interested in your hurt, that He has more important things with which to concern Himself.

To answer these questions, we are going to take a look at the life of Joseph. Let me remind you again not to allow your mind to race to the end of these narratives. If you do, you will miss what God is trying to say. When the Bible presents a particular character's life, the author focuses on those events that are relevant to the theme he is following. This gives the impression oftentimes that the lives of these characters were filled with one supernatural event after another. But that is not the case at all. There were weeks, months, and even years in which nothing special seemed to happen. As we study this Old Testament story, put yourself in the place of the character. Like us, Joseph was forced to deal with the silence of God in the midst of grave adversity.

Just When He Needed Him Most

Joseph's troubles started as a teenager. At seventeen he was his father's favorite, and that did not go over well with his ten older brothers. They were jealous, and their jealousy turned to hatred (see Gen. 37:4). If that was not enough, Joseph had a series of dreams implying that one day his entire family would bow down and worship him. Being young, and perhaps careless, Joseph described these dreams to his father and brothers. The text seems to indicate that his sharing of dreams pushed his brothers over the edge.

Sometime after that, Joseph was sent to Shechem by his father to check on his brothers and the flocks they were tending. Joseph was informed by a stranger that his brothers had moved on to Dothan. Determined to accomplish his mission, he set out to find his brothers in Dothan—about twenty-five miles away. When his brothers saw him coming, they plotted to put him to death. When he arrived, they stripped him and threw him into a pit. Then they sat down to eat dinner.

At this point in the narrative we might expect some divine intervention. If not deliverance, surely some indication that everything was going to work out fine. But nothing happened. God was silent. Joseph sat alone in the bottom of a pit with no guarantee that he would live through the night. No doubt he rehearsed in his mind the events leading up to his imprisonment: his obedience to his father; his willingness to go the extra mile; and now this. It did not make any sense; it was not his fault that his father loved him more than the others. It was not fair. And still, God was seemingly nowhere to be found.

Egypt Bound

As "luck" would have it, a caravan of Ishmaelite traders was passing by. To avoid having the blood of their own kin on their hands, Joseph's brothers sold him to the Ishmaelites. For the next several days, and possibly weeks, Joseph traveled as a slave in the company of the Ishmaelites. Night after night he lay out under the stars wondering, no doubt, why all of this was happening. He knew the stories of his great-grandfather. He had heard how God had spoken to Abraham on several occasions. Certainly he wondered, *Why doesn't God speak to me now?* But God remained silent.

In Egypt Joseph was sold to Potiphar, the captain of Pharaoh's bodyguard. His master recognized that Joseph was special. Every project Joseph undertook prospered. Eventually Potiphar made him the overseer of the entire house. The Bible tells us that Potiphar did not concern himself with anything except the food he ate (see Gen. 39:6).

Now we might be tempted to think, *Well, that is just like a Bible story; everything worked out fine for Joseph.* But what we forget is that Joseph did not show up on Monday and get promoted to overseer on Friday! The best we can tell, Joseph was in Potiphar's service anywhere from five to ten years. And the text seems to imply that Joseph's career as overseer was short-lived. Who knows how long he cleaned out the stables or slopped the pigs? Who knows the type of living quarters he had or who he had to share them with? And regardless of his eventual rank in Potiphar's home, he was still a slave. He was still far away from home. And through all of this, God was silent!

Nothing Lasts Forever

The author of Genesis prepares for the next chapter in Joseph's life when he writes,

> Now Joseph was handsome in form and appearance.
> —Genesis 39:6

It certainly was not Joseph's fault that he was good-looking. Nor was it his choice to be the overseer of Potiphar's home. But the combination of these two things was more than Potiphar's wife could bear:

> His master's wife looked with desire at Joseph, and she said, "Lie with me!"
> —Genesis 39:7

Once again Joseph did the right thing. But the right thing got him into trouble. He refused to get involved with his master's wife. She became angry and accused him of trying to rape her.

Just as things were beginning to pick up, Joseph found himself in prison.

Can You Relate?

I hope that by now you are beginning to relate to Joseph. I sure can. There is nothing more bewildering than doing what is right and then watching things fall apart. Or what about adversity that comes as a result of things over which you have no control? Every time I deal with an individual suffering from something that happened during childhood, I think, *Lord, it was not this person's decision to be born into that home. Why should this person have to suffer?* When I stand at the bedsides of persons suffering from cancer or some other disease, I find myself asking the same question.

You did not pick your parents; yet you may be dealing with things that stem from their problems. You may have lost a job over something that was not your fault at all. But you are the one who is suffering. Maybe you are one of those women who did your best to respond properly to a husband who was impossible to live with, and now he has abandoned you and your children. Situations such as these make for difficult questions. They seem to justify in our minds the line of thinking that goes like this: *If there was a God in heaven, He would not sit idly by while I suffer.* Many people have had irreparable damage done to their faith as a result of adversity. That is why this story is such an important one.

One Step Up, Two Steps Back

There is no way of knowing exactly how long Joseph was in prison. We know he was there for more than two years (see Gen. 41:1). It could have been as many as eight or nine. Imagine spending the next few years of your life in a foreign prison. Not awaiting a trial of any kind. Joseph was a slave. He had no rights or avenue of appeal. There was no one to plead his case to Pharaoh.

No family to pay a visit. He was sent to prison to rot. And for what reason? Faithfulness to a God who certainly did not seem to be showing much faithfulness in return. Joseph had been outspoken about his faith (see Gen. 39:9). He was doing his best to remain loyal. But he received no blessing in return. Things only got worse. And God was agonizingly silent.

As time passed, Joseph was again recognized as responsible and trustworthy. Eventually, the chief jailer made Joseph the supervisor for the whole jail. Remember, however, we do not know how long he was treated like an ordinary criminal. In two verses the writer of Genesis takes Joseph from being a prisoner to being in charge of the prison. But it is not unrealistic to assume that months and possibly even years passed by before Joseph was recognized as one who could be trusted. And even then, God was silent.

Rather abruptly we are introduced to two new characters, the king's baker and cupbearer. There is no apparent connection between these two and Joseph other than the fact that they are thrown into the same prison. And yet as God would have it, these men play a crucial role in fulfilling His plan.

We are not told why these men were thrown into prison, only that they were. As "fate" would have it, the captain of the bodyguard put these men under Joseph's care. The writer tells us that they were there "for some time." This is another indication that the events described here were separated by long stretches of time, perhaps months or even years. One night, after they had been there a while, each of these men had a dream. When they woke up, the expression on each man's face was such that it was clear to Joseph that something was wrong. Joseph asked,

Why are your faces so sad today?

—Genesis 40:7

They answered,

We have had a dream and there is no one to interpret it.

—Genesis 40:8

Once again, Joseph's unshakable faith in God expresses itself:

> Do not interpretations belong to God?
>
> —Genesis 40:8

After all he had been through and with no hope of ever being released from prison, Joseph's faith remained solid, and he was willing to express that faith in God.

Joseph listened carefully as each man described his dream. Then he told them what they meant. The baker was to be executed. The cupbearer, however, would be restored to his previous place of honor. Joseph's response to the cupbearer assures us that Joseph was as human as the rest of us. He said,

> Keep me in mind when it goes well with you, and please do me a kindness by mentioning me to Pharaoh, and get me out of this house. For I was in fact kidnapped from the land of the Hebrews, and even here I have done nothing that they should have put me into the dungeon.
>
> —Genesis 40:14–15

Joseph may have had faith in God, but he wanted out of prison as badly as any of us would. But once again, it seemed as if God had forgotten Joseph. When the cupbearer was restored, the Scripture tells us,

> Yet the chief cupbearer did not remember Joseph, but forgot him.
>
> —Genesis 40:23

Do you ever feel as if God has forgotten you? Maybe you have begged God to change your spouse, but you see no change. You may be addicted to some form of narcotic, and it is as if your prayers get no higher than the ceiling. I can't help but believe that every believer has felt forgotten at one point or another, felt as if God is too busy or has His mind on something else.

A Forgotten Family

Dr. W. A. Criswell, pastor of the First Baptist Church of Dallas, tells a story about a family he went to visit years ago when the oil business was booming. This particular family lived in an area where oil companies were buying the oil rights to people's property left and right. Throughout the area families were becoming wealthy overnight as oil was discovered on their property. When Dr. Criswell drove up to this particular family's property, he noticed a peculiar thing, however. There were no oil wells. On the land adjoining their property there were several wells pumping away, but not a single one on the property of the family he had come to visit.

He was greeted at the door by a very dejected-looking woman whom he assumed correctly to be the lady of the house. Her husband came in, offered Dr. Criswell a seat, and told his "sad" tale. "Pastor," he said, "God has forgotten us. You see, about a year ago oil was found in this area. Engineers came in and assured everyone in our community that eventually we would be rich beyond our wildest dreams. Well, we saw this as the hand of God. A few weeks later crews came in and began digging around on property all over this area. Wells sprung up everywhere. We knew it was just a matter of time until they would begin digging on our property. But it never happened. Dr. Criswell, God overlooked us. They discovered oil on both sides of our property and even on the property behind us—but not a drop on our land. Our neighbors are selling their homes and moving into the city, and we are left out here alone."

I imagine Joseph must have felt pretty lonely sitting in that Egyptian dungeon. We don't know for sure, but he probably felt betrayed as well. For all he knew, the cupbearer purposely did not tell Pharaoh about him. Once again Joseph suffered as a result of trying to do right. And for two more years he remained a prisoner of Egypt. Two years of wondering why God was letting this happen to him. Two years of battling back and forth in his mind as to whether or not the cupbearer had forgotten about him or just did not care. Two years to rehearse mentally the things that had taken place with his brothers, Potiphar, Potiphar's wife, and now this. Two long years—and God was silent.

Meanwhile . . .

> Now it happened at the end of two full years that Pharaoh had a dream, and. . . . it came about in the morning that his spirit was troubled, so he sent and called for all the magicians of Egypt, and all its wise men. And Pharaoh told them his dreams, but there was no one who could interpret them to Pharoah.
>
> —Genesis 41:1–8

It was at this point that the cupbearer finally remembered Joseph. They got him out of the dungeon, shaved him, gave him clean clothes, and brought him before Pharaoh.

> And Pharaoh said to Joseph, "I have had a dream, but no one can interpret it; and I have heard it said about you, that when you hear a dream you can interpret it."
>
> —Genesis 41:15

Put yourself in Joseph's place for a minute. How would you have responded to Pharaoh? I know what I would have said: "Before I interpret any dream, we need to make a little deal. First of all, *no more prison!* Second, where is that sorry cupbearer; I ought to. . . ."

But the words that uttered from Joseph's mouth defy all human explanation. There was no bitterness—though he had good reason to be bitter. He did not speak in anger—though I believe I would have been extremely angry. He did not talk about the wrongs that had been done to him. He simply looked at Pharaoh, the most powerful man in the world at that time, and said,

> It is not in me; God will give Pharaoh a favorable answer.
>
> —Genesis 41:16

And God did give Pharaoh an answer. Pharaoh was so impressed with Joseph that he made him second in command. In one brief moment Joseph went from a hopeless foreign slave to second in command of the most powerful nation on earth. After thirteen years of misery, something good finally happened.

Silent, But Not Still

What happened, however, was much more fantastic than anything Joseph could have ever hoped for. Joseph did not know that God was setting the stage for a key move in His plan to bring salvation to the world. For God had decided to rear His chosen people, through whom the Messiah would later come, as slaves to a pagan nation. Then by miraculously freeing them from a world-renowned power, He would demonstrate to every nation that He was the only true and living God. Along with that, His people would have a heritage of faith and a picture of what the Messiah would one day do for every nation.

The problem (humanly speaking) was how to get His people out of the land He had given to them through Abraham and to the land of a foreign nation. Second, they had to be welcomed there initially and given enough freedom to live together and multiply. So God chose to accomplish all of that through one man—Joseph. Once he was appointed second in command, there was almost nothing he could not do, including invite his entire family to Egypt to settle during the famine that just "happened" to take place a few years later. As long as he was alive, he could guarantee their safety and freedom. Joseph was the key player in one of the most strategic episodes in the story of salvation, and he never knew it!

If anything is clear from the story of Joseph, it is this: God's silence is in no way indicative of His activity or involvement in our lives. *He may be silent, but He is not still.* We assume that since we are not hearing anything He must not be doing anything. We judge God's interest and involvement by what we see and hear.

In the same vein, we are guilty of judging God's involvement in our lives by how favorable or unfavorable our circumstances are. As long as things are great, we have no doubt that God is with us—watching over us, protecting us, providing for us. But as soon as adversity comes along, we think, *Lord, where are You? Why don't You do something? Are You paying attention?*

God's involvement and interest in our lives cannot be judged by the nature of our circumstances. His involvement is measured by two things: first of all, the development of our character, and second, the fulfillment of His plan. Joseph spent about thirteen years facing one adversity after another. And God was involved every step of the way. It was through those adversities that He was accomplishing His will. And God will use adversity to accomplish His will in our lives as well.

In the Meantime . . .

"So what am I supposed to do in the meantime?" you may ask. The answer to that is simple, though it is not necessarily easy. Trust God. That answer may seem too simplistic for your complicated set of circumstances. And in the rest of this book I certainly plan to elaborate. But even if this was the last chapter, consider your options. If you are not going to trust God, what are you going to do? To take things in your own hands is to run the most certain risk of leaping out of the frying pan into the fire. Ask Jonah! Actually, you probably do not even have to think any further than your own experience. When have you ever turned your back on God's plan and come out a winner?

You say, "But you don't understand my circumstances." And you may be right. But think about Joseph. No friends, no family, no church, no freedom, no money, no Bible, no apparent answers from God. Yet he remained faithful—and so did his heavenly Father.

When God is silent, you have only one reasonable option—trust Him; hang in there; wait on Him. He may be quiet, but He has not quit on you.

Back at the Ranch

Now I want to tell you what finally happened to the family who had no oil on their land. A few years later Dr. Criswell ran into the father of that family. He was smiling from ear to ear. Dr. Criswell assumed they had finally found oil on his property. "Quite the contrary," the man replied. "They never found any oil, and I am glad of it." This certainly took the pastor by surprise. "The strangest thing happened," he continued. "All our neighbors moved to the city and bought big expensive houses and new cars. They sent their kids to the finest schools. Most of them joined country clubs. But before too long that lifestyle began to take its toll. One by one their marriages started breaking up. Their kids rebelled. We don't know of any that are still attending church on a regular basis. Pastor, God did us a big favor by not putting any oil on our land. We are all still together and love each other like never before. We thank Him every day for giving us what is important and protecting us from the things that aren't."

God had not forgotten that family. But it took them a while to understand. My friend, God has not forgotten you. He may be silent, but He is not still. Remember, *God's silence is always amplified by the anguish of adversity*. But through even the gravest adversity, He is working to develop your character and accomplish His will for your life.

Chapter 4

JUSTICE FOR ALL

IF GOD IS all-powerful, He certainly has the ability to put an end to injustice. If He is a righteous and just God, He surely must desire to do so. Yet we live in a world full of injustice. What's up?

This question comes in many forms, usually not quite this cut-and-dried. It is the question behind an abandoned wife's tears of sorrow. It is the reason for the doubtful look of a child who has been molested. It is the cause of uncertainty for the man who is fired over some trivial matter only months before retirement. "If God is just, why does He allow injustice to touch the lives of those He loves?"

All of us have asked this question at one time or another. If not on our own behalf, on behalf of a friend or relative. But we are not the first to be slapped in the face with the cold, hard realities of injustice in this world. In the first century the nation of Israel was saturated with injustice of every kind. Having been taken over by the Roman Empire, they were at the mercy of a foreign power. The Romans taxed the Jews heavily in order to pay for their military campaigns in other parts of the world. They confiscated the best land. They took the best produce. They set up their own government and appointed their own governors and magistrates.

At a time when the people desperately needed guidance from their religious leaders, there was none to be found. They had sold out to the Romans. In exchange for places of honor and privilege, the Pharisees had promised to encourage the Jews to work with Rome, not against her. The religious leaders became pawns the Romans used to keep peace.

Into this oppressive atmosphere of injustice befouled by long-standing frustrations walked the Lord Jesus. As news of His ministry spread, so did rumors that this, in fact, might be the Messiah. Expectations began to rise, for the people expected the Messiah to bring about social, political, and religious reform when He came. They were looking to the Messiah to reestablish justice in the land. And so Jesus went about His Father's business knowing that the pressure was on to bring about major reform. The expectations and desires of the people in Jesus' day were much like our own. They wanted justice. They were tired of suffering unjustly. They were ready for God to do something.

In response to the frustration and hopelessness He sensed among the people, Jesus told the following parable:

There was in a certain city a judge who did not fear God, and did not respect man. And there was a widow in that city, and she kept coming to him, saying, "Give me legal protection from my opponent." And for a while he was unwilling; but afterward he said to himself, "Even though I do not fear God nor respect man, yet because this widow bothers me, I will give her legal protection, lest by continually coming she wear me out." And the Lord said, "Hear what the unrighteous judge said; now shall not God bring about justice for His elect, who cry to Him day and night, and will He delay long over them? I tell you that He will bring about justice for them speedily. However, when the Son of Man comes, will He find faith on the earth?"

—Luke 18:2–8

Jesus presents a worst case scenario of a judge who cares about no one and a widow who has very few, if any, rights. She needs justice. And apparently this unrighteous judge is her only hope. Day after day she goes to him begging for help and finds none. Finally this judge thinks to himself, *If I don't do something, this woman is going to drive me crazy. Not only that, she could ruin my reputation.* So he gives in and helps her out.

A cursory reading would seem to indicate that the point of the parable is this: if you bother God long enough, He will grant you justice. But that is not Christ's point at all. The parable is presented in such a way as to set up a comparison between an unrighteous judge and a righteous God. The point Jesus is making is this: if an unrighteous judge can be convinced to bring about justice for a widow with whom he has no relationship or invested interest, how much more confident should we be that a righteous God will bring about justice for His elect. In case His listeners are unclear about the point He is making, Jesus comes right out and says, "I tell you that He [God] will bring about justice for them speedily."

The bottom line is that *God will bring about justice for the elect,* the elect being those who have expressed faith in Christ. I imagine this brought some sense of comfort to His audience as it does to those of us who have wondered from time to time whether or not there would ever be justice on the earth. But I also imagine they had the same burning question you and I are left asking. *When?* When is God going to bring about justice for the elect? When are the unjust going to be punished? When are those who have been treated unfairly going to be avenged?

A Scheduling Problem

Jesus knew His words would raise questions concerning the timing of this promised justice. He knows us so well that He anticipated our response to His answer. So He presents His answer in the form of a question, thereby putting the ball back into our court before we have time to argue. He says, "When the Son of Man comes, will He find faith on the earth?"

There will be justice for the elect when Christ returns the second time. No doubt there were looks of confusion and dismay on the faces of those to whom He spoke that day. They must have thought, *When the Son of Man comes? He is already here!* For us, His response does not bring so much confusion as it does disappointment because we do not want to wait until Christ comes again to see justice prevail. We want it *now*!

It is no wonder. In the past twenty or so years increasing emphasis has been placed on what God will do for us now. Look at the book titles in your local Christian bookstore; listen to the sermons that fill the airwaves every Sunday morning. "Believe today and be healed tomorrow. Give today and God will bless you tomorrow." In our quest to see God do something in our lives we have lost sight of the big picture. We have forgotten what God is doing in the realm of world history. We have overlooked the fact that we live in a sinful, wicked age under a curse from God. Even nature groans waiting to be set free (see Rom. 8:18–25).

The ultimate answer to the problem of suffering and injustice in the world is the return of the Lord Jesus Christ. At His return all men and women must stand and give an account for what they have done. In the book of Revelation the apostle John describes it this way:

> And I saw a great white throne and Him who sat upon it, from whose presence earth and heaven fled away, and no place was found for them. And I saw the dead, the great and the small, standing before the throne, and books were opened; and another book was opened, which is the book of life; and the dead were judged from the things which were written in the books, according to their deeds. . . . and they were judged, every one of them according to their deeds.
> —Revelation 20:11–13

John makes it clear that those who stand at the great white throne judgment will be judged according to their deeds. The apostle Paul echoed the same idea when he wrote,

For we must all appear before the judgment seat of Christ, that each one may be recompensed for his deeds in the body, according to what he has done, whether good or bad.

—2 Corinthians 5:10

This passage is especially interesting for two reasons. First, believers are included in this judgment. Second, the term *recompensed* means "paid back." We will be paid back for our deeds, whether they are good or bad. That means every crooked salesman, every dishonest employee or employer, every unfaithful husband, and on and on we could go. On that day justice will come to God's elect. They will be avenged!

But There's More!

But that is only half the story. Not only will the unjust be dealt with according to what they have done, the righteous will be rewarded. In the Sermon on the Mount Jesus said that those who suffer unjust treatment will have a "great" reward in heaven (see Matt. 5:10). The elect who have been abused, abandoned, stolen from, taken advantage of—all will be rewarded for their pain.

For this finds *favor*, if for the sake of conscience toward God a man bears up under sorrows when suffering unjustly. . . . when you do what is right and suffer for it you patiently endure it, this finds *favor* with God. For you have been called for this purpose, since Christ also suffered for you, leaving you an example for you to follow in His steps.

—1 Peter 2:19–21, *emphasis mine*

Peter says that when we are treated unjustly God looks down from heaven and smiles; He finds "favor" in it. God gets excited when we suffer unjustly. Why? Because that is what we have been called to do. We should not be surprised when we are treated unjustly. In fact, we should be surprised when we are not! Just as Christ suffered unjust treatment, so must we.

To sum up, let all be harmonious, sympathetic, brotherly, kindhearted, and humble in spirit; not returning evil for evil, or insult for insult, but giving a blessing instead; for you were called for the very purpose that you might inherit a blessing.
                                              —1 Peter 3:8–9

Those who suffer unjustly will not only have their cause avenged by God, they will inherit a blessing as well. James refers to this blessing as the "crown of life" (see James 1:12). No one knows exactly what this will be. But the context of these verses seems to indicate that whatever it is it will more than make up for the injustice we have suffered.

First Things First

Think about something for a minute. We want justice now. We don't want to wait for the Lord's return. But did you know that not even the murder of the Son of God has been avenged? The most hideous crime in the history of mankind has yet to come to trial. Somewhere there sits the group of men responsible for the murder of Christ. Though the crime took place many years ago, their case has not yet been tried. God has chosen to wait for Christ's return to judge those who crucified His Son. My friend, if God has chosen to delay justice for that case, who are we to demand that our case take precedent?

God knows when we suffer unjustly. Not only does He know about it, He is taking notes, for the Scriptures promise that we will be judged according to our works. That being the case, then someone, somewhere, must be taking all of this down! God has not abandoned you to the whims and wishes of those who are more powerful. He knows when His children are overlooked for advancement because of their religious views. Young lady, He knows when less talented women are advanced past you because you refuse to compromise morally. He sees the abandoned mother who never knows from month to month if her estranged husband is going to send a check. God is taking it all in. He has already appointed a prosecuting attorney, a jury, and a judge. And they are all the same person—the Lord Jesus. On that court date He will bring about justice for His elect.

Until Then . . .

So what are we to do in the meantime? At this juncture Jesus' question takes on a great deal of meaning.

However, when the Son of Man comes, will He find faith on the earth?

—Luke 18:8

Jesus was asking whether or not any of the elect would remain faithful while justice was delayed. Would He return to find that the elect had taken matters into their own hands? Would He return to find that they had given up hope and abandoned the faith altogether? The very fact that Jesus would ask such a question lets us know how in tune with us He really is. He knows how difficult it is for us to wait. He is aware of the sinking feeling we have felt at some point when we realize we have been taken advantage of or used.

In asking this question, Jesus gives us our assignment: remain faithful; pray for justice; look expectantly for the judge. By faithfulness, He means simply doing all we know to do while trusting Him with everything else. For some, that means picking up the pieces of a shattered marriage and rebuilding from the inside out. For others, it means starting a new career.

If we look beyond the details of our external world, faithfulness can go much deeper. For some, it means repenting of doubt and anger toward God. Perhaps somewhere in your past you were dealt a devastating blow emotionally or even physically. At that point you could not reconcile the conflict of such injustice with the existence of a loving God. And you walked away from the Lord.

My friend, He understands. It is no coincidence that you are reading these lines. Even now God is trying to bring you back to

Himself. Faithfulness for you may mean reestablishing your faith in God, confessing your doubt, and learning all over again to walk by faith.

Let It Go

For some, faithfulness will mean releasing years of bitterness and vengeance that have been stored up on the inside. Perhaps you lie in bed at night and have imaginary conversations with your ex-wife. Or you daydream about getting back at your boss. Or you scheme up ways to embarrass those who have treated you unjustly. Do you realize that by allowing such things to continue, you are in effect saying to God, "I don't trust You to bring about justice in this matter. You need my help"? God does not need your help. He has appointed Christ to judge the wicked and defend the innocent. If you store up hatred and animosity toward those who have hurt you, the injury is only deepened. Those around you will suffer, for bitterness is like poison. It harms everything it touches.

There is no use in allowing persons who have harmed you to harm you further. Release all that anger to the Lord. Tell Him right now that you recognize Him as your judge and your avenger. Ask Him to show you how to put the pieces of your life back together. It won't happen overnight. But He is faithful. And all He requires of you is that you remain faithful as well, knowing that He will bring about justice for His elect!

When the Son of Man returns to claim His own,
He is faithful.
When the Judge of all mankind takes His throne,
He is true.
And when I stand without excuse there in His presence,
Judged for what I did and did not do,
Find me faithful,
Find me true!

Chapter 5

ADVANCING
THROUGH ADVERSITY

Bɪʙʟɪᴄᴀʟ NARRATIVES SUCH as those of Lazarus and Joseph make one point undeniably clear: *God uses adversity in the lives of His children.* Adversity, however, is not simply *a* tool. It is God's most effective tool for the advancement of our spiritual lives. The circumstances and events that we see as setbacks are oftentimes the very things that launch us into periods of intense spiritual growth. Once we begin to understand this, and accept it as a spiritual fact of life, adversity becomes easier to bear.

It is within the context of this principle that Paul was able to say,

> All things work together for good to those who love God, to those who are called according to His purpose.
> —Romans 8:28, ɴᴋᴊᴠ

This is a conditional promise. For the person who does not love God and thus is not interested in knowing Him or growing spiritually, all things do not necessarily work for good because sometimes that "good" is the lesson or depth of character developed as a result of adversity. From God's perspective, it is good if we learn to be patient. It is good if we learn to love those who are unattractive. God values character far more than wealth, prominence, health, or many of the other things we hold dear.

Whose Good?

The "good" of Romans 8:28 is not necessarily the story of a man who loses his job and in the end gets a better one. It may be the story of a man who loses his job and comes to a greater understanding of what it means to trust God daily. The "good" of Romans 8:28 is not necessarily the story of a young woman who loses her love only to find a better catch later on. Instead it could be the story of a woman who through the tragedy of a lost love discovers God's call to enter full-time Christian service.

The reason so many of us struggle so intensely with adversity is that we have yet to adopt God's perspective and priorities. As you read the lives of biblical characters, you will notice quickly that their stories do not end with, "And they lived happily ever after." Oftentimes, their stories seem to end just the opposite way. Moses died in the desert just a few miles from the Promised Land. Paul, according to tradition, was beheaded by Nero. Many of the disciples were martyred.

Are we to conclude from these examples that God has no interest in His children being happy? No! We are told that heaven will be a place of great rejoicing and happiness. But God wants far more for us than simply living a life that is problem-free. The fact is, the people who have no problems as we usually think of them are some of the most unhappy people in the world. They are usually bored. After a while, their boredom drives them to things that cause them problems. It is a mistake to think that a problem-free life is a happy life.

Happiness Defined

Happiness, the way God defines it, "is a state of well-being that reaches deep into the soul of a man or woman." Its context is

*. . . there is
nothing worse
than a life
filled with
adversity from
which nothing
good ever
comes.*

much broader than mere circumstance. Its effect on the emotions goes beyond momentary excitement. And the means by which one comes about it is not by the acquisition of more things. Neither is it the rearrangement of circumstances. The happiness God desires for His children comes only through the process of spiritual growth and maturity. Apart from that, there is no lasting happiness.

God does want us to be happy, but not the happiness advocated by the world. His desire for our happiness is expressed by His desire for us to "grow up" spiritually. The apostle Paul put it this way:

> As a result, we are no longer to be children, tossed here and there by waves, and carried about by every wind of doctrine, by the trickery of men, by craftiness in deceitful scheming; but speaking the truth in love, *we are to grow up* in all aspects into Him, who is the head, even Christ.
> —Ephesians 4:14–15, *emphasis mine*

To remain spiritually immature is to run the risk of eventually abandoning the faith. To adopt a worldview or life philosophy other than God's is to embrace a lie. No one has ever been "happy" for very long embracing a lie. Therefore, spiritual growth is imperative from God's point of view not only for our spiritual well-being, but for our general happiness as well. Continual spiritual growth, then, is the means by which God keeps us in tune with His purposes for our lives.

Since adversity is God's most effective tool insofar as spiritual growth is concerned, the degree to which we desire to grow spiritually corresponds to our ability to handle adversity successfully. Men or women who are only marginally interested in maturing as Christians will have a difficult time with adversity. Their tendency will be to blame God and become bitter. Instead of seeing adversity as something God is trying to do *for* them, they will see it as something He is doing *to* them. It is all a matter of priority and perspective. If our priorities are ease, comfort, and pleasure, we will have little tolerance for adversity. We will see it as an interruption rather than a part of God's plan for us.

But when we allow God to shape our priorities, adversity takes on a whole new meaning. We see it as an integral part of what God is doing in our lives. We begin to understand that adversity is sometimes a means to greater joy and peace. We don't panic and assume God has forgotten about us. Rather, we can rejoice. Why? Because God is in the process of bringing about another good in our life.

Spiritual men and women emerge from adversity excited about what God has taught them. Carnal men and women often emerge bitter and angry with God for what He "put them through." They are quick to point out that "all things don't work together for good," conveniently ignoring the second half of the verse.

An Annual Lesson

It seems that I have to learn this same lesson at least once every year. I am an achievement-oriented person; I like to see projects begun and completed. I like to have several projects going at the same time. I enjoy setting goals. I am always writing out to-do lists. Because of my go-go-go personality and lifestyle, nothing is more frustrating to me than getting sick. What a waste of time! First, I become angry. "Lord, do You know what all I have going on? I don't have time to be sick." Then, I remember I am in the ministry and try to sound spiritual. "Lord, Your work is suffering! If I don't get well quick, what is going to happen to the ministry?"

I finally realize that God is not impressed with my commitment to His work and that He cannot be bribed or manipulated. Only then do I begin to ask the right questions: "Lord, what are You saying to me? What do You want me to learn? What about my lifestyle needs to be changed or eliminated?" For some reason, it is not until I am flat on my back that I am willing to take the time to ask these kinds of questions. The rest of the time I am too busy doing the "work of the Lord."

During these times, God has taught me some of the most exciting things I have ever learned. When I return to the pulpit, I am full of insight and enthusiasm. This has happened so many times now that my congregation gets excited when I get sick. Not because they want me to be sick, but because of the blessing they receive when I am back on my feet and able to share what the Lord has taught me.

That's Easy for You to Say

I realize that the adversity you are facing in your life may be of a far more serious nature than my annual bout with the flu or some other seasonal ailment. And I am painfully aware of the tendency in literature and sermons to oversimplify when it comes to the subject of adversity. But the truth is, God wants to use the adversity you are facing right now to advance your spiritual growth. The Bible gives us plenty of reason to believe that God could erase all adversity from our lives with just a word. But experience tells us He has chosen not to do that. Far more important than our ease, comfort, and pleasure is our spiritual growth.

If we are believers—that is, we have put our trust in Christ's death on the cross to be the payment for our sin—God has us in school. He is in the process of teaching us about Himself: His faithfulness, His goodness, His compassion, and His holiness. Just like any other school, some classes are more appealing than others. And if we are honest, Adversity 101 is not one of our favorite classes. But it is essential if we are to "grow up" in the Lord.

The Old Standby

The most-quoted verse in all the Bible when it comes to the topic of adversity is James 1:2. Unfortunately, verses like this one become so familiar that they lose their punch after a while. That being the case, I purposely waited until this chapter to bring it up.

As much as we may hate to admit it, the truth of James's words is foundational. It serves as the basis upon which our understanding of adversity rests. He writes,

> Consider it all joy, my brethren, when you encounter various trials, knowing that the testing of your faith produces endurance. And let endurance have its perfect result, that you may be perfect and complete, lacking in nothing.
>
> —James 1:2–4

We need to take note of several things in these verses. First of all, our initial response to trials is to be joy. Upon first glance James seems to be demonstrating an incredible amount of insensitivity. When I am facing a crisis in my life, the last thing I want is some preacher telling me to *rejoice!* However, James is not telling us to be joyous because of the trial. There is nothing joyous about trials in and of themselves. We are only deceiving ourselves when we dutifully and unenthusiastically say, "Praise the Lord," every time something goes wrong.

James is very clear as to why we are to be joyous in the midst of adversity. He states it, however, in the form of an assumption rather than a reason. James assumes that his readers are so committed to spiritual growth that when they understand that trials lead to more spiritual growth, they will rejoice because of the end result—growth! The "testing" of our faith produces "endurance." Endurance is a maturing factor. The term *perfect* carries with it the idea of maturity. Whenever persons are forced to endure hardship, they mature in some fashion. James says that endurance can bring about a great deal of maturity in individuals.

James warns that there is a way to interrupt this maturing process. He instructs his readers to "let endurance have its perfect result." The implication is that by reacting to adversity incorrectly, we short-circuit the maturing process. By resisting adversity, we rob ourselves of the work God desires to do in our lives. We put off the very thing God sent the adversity into our lives to accomplish.

I know of several people who are mad at God because of the adversity that has come their way. One particular fellow refuses to step foot inside the church because he did not get the promotion he thought he deserved. Another lady is mad because God did not stop her daughter from marrying an unbeliever. The tragedy in each case is that these people have put themselves on the sidelines spiritually. They cannot advance one more inch spiritually until they change their perspective on adversity. The very thing God allowed into their lives as an incentive to grow has put them into a spiritual coma. Why? Because they refused to "let endurance have its perfect [maturing] result."

Until we are committed to the process of spiritual maturity and growth, we will never be able to take James seriously. There will never be any joy in suffering. James assumed that when the majority of his readers learned that these tests of faith would produce endurance, they would be glowing with excitement.

Rejoice!

You may be thinking, *That is ridiculous. How could anyone be so enthusiastic about growing spiritually as to rejoice when confronted with adversity?* If that is your attitude, the next few verses of this passage are for you.

> But if any of you lacks wisdom, let him ask of God, who gives to all men generously and without reproach, and it will be given to him. But let him ask in faith without any doubting, for the one who doubts is like the surf of the sea driven and tossed by the wind. For let not that man expect that he will receive anything from the LORD, being a double-minded man, unstable in all his ways.
>
> —James 1:5–8

James was not out of touch with the real world. He realized how strange it sounded to tell people to rejoice in the midst of trials. So he followed up by saying, "Hey, if you find that hard to accept, ask the Lord to make it clear to you." That is what he means by asking for wisdom. Wisdom is the ability to see things from God's perspective; it is usually a matter of getting the big picture. The big picture in this case is God's ultimate desire for His children— spiritual maturity.

For a long time I had trouble accepting this connection between adversity and growth. I could grasp the connection mentally, but emotionally it was difficult to take. I thought all this talk about God's using illness and tragedy and other forms of adversity to teach people things was just a way to cover for Him. People like to be able to explain things away, and I assumed this was just another means of dealing with what could not otherwise be explained.

My problem, when I got right down to it, was faith. It was hard for me to accept that God is so intent on bringing us to maturity that He is willing to let us suffer. In His economy, adversity is a small price to pay for the benefits of spiritual growth. As I studied passages such as the ones we have already examined, it became clear to me that the issue was not whether or not I thought adversity was a fair trade-off for spiritual growth. The issue was whether or not I was going to take God at His word and begin viewing adversity from that perspective.

I think my wavering back and forth is exactly what James was talking about when he said we must ask "in faith." That is, when God reveals the answer, we must accept it—not debate it, not simply consider it. We are to take God at His word and live by it. Until we are willing to do that, things will never be clear.

Strangely enough, it was not the adversity I was facing in my life that made this principle so difficult to accept. I could readily see the spiritual benefit that came through the adversity in my life. I was disturbed by the things I saw confronting other people: divorces, serious illnesses, the loss of friends, family, and possessions. I would look at their circumstances and think, *Lord, are You paying attention? These people did not deserve this! What are You doing?*

Over and over again, however, I would go to these people to comfort them and find that God was ministering to them in such a powerful way that they became encouragements to me. Women whose husbands had walked off and left them were praising God for His mercy and provision. I talked to men who lost their jobs but in doing so rediscovered their families and praised God for what happened. I'll never forget a couple who had just lost everything they owned in a fire. After the initial shock wore off, they began to understand why God had allowed it to happen. Before long, they were giving testimony to God's faithfulness and rejoicing that they were able to better understand what really mattered and what does not.

One day I was in a restaurant and noticed that the hostess was wearing a cross. I asked her if she was a Christian. Big tears welled up in her eyes. "You better believe it," she said. As we talked, she told me one of the saddest stories I have ever heard. It was just four days before Christmas, and her husband had walked out on her for another woman. To make matters worse, her daughter and son had turned on her and were planning to spend Christmas with her husband and his girlfriend, leaving this woman with no one to share her holiday. But what issued forth from her lips were not words of criticism and resentment. Instead, she was praising God for His sustaining power. She went on to tell about the people to whom she had been able to witness. I sat there amazed.

Stories like these, along with the clear teaching of God's Word, finally convinced me that God could be trusted in the midst of adversity, that He really could work all things together for good if we would adopt His definition of good and accept His system of priorities. I realized that God knows exactly how much pressure each of us needs to advance in the spiritual life. It was hard for me to stand back and watch others suffer because I was not aware of all God was doing for them on the inside. My perspective was limited to what was taking place on the outside.

Taking the Long Look

Dealing with adversity is like preparing for surgery. By putting our faith in what the doctor has said, we believe we will be better off if we have the surgery. But that does not make it any less painful. By submitting to the hand of a surgeon, we are saying that our ultimate goal is health, even at the cost of pain. Adversity is the same way. It is a means to an end. It is God's tool for the advancement of our spiritual lives.

Perhaps you cannot bring yourself to adopt this attitude. In light of the adversity you or a loved one has faced, it may seem too much like a sugar pill, an excuse Christians use to keep God from looking bad. If that is where you are in your thinking, I want you to contemplate this question: If adversity is not a tool in the hand of God, what is it? What are your options?

You could adopt the philosophy of some who say God is fighting a cosmic battle with evil. In that way of thinking, adversity surfaces when God loses a round. Embracing that form of religion, however, means abandoning Christianity. There is no way the God of the Bible can be made to fit into that worldview. The two are mutually exclusive.

A person could argue that God does not care; therefore, He is unconcerned about the adversity we face. The problem there is that the question of God's love and concern was settled two thousand years ago when God sacrificed what was most precious to Him for the sake of man. The Cross puts to rest any question of love.

One may argue that there is no God. But simply because God does not behave the way *we might expect* Him to certainly does not disprove His existence. That would be like my determining the existence of my wife based upon how I think a wife should act.

This whole problem of injustice in the world kept C. S. Lewis from embracing Christianity. He assumed, like many, that there could not possibly be a good God in light of all the evil in the world. In *Mere Christianity* he describes his pilgrimage as he tried to cope with this perplexing question.

My argument against God was that the universe seemed so cruel and unjust. But how had I got this idea of just and unjust? A man does not call a line crooked unless he has some idea of a straight line. What was I comparing this universe with when I called it unjust? If the whole show was bad and senseless from A to Z, so to speak, why did I who was supposed to be a part of the show, find myself in such violent reaction against it? . . . Of course I could have given up my idea of justice by saying it was nothing but a private idea of my own. But if I did that, then my argument against God collapsed too—for the argument depended on saying that the world was really unjust, not simply that it did not happen to please my private fancies.

To deny the existence of God based on the presence of adversity and pain is to say that in order to validate His existence God must conduct Himself according to my wishes. Clearly, there are multiple problems with that approach.

There really are no good alternatives when it comes to the question of adversity. Adversity is God's tool to promote growth among His children. To resist this principle is to resist all God wants to do in your life; it is to say no to spiritual growth.

The Crown of Life

James ends this section with an interesting promise:

Blessed is a man who perseveres under trial; for once he has been approved, he will receive the crown of life, which the LORD has promised to those who love Him.

—James 1:12

Not only does adversity lead to spiritual maturity in this life, it purchases for us a crown of life in the next. God understands the trauma of dealing with adversity. He has not overlooked the sacrifices we are forced to make when adversity comes our way. Therefore, He has provided a special reward for those who "persevere under trial." Once again we are faced with a conditional promise. This reward is reserved for those who willingly accepted the Christ in their lives. These are the ones who understood that God was up to something, that the adversity they faced was the means by which something good would come about in their lives.

Are you persevering? Are you enduring? Or are you resisting? Are you mad at God for what He is doing? My friend, God wants to advance you through the use of adversity. He wants to grow you up and mature you to the point that your character is a mirror image of Christ's. That is His goal for you. And adversity is the means by which He will accomplish it. Why not trust Him? It is futile to resist. Your sorrow will only be magnified, for there is nothing worse than a life filled with adversity from which nothing good ever comes.

Why not tell the Lord, "Lord, I don't like it, but by faith I rejoice that You are up to something good in my life"? Eventually you will begin to see the "good." You will begin to experience peace. You will begin to advance through your adversity.

Chapter 6

YOUR
ATTENTION, PLEASE!

AN OLD STORY tells of a farmer who had a mule for sale. He claimed that this mule would obey any command it was given. One prospective customer was somewhat leery of this claim and decided to put the farmer and his mule to the test. So he said to the mule, "Sit down." But the mule just stood there. "Sit," the customer yelled. But nothing happened. He turned to the farmer and said, "You claim this mule will do anything it is told, but I can't get the mule to sit down." The farmer just smiled. He reached down and picked up a two-by-four, then walked over and hit the mule in the head. "Sit," he said. And the mule sat right down. Turning to the shocked customer, he said, "First, you have to get his attention."

I am afraid that some of us are like that old mule. One of the reasons God allows adversity into our lives is to get our attention. It is easy to get so caught up in our own activities and busy schedules that we lose sight of God. When we focus on our goals, careers, families, and other personal concerns, we neglect to give God the proper priority in our lives. The result is that we lose our spiritual sensitivity.

This process of becoming spiritually insensitive is not something we are usually aware of. It slips up on us slowly. For me, it is usually a matter of overscheduling and allowing myself to get too busy. Whatever the case, God is acutely aware of when we have become too preoccupied with ourselves and our interests. He knows when it is time to plan an interruption to get our attention.

Is There No Other Way?

The question immediately arises: Isn't there some other way of getting our attention? Does it have to be something painful or tragic? Theoretically, the answer is no. There are certainly other means of gaining one's attention than through adversity. But think about it for a moment. How many sermons have you sat through, keenly aware that what the preacher was talking about applied to you, and then walked right out and did nothing about it? How many times have you heard a testimony that stirred your spirit and sparked a desire in you to live by a higher standard? But again, you were barely out the sanctuary door before some earthly concern flooded your mind and washed away all your noble plans and intentions.

Oftentimes it takes more than a sermon to get our attention. Not even heartfelt conviction is enough. Usually it takes a jolt of some kind to bring us around. C. S. Lewis, in his wonderful little book, *The Problem of Pain*, put it this way:

> God whispers to us in our pleasures, speaks in our conscience, but shouts in our pains: it is His megaphone to rouse a deaf world.

When things are going our way, it is sometimes difficult to turn our thoughts to God. Oh, we all know we should. But it becomes an effort. When all is well, we quickly drift into a state of self-reliance and smugness. Our prayers become lifeless. The Word of God begins to sound unappealing to complacent ears. And to make matters worse, we begin to confuse our sense of well-being with spirituality. *When nothing is wrong, we falsely assume that everything is right.*

Anyone who has done much in the way of evangelism knows what I am talking about. It is next to impossible for an unbeliever who has no pressing problems to see the need for a Savior. When everything is going fine, why mess it up with God? why think about death? For that matter, why even worry about tomorrow?

But come back to that same man or woman following an experience of adversity and you will find a completely different attitude. What was of little concern has become the only concern. What at one time was of great importance holds no attraction at all. Suddenly, God has the individual's attention.

Recently my son, Andy, was invited to a Cocaine Anonymous (CA) meeting to present a one-year chip to a friend of his who had been fighting drug addiction for many years. His comment afterward got my attention. He said, "There aren't any atheists in CA." One of the foundational principles upon which Alcoholics Anonymous (AA), Narcotics Anonymous (NA), and CA are based is that addicts need the help of a higher power if they are to be drug- or alcohol-free. The groups allow members to discover or define for themselves what or who that higher power is. Several confessed that they had little or no time for God before facing up to their addiction. Once they did, however, God, or "the higher power," took on a significant role in their daily lives. All of them recognized their need for help.

Such is the power of adversity. It brings even the strongest and most stubborn of us to our knees. It causes us to loosen our grip on those things that are of little value and cling tightly to the One we know can deliver us.

Blinded by the Light

One of the best illustrations of this principle is what happened to the apostle Paul. He was totally committed to doing what he believed was right—stamping out the existence of the church. He had heard the truth of Jesus preached on several occasions. No doubt he had seen the signs performed by the followers of Christ. But that did not get his attention. He had witnessed the stoning of Stephen. He stood there and watched as Stephen prayed for those who were casting the stones. It is likely that he was one of those who noticed the angelic aura of Stephen's face (see Acts 6:15). But not even that was enough to get Paul's attention.

In the ninth chapter of Acts, Luke records the incident that finally got the attention of the apostle Paul, who was at that time still called Saul of Tarsus. He was on his way to Damascus to seek out and arrest any men or women who were followers of Christ—or "the Way" as it was referred to then. This was not a task he took lightly. Luke informs us that Saul was "breathing threats and murder against the disciples of the Lord" (Acts 9:1). Saul was so given to his task that he is described as one whose every breath was a threat of destruction. He was consumed by his goal.

On his way to Damascus, however, God got his attention. Luke records it this way:

And it came about that as he journeyed, he was approaching Damascus, and suddenly a light from heaven flashed around him; and he fell to the ground, and heard a voice saying to him, "Saul, Saul, why are you persecuting Me?" And he said, "Who art Thou, LORD?" And He said, "I am Jesus whom you are persecuting, but rise, and enter the city, and it shall be told you what you must do." . . . And Saul got up from the ground, and though his eyes were open, he could see nothing; and leading him by the hand, they brought him into Damascus.

—Acts 9:3–6, 8

In one unforeseen moment, God gained Saul's undivided attention by striking him down with a blinding light, humiliating him in front of all his traveling companions. Imagine the thoughts that flashed across his mind as the reality of his condition became apparent. Blind! Envision this man of prominence and prestige down in the dirt as he felt his eyes to make sure they were actually open. No doubt Saul thought he was permanently blind. And that thought must have paralyzed him with fear.

God had Saul exactly where He wanted him. And Saul was more than ready to listen. "Why are you persecuting Me?" the Lord asked. Saul had not thought about what he was doing from that perspective. He never imagined that he was persecuting Jesus; Jesus was dead! Or was He? As the truth settled in, Saul realized his error. And a few days later he was proclaiming Jesus in the synagogues (see Acts 9:20).

When we read or hear a story such as that one, it is easy to see the value of adversity. If indeed it took temporary blindness and humiliation to get Paul's attention, it was certainly worth it, for through him the gospel was preached and churches were planted across the Roman world of his day. Paul was the first to take the Great Commission seriously. He was one of the first to realize that the gospel was to be preached to Gentiles as well as Jews. When we think about all he accomplished, we can understand how God could have justified almost anything to get his attention.

A Look into the Future

But what about you? What could God accomplish through you if He had your undivided attention and loyalty? We forget sometimes that when God looks at our lives, He sees not only our past, but our potential for the future as well. He knows what He could accomplish through our gifts and talents if we were completely His. He is aware of the people watching our lives, judging the merits of Christianity by the consistency of our lifestyle. He sees that lost soul with whom we will have an opportunity to share— if we are spiritually on track at the time of our encounter. He knows who among us could be great preachers or writers or debaters or teachers. He is aware of what could happen through us if we were available for His purposes. And from the perspective of eternity, whatever it would take to get our attention would be worth it.

I Remembered the Lord

The most obvious illustration of this principle in the Scriptures is the story of Jonah. Whereas Paul was ignorant of the truth, Jonah knew the truth all too well, but decided to run from it. Chances are, most of us will probably identify with Jonah more easily than we can with Paul. Rarely are we ignorant of what God wants from us. We are not suffering from a lack of information. What we lack is the willingness to obey. When God uses adversity to get my attention, it is rarely for the purpose of telling me something new. Usually, He is reminding me of something I either have forgotten or have purposely chosen to ignore.

In the case of Jonah, God used adversity to refocus his attention on what he had originally been asked to do. As Jonah sloshed about in the belly of the fish—fighting for his life—he remembered! Jonah said,

> While I was fainting away,
> I remembered the LORD;
> And my prayer came to Thee.
> —Jonah 2:7

I bet it did! He went on,

> Those who regard vain idols
> Forsake their faithfulness,
> But I will sacrifice to Thee
> With the voice of thanksgiving.
> That which I have vowed I will pay.
> —Jonah 2:8–9

To put it mildly, Jonah rededicated his life to the Lord. Why? Because he felt compassion for the lost people in Nineveh? No. In fact he was sorry when they repented. Jonah decided to obey God because in the belly of that fish he got a good dose of reality. Simply put, God is in charge! That is reason enough to obey.

This week I received a letter from an old friend. His story is one I have heard many times in the course of my ministry. At seventeen he felt called to preach. He resisted that call. He fought it through college and graduate school. His struggle finally turned him away from the Lord altogether. It was while he was outside the will of God that he chose both his wife and his career. In time he lost both. Now, almost twenty-five years later, he is ready to serve the Lord. I believe God will use this man—as He has so many others with similar stories. But it was only after He had taken everything this man valued that He finally had my friend's attention.

To some, this whole notion may sound cruel and unfair. And to be honest, in the midst of situations where God was working to gain my undivided attention, I had my doubts as well. But *we* are the ones who are unfair if for one moment we assign to God the label of cruel. Our stubbornness and insensitivity to His Spirit cause Him to resort to those things we find unpleasant. Our preoccupation and infatuation with the things of this world diminish our spiritual sensitivity. If we are really honest, *we leave God no choice.*

If you are facing adversity in your life, God may be trying to get your attention. He may be trying to draw your attention to a specific sin. He may be in the process of steering your affections away from the things of the world. God may know that you are on the verge of making a major mistake in your life; perhaps He wants to intensify His relationship with you during this time of decision making. Whatever your circumstances may be, rest assured that God does not do things without a purpose. If He has allowed adversity to enter your world, He has something exciting in store for you!

Chapter 7

A NOT-SO-GENTLE
REMINDER

It WAS A Saturday afternoon about five o'clock when I heard the door slam shut. From the sound of the footsteps, I knew it was my son. He was seven at the time. I put down my pen, walked to his bedroom, and paused outside the door to collect my thoughts. This was the unpleasant part about being a parent—disciplining my children. There was always the nagging fear that the pain I inflicted through discipline would one day turn them against me. But those thoughts were always overshadowed by my fear that they would grow up thinking that they could get by with things, believing that there were no consequences of sin.

When I stepped into Andy's room, he responded as he always did. "Now, wait, I just want to say one thing." It was a stall. He knew it and I knew it, but it was an unavoidable routine we went through every time he got into trouble. If I had not been so grieved by his disobedience, I'm sure I would have viewed the whole scene as comical. Me standing in the doorway prepared to spank him. Him looking around the room for an escape, talking a mile a minute. "Wait, Dad, I just want to say one thing." By this time the inevitability of what was about to take place was beginning to dawn on him. "What would you like to say?" I would always

269

ask. And as tears would begin to fill his eyes, he would blurt out, "Don't spank me!"

There is a second way in which God uses adversity in our lives. He uses it to remind us of His great love; He uses adversity as a form of discipline. As much as we see pain used in discipline in human relationships, you would think that we would readily accept this principle in the context of our spiritual lives as well. Through the years, however, I have observed that this is a difficult concept for many people to accept. They cannot imagine a loving God inflicting pain on His children. In their minds the concepts of love and pain seem to be diametrically opposed.

But in God's economy, the two go hand in hand, just as they do within human relations. The writer of Hebrews expounds upon this relationship:

> You have forgotten the exhortation which is addressed to you as sons, "My son, do not regard lightly the discipline of the LORD, nor faint when you are reproved by Him; for those whom the LORD loves He disciplines, and He scourges every son whom He receives."
> —Hebrews 12:5–6

There is no conflict in the author's mind when it comes to reconciling pain and love. Love necessitates the possibility and even the probability of pain. Notice he says, "He scourges *every* son whom He receives."

If we think this is strong language in our day, we can only imagine the response this statement must have elicited in the first century. To imply that God "scourges" those He loves must have sent chills down the spines of the early church members. A scourge was a leather whip or a stick used to discipline slaves and criminals. The Romans commonly used a scourge weighted by pieces of bone or metal. This form of punishment was so severe that it was against the law to punish Roman citizens with a scourge. It was not uncommon for men to die as a result of these beatings.

Despite the mental pictures this term must have conjured up, the author of Hebrews felt at liberty to use it when referring to the discipline of God. This is a very sobering thought—or at least it should be. We are not talking about a little whipping here. This is serious!

The writer of Hebrews knew all too well our tendency not to take the discipline of God as seriously as we should. So he warns us, "Do not regard lightly the discipline of the Lord." In other words, the potential severity of God's discipline should be enough to keep us in line. One of the reasons we fall into sin so easily is that we forget God will discipline us when we step out of bounds. We have forgotten that His complete knowledge of sin and its destructive consequences compels Him to take drastic measures with us. As much as He must disdain using adversity to remind us to live a righteous life, the fact is that He will if He knows that is what it takes.

How Far?

The question that occurs to me as I ponder this awesome doctrine is, "How far is God willing to go?" How much pain dare He inflict? Is there a limit to the adversity He might send? He blinded Paul. He brought Jonah within an inch of his life. I think the answer is that *God will do whatever it takes.* As much as He must hate pain, He hates sin that much worse. As much as He must despise suffering, He loves us that much more.

For those of us who do not heed this warning of discipline, the writer offers another piece of advice, "Nor faint when you are reproved by Him." The implication here is that when we are undergoing the discipline of God, we will have a tendency to grow discouraged. We will be dangerously open to suggestions by others that cast doubt on the goodness and justice of God. If we are not careful, we will interpret God's discipline for the opposite of what it really is.

We forget that God treats us as sons and daughters. Instead of expecting discipline from our heavenly Father, we are taken by surprise. We misinterpret this act of supreme love. We view as a threat what was intended for our good. But in reality, the discipline of God is a sign of ownership. It serves as the guarantee of our Father-child relationship with God. So the writer says,

> It is for discipline that you endure; God deals with you as with sons; for what son is there whom his father does not discipline? But if you are without discipline, of which all have become partakers, then you are illegitimate children and not sons.
> —Hebrews 12:7–8

By remembering that God will treat us as His children, we can endure the pain of discipline. To forget that is to run the risk of losing all hope, of becoming discouraged, and of giving up altogether.

A Matter of Respect

Now that my kids are grown, I realize more than ever the importance of discipline. The fears I had in those early years really had no substance. Disciplining my children did not cause them to turn against me. On the contrary, I have no doubt that my discipline paved the way to the harmonious relationship we enjoy today. Discipline develops respect. It deepens relationships. The same is true in our relationship with God.

> Furthermore, we had earthly fathers to discipline us, and we respected them; shall we not much rather be subject to the Father of spirits, and live? For they disciplined us for a short time as seemed best to them, but He disciplines us for our good, that we may share His holiness.
> —Hebrews 12:9–10

If we can understand the value of discipline in the context of an earthly father and his children, certainly we can appreciate to some degree the immense value of a heavenly Father who takes the time to discipline His children. All of us have encountered children who have had little or no discipline. Not only are they unpleasant to be around, but their behavior usually gravitates toward those things that are destructive.

I have noticed among the youths of our church that the teen-agers who have inclinations toward tobacco, drugs, and alcohol are usually those who come from homes where there is little discipline. *Where there is a deficiency in the area of discipline, there is a propensity toward self-destructive behavior.* I am not sure I fully understand the relationship between the two, but I have seen this pattern enough to know that the relationship exists.

God is aware of this relationship as well. He knows that un-less He disciplines us, chances are that we will allow sin to run its destructive course (see James 1:15). He is all too aware of the ultimate consequences of sin when permitted to go unchecked. His love for us will not let Him sit back and watch our lives be destroyed, so He intervenes with discipline.

Ooops!

Every father knows the pain and embarrassment of realizing he has made the mistake of being too harsh in his discipline or, even worse, of disciplining a child who was not guilty. Yet even with those possibilities always looming over his head, a good father continues the routine of discipline, for the value of disci-pline is worth the risk of being wrong occasionally.

If we believe an earthly father should continue disciplining his children—knowing that from time to time his discipline will be unjustified or imperfectly administered—how much more sup-portive should we be of a perfect, omnipotent, heavenly Father who disciplines His children? If we respected our imperfect earthly fathers when they disciplined us, how much more should we respect our heavenly Father? Whereas our earthly fathers dis-ciplined us according to what they knew, we can be assured that the discipline of our heavenly Father will be perfectly suited to our individual needs.

Sharing His Holiness

There is another major difference between the discipline of our fathers and the discipline of God. This one has to do with purpose. Oftentimes the primary reason we were disciplined by our parents was to make us "behave" or be "good." Sometimes their reasons were selfish; they just did not want to be embarrassed. Our heavenly Father has a different agenda. The writer of Hebrews put it this way:

> But He disciplines us for our good, that we may share His holiness. . . . it yields the peaceful fruit of righteousness.
> —Hebrews 12:10–11

God's goal in discipline is not simply to make us behave. His purpose is to make us holy, to bring us into conformity with His Son. He wants to build into our experience a hatred for sin similar to His own—a hatred that will cause us to separate ourselves not only from the practice of evil, but from the very appearance of it as well. Through this process, our character will be fine-tuned to reflect the character of Christ Himself. Because God knows us inside and out, He can tailor our discipline in such a way to accomplish just that.

Sorting It Out

When I stood at my son's door prepared to punish him, there was no doubt in his mind what was about to happen. Neither was there any doubt as to why it was about to happen. I always did my best to administer discipline soon after an offense was committed.

The discipline of the Lord is not always as apparent as human discipline. As a result, there is a great deal of confusion in this area. The Lord does not appear in the night to tell us how and why we are going to be disciplined. In fact, at times it seems as if our sin is going unnoticed. Nothing happens! On the other hand, as soon as something bad happens to some believers, they immediately start looking within to see if they can discover some unconfessed sin. As I close this chapter, I want to give you some guidelines to help you identify adversity that is from God as a form of discipline.

1. *God wants us to know when we are being disciplined.* It does us no good if we are being disciplined but remain unaware of what is going on. What good would it do for a father to spank his child without telling him or her why? Could the father really expect his child to change behavior if the child was not informed as to what was causing the discipline? Of course not. In the same way, God knows that for discipline to accomplish its desired end, we must be informed.

2. *The discipline we incur will be connected in some way to the sin we commit.* This point is related to the principle of sowing and reaping. Paul wrote:

For *whatever* a man sows, *this* he will also reap.
—Galatians 6:7, *emphasis mine*

Notice the italicized words. There is an apparent relationship between what a person does and the consequences that follow. When our children would come in later than the curfew we had set for them, Anna and I would discipline them by setting the curfew even earlier the next time. If the children abused their television privileges, they lost those privileges for a time. Discipline is most effective when there is an obvious relationship between the offense and the result.

Some Christian women cannot have children today because they abused their bodies through drug or alcohol abuse or through an immoral lifestyle involving several sexual partners when they were younger. This is the discipline of God. Some Christian men and women have been caught in adultery and have lost their families and careers as a result. This, too, is the discipline of God.

When a Christian businessman is caught stealing money from his company and loses his job and reputation, this is the discipline of God.

Jonah tried to run from God, and God stopped him from running. Israel was not faithful to God in the land He gave them, so He disciplined them by taking them out of the land. David destroyed Bathsheba's family through his treachery and adultery. God destroyed his family through the treachery of his son, Absalom.

3. *Spiritual insensitivity can hinder a believer's ability to see that God is administering discipline.* I talk to people all the time who are mad at God for the adversity He has allowed into their lives. As we talk, I discover that they have not been walking with God. They are involved in all kinds of sin. And yet they cannot see the connection. They come to me hoping I can press a "magic button" and relieve them of their pain.

God is not about to let up on a believer until He has accomplished what He has set out to do. If a man or woman refuses to give in, God will just turn up the heat. Remember, His ultimate goal for you and me is not ease, comfort, or pleasure. It is conformity to the image of His Son. And He is willing to go to great lengths to accomplish His purpose.

The writer of Hebrews summed it up well when he wrote,

> All discipline for the moment seems not to be joyful, but sorrowful; yet to those who have been trained by it, afterwards it yields the peaceful fruit of righteousness.
>
> —Hebrews 12:11

Saying that discipline "seems not to be joyful" is putting it mildly. Discipline is something we despise for the moment. Like my son at age seven, we all look for a place to run, an excuse with which to stall. No one enjoys it. Yet those of us who have endured it know that the fruit it produces and the pain from which it ultimately spares us makes it worth the agony.

Are you experiencing the discipline of God in your life? Are you suffering from the consequences of sin? Where would you be today if God had allowed you to continue getting away with your rebellion and disobedience? As you look around at others who continue to "get away" with their sin, do you really envy them? Or can you understand that God's love for you moved Him to stop you dead in your tracks and turn your attention back toward Him?

It is true that "all discipline for the moment seems not to be joyful, but sorrowful." But if you will let go and allow God to finish His work, you will experience the "peaceful fruit of righteousness" He has promised to those whom He loves.

Chapter 8

A SELF-EXAMINATION

LINDA NOTICED THAT her bedroom floor made an annoying creaking sound when she walked over a particular area. For the first few weeks she tried to ignore it. Her condominium was brand-new, and she assumed that the noise was simply the result of settling. As the weeks went on, however, the noise grew worse and worse. Finally she called the builder and asked him to take a look. He didn't seem very concerned. "Every new building has its noises," he assured her. But just to be on the safe side he pulled back the carpet and cut a hole in the floor to take a closer look. To his surprise he discovered that the beams designed to join the floor with the supporting wall had been cut too short. They were just barely long enough to make it to the support beam. Not only that, nothing had been done to fasten the floor beams to the support.

The creaking noise Linda had heard was the sound of the floor beams slowly sliding closer to the edge of their supports. Had the problem not been discovered, her floor would have eventually caved in. A crew went to work immediately to remedy the situation. Again, to be on the safe side, the builder had every unit checked. The same problem was found in three other buildings as well. Had it not been for the annoying creak in Linda's floor, she would have never discovered the builder's error. The creak in her floor may have saved her life.

Looking Beneath the Surface

Oftentimes God will allow annoying creaks to occur in the floor of our lives—circumstances or people that are a constant annoyance to us. But as in the case of Linda, these annoyances are God's way of drawing our attention to potentially dangerous blind spots, habits, or emotional baggage from our past. Through them, we are forced to do some serious self-examination. This is the third purpose for which God permits the believer to experience adversity.

In chapter 6 we discussed the fact that God sends adversity to gain our undivided attention. There is some overlap between that principle and the one we will be discussing in this chapter. The primary difference is that in this case we are not talking about a believer who has grown spiritually insensitive or who is running from God. This principle applies to those who are committed to doing the will of God. It presupposes a desire to grow. In chapter 6 we focused on believers who were aware of sin or rebellion but were unwilling to do anything about it. The principle we are examining in this chapter goes a step further.

Step by Step

Spiritual growth is much like physical growth. There are stages of development. Each stage brings with it new expectations and greater freedom. No one would expect a newborn baby to walk. Yet we would be very concerned about a twelve-year-old who was still crawling. We do not think less of a two-year-old because he or she cannot read. But we expect adults to have developed some skill in this area.

Spiritual growth is the same way. God's expectations for new Christians are different from those He has for people who have

*Adversity
removes the
cloak of
"what we are
supposed to be"
to reveal the
truth of what
we are.*

been Christians for many years. Don't misunderstand what I am saying. God's moral standard is the same for every believer. What I am referring to here are things such as character development, discernment, and the surrender of rights and possessions. These are areas of the spiritual life that take a lifetime to develop. Nature clearly demonstrates that the things that grow the strongest usually grow slowly. Only weeds and toadstools pop up overnight.

When people become Christians, they are forced to address certain issues almost immediately: things such as how to handle old friends and how to explain to family members what has happened to them. Usually they are challenged to deal with some sinful habits as well. For the most part, these things are obvious. It does not take a great deal of insight to point them out.

As time goes on, however, and these surface issues are taken care of, God sees fit to begin working on those things that are not so obvious. He is not satisfied with simply calling us to task for our acts of disobedience. He wants to get at the root: pride, prejudices, selfishness, materialism. On and on the list goes to include anger, bitterness, jealousy, grudges, and a judgmental spirit—the kinds of things that seep out subtly in our conversation, our quiet remarks, and our "humor." Along with these, He desires to heal emotional wounds we may be carrying, such as hurts, fears, and insecurities that are the result of things that have happened in our past. He wants to weed out wrong attitudes. He wants to bring to our attention incorrect ideas we were taught as children, things that have caused us to misinterpret the actions of others. He wants to correct our thinking about ourselves as well as our perception of Him. These issues are not dealt with by simply confessing sin. It takes more.

Making Us Aware

Often, we are unaware that these problems even exist. So God sees fit to allow a little adversity into our lives to motivate us to do some self-examination. The winds of adversity blow off the surface issues and force us to cope with things on a deeper level.

God may work through a conflict between you and a friend. He may use your spouse. God may use finances or even one of your children.

God knows how to get our attention. And eventually we become aware of annoying creaks in the floor of our lives. Things quit going as smoothly as they had been. Life is not as easy as it once was. When the structure of life begins falling apart, it may be God's way of saying, "It is time to take a long, hard look within. It is time you discovered what really drives you and causes you to react the way you do."

This is never any fun. It is not the kind of spiritual growth we look forward to or pray for. But during these times of self-examination, we make the greatest strides forward in our relationship with God and others. During these periods of self-examination, God is able to get at the cause of much of our inconsistency and self-will. During these times, we see ourselves for what we really are and not what we pretend to be. If we allow God to reveal all He wishes to reveal, permanent change takes place.

Examine Yourselves!

The apostle Paul commanded the members of the Corinthian church to examine themselves. They were experiencing an unusually high rate of sickness and death among their fellowship. Paul made it clear that this adversity was sent to reveal something about the character of those involved in the church there in Corinth. They were divisive, gluttonous, and disrespectful of the Lord's table (see 1 Cor. 11:19–30). To get their attention, God began disciplining them by striking them with illness and even death! Paul responded by saying,

> But let a man examine himself.
>
> —1 Corinthians 11:28

In other words, "Take an inquisitive look inside and discover what is driving you to such disrespectful behavior." God was not about to allow such confusion to continue, so He sent them some physical ailment to move them back on track.

God does not want negative elements from the past to lie around in our lives and cause us to deteriorate. We are the temple of the Holy Spirit. He wants us to be clean and usable vessels. There is no reason to allow the rubbish of the past to remain in our lives for years and years. When He knows we are able to deal with it, He moves to bring it to our attention. And as painful as it may seem, from God's perspective it is always worthwhile.

Mr. Right

I was talking with a young woman from our singles department who had just been dumped by her boyfriend. She was devastated. Sharla was sure Ben was the "one." She had been praying for God's best since she was in high school. And for some time she felt as if he was the answer to her prayers. They had talked about marriage and even looked at rings. Then with very little warning, he broke off the relationship completely.

As we talked, I felt free to dig a little. I asked her many questions about the relationship. The more we talked, the more transparent she became. She finally admitted that she had been the aggressive one in the relationship. She had pushed Ben, and he finally hit the road. This was painful for Sharla to admit. But with tears in her eyes she admitted that it was her fault he had broken up with her.

Things were going well, so I took the liberty to dig just a little bit deeper. "Why do you think you were so pushy?" I asked.

She shrugged, "I don't know. I have always been that way."

"Always?" I asked.

"As far back as I can remember. My brothers always told me I was 'bossy.' And now that I think about it, they were right."

As we continued to talk, I noticed some familiar patterns in her early family life. Sharla came from a home where a great deal was expected from her. These high expectations coupled with a lack of affection from either of her parents had produced in her an aggressive spirit. She had learned to perform for acceptance. She always did well at whatever she attempted to do. Her reward, however, was not Dad's warm arm of love around her shoulders. Instead she was congratulated with a handshake or some sort of monetary reward.

Eventually, the focus of the conversation shifted away from her and Ben. I began to help Sharla unravel some emotions she had been struggling with for years: the desire to be loved for who she was rather than what she could do; feelings of loneliness and isolation; an inability to wait on the Lord. She was quick to see the connection between these emotional patterns and the environment in which she was reared.

In the months that followed I watched God change Sharla. Her cold aggressiveness disappeared. She became more sensitive toward and accepting of others. Later she admitted to a friend that her breakup with Ben was the best thing that ever happened to her. And I would have to agree, for it was through that tragedy that God allowed her to see a layer of immaturity He was ready to remove.

Why the Pain?

One might wonder if bringing this type of thing to the surface is really worth the emotional anguish. I will admit that sometimes it does not seem worthwhile. But we must remember that God's goal for us is spiritual maturity. The apostle Paul said we are to "grow up in all aspects into Him" (Eph. 4:15). Besides the fact that it is God's will, there are other practical benefits to dealing with conflicts from the past.

The most obvious one is that it protects future relationships from being inundated by the eventual negative overflow from these unresolved conflicts. As much as we may try to suppress it, the undealt-with sin from our past will eventually emerge. It may take a while, but it will seep through the cracks. And usually our families suffer. Therefore, the sooner God reveals these things to us, the better. Every major family counseling session I have been involved in centered on problems that stemmed from some family member's past. Because of this, I begin almost every session with questions about early family life.

Putting It Off

The longer we allow these things to go unsettled, the greater their negative potential; the deeper the roots, the more painful the excavation process and the greater our resistance to let them go. This is why God keeps the pressure on us. He knows that if He lets up, we will return to our old ways. We need incentive to look within. Nobody wants to face what is *really* on the inside. But until we get a good dose of reality, we will make very few changes. The winds of adversity blow away our careful disguises. Adversity removes the cloak of "what we are supposed to be" to reveal the truth of what we are. And as painful as it may be, it is only then that God can complete what He has begun.

A Regular Checkup

Getting a medical checkup is a good idea because it almost guarantees that any threat to health can be detected early before it endangers one's life. Those people who are afraid of what the doctor might find and therefore put off an examination are the ones who get themselves into trouble. It is foolish to ignore the warnings the body sends. It is even more foolish to ignore God's warnings.

Had Linda not called the builder to check her floor, there is no telling what might have happened or how serious the damage might have been—to her and even to others. In the same way, if we don't respond to the adversities that come our way by crying out to the Lord for insight, we, too, run a great risk. Through the winds of adversity, God wants to reveal the hidden things: the characteristics and patterns of behavior that have the potential to ruin future relationships, damage your testimony, and one day destroy your family. Don't run. Don't try to ignore what God is doing. By putting God off, you only hurt yourself.

Looking within may be a painful experience. But remember, whatever you find there, no matter how devastatingly painful it might be, Jesus Himself is there to help you carry that burden to the cross and deal with it once and for all. He has your best interest in mind. He knows that pain sometimes paves the path to complete healing and restoration of the inner man.

In her book *Affliction*, Edith Schaeffer, wife of the late Francis Schaeffer, includes a prayer for those who are struggling with the pain so often involved in the process of sanctification:

> Please let me come out of this closer to You, more mature as Your child, with a skimming off of some of the impurities which are spoiling the reflection of Your face as You look at me.

If you are willing to allow God to surface those hidden and ever-so-subtle inconsistencies and hurts in your life, and if you are willing to cope with them as He directs, you will indeed emerge from the whole process closer to Christ, more mature as His child, and with far greater potential to be a reflection of the love of God.

Chapter 9

A HUMBLING EXPERIENCE

DURING MY THIRTY-SIX years of ministry, I have seen many talented preachers come and go. They explode on the scene like sprinters off the starting blocks. They are invited to the right churches. They are introduced to all the right people. They gather letters of recommendation from the superstars of the evangelical world. They are heralded as the next Billy Graham or Spurgeon. But after a few years in the limelight, they drop out of sight. Some are never heard from again.

Some of these men were personal friends of mine. Others I knew only from a distance. But of the ones I had opportunity to know or minister with, one thing about them stands out in my mind above everything else: they all had a touch of arrogance in their demeanor. I am not talking about overt conceit. In most cases it was more subtle than that.

These promising young preachers suffered from the same ailment that afflicts most men and women who spend too much time in the spotlight. I like to think of it as spiritual amnesia. Instead of forgetting who *they* are, however, they begin to forget the Source of all they are. They forget that God is the voice and that they are simply the mouthpiece. They lose sight of the fact that God could turn off the flow at any time, leaving them high and dry, not only in their spiritual lives, but in their careers as well.

As we would have these men in our home or spend time with them at a conference or convention, it became obvious to Anna and me that they had begun to believe their own press reports. They had taken the applause of man too seriously. An unguarded word or a critical glance revealed to us what would later prove to be true. Lurking beneath the surface of their polished sermons and heartrending prayers was a sinister force slowly chipping away at their foundations. It was a gradual process that in many cases resulted in the destruction of what had taken years to accomplish.

Another Shooting Star

Ben Hillary is a perfect example. Ben was a football star in high school and college. He was outgoing and friendly, and he really had a heart for God. He gave up what promised to be a successful business career in order to become a minister of the gospel. After seminary, he took a church in Florida where he was recognized immediately as a gifted preacher and teacher. His church began to grow by leaps and bounds. After just a short time as pastor, he was heralded as one of the most outstanding young preachers in America.

But something happened. He grew confused as to who really deserved the applause. Pride crept in. It was as if he never got off the football field. He began playing to the crowd. He grew dependent upon the praise and acceptance of men. His twisted perspective began to affect his ability to make decisions. Soon everything he did hinged upon what everybody else would think. After a series of unwise choices, he was asked to leave his church. That was the last I heard of Ben.

God hates pride. It was pride that made sin a reality in God's creation. And it was pride that brought sin into this world:

> The fear of the LORD is to hate evil;
> Pride and arrogance and the evil way
> And the perverted mouth, I hate.
> —Proverbs 8:13

God hates pride so much that He is willing to allow adversity into the lives of His children in order to root it out. As we will see, God has such a disdain for pride that He is even willing to go so far as to send adversity to keep pride from ever becoming a problem. And so the fourth reason God allows adversity in our lives is to conquer our pride.

Why Me?

In his second letter to the Corinthian church Paul spoke of his "thorn in the flesh." Apparently this was some form of adversity—probably physical—that caused him much discomfort and anxiety. This adversity drove him to his knees and caused him to do some serious self-examination. After begging the Lord three times to remove his thorn, he discovered something about himself. During this time of intense soul-searching, God revealed to Paul the reason for this "thorn."

Paul described it this way:

> And because of the surpassing greatness of the revelations, for this reason, to keep me from exalting myself, there was given me a thorn in the flesh, a messenger of Satan to buffet me—*to keep me from exalting myself!*
> —2 Corinthians 12:7, *emphasis mine*

God, foreseeing the possibility of Paul's becoming proud, allowed a messenger of Satan to "buffet" him. The thorn in flesh was God's way of doing some preventive maintenance. It was His way of assuring that Paul's popularity and special spiritual privilege would not cause him to think more highly of himself than he ought. God knew Paul's potential for His kingdom. And He was going to do everything He could to ensure that Paul's ego did not get in the way of his ministry.

Recognizing Your Potential

God knows your potential for His kingdom. He knows what kind of influence you could have. Most believers underestimate their spiritual potential. They think, *What could I do for God? He doesn't need me.* But my friend, it is not a matter of God's *needing* you. The point is that God has *chosen* you to represent Him within your sphere of influence. Your sphere may be your home. It may be your office or the crew you work with. Size is not important. You may be the one person in this world someone at work will listen to. And if you are the difference between heaven and hell for one soul, you have tremendous potential!

Another area of spiritual potential is often overlooked. We tend to focus on the public work of the kingdom. But a private side to the work of God's kingdom is equally (if not more) important—prayer. All of us have great potential through prayer, for the essence of the spiritual life is the struggle occurring in heavenly places (see Eph. 6:12). Prayer is the believer's means of participating in this heavenly battle. Only heaven will reveal the real spiritual heroes. I believe there will be many highly honored people who remained unknown in this life, yet who faithfully supported those in public ministry with prayer.

The Downside

God is not the only One who recognizes your potential. Satan sees it as well. He loves to take a person's success and use it against him or her. He takes great joy in convincing preachers, teachers, and singers that they really are as "wonderful" as people say. He specializes in developing a haughty and critical spirit in those who see prayer as their calling, people who say, "I bet the preacher doesn't even pray as much as I do." He is an expert at confusing counselors as to the source of their insight. Satan knows that nothing forfeits a man's or woman's usefulness to God like pride. No other sin neutralizes a ministry as quickly as pride.

God used Jonah in spite of his rebellion. He used David in spite of his immorality. He even used Abraham after he expressed a lack of faith and lied to Pharaoh. But whenever you find a man in Scripture who gets puffed up with pride, that spells the beginning of the end.

Nebuchadnezzar is a perfect example. One day he was the king of Babylon; the next day he was driven out as a crazy man (see Dan. 4:30–33). Why? Pride. It was Solomon's pride that eventually destroyed his rule as well. Pride will cause God to put a man or woman on the shelf more quickly than anything else, for God refuses to share His glory with anyone.

> Pride goes before destruction,
> And a haughty spirit before stumbling.
> —Proverbs 16:18

> God is opposed to the proud, but gives grace to the humble.
> —James 4:6

A believer who becomes proud is living in opposition to God. The Christian life is designed to be a life of dependency. When pride moves into a life, it slowly wears down the sense of dependency, for the essence of pride is self-sufficiency. By allowing pride to creep into one's personality, a believer develops an attitude toward life that is diametrically opposed to what God intends. God does not help the proud; He does not encourage the proud; He does not assist the proud; He resists the proud.

It's No Wonder

In light of our potential for the kingdom and the devastating effect pride has on our relationship with our heavenly Father, it is understandable why God would go to painfully great lengths to keep us humble. Imagine how much God must have loved the apostle Paul. He allowed him to pen half of the New Testament! Yet He also afflicted Paul with a thorn in the flesh that stayed with him his entire life. The only way to reconcile such privilege with such pain is to realize how much God hates pride—and in Paul's case, even the potential of pride.

If God was willing to head off Paul's pride at the pass through adversity, is it unreasonable to assume that He would do the same for us? Is not our potential for God's kingdom as important to our Lord as Paul's? Is He any less interested in having an intimate relationship with us than He was with the apostle? Of course not. Therefore, the adversity you are struggling with right now may be God's way of taming your pride.

Think about it this way. If you knew that your pride had the potential to hinder you from being all God wanted you to be, would you be willing to ask God to do whatever was necessary to keep it in check? Well, if the thought of praying that kind of prayer causes you to shudder, I have some good news and some bad news. The good news is that you do not need to ask God to send something into your life to tame your pride. The bad news is that He will probably do so on His own initiative!

The tragedy is that some people are smart enough to weasel their way through or around the adversity God intends to use. Through their own ingenuity and determination, they manipulate things in such a way as to temporarily bypass God's plan for keeping them humble. This may work in the short run, but nobody outsmarts or outmaneuvers God! For a while these people are able to continue functioning or even ministering as if nothing has changed. But slowly, what is true privately begins to surface publicly. People begin to notice a change, a lack of power, self-conceit, and sometimes, without their even knowing it, God shelves them.

The Story of Sheila

There was a very talented woman in our church several years ago who was particularly good with young people. The kids in our church were drawn to her as to no one else I have ever seen. Her congenial personality along with her communication skills made her an excellent teacher and role model. But as is true so often with talented people she had a tendency to rely a little too much on the praises of others. I noticed a shift in her attitude toward her work and ministry. The approval of others became more important than the unspoken approval of God. Pride began to take over.

As this transformation was taking place, I watched as God tried twice to humble Sheila. His first effort was through one of her children. Her oldest daughter was born with a physical condition that caused Sheila a great deal of public embarrassment. Instead of embracing her daughter's problem and making a commitment to love her regardless of the cost socially and financially, Sheila rejected Mindy. She criticized her publicly for things that were beyond Mindy's control. Eventually Sheila worked out a situation in which others would care for Mindy until she could care for herself. And all the time Sheila justified her behavior by pointing to the significance of her ministry.

A few years later Sheila's husband lost his job. As a result, he lost his confidence as well. He went for some time without work and finally took a job with the city. Both the type of work he did and the salary he brought home were not what Sheila was used to. Once again she dodged what I believe was another attempt by God to humble her. Instead of supporting her husband in a time when he really needed her, she left him.

I have not seen Sheila for quite some time. After leaving her husband, she went into business for herself. Not long afterward, she dropped all ministry responsibilities at the church. The last thing I heard about her was that she was doing well in her business but was totally away from the Lord. A success in the eyes of the world, she is far from that in the eyes of God.

Painful Love

Just as God had big plans for the apostle Paul, He has big plans for you. There are unsaved people only you can reach. There are hurting saints only you can comfort. And God is not about to allow pride to diminish your potential if He can help it.

Like Sheila, you can resist. But you will hurt only yourself. As painful as it may be, adversity is an expression of God's love. By working to conquer your pride, God works to preserve your potential and your life. Pride is always followed by destruction of some kind. It could be the destruction of your family, your career, or your very life.

Are you struggling with adversity of some kind? Could it be that God has allowed this hardship in your life in order to conquer your pride? If so, are you willing to thank Him? Not for the adversity itself, but for His great love and concern for you and your family. If you can praise Him with sincerity of heart for His active concern and involvement in your life, you have taken a giant step toward advancing through your adversity!

Chapter 10

THE POWER OF WEAKNESS

ONE OF MY favorite Old Testament narratives is the story of David and Goliath. From the way the writer describes this incident, an outsider would have found the whole thing somewhat comical. It seems that every morning the Israelites would line up on the hillside for battle. Just as they were ready to do battle with the Philistines, Goliath would stroll down into the valley. Standing there dressed for battle, with his shieldbearer by his side, he would shout at the Israelite army and dare them to come and get him. At that point the entire Israelite army would turn around and run back to camp (see 1 Sam. 17:1–24).

Apparently this pattern of events had been going on for some time when David appeared on the scene. After a round or two with his brothers, he gathered five stones and went down into the valley to challenge Goliath. Again, to anyone watching from the hillside, this must have been amusing. Imagine—David and his sling going against the giant and his weapons of war. But to everyone's surprise (not the least of which was Goliath) David emerged the victor.

Many great lessons can be drawn from this familiar narrative. And many stirring sermons have been preached concerning

David's faith and courage. But for just a moment let's look at this story from God's perspective. In doing so, we gain great insight into the mind of God and discover another way in which He uses adversity in our lives.

Why did God choose to use David in this encounter with Goliath? He was untrained, ill-prepared, inexperienced, and young. Humanly speaking, he had nothing going for him. There were thousands of well-trained Israelite soldiers present who would have been far more likely candidates. Yet God chose David. Why?

What If . . . ?

Imagine for just a moment that you are the bystander I spoke of a couple of paragraphs ago. You are sitting on the hillside watching all that is taking place. You see Goliath coming down into the valley on his daily run. Then you notice a stirring among the Israelite soldiers. A cheer goes up from their ranks as one of their own takes up his sword and shield and charges down into the valley. Although this fellow is not as big as Goliath, he is certainly no wimp, either. As he positions himself to fight, it becomes apparent that this man has seen many battles and has probably faced great odds before.

Then suddenly the two warriors lunge at each other. For several minutes it looks as if this valiant Israelite warrior has met his match. But then, faster than you could bat an eye, our hero performs an incredible maneuver that catches Goliath off guard. As the giant struggles to regain his advantage, the Israelite thrusts his sword through the Philistine's breastplate and falls with him to the ground. For a minute the two men struggle together on the ground. But the blow proves to be fatal, and soon Goliath's body lies lifeless. The Israelite soldier slowly stands, picks up the giant's sword, and with one swoop separates the Philistine's head from his body. The men of the Israelite army cheer wildly as their enemies flee.

Exciting, huh? But not all that surprising. We have seen the underdog win before. Besides, Goliath made a tactical error, and

*Your biggest
weakness
is God's
greatest
opportunity.*

the Israelite took advantage of it. No big deal. We could chalk the whole thing up to military skill and leave God out of the picture completely. God did not choose to send a soldier for that very reason. He chose a young shepherd instead. He looked for someone who seemed to have not even the slightest chance of success. Someone who would be completely dependent upon Him. An instrument through which He could demonstrate His mighty power in such a way as to get credit for it. When David slew Goliath that day, there was no doubt in his mind who delivered the giant into his hands (see 1 Sam. 17:37). And there was no doubt in anyone else's mind, either.

God's Choice

The point is simply this: *the greater the odds, the better for God.* Our heavenly Father gets far more attention and thus more glory when He works through persons the world considers weak. The apostle Paul put it this way:

> But God has chosen the foolish things of the world to shame the wise, and God has chosen the weak things of the world to shame the things which are strong, and the base things of the world and the despised, God has chosen, the things that are not, that He might nullify the things that are, that no man should boast before God.
>
> —1 Corinthians 1:27–29

Look at that second phrase. God chooses to use the weak things of the world. He does not have to. That is His choice. When He uses what is weak, His power and might are that much more evident.

So how does all of this fit into our discussion of adversity? One of the reasons God allows adversity into our lives is to cause us to rely on *His* strength instead of our own. In doing so, He perfects His power in us (see 2 Cor. 12:9). Relying on His power manifests His sufficiency to us and to all those who are familiar with our situation. David's victory was a source of rejoicing and encouragement to the entire nation of Israel. And so it is when God works through one of His children in spite of the individual's weakness.

Handicaps

Adversities always handicap us in some way. They either slow us down physically or drain us emotionally and mentally. Adversities keep us from functioning at 100 percent. Our minds get divided. Our energy level is low. And even the simplest tasks become major ordeals. Jobs that once took a couple of hours now take all day. Our tempers shorten. And the least little thing irritates us to no end.

Recently I was having to deal with a sensitive family situation. My stepfather is blind and unable to care for himself any longer. This was becoming a terrible strain on my mother. In spite of the pressure that having him at home was placing on her, she did not want me to put John in a nursing home. Back and forth we went. Finally, after much prayer and discussion, I put John in the nicest nursing home I could find. After visiting him one Saturday, my mother decided they were not taking care of him the way they should, so she packed his things and brought him back home. Poor John. For a while there he did not know from week to week where he would be living.

I can remember sitting down to study and struggling to concentrate on my work. My mind kept wandering; I would find myself staring out the window, thinking about my mom and John. It killed me to see her suffering. And yet I did not want to force her to do something against her will. The incident served to handicap me mentally and emotionally.

That is the nature of all adversity. It robs us of the resources we need to function properly. Areas of strength become our greatest weaknesses. Adversity is always unexpected and unwelcomed.

It is an intruder and a thief. And yet in the hands of God, adversity becomes the means through which His supernatural power is demonstrated.

Perfect Power

The apostle Paul certainly understood this principle. After asking God three times to remove his thorn in the flesh, Paul finally received an answer. It was not what he expected. God told him flatly that He would not remove the thorn. He would, however, supply the extra strength Paul needed to carry out the work he had been called to do.

> And He has said to me, "My grace is sufficient for you, for power is perfected in weakness." Most gladly, therefore, I will rather boast about my weaknesses, that the power of Christ may dwell in me. . . . for when I am weak, then I am strong.
> —2 Corinthians 12:9–10

Like all of us, Paul wanted his circumstances to be right. So that is how he prayed: "Lord, get rid of this thorn." But God wanted Paul to live with a handicap. It was His will that Paul remain weak. But not for weakness's sake. God's purpose was to weaken Paul's dependence on his own strength, his own wisdom, his own intellect. God wanted Paul to minister and live out of his weakness, not his strength. This is the idea behind the phrase "power is perfected in weakness."

The term *perfected* does not mean perfect in a moral sense, as in perfect versus imperfect; the idea here is that of being "completed" or "fulfilled." God was giving Paul a general principle. According to this principle, the weaker something is, the greater its need for strength. When what is weak is finally strengthened, the presence of renewed strength is more noticeable by comparison. One of the best ways for God to show forth His power is to manifest it through an otherwise weak or handicapped vessel. For this reason, God allows adversity to enter our experience: not for the purpose of making us weak and incapable of going on with our lives, but for the purpose of enabling us by His strength to do what otherwise would be impossible.

A Painful Priority

From God's perspective, it was more important for Paul to experience supernatural power than it was for him to live a pain-free, adversity-free life. The closer you look at Paul's life, the more difficult that is to accept. He was stoned and left for dead, shipwrecked, beaten, bitten by a snake, and finally imprisoned—all for Christ's sake. When all was said and done, Paul's response was this:

> Therefore I am well content with weaknesses, with insults, with distresses, with persecutions, with difficulties, for Christ's sake; for when I am weak, then I am strong.
>
> —2 Corinthians 12:10

I have seen men and women emerge from far less strenuous circumstances than Paul's full of anger and hostility. They were mad at God for what He did *to* them. But not Paul. Why? Because he recognized that what God allowed to be done *to* him was simply preparation for what He wanted to do *for* him. As Paul grew more and more dependent upon the Lord for strength, it became second nature to him. His faith in Christ grew to the point that he could say with all sincerity, "I am well content with weaknesses."

The whole idea of being content with weakness contradicts the messages society sends us. In an age of power lunches and power ties, it is unusual for people to get very excited about living in a state of weakness. But upon examining the life of the apostle Paul, one hardly gets the impression that he was a weak man. On the contrary, he debated against Christ's apostles over the question of gentile salvation, and he won! He spent his life preaching in the most hostile of circumstances. He planted churches throughout the major cities of Asia Minor and in the port cities along the Aegean Sea. Paul trained the first pastors and elders of these early congregations. And to top it all off, he wrote half of the New Testament!

I don't know what you think, but that certainly doesn't sound like a weak man to me. If Paul had been a businessman, he would have been extremely successful. He knew how to set goals and accomplish them. He understood the principles involved in motivating people. He was a mover and a shaker.

So how do we reconcile Paul's claim to weakness with his amazing accomplishments? Simple, the answer is in the phrase, "when I am weak, then I am strong." A paraphrase of his comment would go something like this: "When I, Paul, in and of my own strength, am weak, then I, Paul, relying on the power of Christ in me, become strong, capable of whatever the Lord requires of me, full of energy and zeal to accomplish His will."

In Search of the Weak

God wants to work through our weaknesses in the same way He worked through the apostle Paul's. You may have been born with characteristics you consider weaknesses. Or you may have been born into a family that did not provide you with the things you think are necessary for success. Perhaps a recent tragedy or illness has left you wondering about your usefulness or self-worth.

If any of these situations sound familiar to you, rejoice! You are just the type of person God is looking for. He wants people through whom He can show off His mighty power, people who know their weaknesses and are willing to allow Him to control and direct their lives. God is looking for men and women who are willing to take on challenges too difficult for them to handle, trusting Him to carry the load. He wants people who understand from experience what Paul meant when he wrote, "My [God's] grace is sufficient for you." Believers who grow accustomed to weakness, but who draw daily upon the sufficiency and power of Christ!

More times than I can remember I have faced challenges that I knew were beyond my abilities to cope with them. I have suffered rejection from men I thought were my best friends. There have been occasions when I have hurt so deeply and cried so intensely that I told God I was ready to die. But in the midst of my pity parties, as I rehearsed for the heavenly Father what I could and could not do, He has always sent a gentle reminder, "Charles, I was not interested in your strength and your ability when I called you. And I am still not interested in them now. What I want to know is, are you available? If so, then let's go. For My grace is sufficient."

I want you to think about something at this point. Your biggest weakness is God's greatest opportunity. Instead of complaining and begging God to change your circumstances, why not ask Him to fill that void with His strength? God has allowed adversity into your life to loosen your dependence on your own strength. It is His desire that you learn to live in dependence on Him for those things you lack. As you grow more and more accustomed to this arrangement, you will actually begin to sense contentment. His power will be perfected in you. And as you make yourself available, His power will be demonstrated through you to the lives of others. And with the apostle Paul you will be able to boast in your weakness. For when you are weak, then *He* is strong!

Chapter 11

FAITHFUL IS HE
WHO CALLED YOU

YOU MAY HAVE heard it said that a person does not really know who his friends are until the bottom drops out. I think there is great truth to that. All of us have experienced the pain of discovering that people we thought would be faithful—no matter what—were simply "fair-weather friends." You know, friends whose loyalty hinges upon the climate of the circumstances. As long as the relationship is enjoyable, they are with you all the way. But when it begins to demand some sacrifice on their part, they are hard to find. The ultimate measure of friends is not where they stand in times of comfort and convenience, but where they stand in times of challenge and controversy. That being the case, apart from adversity of some kind, we would never know who our faithful friends really are.

In the same way, we will never know in a personal way the faithfulness of Christ apart from adversity. As a result, our faith in Him would never increase. It would remain static. One of the primary reasons God allows us to face adversity is so that He can demonstrate His faithfulness and in turn increase our faith. If you are a believer, you have made a decision to trust Christ with your eternal destiny. But you will not experience His faithfulness in that particular area until you die. God wants more from you and for you than simple intellectual acknowledgment of His faithfulness. It is His will that you *experience* it now.

If our lives are free from pain, turmoil, and sorrow, our knowledge of God will remain purely academic. Our relationship with Him could be compared to that of a great-great-grandfather about whom we have heard stories, yet never met personally. We would have great admiration, but no intimacy, no fellowship. There would always be a sense of distance and mystery.

That is not the kind of relationship God wants with His children. Through the death of Christ, God has opened the way for us to have direct access to Him. He went to great lengths to clear the way so that nothing stands between Him and His children. There is potential now for intimacy between us and our Creator. Christ went so far as to say that we are His friends (see John 15:14–15).

God is in the process of engineering circumstances through which He can reveal Himself to each of us. And both history as well as our personal testimonies bear witness to the fact that it is in times of adversity that we come to a greater realization of God's incredible faithfulness to us.

For Example . . .

Imagine how Noah's comprehension of God's faithfulness must have been increased after having been delivered through the Flood. Think about how David's faith was increased through his battle with the lion and the bear that came to steal his sheep. I can't imagine what must have been running through Gideon's mind when God told him he had too many soldiers and he had to get rid of most of them (see Judg. 7)! But after the victory, his faith soared. God used the Red Sea and Jericho to demonstrate His faithfulness to Israel. He used Lot's selfishness in Abraham's life. And on and on we could go. In every case, adversity was the means through which God revealed His faithfulness to His servants.

The psalmist expressed it this way:

> I sought the LORD, and He answered me,
> And delivered me from all my fears. . . .
> This poor man cried and the LORD heard him,
> And saved him out of all his troubles.
> The angel of the LORD encamps around
> those who fear Him,
> And rescues them. . . .
> Many are the afflictions of the righteous;
> But the LORD delivers him out of them all.
> —Psalm 34:4, 6–7, 19

Here is the description of someone who is experiencing the faithfulness of God. An experience that would be impossible apart from "fear," "troubles," and "afflictions." Notice that the writer is not depressed or angry with God. On the contrary, the mood of the psalm is very positive and upbeat. It is a psalm of praise and thanksgiving. Where there is adversity, there is always great potential for praise. The most elaborate celebrations described in the Scriptures always followed an event in which God demonstrated His faithfulness through adversity.

Think back to the last time you genuinely praised the Lord for something He had done. Were the events leading up to your excitement touched by adversity or conflict of some kind? More than likely they were. God's faithfulness through adversity is usually the catalyst for praise. And in the process, faith is stretched and strengthened.

My Latest Cause for Praise

The series of events leading to my most recent experience of praise were full of adversity. For the past week I have been involved in a continuing dialogue with a young lady who had made the decision to end her pregnancy through abortion. She knew it was wrong, but the thought of telling her family and friends was overwhelming. Besides, she had just started a new career, and a baby did not fit into her immediate plans. I met with her and her boyfriend for about an hour and got nowhere. The evening after we had talked, they told a mutual friend that they did not appreciate my trying to scare them.

After several days of not knowing which direction they were heading, I finally got word that the young woman decided to go ahead and have her baby. She called and apologized for her attitude and even thanked me for my help. I have been praising God for His faithfulness ever since. It is not that *He* was any less faithful before, but by allowing me to see and experience His faithfulness in action, *my* faith is increased.

In the Real World

Unfortunately, things do not always work out so well. Sometimes circumstances don't work out at all as we'd like. People we pray for die. Husbands leave their wives and never come back. Children wreck and ruin their lives in spite of the influence of godly parents. Businesses go bankrupt. Christians lose their jobs. And thousands of women *do* have abortions.

But God is no less faithful in these events than He is in the others. His faithfulness, however, takes a different form. Nevertheless, many Christians are quick to doubt God when adversities are not resolved the way they deem appropriate. As a result, they doubt God. Some become angry and turn their back on Him completely. I cannot tell you how many men and women I have counseled who lived for years in rebellion toward God over this very issue. God did not do things the way *they* thought He should, so they wrote Him off as unfaithful and walked away.

God is *always* faithful to His promises. Nowhere, however, did He promise to always work things out the way we think they should be. If that were the case, He would be no more than a magic genie. God's ways are not our ways. And in the same vein, His goals are oftentimes not our goals. But He is always faithful.

Faithful Just the Same

God's faithfulness does not always take the form of deliverance *from* adversity. Many times God demonstrates His faithfulness by sustaining us *through* adversity. Take, for instance, a man marooned on a deserted island. As he explores the island looking for food, he discovers a speedboat washed up on shore. Upon further examination he finds that the tank is full of gas. He cranks the engine, and away he goes. He is delivered from being stranded.

Let's take the same example again. Only this time he does not discover a boat; he discovers a deserted house and fruit orchard. Inside the house he finds all the tools he will need to cultivate the orchard. Although he is still stranded on the island, he has what he needs to survive. He will be able to carry on.

No doubt we would all agree that the first set of circumstances sounds much better. Yet the man in the second scenario could have been much worse off. In both illustrations the man was provided for; the difference was in the form of the provision.

Oftentimes God demonstrates His faithfulness in adversity by providing for us what we need to survive. He does not change our painful circumstances. He sustains us through them. This is what the writer of Hebrews was referring to when he wrote,

> Let us therefore draw near with confidence to the throne of grace, that we may receive mercy and may find grace to help in time of need.

> —Hebrews 4:16

The writer makes an interesting promise. When we are in need, God will provide us with mercy and grace. This verse does not promise us a change of circumstances, freedom from pain, or deliverance from our enemies. It simply states that when we have a need, God will shower us with mercy and grace. Granted, we would rather have God relieve us of pain than sustain us through it. But He is under no obligation to do so. And He is no less faithful either way.

Paul certainly did not lack confidence in God's faithfulness. Yet God opted not to remove his thorn in the flesh. He chose instead to sustain Paul through it. When Paul asked for relief, the answer he received was simply, "My grace is sufficient for you" (2 Cor. 12:9). In other words, "Paul, you will continue to suffer, but if you hang in there with Me, you will make it."

Grace Beyond Measure

In his fascinating book, *A Shepherd's Look at Psalm 23*, Phillip Keller describes God's wonderful faithfulness during his wife's illness and death. As much as Phillip must have desired to see his wife healed, she was not. Yet he writes,

> Again and again I remind myself, "O God, this seems terribly tough, but I know for a fact that in the end it will prove to be the easiest and gentlest way to get me to higher ground." Then when I thank Him for the difficult things, the dark days, I discover that He is there with me in my distress. At that point my panic, my fear, my misgivings give way to calm and quiet confidence in His care. Somehow, in a serene quiet way I am assured all will turn out for my best because He is with me in the valley and things are under His control.
>
> To come to this conviction in the Christian life is to have entered into an attitude of quiet acceptance of every adversity. It is to have moved onto higher ground with God. Knowing Him in this new and intimate manner makes life much more bearable than before.
>
> During my wife's illness and after her death I could not get over the strength, solace and serene outlook imparted to me virtually hour after hour by the presence of God's gracious Spirit Himself. It was as if I was repeatedly refreshed and restored despite the most desperate circumstances all around me.

Could anyone deny God's faithfulness to Phillip? Though God elected not to heal his wife, he was recognizably faithful before, during, and after this painful ordeal. As He did for the apostle Paul, God chose to answer Phillip's cry for help with sustaining grace and mercy.

A Personal Note

I am no different from most people in that I would much rather God deliver me from adversity than sustain me through it. The greatest lessons of my life, however, have been taught to me during times of prolonged adversity. One thing in particular has been a burden on me for twelve years. I have prayed, fasted, and at times literally cried out to God to remove this weight from my shoulders. But His answer every time has been, "Charles, My grace is sufficient for you." And praise God, it is! Every moment of every day it is.

There are times when I operate in my own strength. When I do, I go down under the pressure every time. Then I begin complaining again: "Lord, how do You expect me to be a good husband and father, prepare sermons, and keep everything at church going when I have this extra load to bear as well?" When I finally get quiet enough to listen, He reminds me through His Word or in the privacy of my heart that He does not expect me to do anything on my own. And if I will let Him, He will provide grace and strength in my time of need.

Through all of this I have emerged with a greater sense of who God is. I understand in a much deeper way His commitment to His children. I know beyond a shadow of a doubt that we serve a faithful God, a God who can be trusted in even the darkest valleys, one whose grace is always sufficient and always on time.

Dear friend, I do not know the nature of the adversity you are facing at this time. But I do know that if you will allow Him to, God will use this trial to deepen your faith in His faithfulness. He will reveal Himself to you in ways that are afforded Him only in times of difficulty and heartache.

At no other times are we forced to depend so completely upon the mercy and grace of God. And it is only after we are driven to rely upon His sustaining power that we know it to be adequate; and it is only then that we know in our experience that He is faithful.

Perhaps God has chosen to leave your circumstances the way they are. You may never feel any better. Your spouse may never return. You may never recover financially to the economic level you had previously attained. But God is no less faithful, for He will provide you with mercy and grace in time of need.

The Lord did not say to Paul, "My grace *will be* sufficient for you," or "My grace *has been* sufficient for you." He said, "My grace *is* sufficient." That's in the present tense; that means right now. And so it can be in your experience if you will choose to trust Him. Then you will be able to say with the apostle Paul,

Most gladly, therefore, I will rather boast about my weaknesses, that the power of Christ may dwell in me.
                                        —2 Corinthians 12:9

Chapter 12

COMFORTED TO COMFORT

As SOON AS Bill Jackson entered my office and sat down, I knew he was hurting. Bill was the pastor of a church in another state. He and his family were just finishing their summer vacation and decided at the last minute to swing through Atlanta and visit our church. That last-minute decision proved to be ordered by God.

Bill had been called to River Park Baptist Church about eighteen months prior to his visit with me. During Bill's first year and a half there, God, had richly blessed the church. People were being saved, families were being reunited, and there was numerical growth in every area. But some "leaders" were not excited about what was going on. They had been in control for many years, and they felt their control slipping away. Instead of rejoicing over what God was doing, they had begun to speak critically of Bill and his family. They said he was neglecting the elderly. They accused him of preaching too many evangelistic sermons. And they did not like his style of leadership—whatever that meant.

As Bill poured out his heart, I had no trouble identifying with everything he was feeling. I had faced a very similar set of circumstances when I came to First Baptist in Atlanta. When he finished, I told him my story. I explained the best I could the hurt I experienced during that time in my life. I described my anger and frustration, my desire to tell the whole crowd what I thought about them. I told him about the times I wanted to walk out.

Then I described for him the amazing ways in which God demonstrated His faithfulness to my family and me. I showed him the passages of Scripture that sustained me. I related the events that finally turned the tide. Then I brought him up to date on all that God has done in our fellowship since then. By the time we were finished, his whole attitude had changed. He was excited about what God was up to at River Park.

As he was leaving, he turned and said, "You know, I really didn't think I would be able to get in to see you. And to be honest, I really didn't think you would be able to understand where I was coming from. Thank God, I was wrong on both counts! I am so encouraged."

That was not the first time I heard a story like Bill's. Neither was it the last. And I have no doubt that God will continue to bring discouraged pastors into my life so that I can share with them and offer encouragement to them. How do I know? Because part of the reason God allowed me to go through that season of adversity was to prepare me for that very thing—to comfort and encourage others who are facing similar circumstances.

God wants each of us involved in the ministry of comforting others. But before you rush to volunteer, keep one thing in mind. It is a very poor *comforter* who has never needed *comforting.* So we come to yet another reason God allows adversity to touch our lives: to equip us to comfort others.

Learning the Hard Way

Like so many lessons, I had to learn this one the hard way. For years I had a very simplistic approach to marriage counseling. I believed that if people would just confess their sin, they would live happily ever after. So a couple would come in and tell me

*It is a
very poor
comforter who
has never
needed
comforting.*

their story. I would point out their sin, instruct them to confess it, give them a few verses to memorize, pray with them, and send them on their way. It was a great system because I rarely had to schedule a second appointment. The reason for that, however, was not my tremendous success rate, but people's reluctance to waste any more of their time talking to me.

My problem was that I had never seen a married couple deal with problems from a Christian perspective. My stepfather was not a believer. He and my mother never successfully resolved any of their differences when I was growing up. Up until that point Anna and I had never disagreed about anything major. I really thought that if a couple loved God and kept their sins confessed, everything would be fine. You can imagine what kind of "comforter" I must have been to husbands and wives who were hurting.

Then God took advantage of a change in circumstances to increase my sensitivity. In 1970 we moved to Atlanta, and I got too busy. I became married to the ministry and began to neglect my family. It took me several years to see how I was at fault and to put things back in order. Anna experienced a great deal of hurt and rejection during that time. There were moments when I was not sure either of us could go on.

But during that painful process, God made comforters out of each of us because in our low moments He ministered to us in the sweetest ways. Sometimes through understanding friends. Other times through His Word. On many occasions there was just unexplainable peace that permeated my soul. God was our Comforter, our Encourager and, in a literal sense, our Savior.

Today I can feel the hurt of a man or woman who sits in my office and cries. I can identify with the husband who wants desperately to change but is not sure where to begin. I know firsthand the frustration of a woman who loves her husband but feels that her love is not reciprocated. And more important than being able to identify with their hurts, I know how to comfort them, not simply counsel them.

The God of All Comfort

For a long time I believed a person's ability to comfort another was simply a by-product of having experienced suffering. But notice what the apostle Paul says in his letter to the Corinthians:

> Praise be to the God and Father of our LORD Jesus Christ, the Father of compassion and the God of all comfort, who comforts us in all our troubles, so that we can comfort those in any trouble with the comfort we ourselves have received from God. . . . If we are distressed, it is for your comfort and salvation; if we are comforted, it is for your comfort, which produces in you patient endurance of the same sufferings we suffer.
>
> —2 Corinthians 1:3–4, 6, NIV

According to Paul, God does not comfort the believer for the believer's sake only. Part of His reason for comforting us in our times of distress is so that we can more effectively comfort others. The apostle portrays himself as one who is passing along to other believers the very comfort God used to comfort him.

He goes on, however, to make a strong statement concerning the purpose of suffering in general. He says, "If we are distressed, it is for your comfort." The implication is that part of the *purpose* for the adversity he was facing was to better enable him to comfort the Corinthian believers. In other words, God sent adversity into his life just to make him a more effective comforter. This was more than a by-product of suffering; it was part of God's purpose.

What was true for the apostle Paul is true for all believers. God allows tragedy to interrupt our lives so that He can comfort us. Once we have dealt with our hurt, He will bring someone across our path with whom we can identify and therefore comfort. As strange and as unnecessary as it may seem on the surface, this is part of God's strategy in maturing us. God is in the business of developing comforters. And the best comforter is one who has struggled with pain or sorrow of some sort and has emerged from that experience victorious through the comfort of another.

Defining Terms

To comfort others is "to impart strength and hope" to them. By strength, I mean Christ's strength. For as I said in a previous chapter, God wants to use adversity to teach us to rely upon Him. The job of a comforter, then, is to move the other persons from relying on their own strength to that of Christ. When we have been used to do that, we have imparted strength.

Every time I read the biography of a great saint I am encouraged by God's grace to that person in times of adversity and difficulty. I come away thinking, *If God sustained that individual through such trials, He will sustain me as well.* In that way, the testimony imparted strength to me. It motivated me to go on and forget about giving up.

To impart hope is to enable others to take their focus off their immediate circumstances and place it on eternal things. Much of our suffering will not be completely understood or justified in our minds until we see Jesus. In His presence all the loose ends will tie together. All the questions will be answered. The apostle Paul described our hope when he wrote,

> Therefore we do not lose heart. Though outwardly we are wasting away, yet inwardly we are being renewed day by day. For our light and momentary troubles are achieving for us an eternal glory that far outweighs them all. So we fix our eyes not on what is seen, but on what is unseen. For what is seen is temporary, but what is unseen is eternal.
> —2 Corinthians 4:16–18, NIV

Why did Paul not lose heart when faced with great difficulty? Eternal glory; that which is unseen. Paul's hope was that which is yet to come. That was where he found great comfort. So it is with all of us when the questions raised by adversity run too deep for simple answers. It is not a cop-out to talk about finding answers in heaven. Pointing a person toward eternity is not an act of desperation; it is certainly not a last resort.

In Scripture, the return of the Lord Jesus Christ and His ensuing judgment are almost always presented as encouragements to those undergoing difficulties and trials. In fact, John wrote the entire book of Revelation with that purpose in mind. The Christians of his day were in despair because of the physical persecution they were experiencing from Rome. As the pressure on them continued to mount, the Holy Spirit moved John to write this stirring account of the last days. By his presentation of the fall of Satan and the ultimate and eternal reign of Christ, the believers of his day were encouraged to take heart and endure to the end. John imparted hope to them!

Experience Is Not Enough

Simply experiencing adversity does not automatically prepare a person to comfort others. Only those who have *received* comfort are capable of giving it. Simply going through hard times is not enough. Comforting someone is more than saying, "I understand" or "The same thing happened to me." Paul said he comforted others with the same comfort he had received from God (see 2 Cor. 1:4). Only persons who have allowed God to comfort them are ready to comfort others.

Your response to adversity will determine whether or not God can use you to comfort others. Many Christians are so thrown off course when adversity strikes that instead of turning to God for comfort, they turn away in anger. When that happens, they miss the purpose for which God allowed adversity to strike in the first place. Not only that, they disqualify themselves as comforters. People who are harboring anger in their hearts cannot truly comfort anyone. As long as their hurt is unresolved, they cannot impart to others the strength of Christ. As long as they are buried under their own circumstances, they cannot offer hope.

The individuals who have allowed (or are allowing) God to walk with them through trials are the ones prepared to comfort others. These people have faced their hurts squarely, drawn on the power of Christ within them, and then put it all in perspective and moved on. These men and women are ready to comfort others.

Allow me to clarify one thing. When I refer to comforters as having dealt with their hurt, I do not mean that they are never bothered by it again. I know people who are forced to deal with certain physical ailments every day of their lives. I am not saying persons in such conditions should come to the point of dealing with their pain once and for all. Neither do I mean that there are no painful memories from past hurts. There are things from my childhood that still bother me to talk about. Both those with continuing adversity as well as those who suffered in the past can be used by God if they have allowed (or are presently allowing) God to comfort and strengthen them.

In Search of Comforters

God is in the process of making you a comforter. He is structuring your experience in such a way as to prepare you for a ministry in someone else's life. As Edith Schaeffer says in *Affliction:*

> No one can really comfort anyone else unless there has been a measure of the same kind of affliction or some kind of suffering which has brought about an understanding and in which we have ourselves experienced the Lord's comfort.

Are you aiding the process by drawing on His divine power? Or are you working against Him by questioning His goodness and love? To resist Him is to miss out not only on the lessons He wants to teach you, but the ministry He is preparing for you in the life of another. It is not a matter of having the right words to say. Neither is it just having experienced the same pain or heartbreak. A comforter is one who has known pain, but along with the pain is the healing, comforting grace of God that ministers strength and hope and encouragement to carry on!

In my book *How to Keep Your Kids on Your Team* I used an illustration that I think bears repeating here. It is a perfect picture of the attitude we are to have toward the adversities we face in light of God's desire to make a comforter of each of us.

A farmer had some puppies he needed to sell. He painted a sign advertising the pups and set about nailing it to a post on the edge of his yard. As he was driving the last nail into the post, he felt a tug on his overalls. He looked down into the eyes of a little boy.

"Mister," he said, "I want to buy one of your puppies."

"Well," said the farmer, as he rubbed the sweat off the back of his neck, "these puppies come from fine parents and cost a good deal of money."

The boy dropped his head for a moment. Then reaching deep into his pocket, he pulled out a handful of change and held it up to the farmer. "I've got thirty-nine cents. Is that enough to take a look?"

"Sure," said the farmer. And with that he let out a whistle. "Here, Dolly!" he called. Out from the doghouse and down the ramp ran Dolly followed by four little balls of fur. The little boy pressed his face against the chain link fence. His eyes danced with delight.

As the dogs made their way to the fence, the little boy noticed something else stirring inside the doghouse. Slowly another little ball appeared; this one noticeably smaller. Down the ramp it slid. Then in a somewhat awkward manner the little pup began hobbling toward the others, doing its best to catch up. This was clearly the runt of the litter.

"I want that one," the little boy said, pointing to the runt.

The farmer knelt down at the boy's side and said, "Son, you don't want that puppy. He will never be able to run and play with you like these other dogs would."

With that the little boy stepped back from the fence, reached down, and began rolling up one leg of his trousers. In doing so he revealed a steel brace running down both sides of his leg attaching itself to a specially made shoe. Looking back up at the farmer, he said, "You see, sir, I don't run too well myself, and he will need someone who understands."

My friend, the world is full of people who need someone who understands. That is the ministry to which God has called each of us.

Chapter 13

NOT I, BUT CHRIST

WHEN OUR KIDS were in elementary school, Anna and I decided it was time to begin teaching them to make decisions for themselves. We began with small things, such as what to wear, where the family should eat, and where we should go for vacation. Every once in a while, however, our system hit a snag. Like most youngsters, our kids had an unquenchable desire to please Mom and Dad—that is, most of the time. Consequently, there would be times when we would leave a decision in their hands, and their response would be, "What do you want us to do?" Our natural tendency was to tell them. But we realized that to do so would simply interfere with the development of their decision-making skills. We tried to stay involved with the decision-making process, but we allowed them to make the final decision.

Oftentimes this created a frustrating situation for the kids. "Why won't you just tell me what you want me to do?" one of them would ask. "We want you to learn to make decisions on your own," we would reply. "I don't want to make decisions. I want to do what you want me to do," our child would answer.

As I think back on those somewhat comical exchanges, I am reminded of our relationship with the heavenly Father. The reason we and the children went round and round about the simplest issues is the same reason we are confused by much of what our heavenly Father allows. We had different goals. Anna and I were trying to prepare our kids for life. They just wanted direction. To have always given them answers would have made it easier on them in the short run, but it would have handicapped them later. There was bound to be conflict either way. If, however, the children would have understood then how important it was to learn to make decisions, and if somehow, as youngsters, they could have developed the same perspective and goals that Anna and I shared, things would have been easier all the way around.

Our goals and perspective on life determine our response to adversity. If your ultimate aim in life in any way conflicts with that of our heavenly Father, confusion is inevitable. Somewhere down the line He will structure your experience in such a way that it appears as if He is working against you rather than for you. Your natural reaction will be to wonder if He is paying attention, if maybe He has forgotten about you. But in reality He is just involved in the next stage of your development. What is progress to Him will likely have every appearance of abandonment to you.

This past week I was talking to a woman in our fellowship who is undergoing chemotherapy. As a result she has lost all of her hair. Following each treatment, she spends fifteen to sixteen hours throwing up. She has no energy. Every area of her life has been affected. Her response?

Pastor, I thought for sure I would be able to minister to patients in the waiting room. But I realize now that it is my nurse who God wants to speak to. She cannot figure out how my husband and I have such a good attitude about this whole thing. We had a wonderful opportunity to explain how God uses those in the medical profession as His tools while He does the actual healing.

I stood there in amazement. No bitterness. No doubts. Just pure, childlike faith that God was still in control. Her perspec-

*Our goals
and perspective
on life determine
our response
to adversity.*

tive was right in line with her heavenly Father's. She was looking for the good He would no doubt bring about through this
whole ordeal. She did not deny the pain and the occasional fear
she experienced. But she refused to allow her thoughts to remain
there. Instead she was looking for God's hand at work in the midst
of her adversity, just as she had always looked for His hand during times of health and prosperity. Again, your goals and perspective on life will determine your response to adversity.

What's the Point?

As I have stated earlier, God's goal for you and me is not ease,
comfort, or pleasure. Neither is it that we simply avoid eternal
condemnation. Many Christians believe, however, that these two
ideas are the sum total of God's will for their lives. Listen to their
prayers. They are filled with references to health, protection,
guidance, and safety. Then to top it off they pray, "Lord, please
be with us as we go." What do they think He is going to do? Wait
there until they come back? Again, the implication is, "Lord, we
know Your number one concern is our safety, health, and protection. Go with us now and keep us safe."

In the last few chapters I have discussed several reasons God
allows adversity. Each of these can be thought of as a spoke in
a wheel. In this chapter I want to concentrate on the hub. What
is God really trying to accomplish in all of this? Why deal with
our pride and independence? Why discipline us? Why make us
better comforters? The answer goes back once again to God's
goal for His children. The apostle Paul described that goal this
way:

Blessed be the God and Father of our LORD Jesus Christ, who
has blessed us with every spiritual blessing in the heavenly
places in Christ, just as He chose us in Him before the foundation of the world, *that we should be holy and blameless
before Him.*

—Ephesians 1:3–4, *emphasis mine*

What is His goal for us? That we should be "holy" and "blameless." Paul made a similar statement in Colossians:

> And although you were formerly alienated and hostile in mind, engaged in evil deeds, yet He has now reconciled you in His fleshly body through death, *in order to present you before Him holy and blameless and beyond reproach—* if indeed you continue in the faith firmly established and steadfast.
>
> —Colossians 1:21–23, *emphasis mine*

And again in Romans:

> For whom He foreknew, He also predestined to become *conformed to the image of His Son,* that He might be the firstborn among many brethren.
>
> —Romans 8:29, *emphasis mine*

God's ultimate goal for us is that we be conformed to the "image" of His Son—in other words, Christlikeness. This is what we were made for. But what does that mean? I have heard it said that Christlikeness is simply doing what Christ would do in every situation. Along the same line, some say it is a matter of imitating Christ. I believe there is a place for this kind of thinking and application in the Christian life. But what Paul is referring to goes much deeper than that. A lost person could imitate Christ. Many good and moral men and women have lived lives that put many Christians to shame, and yet they never put their faith in Christ. Certainly they were not holy and blameless before God. What, then, is Paul referring to?

Imitation Versus Impartation

God's goal for us is not that we merely imitate the life of Christ. His desire is that the life of Christ be lived through us. The difference is this: we can do many good, Christlike things and still be controlled by "self." Think about our motives sometimes for the "Christlike" things we do. We pray when we have a need. We read the Bible for comfort or direction. We are kind to people so they will be kind in return. We give because the preacher asks us to. We witness only when highly motivated. We attend church out of habit. Does that sound like Christ? Yet all those activities are things He did on earth. Something is wrong.

The problem is that we can be totally controlled by "self" and yet be busy about the "Lord's work." We rarely take time to look beneath the surface and examine why we do what we do and in whose strength we operate. Think about your prayers. Who do they center on? Oftentimes it is "self." God becomes a means to an end. Instead of getting involved with God's agenda, we spend our energy trying to get Him involved with what is significant to us: prosperity, peace, acceptance, and so on. As a result we become very religious but not very Christlike.

Remember how Christ prayed? *"Thy will be done,* on earth as it is in heaven." When is the last time you prayed an open-ended prayer like that? "Lord, whatever You want to do, do it. However You want to use me, use me. Whatever You want to accomplish through me, Thy will be done!" "Self" does not like prayers like that. There is too much to lose, too much sacrifice involved. "Self" always has an agenda that benefits itself.

Christ's agenda was to please the Father and accomplish His will at any cost. On the eve of His death we find Him saying,

My Father, if it is possible, let this cup pass from Me; yet not as I will, but as Thou wilt.

—Matthew 26:39

That is the attitude God wants to develop in each of His children. Total surrender to the unannounced will of God. An attitude that says, "Yes, yes, yes. Now, what is it You want me to do?" Christlikeness is not "self" camouflaged in Christlike activities. It is an attitude that flows from the very life of Christ Himself as He indwells the believer.

Adversity?

At this point you are probably wondering what all this has to do with adversity. God is not satisfied with well-mannered, respectable "self" on the throne of our lives. He wants to remove all traces of "self" so that we can be presented to Christ holy and blameless. One way God accomplishes that is by sending adversity into our lives. Adversity stirs us up and causes us to look at life differently. We are forced to deal with things on a deeper level. Nothing causes "self" to cave in like suffering. And once our religious facade begins to wear thin, God moves in and begins teaching us what real Christlikeness is all about.

"Self's" first reaction to adversity is to begin looking for sin to confess. But it is not because "self" is concerned with holiness. "Self" is concerned with preservation. And if confessing sin will influence God to turn off the heat, then so be it. When that does not work, "self" becomes desperate. Oftentimes "self" will then bury itself in religious service, saying, "Certainly God would not allow a diligent servant like me to suffer." But God just turns up the heat.

Death to Self

God's goal for "self" is clearly outlined in Scripture. The apostle Paul summed it up this way:

> I have been crucified with Christ; and it is no longer I who live, but Christ lives in me; and the life which I now live in the flesh I live by faith in the Son of God who loved me, and delivered Himself up for me.
>
> —Galatians 2:20

God wants the "self" life crucified. He does not want it dressed up, patched up, under control, decorated, or ordained. He wants it crucified. Paul said that there was a sense in which he was crucified with Christ. And the life he lived was no longer his life.

That is, the life expressed through him was not "self" trying to imitate Christ. He said Christ was living through him. The actual life of Jesus Christ was being expressed through his body, through his flesh and blood. He describes the same experience a little differently in Romans:

> Or do you not know that all of us who have been baptized into Christ Jesus have been baptized into His death? Therefore we have been buried with Him through baptism into death, in order that as Christ was raised from the dead through the glory of the Father, so we too might walk in newness of life. . . . knowing this, that our old self was crucified with Him, that our body of sin might be done away with, that we should no longer be slaves to sin; for he who has died is freed from sin.
>
> —Romans 6:3–4, 6–7

Paul says our "old self" was crucified with Him. As a result we now have the privilege of walking in "newness of life." Whose life? Christ's life. *Christlikeness is not simply the imitation of a life. It is the impartation of new life—His life!*

This is the experience into which God wants to bring all of His children: personal identification with Christ, specifically, the death and resurrection of Christ. Ultimately, this is accomplished on a daily basis through faith. Believers go about their daily responsibilities trusting Christ to express Himself through their individual personalities.

Back to the Drawing Board

Many believers are ignorant of this doctrine. Once they trust Christ as their Savior, they immediately try to Christianize "self." Consequently, many well-meaning Christians spend years trying to make "self" look and act like Christ. Layers and layers of good works are piled on. Hours and hours of prayer are added. All of this is fortified by sermons and seminars and tapes and books, and on and on it goes.

In many respects they are actually hindering the will of God in their lives. Sooner or later, because of His unwavering commitment to finish what He has begun, God begins to peel away the layers of "self." This is usually a painful process because it involves exposing the inadequacy of "self." That means failure at those things that were once considered one's forte.

Oftentimes this process involves a stripping away of self-confidence. Sometimes God moves in on "self" through a person's finances. Other times it is through health. Everybody is different. And everybody's "self" life has its own makeup. But God knows just how to peel away the layers so as to force His children to deal with their Christian life on a completely different level. "Self" always has an Achilles' heel. And God knows just where it is.

Losing to Win

Through the years, I have watched God perform some radical "self" removals on folks. Although their circumstances differ, the pattern is somewhat the same. God is in the process of breaking a man on our maintenance staff even now. When I first met Phillip, he was a few days away from becoming one of Atlanta's many street people. He had come to the end of his financial resources, and he had nowhere to go but the streets. At one time he had been a successful businessman. Slowly his luck turned sour. First, he lost his business. To make ends meet, he went to work for a company doing the same type of work at which he had been successful for years. He failed miserably and was laid off. As a result of his financial situation, his wife left him and went to live in another state. Phillip turned in his company car, packed up his few belongings, and hitchhiked to Atlanta. To this day, he is not sure why he chose our city.

We found Phillip a place to live and gave him a job. After talking with him a few times, I realized he was dealing with deep depression over all that had transpired. I also recognized God's hand at work in Phillip's life. God was marching "self" to the cross. Every time I passed Phillip in the hall I would ask him how it was going. For the first couple of months he would hang his head and tell me how lonely and angry and frustrated he was. "I don't know how much more I can take. It seems I can't do anything right. Nothing is working out. I used to be responsible for buildings twice this size. And here I am back doing the kind of work I was doing ten years ago."

In the months that followed, God began to transform Phillip. Through counseling, he began to understand what it meant to be identified with the death of Christ. It began to get through to him that he had been given new life. For a while when I would check on him, he would smile and say, "I don't understand all of this yet, but by faith, Christ is my life."

Then I got news that Phillip's wife had called and said she was never coming back. I knew this would devastate him. We had been praying that God would soften her heart and restore their marriage. Now it looked as if there was no hope.

I found Phillip busy at work by the kitchen. I put my arm around him ready to provide the comfort I imagined he would need. But the look on his face told me a different story. "I understand now," he said. "Christ is my life. I still don't understand it all, but praise God, I don't have to understand it to experience it." I asked him how he was doing in view of his last conversation with his wife. "Great," he said. "I don't know why, but I am doing great. It is all in the hands of the Lord now, and He is my life."

Only the Lord knows what is going to happen with Phillip's marriage. His wife has not changed her position. But Phillip is going to make it. In our last conversation Phillip admitted that he would never have come to understand his identification with Christ apart from losing everything else he was dependent upon.

The Way of the Cross

"So," you ask, "can people come to the cross without having their whole lives ripped apart?" Absolutely. The path to the cross is not the same for everybody. It is far easier for some than others.

The thing to remember is that marching "self" to the cross is God's number one goal insofar as a person's sanctification is concerned. Once He begins, He will not let up until "self" is dethroned and crucified. Then, and only then, will you be free to experience the very life of Christ flowing through your personality. Your whole Christian experience will be radically different. God will no longer be a means to an end; He will be the end. To know Him will be enough.

The idea of total surrender will no longer leave you paralyzed with fear. On the contrary, it will become the most exciting challenge in life. Every day will bring with it new opportunities for the very life of the Savior to be poured out through you. "Newness of life" will no longer be a theological concept; it will be your experience. Christianity was never meant to be a form of self-improvement. God is not interested in improving "self"; His concern is with crucifying it.

Dear friend, is God marching you to the cross? If so, is He having to drag you kicking and screaming, or are you going willingly? Refusing to surrender only prolongs the pain. Remember, the One who has engineered what may appear to be unbearable conditions is the same One who gave His only begotten Son to die for your sins. As much as it may seem that He has turned against you, that is not the case. The situation can be compared to that of an earthly father who has set about to remove slivers of glass from his child's foot. To run would be to inflame the wound. To cry out in protest only delays the inevitable.

In his classic work *Mere Christianity*, C. S. Lewis has this to say about Christ and the "self" life:

The terrible thing, the almost impossible thing, is to hand over your whole self—all your wishes and precautions—to Christ. But it is far easier than what we are all trying to do instead. For what we are trying to do is to remain what we call "ourselves" to keep personal happiness as our great aim in life, and yet at the same time be "good." We are all trying to let our mind and heart go their own way—centered on money or pleasure or ambition—and hoping, in spite of this, to behave honestly and chastely and humbly. And that is exactly what Christ warned us you could not do. As He said, a thistle cannot produce figs. If I am a field that contains nothing but grass-seed, I cannot produce wheat. Cutting the grass may keep it short: but I shall still produce grass and no wheat. If I want to produce wheat, the change must go deeper than the surface. I must be ploughed up and re-sown.

Is God in the process of plowing you up? If He is, don't resist. Your heavenly Father loves you too much and has paid too high a price to let you go your own way. He wants you to come to the end of yourself. He wants you to admit defeat. He wants you to entrust your life, your future, your possessions, your relationships, your all to Him. And then just when you think all is lost, He wants to replace what He has taken, not with things, but with Himself. C. S. Lewis interpreted God's intent in this way:

Hand over the whole natural self, all the desires which you think innocent as well as the ones you think wicked—the whole outfit. I will give you a new self instead. In fact I will give you myself.

Amen!

Chapter 14

ONE MAN'S STORY

I AM USUALLY leery of autobiographies. It is next to impossible to interpret one's own experience with much objectivity. An individual's story as described by someone who knew the person usually offers a more realistic picture. On the other hand, once I have been exposed to and encouraged by the experience of another as portrayed in a biography, I oftentimes wish for a personal interview, an opportunity to know firsthand what drove that person and what thoughts occurred during challenging circumstances and how successes and failures were handled.

After reading the biography of C. T. Studd, I had a burning desire to know how he dealt with the loneliness of being separated from his wife all those many years while serving God on separate continents. I think about Jim Elliot and the courage he displayed as he confronted the Auca Indians. What was running through his mind in the moments just preceding his death at the hands of those whom he had come to serve?

The ideal situation would be to have a biography written by an objective observer along with an autobiographical commentary of what the character was feeling and thinking in the events of life. With two accounts we would have a trustworthy historical sketch as well as personal insight into the man or woman.

An Ideal Situation

God has been gracious enough to provide us with just such an ideal account. In the book of Acts, Luke gives us a running narrative of Paul's trials and tribulations. Luke was a companion of the apostle Paul. Throughout the book he refers to "we" and "us" when speaking of the events Paul encountered (see Acts 16:10–17; 20:5–21; 27:1—28:16). Luke accompanied Paul to Macedonia. He headed up the work in Phillippi. Eventually he ended up with Paul in Rome during the apostle's house arrest. It was probably during this period that he wrote the book of Acts.

When Paul talks about affliction and trials and persecutions, it is not just his word that we have to go on. Luke was an eyewitness to much of what Paul claims to have experienced and there would be no reason for him to lie. Luke was motivated to record these things so that there would be an accurate historical record (see Luke 1:1–4). In light of all this, we can have confidence that the suffering Paul claims to have experienced was real.

But that is only half the good news. Not only has God provided us with an eyewitness account of Paul's trials, He has allowed us to possess Paul's own commentary of these same events. We don't have to wonder *why* Paul endured. We are not left to speculate as to *how* he remained faithful through his various trials. Neither are we forced to depend totally on someone else's interpretation of Paul's inner battles with pain and suffering. We have his personal testimony.

We should take advantage of this unique combination of documents in our possession and dig out every nugget of truth concerning adversity. In Paul, we have a man who suffered extensively on every level, and yet remained faithful to the end— something that cannot yet be said of you or me.

What did Paul have to say about adversity? What did he learn? What was his secret? How did he keep picking himself up over and over again when most men would have quit? The answer to almost all these questions can be found in one section of Paul's second letter to the church in Corinth:

> And because of the surpassing greatness of the revelations, for this reason, to keep me from exalting myself, there was given me a thorn in the flesh, a messenger of Satan to buffet me—to keep me from exalting myself! Concerning this I entreated the Lord three times that it might depart from me. And He has said to me, "My grace is sufficient for you, for power is perfected in weakness." Most gladly, therefore, I will rather boast about my weaknesses, that the power of Christ may dwell in me. Therefore I am well content with weaknesses, with insults, with distresses, with persecutions, with difficulties, for Christ's sake; for when I am weak, then I am strong.
>
> —2 Corinthians 12:7–10

Of all the hardships and abuse Paul suffered, his "thorn in the flesh" bothered him most. As stated earlier, no one is sure what Paul is referring to here. Some have said it was his wife. Others say it was sexual temptation. I believe it was a physical problem of some sort.

The term itself is used in literature of the same period to refer to a splinter. When used figuratively, this word refers to anything that is a constant annoyance. In the context of Paul's discussion, this may be somewhat of an understatement. Although his thorn was constant, it was more than just a little annoying. Paul's thorn was a source of great concern.

Paul's Discoveries

As we have observed in previous chapters, God chose not to remove this thorn, and Paul learned to live with it. In the process, however, Paul made some fantastic discoveries about adversity that enabled him not to merely survive his circumstances, but to "glory" in them and emerge victorious. So what did Paul discover?

1. THERE IS A DIVINE PURPOSE BEHIND ALL ADVERSITY.

And *because* of the surpassing greatness of the revelations, *for this reason*, to keep me from exalting myself, there was given me a thorn in the flesh.
—2 Corinthians 12:7, *emphasis mine*

Paul understood that God was always using adversity to further His cause; it always had a purpose. In the preceding chapters we examined in detail several of God's purposes in allowing adversity to touch our lives. Unfortunately, they are not always easily identified, and there is oftentimes a gap between our experience and our understanding. We can go for days, weeks, years, and sometimes a lifetime without knowing God's purpose.

Job went to his grave without ever knowing why he suffered. Paul says he entreated the Lord three times before receiving an answer. The way the verse reads, it sounds as if Paul asked God once in the morning, once after lunch, and then one more time in the evening. But we do not know how much time elapsed between his petitions. Like us, Paul knew the frustration of trying to maintain faith in God while at the same time wondering why He did not respond.

What Paul learned, and what we must learn as well, is that when God does not remove our "thorn," it is not without reason. God would not have us suffer for the sake of suffering. There is always a purpose.

2. GOD MAY CHOOSE TO REVEAL THE PURPOSE FOR OUR ADVERSITY.

In Paul's case, God chose to indicate why he was given the "thorn." It was to keep him from becoming proud. It is interesting that God did not reveal this to Paul the first time he prayed. There is a reason for that. Notice that Paul prayed, "Concerning this I entreated the Lord three times that it might depart from me." Paul did not even ask God *why*. He was asking that it be removed.

It is not uncommon for God to reveal the reason for suffering. He revealed to Moses the reason he was not allowed to enter the Promised Land. God told Joshua why he and his army were defeated at Ai. Jesus told the disciples that they could expect trouble and why. John wrote to the churches of his day and explained why they were experiencing trials. And James used the first part of his epistle to explain why the believers of his day were suffering. God is not necessarily silent concerning the question of *why*. But He answers according to His schedule, which is usually slightly behind ours.

3. GOD NEVER SCOLDS US FOR ASKING WHY OR FOR REQUESTING THAT THE ADVERSITY BE REMOVED.

There is no evidence that God scolded Paul for asking that his thorn be removed. God understands our weakness. He expects us to cry out to Him when we are experiencing hurt or frustration. He desires that we cast our cares on Him. Why? Because in doing so we are expressing faith, and faith is the foundation of our entire relationship with Him.

Paul was not the first to cry out to God for help. His own Son found Himself facing pain and rejection of the worst kind. In His own way, He, too, asked that a thorn be removed—the cross.

And He went a little beyond them, and fell on His face and prayed, saying, "My Father, if it is possible, let this cup pass from Me."

—Matthew 26:39

You need not feel guilty for asking God to remove adversity from your life. He expects it. At the same time, as we have seen, your prayer may not be answered in the fashion or moment you would prefer. But nevertheless, you should ask, for it was during the process of asking for relief that Paul received a word from God.

In the same way, we should not be afraid to ask God *why*, either. So often I hear people say, "I am not asking God why He allowed this; I am just trusting that He is in control." I understand the motivation behind such a statement. It is meant as an expression of faith and trust in the sovereignty and presence of God. And I would never fault individuals for their faith. But nowhere in Scripture are we admonished to refrain from asking *why*. As we have already seen, there are plenty of examples in Scripture where God was more than willing to answer that question.

James actually instructs believers to ask God for an answer to the *why* question. After encouraging his readers to focus on how God is using adversity in their lives, he says,

> But if any of you lacks wisdom, let him ask of God, who gives to all men generously and without reproach, and it will be given to him.
>
> —James 1:5

In effect, he is saying, "If in the middle of all these trials you have any questions, go ahead and ask God." Then notice the second half: "Who gives to all men generously and *without reproach*." God is a generous God. Not only that, He is not going to get upset if we question Him as to what is happening.

The question of *why* becomes a problem when it is asked in doubt. That is, we assume that because *we* see no purpose in suffering, there is none. To the one who asks *why* from that point of reference, James says,

> Let not that man expect that he will receive anything from the Lord, being a doubleminded man, unstable in all his ways.
>
> —James 1:7–8

Just as an earthly father desires to comfort his children in times of distress, so our heavenly Father desires to comfort us. And when in His wisdom He believes the answer to the question of why is important for us to know, He will reveal it.

4. ADVERSITY MAY BE A GIFT FROM GOD.

When we think of adversity, we are oftentimes prone to think of it as something God does *to* us. Our prayers reflect that attitude: "Lord, why did this happen *to* me?" "Father, why are You allowing this to happen *to* me?" Prayers such as these reflect our basic heartfelt conviction—adversity at best is bad! And so it is viewed as something that happens *to* us.

Paul did not view it that way at all. Notice his phraseology when referring to his thorn in the flesh:

> For this reason, to keep me from exalting myself, there was *given* me a thorn in the flesh.
>
> —2 Corinthians 12:7, *emphasis mine*

Paul had the faith to believe that this constant irritation was a gift. As godly a fellow as the apostle Paul may have been, I doubt that his attitude started out this positive. But as he grew to understand what God was doing in his life, his attitude began to change. And in the process he saw his thorn for what it was— a gift.

It was a gift in that it was through this irritation that God protected Paul from the thing he feared the most—spiritual disqualification (see 1 Cor. 9:27). Paul had a burning desire to end well, to finish the course God had set before him. He knew from watching others that nothing destroys a man's or woman's effectiveness for God as quickly and as thoroughly as pride. Therefore, if his thorn in the flesh would protect him from pride, it was indeed a *gift* from God. He could with all sincerity view it as something God did *for* him rather than *to* him.

5. SATAN CAN BE THE AGENT OF ADVERSITY.

Things certainly become confusing at this point. Paul just finished saying that God was the One who arranged for him to live with this thorn in the flesh. Then he explained that it was really a gift in light of its intended result. Just as things were making good sense, he stated,

> There was given me a thorn in the flesh, *a messenger of Satan* to buffet me.
> —2 Corinthians 12:7, *emphasis mine*

Now wait, is God behind this, or Satan? How is it that a messenger of Satan is now working for the good of one of God's servants? That seems like a total contradiction. Everybody has an opinion at this point. But we stay on solid theological ground if we take the text at face value. And the implication is that God uses messengers of Satan in the lives of His servants. What more can we say?

Actually, this point should be very comforting. When we take what is stated here and compare it to the life of Job, we gain a clearer picture of God's sovereignty. Even the schemes of the devil can be used to benefit us and further the kingdom of God. Think about it. Even Satan's host works under the watchful eye of our Father in heaven.

6. GOD WILL COMFORT US IN OUR ADVERSITIES.

The answer Paul received from God concerning his thorn in the flesh was not what he expected. We know from his prayer that it was not what he really wanted, either. Yet Paul was able to take great comfort in the fact that he received an answer. God's response to Paul served to assure him that he had not been abandoned. He was not suffering alone. God was still in control and still at work in Paul's life.

Our Lord has promised never to leave or forsake us. He made this promise at a time when those who had followed Him faithfully were about to launch out into a work that would be difficult. God demonstrated His faithfulness to those men, and He will do the same in your life and my life.

The primary reason we are not aware of God's comfort during

times of adversity is that we don't look for it. We give up. We begin to doubt His wisdom, His goodness, and at times His very existence. *Doubt diminishes our ability to recognize the comforting hand of God.* It clouds our spiritual vision. Once we doubt God's goodness and faithfulness, we will miss His efforts to comfort us.

7. GOD'S GRACE IS SUFFICIENT DURING TIMES OF ADVERSITY.

God did not give Paul what he requested. But what He gave him was far better in the long run. God granted Paul the grace he needed to bear up under the pressure brought about by his thorn in the flesh. To say that Paul was able merely to bear up under the pressure is to understate the case, however. Paul endured his hardship victoriously! Notice how he describes his situation:

And He has said to me, "My grace is sufficient for you, for power is perfected in weakness." Most gladly, therefore, I will rather boast about my weaknesses, that the power of Christ may dwell in me.

—2 Corinthians 12:9

This does not sound like a man who is just barely getting by. We don't find Paul dwelling on his hardships and his trials in a depressing manner. Rather, we find him rejoicing over weaknesses. He is not excited about the weaknesses themselves; he is exultant over the fact that God's grace empowers him to reign victoriously over his weaknesses.

Paul discovered what many believers miss throughout their whole lives. That is, God's power is most evident to us when we are weak. It is most evident then to others as well. Paul understood he was far more effective when forced through weakness to rely on God's power through him, and so he says he gladly boasts about his weaknesses.

Paul's testimony is an encouragement to me in this one area

more than any other. If God's grace was sufficient for a man who left his family, his home, and his friends to plant churches in hostile environments; who was shipwrecked, imprisoned, stoned, and left for dead; I am confident His grace is more than sufficient for anything I will encounter.

8. GOD MAY NOT SEE FIT TO REMOVE THE ADVERSITY.

This is the most difficult principle of all to accept—not only in the context of our own lives, but in the lives of those we love as well. How many times have you seen someone suffering and thought, *Lord, why don't You do something?* There is a woman in our fellowship who has calcium deposits all along her spinal column. Her back is bent over so far that she is unable to look up. Every Sunday one of our faithful men and his daughter bring her to church. As they lead her down the aisle to her regular pew, I always think, *Lord, how great it would be if You would heal that dear saint.* And yet it seems that this is an adversity He has chosen not to remove.

Many Christians have the idea that if they pray enough and believe enough, they can force God's hand; they think He will be compelled to remove their adversity. They misuse Scripture to build a case for the divine healing of every disease and affliction. The Scriptures, however, make no such claim. I certainly believe in divine healing. In fact, all healing is divine. But nowhere in the Bible are we promised exemption from disease and illness in this life. This world is still under a curse. And these dying and decaying bodies of ours are cursed right along with everything else.

I think about Joni Eareckson Tada, who is a beautiful testimony of God's grace in a life. She does not suffer from a lack of faith. It takes far more faith to endure confinement to a wheelchair than it does to believe Jesus can heal. Joni realizes that Jesus could heal her in a moment. But she has realized that for the time being He has chosen to use her as she is.

Jesus never promised to remove our pain and suffering in this life. Certainly there are cases in which He does. Some are quite miraculous. But these are the exceptions, not the rule. Jesus told His disciples,

> In the world you have tribulation, but take courage; I have overcome the world.
>
> —John 16:33

Paul knew what it meant to live with adversity. He knew the frustration of realizing that relief would never come; having asked three times, he was denied. Yet he did not complain and grow bitter; he did not doubt the goodness and mercy of God. He experienced instead the power of God. Paul learned to depend daily on God's grace. He was even able to accept the fact that God would be doing him a disservice by removing his thorn in the flesh. And so he learned to be content, even in the midst of constant suffering.

No one likes to suffer. In our hearts, we all desire immediate relief from pain and grief. God understands our weakness and our sorrow. There are times, however, when despite our inconvenience, He allows adversity to persist. The best thing we can do is simply submit to His sovereign decision, knowing that His grace will be sufficient for anything we might face.

9. CONTENTMENT DOES NOT HINGE ON THE NATURE OF OUR CIRCUMSTANCES.

I have met many discontented people in my life. Always on the move. Forever arranging and rearranging their lives. Never satisfied with themselves or their circumstances. The underlying promise from which most of their decisions flow is that personal contentment is inextricably linked to one's circumstances. In other words, a person's surroundings—job, spouse, income, residence–determine peace of mind and satisfaction. Consequently, when they become dissatisfied with life, they begin changing things. They quit their job. They sell their house. They trade their car. Or in some cases, they look for a new marriage partner. Soon, however, that same feeling begins gnawing at them again. And off they go, making more changes.

Now if you will think about it, nobody needed a change of scenery more than the apostle Paul. His life seemed to go from bad to worse. In this same letter he lists the perils he faced in his attempt to spread the gospel:

> Five times I received from the Jews thirty-nine lashes. Three times I was beaten with rods, once I was stoned, three times I was shipwrecked, a night and a day I have spent in the deep. I have been on frequent journeys, in dangers from rivers, dangers from robbers, dangers from my countrymen, dangers from the Gentiles, dangers in the city, dangers in the wilderness, dangers on the sea, dangers among false brethren; I have been in labor and hardship through many sleepless nights, in hunger and thirst, often without food, in cold and exposure.
> —2 Corinthians 11:24–27

Having experienced all of that, he is still able to say,

> Therefore I am well content with weaknesses, with insults, with distresses, with persecutions, with difficulties, for Christ's sake; for when I am weak, then I am strong.
> —2 Corinthians 12:10

He echoes the same idea in his letter to the Philippian believers:

> Not that I speak from want; for I have learned to be content in whatever circumstances I am. I know how to get along with humble means, and I also know how to live in prosperity; in any and every circumstance I have learned the secret of being filled and going hungry, both of having abundance and suffering need.
> —Philippians 4:11–12

If Paul was able to find contentment in the midst of those hostile environments, I think it is safe to say that contentment does not hinge on one's circumstances. Paul faced adversity at every level—everything from prison to sickness to rejection by his own people. Yet he claimed to be "well content."

Paul's "secret," as he referred to it in Philippians, was his relationship with Christ. He discovered that true and lasting contentment is found not in things, but in a Person. He could be content in the most adverse circumstances because his aim in life was to be pleasing to the Lord (see 2 Cor. 5:9). Knowing that he was where his Lord wanted him to be was enough. He did not need material props to bring him satisfaction.

You may say, "Well, that sounds mighty spiritual, but how realistic is it to think that we can find contentment outside the realm of our circumstances?" I believe it is extremely realistic. And I don't believe this is a principle that applies to some elite group of believers. This kind of contentment is for all Christians. Otherwise we will spend the bulk of our time and energy trying to better our circumstances rather than serving Christ. I am not against self-improvement. But I have a real problem with believers who are so caught up in upgrading their lifestyle that they have little time for God and His church.

For Paul, learning to be content in every circumstance was a necessity. He would not have survived if this principle did not work. Yet as we have seen, Paul did more than simply survive; he "reigned" in life through Christ (see Rom. 5:17). Contentment is available to all of us, regardless of our circumstances, if we will only commit our lives to the purposes and plan of God.

10. THE KEY TO ADVANCING THROUGH ADVERSITY IS TO VIEW IT AS FOR CHRIST'S SAKE.

Paul understood that his purpose in life was to bring glory to God by preaching the gospel of Christ. Therefore, anything that happened to him in the process of obeying God was really for

Christ's sake. That is, people were not rejecting him. They were rejecting his message and thus Christ.

> Therefore I am well content with weaknesses, with insults, with distresses, with persecutions, with difficulties, *for Christ's sake;* for when I am weak, then I am strong.
> —2 Corinthians 12:10, *emphasis mine*

Paul did not take what was happening to him personally. He realized that his suffering was the direct result of his mission in life. Even his thorn in the flesh was for Christ's sake. It was given to him to keep him from forfeiting his ministry and damaging the cause of Christ. Paul was not glorying in suffering for suffering's sake. It was for Christ's sake. There was purpose in all he experienced.

Your mission in life is to bring glory to God through the spreading of the gospel of Christ. You may never stand in a pulpit. You may never leave your hometown. Regardless of where you go or the opportunities you have, your mission is still the same. When you become consumed by God's call on your life, everything will take on new meaning and significance. You will begin to see every facet of your life—including your pain—as a means through which God can work to bring others to Himself. When God uses the adversity in your life to draw people to Himself, you have suffered for Christ's sake.

We know God can use our time, our money, and our talent. Why not our suffering? I have heard many invitations in which preachers have asked people to dedicate children, homes, and businesses to the Lord's service. I have yet to hear a preacher challenge his people to dedicate their adversity to the Lord. Yet nothing gets the attention of the lost world more quickly than a saint who is suffering successfully. Sorrow and grief are powerful tools in the right hands.

For whose sake are you suffering? Most people suffer for their own sake. Consequently, they become bitter, angry, and difficult to live with. Paul realized his suffering was for Christ's sake. It was just one more means of expressing the glory and grace of God to a lost world. God may want to relieve you of the adversity in your life. But He may choose to delay your deliverance that He might use your suffering for His sake. Cruel, you ask? It may seem so now. But remember that He spared not His own Son. You and I have eternal life today because Christ suffered and died for His Father's sake. It was through the Lord's pain that many were reconciled to God. And we who say we know Him ought to walk even as He walked. That is, we should make our pain available to God for Him to use as He desires. And then we, too, will endure these things for Christ's sake.

Looking Back

As I think back over these ten lessons Paul learned about adversity, he almost appears larger than life. He makes it sound so simple. It appears that way because by the time Paul penned this letter to the church in Corinth he had assimilated these principles into his lifestyle. It is just like watching players in a professional tennis match. They make it look so simple. I find myself wanting to go home, get out my racket, and start smashing tennis balls as hard as I can. Because it looks as if that is all they are doing. What I don't see are the hours and hours of practice and evaluation they go through before they ever get to the match.

As we read the life of Paul, in Acts and in his various epistles, we are seeing him at his best, at the end of a lifetime of learning. That is not to take away from what he says. On the contrary, what we read in 2 Corinthians 12 should be very encouraging. It sets before us what is possible if we press on. It serves as a constant reminder of God's abiding grace. It stands as a warning to those who would shake their fist at God when adversity strikes. Paul's life was filled with such extreme suffering that each of us must think, *If God could sustain him through that, I don't have anything to worry about.*

You really don't have anything to worry about. God's grace *is*, even now as you are reading, sufficient for whatever you are fac-

ing. Your responsibility is to submit yourself to the lordship of
Christ and say,

> Have Thine own way, Lord, have Thine own way;
> Thou art the potter, I am the clay;
> Mold me and make me, after Thy will;
> While I am waiting yielded and still.

When that becomes the sincere prayer of your heart, you, too,
will become well content with weakness. And you will have
taken another giant step toward advancing through adversity.

Chapter 15

RESPONDING TO ADVERSITY: THE CHOICE IS YOURS

WE BEGAN IN chapter 1 by looking at the possible sources of adversity. We found there were three: God, Satan, and sin. But it is not always easy to discern the source of our adversity. We have even seen cases in the Bible where they appear to overlap. It is evident that God's primary concern is not that we always understand the source of our adversity. Otherwise He would have made it clear. God is, however, extremely interested in how we respond to adversity because our response determines whether or not adversity is going to bring about its intended result.

The nature of our adversity alone does not determine its spiritual value in our lives. It is our reaction to it, the way we deal with it, that makes suffering valuable. We have all seen people who faced tough times and folded under the pressure. Some pull themselves back together and go on to learn whatever God wants to teach them. Others never recuperate.

The Blame Game

When adversity strikes, our first response oftentimes is to blame somebody. I can remember standing at the scene of an automobile accident listening to a college student trying to explain to the police officer why he had turned in front of a lady. He was sure that it was not his fault; something about the angle of the traffic light threw him off. He was clearly to blame. But this young man was so angry at having wrecked his car, he could not stand the thought of its being his fault.

We all have a tendency to strike out at those around us when things go wrong or we are hurt. Remember Mary and Martha's response: "Lord, if You had been here. . . ." Some people blame God. Others blame Satan. But usually we pin the blame on another person in an attempt to escape personal responsibility.

If blaming it on someone else does not get us anywhere, we may find ourselves fighting the problem. We attempt to manipulate or reshape our circumstances so as to rid ourselves of pain and inconvenience. This is the reason behind many lawsuits. People who have been fired or passed by for a promotion may sue the company. They feel impelled to fight for their rights.

Another way people react to tragedy is denial. They simply will not face what has happened. They act as if nothing is wrong. I see this in situations where someone has lost a loved one. And a parent or friend refuses to accept the separation as permanent. This is usually a temporary situation. In time, most of these people are able to accept what has happened.

Any of the preceding responses can easily turn into bitterness —bitterness toward the person or organization through which adversity comes or even bitterness toward God. When people become bitter, the very thought of the person who hurt them causes their stomach to turn. Bitterness forces people to overreact to circumstances that remind them of those through which they were wronged.

At this stage people may think about revenge. All of us are guilty at one time or another of rehearsing in our minds what we would like to do to somebody if we thought we could get away with it. We imagine ourselves walking into the office of our boss and letting him have it. Or perhaps calling our parents and telling them just what we think. Whatever the case, whenever there

But the man or woman who has God's perspective on this life and the life to come will always emerge victorious!

is a routine of imaginary confrontations, that is a good indication that bitterness has set in.

Bitterness toward God is much the same. A person who is bitter toward God cannot discuss religion objectively. There is always emotion involved. I have met a couple of self-proclaimed atheists who got so upset when the subject of God came up that they turned red! One would think that talking about something that did not exist would lend itself to an intellectually oriented discussion. But these people's atheism stemmed not from research and intellectual pursuits, but from hurt. At one time they had believed in God. But He did not act the way they thought He should, so they decided He did not exist. Such is the power of bitterness.

The Pity Party

Another common way of dealing with adversity is self-pity: "Oh my, what am *I* going to do? Nobody cares about *me* anymore. Look at *my* situation. *I* am hopeless. Before long *I* won't have any friends. *I'll* be alone. . . ." Self-pity results from focusing exclusively on oneself rather than God. Individuals suffering from self-pity have drawn an imaginary circle around themselves and their circumstances. The only people they will allow in are those who want to join them in their misery. Consequently, they do oftentimes end up alone. No one wants to be around that type of person for long. This solitude serves to reinforce their negative perspective, and they cling to it even more tightly.

It is not unusual for these people to become depressed. Hopelessness overwhelms them, and they see no reason for going on with life. Depressed persons are unable to interpret accurately the events around them. Thus, if left alone, they tend to get worse.

Responding the wrong way to adversity will always have a devastating effect. People who react in any of the ways just described will always come out the losers. It is understandable why those who are hurt react the way they do. But regardless of how understandable their response may be, if it is a wrong response, they will suffer just the same.

Holding on to anger and bitterness is always self-destructive. Both are poisons. They poison your relationships, your decision-making ability, and your testimony. You cannot carry anger and bitterness and emerge from adversity a winner. Responding incorrectly to adversity only prolongs the agony. This is especially true if there is something specific God wants to teach you. He will not let up until He has accomplished His will.

There have been times when I felt as if I was on a Ferris wheel. Round and round I would go, experiencing the same hurt over and over again. "Lord," I would say, "what are You doing? I've already been through this." It was as if He said, "You're right, and when you respond correctly, I'll let you off."

God wants to use our pain and sorrow for something positive. When we respond incorrectly, we can rest assured He will devise another way to give us a second or third chance to handle it right.

In his book *Don't Waste Your Sorrows*, Paul Billheimer states the same principle this way,

> Yielding to self-pity, depression, and rebellion is a waste of sorrow. Those who have unsuccessfully sought healing and who submit to resentment, discontent, impatience, and bitterness against God are wasting what God intended for growth in love and thus for enhanced rank in the eternal kingdom.

God intends to use adversity in our lives. That being the case, the wisest thing we can do is to learn to respond correctly. By doing so, we work with God rather than against Him.

The Right Response

I have divided this discussion into two parts. First, we will deal with how to respond to adversity that is the result of sin. Following that, we will focus on what our response should be when adversity originates with God or Satan.

The Wages of Sin

Sin always results in adversity of some form. Some types are certainly more obvious than others. And some are more devastating in their effect. But there is always a consequence of some sort, even if it is only guilt. The following are some steps I have found helpful in dealing with the consequences of sin.

1. ASSUME THE RESPONSIBILITY.

Don't look for someone else to blame. Don't think about what would have happened if someone had done something differently. Take the responsibility; own up to it. Admit to yourself that you are facing adverse circumstances because of your own doing.

2. CONFESS AND REPENT OF YOUR SIN.

To confess is to agree with God. Tell God you have sinned. Not that you have made a mistake. Not that you have had an accident. Simply agree with Him that it is sin. Then repent of your sin. Make a decision not to return to it. That may entail ending a relationship. It may mean leaving your place of employment. You may have to go back to people you have wronged and apologize. Perhaps you have stolen from someone. Repentance would involve returning what you have taken. To repent is to make every arrangement necessary not to go back to the same sin. That way God knows you are serious.

3. DO NOT COMPLAIN.

If you are suffering because of something you have done, you have no right to complain. You brought this on yourself. Don't spend your time trying to gain people's sympathy. Use your energy to get things right with God.

4. ASK GOD TO HELP YOU DISCOVER THE WEAKNESS THROUGH WHICH SIN CREEPED INTO YOUR LIFE.

Is there a flaw in your thinking? Have you adopted ideas into your philosophy of life that are contrary to Scripture? Do you have an area of insecurity you have never dealt with? Do you have friends who drag you down? Is there someone in your life who is a constant source of temptation? Questions like these can help you pinpoint the door through which sin has entered and found a resting place in your life.

5. RECOGNIZE THAT GOD WANTS TO USE THIS ADVERSITY IN YOUR LIFE.

Regardless of the source, adversity is always a tool when entrusted to the hands of the Lord. Tell Him, "Lord, I know that I am suffering because of my own doing. But I trust that You will use this time of adversity to deepen my faith and strengthen my commitment to You."

6. THANK GOD FOR NOT ALLOWING YOU TO GET BY WITH YOUR SIN.

True repentance is followed by genuine gratitude. When you see your sin for what it is and if you believe God disciplines those He loves, it makes sense to thank Him for sending adversity into your life if that is what it took to keep you from hurting yourself any further. No one enjoys adversity. But you can and should be grateful for what adversity accomplishes.

Adversity from Above and Below

Responding to adversity when it originates with God or Satan is different from merely responding to the consequences of sin. Yet, the way you respond when God is behind it and the way you respond when Satan is behind it is identical. This may come as a surprise. But think about it. Most of the time you really do not know who is behind it. And it really does not matter. What is important is your response.

Beyond that, however, another principle becomes a factor. You know if God is behind it, He is going to use it for your good. If Satan is behind it, you know he works under God's supervision. As you have seen in the life of Paul, God uses even Satan's schemes to accomplish His will. You are not pressed to discover the source, but you are expected to respond correctly.

You may think, *But shouldn't I resist the devil? Shouldn't I stand against him with Scripture and prayer?* Absolutely—when he comes at you with temptation. For you know that God has no part in tempting you. But we are not talking about temptation. The focus is adversity, unexpected tragedy, suffering. When these things occur, and you are sure it is not the direct result of your sin, here is how you should respond.

1. REAFFIRM YOUR POSITION IN CHRIST.

Remind yourself of who you are and what you have in Christ It helps to do it aloud. You can say something like this:

> I know that I am a child of God. I am saved. I have been placed into Christ. I am sealed with the Holy Spirit. My eternal destiny is determined, and nothing can change that. The LORD will never leave me or forsake me. The angel of the LORD encampeth round about me. Nothing can touch me apart from what my loving heavenly Father allows. All things will work together for my good since I love God and have been called according to His purpose in Christ Jesus.

In his book, *God's New Creation,* Jack Taylor lists 365 statements of truth about the believer. He calls them "New Creation Confessions." They came to him in a moment of his life when he, too, was struggling with adversity. He writes,

One day, far away from home and alone, I seemed to be enshrouded in a cloud of anxiety, uncertainty, and depression. I could not pinpoint the exact source of my problem, but the feelings had to do with my real standing with God. The more I thought, the more exasperated I became. At last I spoke to God these words, "I would really love to know what you think of me." The LORD began to communicate with my troubled heart urging me to go to the Word as if saying, "I have already made clear what I think of you in my Word. . . . read it!"

From that experience, Jack developed these 365 confessions. Truths such as these are essential to maintaining the right perspective on adversity. The reason is that self-esteem and confidence in God are usually the two things affected most by tragedy: "How could *God* allow this to happen to *me?*" In moments of despair you need a good strong dose of the truth to relieve your troubled heart.

2. ASK GOD TO REMOVE THE ADVERSITY FROM YOUR LIFE.

This is usually where we begin. And I am sure the Lord understands. But it is best to ask after we have regained some perspective. Paul asked that his adversity be removed. God did not chastise him for that request. God will not be displeased by your request, either. Even your prayer for mercy is an expression of dependence and faith. God is always pleased when we demonstrate our faith.

3. REAFFIRM THE PROMISE OF GOD'S SUSTAINING GRACE.

As we have seen, God may choose not to remove adversity from your life immediately. When that is the case, it is imperative that you rely on His grace rather than your own strength. People who try to endure suffering in their own strength go down under the weight of it all. Admit right up front that you do not have the power to withstand the pressure. Cry out to God for mercy. He will hear you. His grace will be sufficient moment by moment to get you through.

4. THANK GOD FOR THIS UNIQUE OPPORTUNITY TO GROW SPIRITUALLY.

You must look for God's part in your adversity, or you will miss it. You are not simply to endure suffering; you are to grow and mature through it. From the very outset you must look for the lessons God wants to teach you. The best way to develop this attitude is to thank Him every day for the spiritual growth He is bringing about in your life.

5. RECEIVE ADVERSITY AS IF IT WERE FROM GOD.

It does not matter if the adversity you are facing originated with Satan. Receive it as if it were from God. You know that nothing can happen to you unless He allows it. And if He allows it, He must certainly have a purpose in it. Therefore, as long as God is accomplishing His purpose through the adversity in your life, you can receive it as if it were from Him. When you respond to adversity as if it were from Satan, the tendency is to fight it. When it lingers, you may begin to doubt God.

I learned this principle during one of the most difficult periods of my life. After being at First Baptist Church for only a year, several deacons began a move to get me out of the church. As I prayed, I knew beyond any doubt that God wanted me to stay. Things got pretty rough for a while. People who I thought were my friends turned on me. I never knew where I stood from week to week.

On the one hand, I knew that if God wanted me to stay at FBC and they wanted me to leave, they certainly were not being led of the Spirit. That left only one option. Satan was clearly behind the controversy. Yet on the other, I knew that somehow the Lord was in it as well. One day I was in my office praying, and a thought came to me that I know now was from the Lord: *The only way to deal with this is not to look at men, but to keep your eyes on Me. It doesn't matter who says what, when, where, or how. You must see all this as coming from Me.*

From that moment on, I began thanking God for what He was doing. Things got worse before they got better. But God was faithful. He accomplished many great things through that time—both in my life and in the life of the church. In spite of all the rejection and deception, I never grew bitter. To this day I am not resentful. The thing that got me through it was trusting that somehow God was in it and that when He had accomplished His purpose, things would change. In the meantime my responsibility was to remain faithful.

As long as you are able to believe that God is involved in the adversity you are facing, you will have hope. Regardless of who initiated it, God is in it! And if He is in it, His grace for you will be sufficient. It does not make any difference who the source is. It matters very little who the messenger is. As long as you respond as if it were from God, you will come out a winner.

6. READ AND MEDITATE ON SCRIPTURES DESCRIBING THE ADVERSITIES OF GOD'S SERVANTS.

Read the story of Joseph. Put yourself in the place of Moses when he was told he could not enter the Promised Land. Look at the way God provided for Abraham when he was left with the least desirable land. Imagine how foolish Noah felt while building the ark. The Bible contains illustration after illustration of God's faithfulness in adverse circumstances. Fill your mind with these truths. Ask Him to open your eyes to the human side of these characters that you might be able to identify with their pain and their sorrow. Then dwell on Christ's promise to care for those who love Him (see Matt. 6:25–34). Just as He was faithful to those whose stories are in the Old and New Testaments, so will He demonstrate His faithfulness to you.

A Final Word

Suffering is unavoidable. It comes without warning; it takes us by surprise. It can shatter or strengthen us. It can be the source of great bitterness or abounding joy. It can be the means by which our faith is destroyed. Or it can be the tool through which our faith is deepened. The outcome hinges not on the nature or source of our adversity, but on the character and spirit of our response. Our response to adversity will for the most part be determined by our reason for living, our purpose for being on this earth, as we see it.

If you are a child of God whose heart's desire is to see God glorified through you, adversity will not put you down for the count. There will be those initial moments of shock and confusion. But the man or woman who has God's perspective on this life and the life to come will always emerge victorious!

Book Three

THE GIFT
OF
FORGIVENESS

To my loving and loyal family,
Anna, Becky, and Andy

CONTENTS

Acknowledgments

I especially want to thank my son, Andy, for his help in research and editing and my publisher, Victor Oliver, for his encouragement and assistance.

PREFACE

It was Sunday morning. As I drove toward the church, I rehearsed in my mind the events of the past months. I had been filling the pulpit as an associate pastor at the First Baptist Church of Atlanta while a committee searched high and low for a senior pastor to replace the man who had resigned. It was not long until the people began taking sides. One group wanted me as the pastor; another group wanted an older, more experienced, more well-known man. I was caught in the middle. My responsibility was simply to preach while the congregation battled it out among themselves.

The internal struggle that ensued left my family and me emotionally drained. I had been asked to leave on several occasions, and I would have been glad to go except for one reason. God said, "Stay." As my wife Anna and I prayed, we knew God was making it clear that we were to trust Him and remain where we were.

Now, after twelve months, it appeared that the end was in sight. In a very turbulent business meeting that lasted three hours I had been elected the pastor of the church. It seemed as if we had hurdled all the major obstacles. Little did I know, however, that the greatest obstacle—the obstacle of forgiveness—was yet to come.

The following pages flow from my struggle to forgive people whom I trusted and loved as my friends, yet they proved otherwise. More than anything, this book is simply an invitation to deal with the poison of an unforgiving spirit. It is a poison capable of ruining not only your life, but the lives of those around you as well. It is my prayer that in these pages you will discover the freedom that comes from putting behind you once and for all the hurts and injustices of yesterday.

You shall know the truth,
and the truth
shall make you free.

John 8:32

Chapter 1

FORGIVENESS AND FREEDOM

"Forgive him? Are you kidding? After what he has done to me? I can *never* forgive him!"

"Forgive me? How could God forgive me? You don't know what I have done."

"How could I have done such an awful thing? I can never forgive myself."

These are the confessions I hear every day as a pastor. Confessions from people who have grown up in churches, grown up with godly parents, and yet grown up without ever fully understanding God's forgiveness and its intended effect on every level of their lives.

The tragedy of all this is the bondage people find themselves in when they do not grasp the immensity of God's forgiveness. It is a bondage that stifles their ability to love and accept those they know in their hearts most deserve their love. It is a bondage that cripples marriages from their outset. It is a bondage that is often passed from generation to generation. It is a bondage that chokes out the abundant life Christ promised to those who would believe.

That is why I felt compelled to write this book on forgiveness. Only by truly understanding God's forgiveness and making it a part of their lives will people be delivered from this bondage. Only then will they be able to enjoy the freedom that ensues and be able to live the Christian life to its fullest.

What Is Forgiveness?

Forgiveness is "the act of setting someone free from an obligation to you that is a result of a wrong done against you." For example, a debt is forgiven when you free your debtor of his obligation to pay back what he owes you.

Forgiveness, then, involves three elements: *injury*, a *debt* resulting from the injury, and a *cancellation of the debt*. All three elements are essential if forgiveness is to take place. Before we look in more detail at this process, however, we need to trace the sequence of events that lead to bondage when this process is abandoned. This is important because I believe most people who suffer from an unforgiving spirit do not know that unforgiveness is the root of their problem.

All they know is that they just "can't stand" to be around certain people. They find themselves wanting to strike out at people when certain subjects are discussed. They feel uncomfortable around certain personality types. They lose their temper over little things. They constantly struggle with guilt over sins committed in the past. They can't get away from the ambivalence of hating the ones they know they should love the most. Such feelings and behavior patterns often indicate that people have not come to grips with the forgiveness of God and the implications of that forgiveness.

Taking Hostages

We are all painfully aware of what it means for somebody to be taken hostage. We are outraged when the news of such an atrocity reaches us. And yet when we refuse to forgive others (or ourselves, for that matter), there is a sense in which we hold them hostage. Let me explain.

When a person is taken hostage on the international scene, the abductors usually want something. It may be money, weapons, or the release of prisoners. The message they send, in essence is, "If you give us what we want, we will give you back what we have taken." There is always some type of condition, a ransom of some sort.

When individuals refuse to forgive others for a wrong done to them, they are saying the same thing. But instead of holding people hostage until they get their demands, they withhold love, acceptance, respect, service, kindness, patience, or whatever the others value. The message they send is this: "Until I feel you have repaid me for the wrong done to me, you will not have my acceptance." If we go back to our definition, we can see that the element missing from this scenario is *cancellation of the debt*. Persons who refuse to forgive refuse to cancel the debt.

The Real Loser

A person who has an unforgiving spirit is always the real loser, much more so than the one against whom the grudge is held. This is easy to see when we take a closer look at the things most people withhold from those they feel have wronged them. Unforgiveness, by its very nature, prevents individuals from following through on many of the specifics of the Christian life and practically necessitates that they walk by the flesh rather than by the Spirit.

Think about your own experience for a moment. Think back to the last time someone really hurt you or wronged you or took something that belonged to you, whether it was a possession or an opportunity.

Immediately following the incident, did you feel like running out and doing something kind for the person, or did you feel like retaliating? Did you consider responding in gentleness, or did you think about letting loose with some well-chosen words? Did you feel like giving in and accepting the situation, or did you feel like fighting for your "rights"?

If you were honest, you probably identified more with the latter option in each case. These are the normal responses to being hurt or taken advantage of. But think of these responses in light of what Paul says, and you will begin to understand why an improper response to injury automatically impairs a person's walk with God.

> But the fruit of the Spirit is love, joy, peace, patience, kindness, goodness, faithfulness, gentleness, self-control; against such things there is no law. . . . If we live by the Spirit, let us also walk by the Spirit.
>
> —Galatians 5:22–23,25

In a broad sense Paul's list here includes all the things we naturally want to hold hostage from the people who have hurt us. We rarely want to give our love to individuals who have hurt us. We certainly have no joy or peace when others have injured us in some way. We are not generally patient with or kind to people who have wronged us. We could go right down the list.

Paul accurately describes the responses of the unforgiving person:

> Now the deeds of the flesh are evident, which are . . . enmities, strife, jealousy, outbursts of anger, disputes, dissensions, factions, envying, . . . and things like these, of which I forewarn you just as I have forewarned you that those who practice such things shall not inherit the kingdom of God.
>
> —Galatians 5:19–21

An unforgiving spirit prevents a person from being able to walk consistently in the Spirit. The only choice is to walk according to the flesh. The consequences of such a life are devastating, and Paul discusses what will happen:

> Do not be deceived, God is not mocked; for whatever a man sows, this he will also reap. For the one who sows to his own

flesh shall from the flesh reap *corruption*, but the one who sows to the Spirit shall from the Spirit reap eternal life.

—Galatians 6:7–8, *emphasis mine*

The corruption Paul mentions has nothing to do with hell. He is talking about the consequences on this earth. If a person—believer or nonbeliever—makes decisions according to the impulses and desires of the flesh, the result will always be corruption—a wrecked and ruined life. Those persons who have not come to grips with the concept of forgiveness have by the very nature of unforgiveness set themselves up to walk according to the flesh. When that happens, they are losers every time. By withholding patience, kindness, gentleness, self-control, and the rest, the individual is held hostage by the flesh and, thus, is the ultimate loser.

A Consuming Corruption

The destructive nature of an unforgiving spirit is such that it is not limited to one relationship. Resentment and other negative feelings spill over into other relationships. This is the second reason a person with an unforgiving spirit loses out in life.

Unfortunately, people are rarely aware when hostility from one relationship affects their ability to get along with others. So they try and try—unsuccessfully—to work out their differences with others, never recognizing the real source of the problem. Once they tire of trying to change, they excuse their insensitivity as part of their personality and expect people to "work around" them emotionally speaking. They develop a take-me-or-leave-me-but-don't-try-to-change-me attitude, and in the process they hurt people they love the most.

I see this spillover most often in marital relationships. When a husband and a wife come in for marriage counseling, I begin by asking about their relationships with their parents. Almost without fail, one of them feels some bitterness or resentment toward a parent (or parents). Sometimes both of them have these feelings. Oftentimes the root of their marriage problems is found in some hostility they have been hauling around, sometimes since childhood.

In almost every case, the counselees have a legitimate complaint; they have really been wronged by their parents. But their inability or unwillingness to forgive ends up hurting them, not their parents!

The Rejection Connection

The third reason a person with an unforgiving spirit loses out in life is closely tied to the other reasons we've just discussed. When a person is wronged in some way, whether in marriage, business, friendship, or some other relationship, rejection occurs. The classic case would be when a guy breaks up with his girl friend because he has found another girl. In her struggle with rejection the girl swears she will never trust another male.

It is easy to see where hurt resulted from rejection. But if we plug this concept into other sets of circumstances, we can see it holds true in every case where forgiveness is needed. The following incident, which set my son and me at odds for years, illustrates how an unforgiving spirit has feelings of rejection at its roots.

When Andy was about fourteen, he discovered he had some musical talents. He began spending a great deal of time playing the piano, primarily by ear. That meant a great deal of pounding chords with very little melody. To me, it sounded all the same.

One day on my way upstairs I stuck my head in the living room and said, "Andy, is that all you know?" To my uninformed ear, it sounded as if he had been playing the same song for hours! He immediately stopped playing. And he never played for me again. He would wait until my wife and I would leave the house, and then he would spend hours practicing and practicing. I began hearing from others what a fine pianist Andy was, but I never heard another sound from the piano in the living room.

Some years later—when Andy was in his twenties—our conversation turned toward his music. He gave me his version of what happened in the living room that afternoon, and he confessed that he had resented me from that day on. Why? It really was not a big deal to me. I did not mean anything serious by what I said. But to Andy, as a teenager, what I communicated was this: "I do not accept you or your music."

He was too young to understand that my comment was directed at his music, not at *him* as my son, And I was too insensitive to understand that the budding young artist saw little distinction between his work and his personhood. And so I crushed him; and he held it against me. By Andy's own admission, the resentment he held in his heart toward me spilled over into other relationships in his life, primarily those having to do with authority.

What I want you to understand is that the cause of his resentment was perceived rejection. I say "perceived" because I did not intend to reject him. His response, however, was the same as if it had been intentional.

LOST AND FOUND

After years of listening to people recount how they have been hurt and mistreated by parents, spouses, kids, employers, and even pastors, I am convinced that at the beginning of each story is an experience that has been interpreted as rejection. As the rejection evolves into an unforgiving spirit, and eventually into bitterness, it takes a terrible toll. The person is left with a deep sense of emptiness, an inner sense that something is missing. Consequently, the individual seeks to regain what has been lost— and almost always in the context of relationships that are unrelated. Let me give an example to illustrate.

A counselor I know told me the following story. He said a father brought his daughter in for counseling after the father learned she had recently had an abortion. As the father began conveying his concern about the spiritual welfare of his daughter, it became apparent to my friend that the girl deeply resented her father. It was also clear that the daughter felt no remorse about what she had done, and she frankly did not want to be there.

She paid no attention to anything being said until the counselor began to explain the usual sequence of events that leads a young girl to become sexually active. Then he described what a father-daughter relationship should be like: how a father should spend time with his daughter, how he should show her proper affection and praise her for her character and accomplishments. He explained that when a father loves his daughter, she does not feel compelled to look for love the way his daughter had.

Before he could finish what he was saying, the girl interrupted. Looking at her father, she said, "You never loved me that way! You never spent time with me! You never listened to anything I had to say!"

Then to the shock of my friend, she turned to him and said, "I have never had love the way you described it, but I am willing to give anything to get it." As she spoke, she slowly slid her skirt up several inches.

An extreme example? Maybe, but not unrealistic. Some people will go to almost any extreme to find what they have lost through intentional or unintentional rejection. People harboring unresolved resentment can feel driven to explore all kinds of avenues—usually ones that are not in keeping with the Christian life.

The Waiting Game

There is a fourth reason an unforgiving spirit can devastate a life. Since the person with the unforgiving spirit is usually waiting for the other person to make restitution, a great deal of time may go by. During this time, fleshly patterns of behavior and incorrect thought processes develop. As I mentioned before, other relationships are damaged. Even after an unforgiving spirit is corrected the side effects can take years to deal with, especially in the area of relationships.

The irony of the situation is this: By refusing to forgive and by waiting for restitution to be made, individuals allow their personal growth and development to hinge on the decision of others they dislike to begin with. They allow themselves to be held hostage. They say, "If he apologizes." "If she comes back to me." "If he rehires me." "If they invite me." They play the game of waiting for others to make the first move. In the meantime they allow an unforgiving spirit to weave its way into the total fabric of their lives.

Another ironic element is that sometimes the person who has done the wrong has no idea anything is wrong. A senior in the high-school department of our church had a good relationship with my son who was serving as youth pastor at the time. Andy began to notice that Kim was not as friendly as she had been and that she became less and less involved in the youth department. He would make a point to speak to her, but his kindness was rarely returned.

After several months went by, he took the youths skiing. It so happened that late one evening on the trip Kim approached Andy and said she needed to talk. She began by apologizing for her attitude. She admitted she had been hurt by Andy and she had been holding something he said to her against him for some time. Then she asked him if he knew what he had said that hurt her so badly. Andy thought and thought and came up with nothing.

She looked surprised, reprimanded him for his insensitivity, and said, "Several months ago, I spoke to you in Sunday school and told you our family had just bought a new pet."

Andy still drew a blank.

She continued, "You asked me what we got, and I told you it was a bird. Do you remember what you said then?"

At that point Andy remembered the conversation as well as his response to the news that her family had acquired a bird. "Yes," he said, "I do remember. I told you birds were messy and asked why you didn't get something more useful like a dog."

Andy immediately apologized, and his friendship with Kim was restored. Unfortunately, months were wasted because she would not deal with her hurt, and he did not know he had done anything.

A great deal of the hurt and rejection we face is unintentional.

The seeming lack of concern on the part of those who hurt us is often not an attempt on their part to be insensitive.

Some Choose to Lose

From what we've examined in this chapter, I hope you clearly understand this: A *person who harbors unforgiveness always loses*. Regardless of how wrong the other person may have been, refusing to forgive means reaping corruption in life. And that corruption begins in one relationship including the relationship with God, and works its way into all the rest.

Holding on to hurt is like grabbing a rattlesnake by the tail; you are going to be bitten. As the poison of bitterness works its way through the many facets of your personality, death will occur— death that is more far-reaching than your physical death, for it has the potential to destroy those around you as well.

Making the Plunge

Have you been hurt? Has somebody, somewhere in your past, rejected you in such a way that you still hurt when you think about it? Do you become critical of people in your past the minute their names are mentioned? Did you leave home as a child or a college student with great relief that you were leaving, swearing you would never return?

Have you worked hard all your life not to become like your parents? Are there people in your past upon whom you would enjoy taking revenge? Have you made a pastime out of scheming about how you could get back at them or embarrass them publicly. Were you abused as a child? Maybe even molested? Did you suffer through your parents' divorce as a child? Were your parents taken from you when you were very young?

Were you forced by circumstances to pursue a different career from the one you originally wanted to pursue? Were you unable to attend the school of your choice because of financial reasons?

Were you pushed out of a job opportunity by a greedy friend? Were you promised things by your employer that never came about?

If you answered yes to any of these questions, you may be on the brink of being set free from a bondage that you did not even know was keeping you a victim. You may be about to understand for the first time why you act the way you do in certain circumstances and why you cannot seem to control your temper. You may be on the verge of receiving the God-given insight you need to restore your war-torn home—this time for good.

Whatever your situation, whatever has happened in your past, remember that you are the loser if you do not deal with an unforgiving spirit. And the people around you suffer, too.

I am writing so that you may be set free. In the process you may experience some pain. In some instances, it may be pain you have worked for years to avoid. Yet that pain is necessary for healing to take place.

It is my prayer that you will read each chapter carefully and prayerfully. It is my goal to bring old truths to bear on the damaging experiences of your life. And in doing so, I hope to give the Holy Spirit an opportunity to make you whole.

Questions for Personal Growth

1. What does the word *forgiveness* mean?

2. What are the three essential elements of forgiveness?

3. Name four reasons why the person with an unforgiving spirit is the real loser?

4. What insights have you gained with regard to your past circumstances and your present actions?

*Those who err in mind
will know the truth,
and those who criticize
will accept instruction.*

Isaiah 29:24

Chapter 2

THE BIG PICTURE

Attitudes are difficult things to change. I can remember as a child being told to "change my attitude," as if there were some button I could push that would instantly cause something to happen inside my head! In dealing with an unforgiving spirit—or a grudge as some call it—people need a big change in attitude. The following story illustrates how attitudes may actually be changed.

Once there was a boy who lived with his mother and grandfather. His grandfather was not really an elderly man, but he was confined to a wheelchair and had very little use of his arms. His face was badly scarred, and he had a difficult time swallowing his food.

Every day the little boy was assigned the task of going into his grandfather's room and feeding him lunch. This the little boy did faithfully, but not joyously. It was quite a mess to feed Grandfather.

As the boy grew into adolescence, he became weary of his responsibility. One day he stormed into the kitchen and announced that he had had enough. He told his mother, "From now on, you can feed Grandfather."

Very patiently his mother turned from her chores, motioned for her son to sit down, and said, "You are a young man now. It is time you knew the whole truth about your grandfather." She continued, "Grandfather has not always been confined to a wheelchair. In fact he used to be quite an athlete. When you were a baby, however, there was an accident."

The boy leaned forward in his chair as his mother began to cry.

She said, "There was a fire. Your father was working in the basement, and he thought you were upstairs with me. I thought he was downstairs with you. We both rushed out of the house leaving you alone upstairs. Your grandfather was visiting at the time. He was the first to realize what happened. Without a word he went back into the house, found you, wrapped you in a wet blanket, and made a mad dash through the flames. He brought you safely to your father and me.

"He was rushed to the emergency room suffering from second- and third-degree burns as well as smoke inhalation. The reason he is the way he is today is because of what he suffered the day he saved your life."

By this time the boy had tears in his eyes as well. He never knew; his grandfather never told him. And with no conscious effort on his part, *his attitude changed.* With no further complaints, he picked up his grandfather's lunch tray and took it to his room.

"Now I See . . ."

Attitudes change when we get all the facts, when we see the big picture. In this chapter and the one that follows it we will be taking a look at the big picture concerning forgiveness. We will be gathering facts that will give us the perspective we need to understand the basis of God's forgiveness.

Where It All Began

Sin creates a deficit in God's economy. Whenever there is sin, something is taken or demanded from the sinner. In Genesis 3 the serpent lost its standing in the animal kingdom because of its part in the temptation of Adam and Eve (v. 14). Adam and Eve lost the perfect harmony that once characterized their relationship (v. 16). Adam and Eve lost their home in the Garden of Eden (v. 24). Chapter 4 of Genesis records that Cain lost his ability to effectively cultivate the ground. He also lost his place among men (vv. 12–14).

We could go right through the Scriptures illustrating this principle. Whenever there is sin, the sinner loses something that is outside the sinner's power to regain.

Another principle, however, runs parallel with this one. Historically, whenever human beings sin against God, He provides a channel through which fellowship can be reestablished and maintained. This is an important concept as we look into the idea of forgiveness because we see in it God's desire to have fellowship with sinful, disobedient men and women.

This principle demonstrates God's willingness to give the human race a second chance. As we look closer at this second principle, we will see that all of history is the outworking of God's strategy to bring humankind back into fellowship. The groundwork for your forgiveness and mine was laid immediately after the first sin was committed, and God has been building on that foundation ever since then. The first clear example of this principle is in the case of Cain and Abel.

> So it came about in the course of time that Cain brought an offering to the LORD of the fruit of the ground. And Abel, on his part also brought of the firstlings of his flock and of their fat portions. And the LORD had regard for Abel and for his offering; but for Cain and for his offering He had no regard.
> —Genesis 4:3–5

The Bible does not give us all the details surrounding this narrative, but some things are clear by way of implication. First, both Cain and Abel knew that they were to bring an offering to the Lord. Second, there was a distinction between a *proper* offering and an *improper* offering. Third, Cain and Abel knew what God considered proper and improper offerings. This is evident from God's response to Cain when He said. "If you do what is right, will you not be accepted?" (4:7 NIV).

This narrative is important to our discussion because it illustrates God's desire to have fellowship with members of the human race. The implication of the text is that immediately after the Fall, God instituted a way through which His people could restore fellowship with Him. God had every right in the world, humanly speaking, to break off His relationship with humankind after Adam and Eve sinned in the Garden. But God's love for us is so strong He delayed His wrath to give us a second chance.

Looking Ahead

Another Old Testament example of God's desire to have fellowship with men and women is found in the sacrificial system as practiced in Israel. The book of Leviticus describes in detail the procedure an individual had to go through to maintain fellowship with God. To us, it seems complex; it looks as though God went out of His way to make it difficult for His people to get to Him. But the whole sacrificial system is actually a picture of God's grace because He provided a way for His people to get to Him.

Here is a brief overview of how the sacrificial system worked:

Then the LORD called to Moses and spoke to him from the tent of meeting, saying. "Speak to the sons of Israel and say to them. 'When any man of you brings an offering to the LORD, you shall bring your offering of animals from the herd or the flock. If his offering is a burnt offering from the herd, he shall offer it, a male without defect; he shall offer it at the doorway of the tent of meeting, that he may be accepted before the LORD. And he shall lay his hand on the head of the burnt offering, that it may be accepted for him to make atonement on his behalf.'"

—Leviticus 1:1–4

The sacrificial system was a reminder that the penalty for sin is death. Instead of the sinner being put to death, however, an animal was put to death. To signify that the animal was the substitute, the person offering the sacrifice placed a hand on the head of the animal. As a result, the person was accepted before the Lord. The term *accepted* denotes fellowship with Him.

The system was God's way of allowing sinful men and women to carry on a relationship with the sinless Creator. God was under no obligation to provide such a system. Yet His desire for fellowship with His people was so strong He willingly went the extra mile to make such fellowship possible.

The Cover-up

The Old Testament uses an interesting word in connection with the forgiveness of God. That word is *atonement*. In Leviticus 6 we read,

> And as a penalty he must bring to the priest, that is, to the LORD, his guilt offering, a ram from the flock, one without defect and of the proper value. In this way the priest will make atonement for him before the LORD, and he will be forgiven for any of these things he did that made him guilty.
>
> —Leviticus 6:6–7 NIV

Atonement means "to cover." It is the same Hebrew word translated "coat" in Genesis where God instructs Noah in how to build the ark: "So make yourself an ark of cypress wood; make rooms in it and coat it with pitch inside and out" (Gen. 6:14 NIV).

The significance of this term is that the sacrificial system was adequate for the time being, but it was temporary in nature. The sins of those living under the Levitical system were *covered* for the time, but not *forgiven* in the absolute sense of the word. Why not? Because the blood of animals cannot be sufficient payment for the debt incurred by sinners. The testimony of the New Testament affirms that fact:

But those sacrifices are an annual reminder of sins, because it is impossible for the blood of bulls and goats to take away sins.

—Hebrews 10:3–4 NIV

At the beginning of this chapter I said that sin creates a deficit in God's economy. Whenever there is sin, something is taken or demanded from the sinner. What God ultimately requires of the sinner as a result of the sin is death—the death of the sinner. This is clear from God's warning to Adam in the Garden:

And the LORD God commanded the man, saying, "From any tree of the garden you may eat freely; but from the tree of the knowledge of good and evil you shall not eat, for in the day that you eat from it you shall surely die."

—Genesis 2:16–17

Paul confirms this:

Therefore, just as through one man sin entered into the world, and death through sin, and so death spread to all men, because all sinned.

—Romans 5:12

As we study further in Scripture, we find that this death entails more than the giving up of physical life. It means eternal separation from God.

And if anyone's name was not found written in the book of life, he was thrown into the lake of fire.

—Revelation 20:15

What's the Holdup?

So some questions arise: If the penalty for sin is death, why did God not immediately snuff out the lives of Adam and Eve?

Did He not say that on the "day" they sinned they would "surely die"? Why does He not do the same for all sinners? What is He waiting for? Why did He provide Cain and Abel and later Israel with a system through which fellowship could be restored if sin ultimately resulted in death?

The answer is simple yet life-changing in its profundity. There is something God wants more than retribution. There is something He desires more than simply being paid back for the disrespect shown Him. God wants fellowship with us. And He was willing to put His own system of justice on hold while He made provision for sinful men and women to be rescued.

Notice I did not say God "bypassed" His system of justice. He could not do that, because the system by which He abides is an expression of His very nature. What He did, as we have seen, was to come up with a temporary system through which His own righteous standards could be served.

Is There Any Doubt?

Before we go on, consider this crucial question: Do you realize that the God of the universe desires to have fellowship with you? You may say, "But you don't know what I've done!" I know this. Whatever you have done pales into insignificance beside the sin of Adam and Eve. They brought sin into the human race (Rom. 5:12). Their sin brought about God's curse on the whole earth (Gen. 3:17). Their sin made death a reality for all that breathes, both human and animal.

Yet after all that, God still cared enough about Adam and Eve to slay an animal and make garments of skin to cover their nakedness and hide their shame (Gen. 3:21). Although their sin was not taken away, it was covered until something permanent could be done. When an animal was slain to provide the skins for Adam and Eve, a sacrificial system was begun. It was a system that would allow God and His people to have fellowship once again.

If God was willing to move that quickly to restore fellowship with Adam and Eve, does it make sense that He would move any less quickly to restore fellowship with us? And if the heavenly

Father was willing to move that quickly to restore fellowship with sinners, how much more quickly should we move to restore fellowship with those who have wronged us?

The big picture is simply this. People turned their backs on God and God immediately went to work to regain fellowship. These observations from the Old Testament should be enough to convince us that God is a God of love and forgiveness. He forgives because He desires to forgive, not because He is under some constraint. His forgiveness is not handed out on an individual basis depending upon the sin committed. On the contrary, in the Old Testament God set up a system by which *any man or woman could come to Him regardless of the sin committed.* In the New Testament we find that these same principles of forgiveness apply. (In the next chapter we will look at God's permanent solution to the problem of sin.)

His Way or Your Way?

A major hindrance to the ability to experience God's forgiveness is the unwillingness to accept God's frame of reference concerning sin and the individual's inability to do anything about it. Instead some people create for themselves a procedure for finding forgiveness and impose it upon God. In time their emotions become so attuned to their own way of thinking that it is almost impossible for them to accept any other way. Usually, their alternate systems underestimate the consequences of sin and overestimate their ability to remedy the situation.

You may be one of these people. I urge you to think about two things. First, God and God alone fully understands the reality of your sinful condition. Only God understands your need in terms of your relationship with Him. Therefore, regardless of what your mind and emotions may tell you, regardless of what may seem fair or unfair, God's plan for forgiveness is the only plan in which you can put your trust with any assurance.

Second, since that is true, are you willing to examine your heart and ask God to reveal any alternative systems you may have been clinging to? Are you willing to lay aside those things and ask God to show you *His way* to true forgiveness?

Cain decided to approach God his way, according to what made sense to him. The result of his decision was disastrous. If you insist on seeking forgiveness any way but God's, the result will be no less disastrous for you. But if you will look at your sin and God's provision for dealing with it from His perspective, you will experience freedom that comes with knowing *you are truly forgiven!*

Questions for Personal Growth

1. How does sin create a deficit in God's economy?

   What is required to balance the economy?

2. What does the word *atonement* mean?

3. What does God want more than retribution?

   Why?

4. What is the major hindrance to experiencing God's forgiveness?

   Have you been clinging to alternative systems of forgiveness?

*Through His name
everyone who believes
in Him receives
forgiveness of sins.*

Acts 10:43

Chapter 3

THE ONLY SOLUTION

ONE OF MY more memorable seminary professors had a practical way of illustrating the concept of grace for his students. At the end of his evangelism course he would hand out the exam with the caution to read it all the way through before beginning to answer it. This caution was written on the exam as well.

As we read through the exam, it became unquestionably clear to each of us that we had not studied nearly enough. The further we read, the worse it became. About halfway through, audible groans could be heard throughout the lecture hall. By the time we were turning to the last page, we were all ready to turn the exam in blank. It was impossible to pass.

On the last page, however, there was a note that read, "You have a choice. You can either complete the exam as given or sign your name at the bottom and in so doing receive an A for this assignment."

Wow! We sat there stunned. "Was he serious? Just sign it and get an A?" Slowly, the point dawned on us, and one by one we turned in our tests and silently filed out of the room. It took the rest of the afternoon for me to get over it. I had the urge to go back and check with him one more time to make sure he was serious.

When I talked with him about it afterward, he shared some of the reactions he had received through the years as he had given the same exam. There were always students who did not follow instructions and began to take the exam without reading it all the way through. Some of them would sweat it out for the entire two hours of class time before reaching the last page. Their ignorance caused them unnecessary anxiety.

Then there were the ones who would read the first two pages, become angry, turn in their paper blank, and storm out of the room. They never realized what was available. As a result, they lost out totally.

One fellow, however, topped them all. He read the entire test, including the note at the end, but he decided to take the exam anyway. He did not want any gifts; he wanted to earn his grade. And he did. He made a C+, which was amazing considering the difficulty of the test. But he could have easily had an A.

Actions and Reactions

This story vividly illustrates many people's reaction to God's solution to sin. Many are like the first group. They spend their lives trying to earn what they discover years later was freely offered to them the whole time. They spend years sweating it out, always wondering if God is listening to their pleas for forgiveness, always wondering if they have finally pushed Him too far. They hope God has forgiven them; they suppose He has. They do all they know to do to get forgiven. But insofar as God is concerned, they do not want to be presumptuous. So they live their lives with doubts.

Many people respond like the second group. They look at God's standard—moral and ethical perfection—and throw their hands up in surrender. *Why even try?* they tell themselves. *I could never live up to all that stuff.* They live the way they please, not expecting anything from God when they die. Often they decide there is no God. Their acknowledged inability to live up to His standard drives them to this conclusion. Instead of living under constant pressure and guilt, they choose to completely abandon the standard. What a shock it will be for them when they stand before God and understand for the first time what was available had they only asked!

Then there is the guy who took the test anyway. I meet people like him all the time who are unwilling to simply receive God's gift of forgiveness. Striking out to do it on their own, they strive to earn enough points with God to give them the right to look to their own goodness as a means of pardon and forgiveness. They constantly work at "evening the score" with God through their good works. "Sure, I have my faults," they say. "But God does not expect anyone to be perfect."

When it comes to forgiveness, there is no room for boasting in one's own ability. As we will see, forgiveness is not a team effort. It is not a matter of God's doing His part and us doing ours. Unlike my professor's test, in God's economy anything less than 100 percent is failing.

The Bottom Line

The bottom line is that through Christ, God did away with the problem of sin insofar as its ability to keep us from having a relationship with Him. Let's examine how He did that.

As we have discussed, the entrance of sin into the world meant that members of the human race lost physical life (a gradual process) and righteous standing before God. Fellowship with the sinless Creator was interrupted.

There was another angle to sin and its relationship to death. God demanded the life of the sinner: "For the wages of sin is death" (Rom. 6:23). Sin earned the sinner death.

Although sin deserved immediate action on God's part, God in His mercy did not immediately judge humankind. He chose to suspend judgment to give His people a second chance.

Time is the key factor. Every individual has the length of a lifetime to restore a personal relationship with God. Once life ends, however, judgment comes: "And inasmuch as it is appointed for men to die once and after this comes judgment" (Heb. 9:27).

Because of His unexplainable love, God desired (and still desires) to have fellowship with men and women. As we saw in chapter 2, He established a temporary system through which fellowship could be restored and maintained and sin could be covered—but not forgiven. Sin would have to be forgiven before the problem of sin could be solved once and for all. That is where Christ entered the picture.

God's Economy

To understand how the coming of Christ facilitated the forgiveness of sin, we must understand some basics about the nature of God. God's righteousness, that is His sinlessness and holiness, by definition set up a standard that all those who would have fellowship with Him must meet. To put it another way, certain things must be true about people to be acceptable to God.

When I say this standard is set up by definition of His righteous nature, I mean that God did not arbitrarily establish this standard as we would establish the rules of a game. If that were the case, He could just change His standard and everybody would be acceptable. God's righteous standard flows from His unalterable nature.

God's righteousness can be compared to fire. Certain things must be true of any material that is to survive being exposed to fire. The nature of the fire determines what will and will not last.

God's righteousness can be compared to water. Certain things must be true of any animal that is to live under water. The nature of water demands that these things be true. Any animal that does not meet these standards will not survive. Furthermore, the standards cannot be changed because they flow from the very nature of water.

So it is with God. His nature demands that certain things be true of those who desire to have uninterrupted fellowship with

Him and who desire to someday dwell in His very presence. Specifically, His nature demands sinlessness, or perfection, but the presence of sin makes us unacceptable to Him. Paul expresses this concept when he writes, "For all have sinned and fall short of the glory of God" (Rom. 3:23).

Our sin causes us to "fall short." Our sin disqualifies us in light of God's standard. Sin puts us in a relationship with God wherein we owe Him something. We must pay for what we have done much like common criminals must repay society for the crimes committed. Thus, the solution must in some way remove the consequences of our sin and restore us to a state in which our sin is no longer counted against us. Somehow, what was done through sin must be undone. So, how can that happen? How can the sinful be made the sinless?

All Right Already!

By now you are probably wondering why we don't move along a little faster. I have repeated some significant points because we need to understand as much as is humanly possible about God's forgiveness. Until it all clearly fits together, we are not likely to abandon the unbiblical ways of thinking we have grown comfortable with through the years. Until we see how the whole thing fits together, it will be difficult for us to change our prayer habits. And until we are confronted with (and have accepted) God's unconditional goodness to us, we will have a difficult time forgiving others.

Now You See It . . . Now You Don't

To help us better understand how God can undo what has been done insofar as our sinfulness is concerned, we can look at one aspect of our present legal system. If people are convicted of a serious crime, such as a felony, they lose their civil rights. They are not allowed to vote. They are not allowed to hold public office. These rights can be restored only through the granting of a pardon by a governor of a state or by the president if it is a federal case.

The interesting thing about a pardon is that it is not conditional upon guilt. That is, when someone receives a pardon, it is not necessarily an indication of innocence. It simply means that the person does not have to pay the penalty for the offense; there are no legal or civil consequences. For example, when President Ford pardoned Richard Nixon, it was out of respect for the office he had held, not because Nixon was proved to be innocent. According to the law, then, a governor or the president in effect has the power to allow a guilty individual to go free; the crime is never paid for; the person suffers none of the regular consequences.

Like persons convicted of a felony, we lost our citizenship. Sin resulted in the forfeiture of our right to enter the kingdom of God. Like a governor, God has the power to pardon those who are guilty. There is one major difference, though. In our system of law a crime does not have to be paid for. A governor can pardon a convicted person, and that is the end of it. But the nature of God requires that those who dwell in His presence must be sinless, which means we must have committed no sins or have no sin that has not been paid for. God's nature will not allow Him to simply overlook sin. Sin carries with it a penalty that must be paid. The author of Hebrews sums it up this way: "Without the shedding of blood there is no forgiveness" (Heb. 9:22 NIV). On the other hand, once sin has been paid for, nothing hinders our relationship with God.

Think of it like this: A builder cannot make the payments on his bank loan. He goes to the president of the bank and apologizes for being so irresponsible. He asks the president to forgive him and then expresses an interest in doing business with the bank in the future. Regardless of how kind and understanding the president of the bank is, the nature of his job restricts him from simply patting the builder on the back and saying, "No hard feelings. We understand. Forget about the money and try to be more careful next time." It does not work that way. The builder will not be in good standing with the bank until his debt is paid.

Our sin and the debt that resulted left us in a position wherein we needed both *pardon* and *payment*. The situation was hopeless. We did not have the potential to regain for ourselves what was necessary to make us acceptable to God. It was checkmate; the game was over; there were no more moves for us to make. And it was nobody's fault but our own. Yet in our darkest hour, God gave us an extra Player and, in doing so, a second chance.

Bad News/Good News

As you think about what has been said so far, you will notice that neither the *degree* of sin nor the *quantity* of sin has been mentioned. That is because both are irrelevant. Yet if you are like many people I talk to every week, these are the two issues you may be wrestling with as you question God's willingness or ability to forgive you. The bad news is the good news. It took only one less-than-perfect move to forfeit the right to a relationship with God. That is the bad news. The good news is that there are no degrees of separation.

Perhaps this example will clarify what I mean. It is similar to the situation of two people who lost their jobs. One was fired for coming into work late; the other for stealing from the cash register and falsifying his time card. What the first guy did was not even in the same league with the actions of the second. But fired is fired, and neither had a job.

If you can understand that everyone is in the same boat in terms of separation from God, it will be far easier for you to accept God's solution to the sin problem. Paul expresses the same idea:

> So then as through one transgression there resulted condemnation to *all* men, even so through one act of righteousness there resulted justification of life to *all* men. For as through the one man's disobedience the *many* were made sinners, even so through the obedience of the One the *many* will be made righteous.
>
> —Romans 5:18–19, *emphasis mine*

Paul lumps everybody into one of two categories, *condemned* or *justified*. He does not mention quantity or quality of sins.

Another truth in this passage is extremely important to recognize. We have seen how our sin incurred for us a debt that was nonnegotiable in view of the nature of God and was unpayable in regard to our ability to pay it. Yet what Paul implies in these verses, and is straightforward about saying in other places, is that just as one man's (Adam's) sin had the potential to affect every man and woman, so one Man's (Christ's) righteous act had the potential to undo what had been done by Adam. If one man had the potential to damage the entire human race, certainly the Son of God had the potential to make everything right. In other words, Christ had the ability to cancel our indebtedness by assuming our debt and paying the penalty that was required.

Paid in Full

Using the analogy of indebtedness when talking about sin and its consequences fits perfectly with the New Testament's approach to the subject. Paul writes,

> And when you were dead in your transgressions and the uncircumcision of your flesh, He made you alive together with Him, having forgiven us all our transgressions . . .

And then he illustrates what he has just written by adding:

> . . . having canceled out the certificate of debt consisting of decrees against us and which was hostile to us; and He has taken it out of the way, having nailed it to the cross.
> —Colossians 2:13–14

Paul's use of the word *having* implies the idea of means. We could restate verse 13 this way: "He made you alive together with Him by means of forgiving us all our transgressions." Forgiveness is the way in which God made us alive.

The phrase "having forgiven us all our transgressions" means the same thing as "having canceled out the certificate of debt consisting of decrees against us." Forgiveness, then, is the cancellation of a debt.

Paul is referring to a practice familiar to his first-century audience. In those days a man who owed another man would write out a *certificate of debt*. The certificate would include all that was owed along with the terms of payment. The debtor, the lender, and a witness would sign the document.

In a sense each of us had a certificate of debt against us, and Christ's death canceled the certificate. Paul says, "He has taken it out of the way, having nailed it to the cross." Often an ex-debtor would nail up his canceled certificate of debt in a public place so all would know his debt had been paid. Paul picks up on this practice and says that our debt was nailed to the cross with Christ signifying that it had been paid in full; it was no longer legally binding.

If we have correctly understood Paul's analogy, there should be no question that total forgiveness of sin comes through Christ. And that includes all sins—the ones we have already committed and the ones we will commit. From the perspective of the Cross, they were all future. And it was from that perspective they were dealt with. So Paul could say to believers he had never met, "He made you alive together with Him, having forgiven us all our transgressions" (Col. 2 :13). He did not need to know how many sins the Colossian believers had committed. He did not need to know the nature of their sins. All he needed to know was that they had approached God for forgiveness through Christ. That was enough then—and that is enough for us today!

I can say to you, with perfect assurance, that if you have trusted Christ's death on the cross to be the payment for your sins, your sins are forgiven. I don't know you any more than Paul knew all the Colossians or Ephesians or Romans who read his letters. But it does not matter. We are all condemned apart from Christ, and we can all be forgiven through Him. No matter what you have done, how many times you have done it, or who you hurt in the process, God has forgiven you.

If doubts about your particular situation remain in your mind, it should be obvious that you are still thinking about forgiveness according to your own artificial standards. If what I have said thus far is true, through Christ you have forgiveness (Eph. 1:7). Right now as you read, you are a forgiven child of God. The guilt you continue to carry around because of past sins is unnecessary. Later I'll explain how to deal with false guilt. But to begin with, you must accept the truth about your past hopelessness as well as your present forgiven state. *You are forgiven.*

"My God, My God"

At this point you may be asking, "If our sin demanded a death—but this death involved eternal separation from God—how could Christ pay the penalty for our sin and still sit at the Father's right hand? If He took our place, it would seem He should go to hell. That is where we were heading, wasn't it?" In searching for answers, we are once again confronted with God's insatiable desire to restore fellowship with humankind. As we will see, Christ did have to suffer the punishment we would have had to suffer.

Mark described the events surrounding the crucifixion of Jesus:

> And when the sixth hour had come, darkness fell over the whole land until the ninth hour. And at the ninth hour Jesus cried out with a loud voice, "Eloi, Eloi, lama sabachthani?" which is translated, "My God, My God, why hast Thou forsaken Me?"
>
> —Mark 15:33–34

While hanging on the cross, Christ experienced for our sake separation from His heavenly Father. The separation was so deep that Christ even addressed Him differently. Until that time He had spoken of God as His Father. All of a sudden He cried out, "My God." There was no longer the intimacy, the warmth, or the closeness. Gone was the assurance He had just a few hours earlier when He said to His disciples,

Behold, an hour is coming, and has already come, for you to be scattered, each to his own home, and to leave Me alone; and yet I am not alone, because the Father is with Me.

—John 16:32

Why the change? Because sin required separation from the Sinless One. In taking on the responsibility of our sin (2 Cor. 5:21), Christ voluntarily put Himself in a position in which He no longer had fellowship with the heavenly Father. Just as Adam was cast out of the Garden, so Christ, in a sense, was cast out of His privileged position with God.

Think for a moment. What if the person you loved the most—the person whose approval you valued more than anyone's—suddenly walked out on you? You may have experienced pain just like that, the type of pain you would not wish on your worst enemy. Yet Christ volunteered to suffer that kind of pain multiplied ten thousand times because it was the only way God could get you back. It was the only way He could arrange for your forgiveness. God wanted you, and He wanted you badly!

After becoming sin for our sakes and suffering the punishment we deserved, Christ was accepted back into fellowship with His heavenly Father.

But He, having offered one sacrifice for sins for all time, sat down at the right hand of God, waiting from that time onward until His enemies be made a footstool for His feet. For by one offering He had perfected for all time those who are sanctified.

—Hebrews 10:12–14

Christ was accepted back into fellowship based upon His own righteousness. He needed no sacrifice for His sin. He had no debt that needed paying. Because He was sinless, He had the right through His own merit to sit at the right hand of God.

Take It or Leave It

There we have it, Christ is God's solution for dealing with sin. Only through Christ can we find forgiveness. But once it has been found, it is a settled issue—past sin, present sin, and future sin. The details of what we have done, why we did it, and how many times we did it are irrelevant. Sin is sin; lost is lost; paid is paid; forgiven is forgiven. Either we have it, or we don't.

Are there sins from your past that continue to hang over you like a dark cloud? When you pray, does something inside you cause you to doubt that God is going to listen to you because of your past? Do you feel that your potential for the kingdom of God has been destroyed because of your past disobedience? If you answered yes to any of these questions, you have not yet come to grips with God's solution to your sin. You are still holding on to a way of thinking that will keep you in bondage the rest of your life. You have set yourself up to live a defeated life in which you will never reach your potential for the kingdom of God.

I want you to be free. More important, God wants you to be free. And because He does, He sacrificed what was dearest to Him. I encourage you to meditate on the concepts of this chapter. Ask God to sink them deep into your subconscious so that they become the grid through which you interpret the experiences of life. Not until you are able to see yourself as a forgiven child of God will you begin to enjoy the fellowship that the death of His Son made possible.

Questions for Personal Growth

1. Name three ways people may react to God's offer of forgiveness.

   What is wrong with these reactions?

2. Explain how God's forgiveness is like an executive pardon.

   Why is the guilt of the person who is pardoned *not* an issue?

3. Why does the *degree* or *quantity* of sin make no difference in the judgment of guilt?

   Why is forgiveness a settled issue—even for future sins— once it has been found?

4. What past sins are still hanging over your head?

   Have you come to grips with God's solution?

Your faith
has saved you;
go in peace.

Luke 7:50

Chapter 4

FAITH AND FORGIVENESS

ONE OF THE most difficult habits for me to break was playing what I call the time game. It went like this. I would sin. I
would feel guilty. I would ask God to forgive me. Then, depending on the magnitude of the sin, I would allow a certain amount
of time to pass before I would ask God for things again. Sometimes I would wait an hour. Sometimes I would wait until the
next day. I realize now that this was my way of punishing myself. But on the conscious level, I did it out of respect for God. I
mean, God is forgiving and all that, but I felt I needed to give Him
a little time to cool off before I started right back in with Him; I
could not go on as if nothing happened. I understood all about
the theology of forgiveness, but what I knew in my head had not
taken hold of my heart and my emotions and my actions.

Many people share this problem. They nod their heads in agreement as the preacher expounds on the unconditional love of God
and His desire to restore fellowship with lost men and women.
Then you ask them, "Do you think God has really forgiven you?"
And they reply, "I hope so," or "I guess we really don't know until
the end." For many Christians, a seed of doubt remains that all
their personal sins are really forgiven, that God is genuinely not
holding anything against them.

Until we are sure, until we settle the issue of forgiveness once and for all, two things will always be true. First, we will never have much confidence when we petition our heavenly Father. We will always feel that God is holding something against us. Second, we will put others on the same scale we put ourselves on. Since we are always trying to do something to ensure our forgiveness, we will subconsciously pressure others to perform to gain our forgiveness. We will have a tendency to remind others of their failures and their need to make up for them in some way.

A believer who functions in a "payback" mode in relation to personal standing before God is like a man who wins a car and continues to walk everywhere he goes. People comment on how beautiful it is, and he agrees. He keeps it clean. He reads the owner's manual several times until he is thoroughly familiar with every facet of the car. Yet it does not accomplish for him what it was intended to accomplish. And it is all his fault. The car is no less his. But practically speaking, he might as well not own it. So it is with the believer who does not accept the forgiveness of God.

Making Sure

God wants us to live with perfect assurance that we are completely forgiven. To facilitate this, He has provided directions for making sure His gift of forgiveness has been applied to each individual's situation. In chapter 3 we looked at the mechanics of forgiveness, how it all fits together. In this chapter we will look closely at the door through which each individual must pass to become a partaker of God's forgiveness.

My purpose here is twofold: to provide assurance for some and instruction for others. I want those of you who have passed through this door to walk away with perfect assurance that you have no need to ever doubt your forgiveness again, because you have done it God's way. For those of you who may never have understood exactly how to get in on God's plan for forgiveness, I want to clarify it so that you, too, can share in it.

If the last chapter can be thought of as putting together the elements of a contract, this chapter can be approached like the signing, the time when the lawyer points to the line at the bottom and hands you the pen to sign your name. Only then do the conditions of the legal document apply to you.

In the same way, God has left us instructions as to how we are to sign His contract for forgiveness. Yet many Christians have a tendency to complicate them, add to them, and attempt to redefine the terms. But if what we have seen so far is true, that God intensely desires fellowship with us, it makes sense that He would keep the instructions as simple as possible.

The Dotted Line

The Old Testament Levitical laws delineated how an individual became a beneficiary of God's offer of atonement. Let's look once again at the sacrificial system:

> And he shall lay his hand on the head of the burnt offering, that it may be accepted for him to make atonement on his behalf.
>
> —Leviticus 1:4

A man had to bring a sacrifice that met certain standards and sacrifice it on the altar. As I pointed out in chapter 2, not only did the one making the sacrifice have to bring an animal, he had to place his hand on its head as it was sacrificed. Thus, he identified with the dying animal, and God's promise of atonement was appropriated to his account.

What, then, is the New Testament equivalent to the placing of the hand on the head of the sacrifice? Just as the Old Testament saints had to have a way of appropriating God's promises concerning forgiveness, so must we.

The point of identification for New Testament Christians is *faith*. Perhaps a better word is *trust*. To make God's gift of forgiveness our own, we must exercise faith. We must trust Him to apply His work through Christ to our account when we sign on the dotted line of the certificate of pardon.

Now we need to consider something. Do we realize that every time we play the time game or whatever games we play with God, we are turning our backs on His means of ensuring our forgiveness and creating our own? What is worse, we are abandoning a system of faith for a system of works.

When we punish ourselves, whether it is by depriving ourselves of something or doing more than what is expected in some area, we treat God as if He requires some penance for our sin. We act as if a demonstration of our sorrow earns forgiveness for us. We may feel better about ourselves when we demonstrate our sorrow in some way, but self-punishment has nothing to do with God's willingness to forgive. It has nothing to do with forgiveness at all. Yet every time we consciously or subconsciously work out some trade-off with God in regard to sin, we are abandoning His way for our way.

If we have placed our trust in God's system of forgiveness, we live in a forgiven state. From God's perspective, that means there is no difference between the sins we have committed, are committing, and will commit. None! Remember, forgiven is forgiven. In one sense, living in a state of forgiveness can be compared to having a checking account with unlimited funds available. In that financial condition we do not have to ask someone else to pay our debts for us. It would be impossible for us to incur debts as long as we write checks and continue to draw on our account.

This is exactly Paul's point when he writes:

And the Law came in that the transgression might increase; but where sin increased, grace abounded all the more, that, as sin reigned in death, even so grace might reign through righteousness to eternal life through Jesus Christ our Lord.
—Romans 5:20–21

There is always more grace than there is sin. Regardless of what is done or how many times it is done, it is already covered by God's grace. That is His willingness to consider it paid for in view of Christ's death. To work out our own system of merit is to say that God's grace is not sufficient for our sin, that He needs our help in dealing with our sin.

Our natural tendency is toward a work ethic in terms of our forgiveness. We find it difficult not to do *something* on our behalf. We are quick to give lip service to concepts such as *forgiveness comes through faith* and *we can do nothing to merit forgiveness*, but when it comes down to everyday living, we revert to a works plus faith system. That being the case, we need to understand the nature of faith and how it functions as the door into the realm of forgiveness. When we have made this idea our own, our behavior will be transformed. Our relationship with God and with others will be in accordance with what God intends for us, not what we intend for ourselves.

"I Believe! I Think?"

What is faith? What does it involve? These may seem to be somewhat elementary questions, but Christians answer in various ways and rarely do they respond with answers that fit the biblical data. A whole host of people seem to be confused about whether or not they have *really* believed. On the other hand, some people are certain that they believe, but when pressed for details, they are not exactly sure *what* they believe; the content of their faith is undefined. Confusion or a lack of assurance in this area logically leads to confusion and doubts about forgiveness as well.

The use of the term *believe* in connection with forgiveness is not parallel to common uses of the term. For instance, someone might say, "I believe it will snow tonight." In that case the term *believe* carries with it the idea of "calculated hope." That is, there is no guarantee it will snow; it is just a personal impression. Or a person might say, "I believe in God." In this case *believe* denotes mental assent to an idea. There is no sense of trust or commitment, just an acceptance of facts. (For a more complete discussion of this idea, see H. Phillip Hook, "A Biblical Definition of Saving Faith:" *Bibliotheca Sacra* [April 1964]).

If we take these two unbiblical uses of the term *believe* and apply them to a discussion of forgiveness, we can understand how an individual can express belief in something and yet have no personal assurance. A person can say, "I believe God forgave me of my sin," and then turn right around and say, "I hope I am forgiven." There really is no contradiction for the person who uses the term to refer to a calculated hope.

In the same way an individual who understands faith as mental assent to facts can say, "I believe God offers forgiveness through Christ," and yet have never had God's forgiveness applied to personal sin. Think about that. A man or a woman can verbally express faith and not be forgiven. The problem is that neither has expressed biblical faith.

Biblical Faith

In discussing the meaning of biblical faith, the term *trust* should be substituted whenever *faith* or *believe* is being used in connection with forgiveness or salvation in general. *Webster's Third New International Dictionary* defines *trust* as

> assured reliance on some person or thing: a confident dependence on the character, ability, strength, or truth of someone or something.

The concept of trust denotes personal involvement. It assumes a relationship of some sort between the one expressing trust and the person or thing being trusted. The difference between belief and trust is the difference between acknowledging that the bridge is capable of holding a person's weight, and actually walking out on the bridge. The former is simply the acknowledgment of something, with no involvement on the part of the one expressing faith; the latter is actual dependence.

Biblical faith, the type of faith that serves as the door to forgiveness, assumes a relationship of actual dependence and reliance. To state it in *Webster's* terms, biblical faith, or trust, is the assured reliance on God: A confident dependence on the character, ability, strength, and truth of God and His promises.

The biblical support for this understanding of the term *believe* comes from a grammatical construct that occurs repeatedly when faith is spoken of in connection with forgiveness and salvation. This construct consists of the Greek word that means "believe" followed by a little word that is translated "in" or "on," depending on the context of the passage and the Bible version used.

I emphasize the use of these two words together because the expression was original with the New Testament writers. They used it forty-five times. Yet there is no parallel to this construction in either the Greek version of the Old Testament or the secular Greek literature of the day. (For more on this, see Gerald F. Hawthorne, "The Concept of Faith in the Fourth Gospel," *Bibliotheca Sacra* [April 1959]).

This means that the New Testament writers had to develop terminology as original as their message. So John wrote the following:

But as many as received Him, to them He gave the right to become children of God, even to those who *believe in* His name.

—John 1:12, *emphasis mine*

Now when He was in Jerusalem at the Passover, during the feast, many *believed in* His name, beholding His signs which He was doing.

—John 2:23, *emphasis mine*

The object of biblical faith, as regards forgiveness, is always the person or words of Jesus, by "object" I mean what people are being asked to put their faith in. For example, in the statement, "Trust the car to get you there," the car is the object of faith. This is an important point because many people have faith, but it is directed in all sorts of inappropriate directions—or no direction at all.

The object of forgiving faith must be Christ, not simply God, the goodness of God, or faith itself. Jesus points to this truth when He says,

> Let not your heart be troubled; believe in God, believe also in Me. . . . I am the way, and the truth, and the life; no one comes to the Father, but through Me.
>
> —John 14:1,6

Jesus parallels *believing in Him* with *believing in God*. Then He turns right around and says that "no one" gets to God except through Him.

I mention this because many people have faith *in God*, yet have never expressed faith *in Christ*. I meet men especially who express faith in God, but they leave Christ out of the picture altogether. They have faith, but the object of their faith is wrong or, perhaps I should say, limited.

Many people have faith in another god. They often respond by saying something to the effect that "all religions lead to God; you choose your way, and I'll choose mine." This sounds so just and fair. And once again there is a genuine expression of faith. But it is faith man's way, not God's. It is real faith without a real foundation. It is sincere, but uninformed, faith. Forgiveness is available only to the man or woman who has put personal trust in Christ. For faith to accomplish its intended purpose, it must be focused in the right direction.

The New Testament writers were calling people to place their trust in the person of Jesus Christ for the forgiveness of their sins and the promise of eternal life. They were asking people to rely on or depend on Christ as the way to God and thus to forgiveness of sin. It was more than acknowledging that Christ was from God. It was more than hoping that what He said was true. It was a personal commitment to dependency upon Him for forgiveness. It was a matter of casting hopes for eternity upon the claims and promises of Jesus Christ. Such faith was (and still is) the way to forgiveness.

For God so loved the world, that He gave His only begotten Son, that whoever *believes* in Him should not perish, but have eternal life.

—John 3:16, *emphasis mine*

Appropriating the Gift

God's gift of forgiveness must be appropriated; that is, it must be accepted on an individual basis. Although it is a universal offer, it has no effect on the sin debt of a man or a woman who has not personally put trust in Christ. It is like a paycheck that is never picked up; it is like a gift certificate that is not redeemed; it is like a lifeline that is ignored by a drowning person.

Christ creatively communicated the concept of appropriation. Through the use of word pictures and parables, He drove home His point to "put your trust in Me." He told the woman at the well to ask for "living water" (John 4:10). He instructed the Jews to come to Him to receive "life" (John 5:40). He told one group they would have to "eat the flesh of the Son of Man and drink His blood" (John 6:53). To the leaders of the Jews, He said, "If anyone keeps My word he shall never see death" (John 8:51). He presented Himself to the Pharisees in this way: "I am the door; if anyone enters through Me, he shall be saved, and shall go in and out, and find pasture" (John 10:9). He used every conceivable illustration to show His audience that they needed to personally and individually appropriate God's gift of eternal life for themselves.

Christ constantly reiterated the need to appropriate His offer because the Jewish mind-set was such that the Jews believed they were automatically included in God's plan simply because of their nationality. Their confusion was similar to the confusion I find in many people today. Most people want to avoid the subject of accountability to God. Hearing the gospel may be bearable, but making a decision to place their trust in Christ to be the payment for their sin is going a step too far. They would much rather go on thinking about God as some benevolent force in the sky who loves everybody and who would not dare send anybody to hell. What they overlook is their responsibility to appropriate, through faith, God's gift of forgiveness.

What About You?

That brings us to some important questions. Has there been a time in your life when you personally placed your trust in the death of Christ to be the payment for your sin? Have you appropriated His payment for your debt? Have you tasted the living water? Have you walked through the door that leads to salvation? Have you received eternal life?

Remember, *knowing* the truth is not enough. Understanding what Christ did is only the first step. Forgiveness comes through *trusting* in Christ. Regardless of what you have done or how many times you have done it or who you hurt in the process, complete forgiveness is available if you are willing to receive it. But it is available only through the death of Christ.

If, on the other hand, you know that you have placed your trust in the death of Christ for the payment of your sin, I can say to you with full assurance, "You are forgiven!"—past, present, and future. No more saying, "I hope so" or "I think so." You can say, "I *know* so!"

Memorials and Reminders

You may be thinking, *That is easy for you to say, but I am plagued by memories of the past. Every time I pray I think about the things I have done, and I feel alienated from God. I cannot pray with any confidence or assurance.*

If that is your situation, let me offer a practical exercise that will turn things around for you. First, you must settle in your mind once and for all that your sins are forgiven; that God is in no way holding them against you; that from His perspective, they are no longer obstacles to fellowship. That takes care of the mind aspect, now for the emotions.

Second, you must begin to view your past failures as reminders of God's grace. Your past sins should become memorials to the grace of God in life. When Satan accuses you of being unworthy because of things you have done in the past, you can respond by saying (and I recommend actually speaking out loud), "That is exactly right. I did do that, and that's not all. But before I ever committed my first sin Jesus Christ died and paid for my sins—not just the ones you have reminded me of—all of them. Now they stand in my past as memorials, reminders, of God's goodness and grace toward me. Thanks for the reminder."

This may seem like just a mental exercise, but more important, it is also a confession of truth. It confesses the truth you need to combat the lies of Satan. In time you will be able to rejoice at the thought of your past in connection with the grace of God as it was demonstrated at Calvary. Soon what once destroyed your assurance will become your greatest source of assurance.

As we close this chapter, I want to ask you one more time if you know for sure that you have expressed personal trust in the death of Christ for the payment of your sins. If not, there is a sense in which God just slid His eternal contract in front of you and now waits for you to sign. You can do that right where you are by simply confessing your sins and telling Him that you are putting your trust in His Son's death to be the payment for your sins. Once you do that, *you are forgiven!*

Questions for Personal Growth

1. Explain the time game and give some examples of how you may have played it?

2. How does *faith* function as the door to forgiveness?

3. Biblical faith involves faith in the person or words of whom? Explain why "faith in God" is a limited faith.

4. How is forgiveness appropriated?

Have you personally trusted in the death of Christ for payment of your sins?

Father, forgive them;
for they do not know
what they are doing.

Luke 23:34

Chapter 5

OUR FORGIVING FATHER

W HEN MY CHILDREN were younger, we would have family meetings to discuss chores, summer plans, or other family business. Although they were for the most part planning sessions, when I would "call" the meetings, my kids would usually look at me with great concern and say, "Did we do something wrong?"

I was puzzled by their reaction until my wife pointed out that the tone of my voice was very serious when I announced the meetings, much like it was when I disciplined the kids. So it was natural for them to respond the way they did.

My kids' attitude is similar to that of many believers when they have to "do business" with God. They come to Him confident of only one thing—they have blown it, they have done something wrong and forgotten to ask God to forgive them. They know all about the substitutionary death of Christ and all that, but they picture God as an angry old man who just puts up with them. I have talked with folks who even make a differentiation between Christ's attitude toward them and the Father's. They view Christ as the Friend who is working to hold back the wrath of God the Father. They understand Christ's role, as the One who paid for their sins, to mean that He is the only One preventing God from giving them what they really deserve. The assumption is that God wishes He could give them what they deserve, in spite of Christ.

You may never have pictured God the Father exactly like that. But how do you picture Him when you think about your sin? What do you think His expression is when you come to Him with the same old sin time and time again? What do you think His attitude is toward you in light of your failures? What do your emotions tell you when you contemplate these questions? Like most Christians, you would probably acknowledge that God loves you. But do you think He *likes* you? Or do you think He just puts up with you because, after all, His Son did die for you?

For many people, these are especially difficult questions. The term *Father* does not bring with it feelings of love and acceptance. Instead it conjures up feelings of fear, dread, hurt, and disappointment. I have counseled with enough people to know that these feelings associated with an earthly father have the potential of robbing them of the assurance of forgiveness the heavenly Father sacrificed so deeply for them to experience.

We have seen a great deal of biblical evidence to illustrate that our heavenly Father desires to have fellowship with each of us. He desired that while we were still sinners, still separated by the debt of sin. Paul writes, "But God demonstrates His own love toward us, in that while we were yet sinners, Christ died for us" (Rom. 5:8). Until all aspects of this verse sink deep into our emotional being, we will never be free of the feelings of condemnation that accompany sin. The strategy that secured our forgiveness was God's idea; He initiated it. He wants us for His very own.

So What's New?

We are not the first generation to struggle with a distorted view of God's attitude toward sinners. The Jews of Jesus' day had the same misperception. From the premise that God could not tolerate sin along with the guidelines of the Ten Commandments, they developed a system to rate where people stood with God based on the degree of their sin. The worse the sin, the less acceptable a person was. In time this thinking developed to the point where God was perceived as "despising" sinners altogether.

In addition, those whose job or position in life kept them from remaining ceremonially clean as prescribed in Leviticus were considered unacceptable. Shepherds, tax collectors, and butchers were included in this category.

As a result, two mind-sets polarized the Jews of Jesus' day. One group—the majority of the people—felt as if God would never accept them because they could not live righteous and ceremonially clean lives. The other group thought their personal righteousness was enough to make them acceptable. They looked down upon and despised the others, the "sinners."

To correct this thinking, Jesus told a series of parables. The last in the series we know as the parable of the prodigal son. Christ's motivation in telling this parable was to explain to His contemporaries His Father's true attitude toward sinners. We know this from the way the parable is introduced:

> Now all the tax-gatherers and the sinners were coming near Him to listen to Him. And both the Pharisees and the scribes began to grumble, saying, "This man receives sinners and eats with them." And He told them this parable.
>
> —Luke 15:1–3

The religious leaders could not understand how a Man who said He was from God could be so attractive to and attracted to such unholy, unclean people. They thought, *God has rejected these people. So why does this prophet spend so much time with them?* Christ's actions did not fit with their notion of God the Father's attitude toward sinners. So Christ set out to straighten them out.

Changing The Picture

By looking at this insightful parable, we can pick up on God's attitude toward sinners and His motivation for sending Christ to die. I believe it is the best illustration of the forgiving nature of our heavenly Father in the whole Bible.

It is my prayer that through this chapter God will begin to deal with you on an emotional level so that whatever is keeping you from experiencing the joy and peace of knowing you are forgiven will be put to rest. Whether you are a victim of incorrect teaching or you were mistreated by your earthly father—whatever the stumbling block may be—God wants to take it out of the way and flood you with the assurance of His forgiveness and acceptance. He wants you to live with a sense of security and intimacy with Him.

Take some time to refamiliarize yourself with the parable.

A certain man had two sons; and the younger of them said to his father, "Father, give me the share of the estate that falls to me." And he divided his wealth between them.

And not many days later, the younger son gathered everything together and went on a journey into a distant country, and there he squandered his estate with loose living.

Now when he had spent everything, a severe famine occurred in that country, and he began to be in need. And he went and attached himself to one of the citizens of that country, and he sent him into his fields to feed swine. And he was longing to fill his stomach with the pods that the swine were eating, and no one was giving anything to him.

But when he came to his senses, he said, "How many of my father's hired men have more than enough bread, but I am dying here with hunger! I will get up and go to my father, and will say to him, 'Father, I have sinned against heaven, and in your sight; I am no longer worthy to be called your son; make me as one of your hired men.'"

And he got up and came to his father. But while he was still a long way off, his father saw him, and felt compassion for him, and ran and embraced him, and kissed him. And the son said to him, "Father, I have sinned against heaven and in your sight; I am no longer worthy to be called your son." But the father said to his slaves, "Quickly bring out the best robe and put it on him, and put a ring on his hand and sandals on his feet; and bring the fattened calf, kill it, and let us eat and be merry; for this son of mine was dead, and has come to life again; he was lost, and has been found." And they began to be merry.

—Luke 15:11–24

Jesus gives us this parable of the lost son to help us understand God the Father's attitude toward us when we sin against Him. Since He illustrates His point by reference to a father-son relationship where the son has sinned against the father, it should be obvious that the message is for those who are already of the household of faith, that is, believers. It is particularly aimed at those persons living under the awesome load of uncertainty of knowing they have displeased God.

A Worse Case Scenario

When we understand the culture of the day, we see that Jesus could not have pictured the prodigal in a more degrading manner. First of all, in his selfish egotism he asked for his share of the inheritance. The custom was for the father to give the inheritance at the time he chose. It would have been unheard of for a son, especially a younger son, to ask for his inheritance. Jesus' audience would have viewed his actions as a sign of great disrespect, maybe even as grounds for disinheritance.

Second, he took it all and left. The custom would have been for him to stick around and care for his aging parents. Sons were to make sure that their fathers were buried properly and that their mothers were provided for. This son took off with no regard for his family. Again, his behavior would have been disturbing to Christ's first-century audience.

Third, he spent his entire inheritance in a relatively short time. His father had taken a lifetime to accumulate it, and it represented years of hard work and wise stewardship. Yet the younger son spent it all on short-lived pleasure. It would seem that Jesus could have added nothing to make the son sound any more disreputable. The father had every right in the world to write him off as a sluggard and an embarrassment to the family.

But Jesus took him even one step further. After he had run out of money and the famine hit, he did the most despicable thing a Jewish man could do—he took a job caring for hogs. Not cows or sheep, but pigs. Jesus could have said nothing about the young man that would have been more horrifying to the Pharisees.

Why So Bad?

Why did Jesus picture the prodigal in such an extreme fashion? He was trying to help us understand something basic about forgiveness. The young man's sinfulness was such that there was nothing left in him that could motivate his father to forgive him. His father forgave him because it was his nature to love and thus to forgive. And that was Jesus' point exactly.

Like the father in the parable, God forgives because it is His nature to forgive. Nothing we can do on our own can prompt God to forgive us. It is His character that moves Him, not ours. Earlier we discussed God's initiating the forgiving process, and Jesus' vivid word picture of a father and son portrayed just that.

A Surprising Response

When Jesus got to the part of the story where he described the son's desire to return home, I can only imagine the Pharisees' feelings as they thought about what they would do if they had a son who behaved in such a manner. No doubt they were shocked at how Jesus closed the story.

The son finally realized the futility of his ways and decided to go home. There was no mention of his cleaning himself up. As far as we know, he did not even attempt to make himself presentable to his father. He just headed home in the most despicable condition possible.

When the father saw his son coming down the road, he ran toward him, hugged him, and kissed him. He showered his affection upon the dirty, bedraggled, hog-feeding son of his who had squandered his inheritance and embarrassed the family. He seemed unconcerned about where his son had been or what he had done; his focus was on his son who had returned.

How Far Is Too Far?

This "surprise ending" reveals several marvelous facets of God's attitude toward returning sinners. First, *our heavenly Father's love has no limits*. If there had been a limit on how far the father was willing to stretch before cutting his son off completely, certainly the young man would have gone too far. He did everything wrong.

The point is clear. A man or a woman cannot go so far that God's love and forgiveness are no longer offered. The father would have accepted the son back at any time. The implication, therefore, is that the son was forgiven before he ever returned. From the father's perspective, there was no condemnation. That is why he accepted his son back into the family so quickly.

Regardless of what you have done, you have not stretched God beyond His limits. His love knows no limits. Your sin was dealt with two thousand years ago when Christ died. As far as He is concerned, you live in a state of forgiveness.

How Long Is Too Long?

We do not know how long the son had been gone. It was long enough for him to spend a great deal of money, suffer through a famine, and hold down a job. Jesus did not give us a time frame. It was really irrelevant to His point. And yet it was part of the point. *Our heavenly Father's love is patient*. The story seems to indicate that the boy's father made it a habit of looking in the direction the boy had gone, hoping to see him returning. He was willing to restore his son no matter when he returned.

In the same way your heavenly Father waits patiently for you when you leave for a season of sin. He does not sit and scheme about the things He will do to you once you return. Because He desires to have unbroken fellowship with you. He wants you to return. He wants you to take advantage of the depth of relationship He has made possible for you through Christ.

Patient But Eager

Third, *God is also eager to express His love.* Jesus made this clear when He said, "But while he was still a long way off, his father saw him, and felt compassion for him, and ran and embraced him, and kissed him" (Luke 15:20). In New Testament times no one who had any dignity ran in public. But when the father saw the son coming down the road, he ran.

This detail must have stunned the scribes and Pharisees. "God, eager to restore fellowship with sinners? How could this Jesus be so brazen as to portray the God of the universe running to a sinner and throwing His arms around him?" That was not the way they imagined God at all. They saw Him as a God who delighted in chastising sinners.

Do you realize that God is more eager to reestablish fellowship after you sin than you are? You can be assured of that by looking at what He did to make fellowship with Him possible to begin with. He can't wait for you to turn back to Him.

God is not sitting on His throne with a black notebook in one hand and a whip in the other waiting for you to return so that He can read off all you have done and chastise you for it. Like the father in the parable, He is eagerly waiting for you to return so He can restore you and clean you up. God's pardon is not miserly. Paul had this in mind when he wrote, "He who did not spare His own Son, but delivered Him up for us all, how will He not also with Him freely give us all things?" (Rom. 8:32).

The Focus Of The Father

A fourth facet of God the Father's attitude is that *His focus is on the sinner*, not the sin. Upon returning, the son immediately began to recite his prepared speech: "Father, I have sinned against heaven and in your sight; I am no longer worthy to be called your son" (Luke 15:21). His focus, like ours, was on his sin, his unworthiness. In essence he was begging for mercy. He readily acknowledged his father's right to reject his request for charity. He knew what he deserved, and he was willing to take what was coming.

The father, however, had an entirely different focus; his focus was on his son. The father seemingly ignored his son's speech. He began shouting orders to everyone:

Quickly bring out the best robe and put it on him, and put a ring on his hand and sandals on his feet; and bring the fattened calf, kill it, and let us eat and be merry.

—Luke 15:22–23

"But what about the son's sin? What about all the money he wasted? What about the embarrassment he caused the family?" we may ask. Those were not the father's concerns. He had one thing, and one thing only, on his mind: "For this son of mine was dead, and has come to life again; he was lost, and has been found" (Luke 15:24).

God has dealt with your sin. It is no longer His focus. *You* are His focus. To God, your sin is no longer a hindrance to His fellowship with you. It is a hindrance only as long as you allow the guilt that accompanies sin to blind you to the fact that God is eager to reestablish fellowship with you. (We will deal more with this and the place of confession in the next chapter.)

Once you turn back to God, He is eager to take you back immediately. What you have done or how long you have done it is never a consideration. The father in the parable did not know what had happened to his son, where he had been, or how he had lost his money. And he did not ask. His son was back, and that was the only thing that mattered.

A Joyful Welcome

We need to consider a fifth and final facet of God's attitude toward returning sinners. This one gives us great insight into the heart of God. *God receives the sinner back into fellowship joyfully.*

We see this in two statements Jesus made. First, He said, "But while he was still a long way off, his father saw him, and felt compassion for him" (Luke 15:20). Think about this. Jesus portrayed the heavenly Father in such a way that His immediate response to a returning sinner was compassion. Not anger, not frustration, not indignation—all of which we might think He would have been justified in feeling—but compassion.

When we are confronted with people who have hurt us or abused our relationship with them, our initial response—the one that just happens without our planning it—is usually anger or hurt. Then if we are really "spiritual," we may try to deal with those emotions by asking God to help us see things from His perspective. In time we can usually relate to those individuals in a civilized manner without blowing up and telling them how we feel.

That is what makes the father's first emotional response even more amazing to us. Out of his compassion he identified with the hurt and misery of his son, and he wanted to alleviate that pain. His own hurt did not get in the way of his ability to identify with his son's hurt.

So it is with the heavenly Father when you return to Him from your sin. He has dealt with the personal hurt sin caused Him. His focus is now on your hurt. Alleviating your pain and sorrow results in joy on His behalf.

We also see this idea of joy in Jesus' statement: "And they began to be merry" (Luke 15:24). It was a time of celebration for the father, and he threw a big party. His greatest desire had been fulfilled; his son had come home.

Jesus underscored this element of joy in each of the two parables preceding this one. When the shepherd found the lost sheep, he said, "Rejoice with me, for I have found my sheep which was lost!" (Luke 15:6). And then concerning the woman who lost her coin, "And when she has found it, she calls together her friends and neighbors, saying, 'Rejoice with me, for I have found the coin which I had lost!'" (Luke 15:9). Jesus then summed up both parables by saying, "In the same way, I tell you, there is joy in the presence of the angels of God over one sinner who repents" (Luke 15:10).

When you or any child of God turns from sin, God rejoices. If it is possible to assign emotions to the heavenly Father, He "feels" compassion for you and therefore experiences joy at your homecoming. He does not wrestle with feelings of hurt and jealousy. He has dealt with that once and for all. Instead, He identifies with your hurt and frustration and takes joy in seeing you set free.

Accept God's True Character

I imagine it was difficult for many of those listening to Jesus to change their thinking about God and His attitude toward sinners. Those who did, however, opened themselves to lives of fellowship with their heavenly Father that had been unknown to them until that time. Those who refused to listen or who were too overwhelmed to believe remained in bondage to pride or despair. What about you? Are you willing to accept what Christ said about your heavenly Father? Are you willing to allow God to tear down the barriers that keep you from accepting Him as He really is?

You have a forgiving Father whose love and patience are unlimited. You cannot push Him too far. He is eager to have fellowship with you. You have a heavenly Father who is free to identify with your situation and who takes great joy in seeing you restored to your rightful place as His child. Your forgiving Father's greatest concern is *you*, not your sin. His focus is on you and your willingness to comply with His will for your life.

For some of you, this may come easy. For others, it may take some time to change your attitude about who God is and how He perceives you. Begin renewing your mind by thinking about these five tremendous facts about the character of God. To a great extent, they summarize everything we have discussed so far, and these principles come alive in the parable as we see them acted out in the response of the father toward his rebellious younger son.

A good way to start would be to recite this simple prayer that incorporates all that we have seen about the character of God in this chapter.

> *Heavenly Father,*
> *Sometimes it is difficult for me to see You as You really are.*
> *By faith in the testimony of Jesus, however, I accept You as my forgiving heavenly Father.*
> *A Father who loves me with unlimited love;*
> *A Father whose patience is inexhaustible;*
> *A Father who is eager to have fellowship with me:*
> *A Father who focuses on me and my position as Your child, not on my sin;*
> *A Father who rejoices when I turn to You from my sin, whether it be one single act or a season of rebellion.*
> *Expose the errors in my thinking toward You and fill me with the truth, for I know that in discovering the truth I will be set free. Amen.*

Questions For Personal Growth

1. What feelings do you have when you think about your earthly father? (Do you have feelings of love and acceptance or feelings of fear, dread, hurt, and disappointment?)

How do you picture God the Father?

2. What two mind-sets polarized the Jews of Jesus' day?

3. What five aspects of God's attitude toward returning sinners are revealed in Jesus' parable of the lost son (Luke 15:11–24)?

4. Are you willing to accept what Christ said about your heavenly Father?

*He who conceals his
transgressions
will not prosper,
but he who confesses
and forsakes them
will find compassion.*

Proverbs 28:13

Chapter 6

FORGIVENESS AND CONFESSION

Now THAT WE have examined God's part in forgiveness, what about our responsibility? You may be asking at this point, "Do we even have a responsibility? It sounds as if God has taken care of the whole thing from beginning to end." Remember, however, that the parable of the prodigal son portrays not only a forgiving father, but also a returning son. What about him?

The Scripture reads,

> But when he came to his senses, he said, "How many of my father's hired men have more than enough bread, but I am dying here with hunger! I will get up and go to my father, and will say to him, 'Father, I have sinned against heaven, and in your sight; I am no longer worthy to be called your son; make me one of your hired men.'" And he got up and came to his father.
>
> —Luke 15:17–20

Out of a spirit of futility, hopelessness, and humility he made a decision to return to his father. Notice that he rehearsed what he would say, "I have sinned against heaven, and in your sight; I am no longer worthy to be called your son." And upon falling into his father's arms, he confessed just that: "I have sinned against heaven and in your sight: I am no longer worthy to be called your son." He confessed his sin to his father.

The Father And Confession

It is vital to note that before the prodigal could confess his failure to his father, "his father saw him, and felt compassion for him, and ran and embraced him, and kissed him." The son's acceptance and forgiveness were not conditional upon his confession. As we discussed in the last chapter, the father was not motivated to forgive based on his son's confession of a life of sin. He fell into the arms of a father whose forgiveness was constant from the moment he walked away.

Confession And Forgiveness

Then why does the Bible teach we are to confess our sins if we are already forgiven? What is the role of confession? If we are already forgiven, it seems unnecessary, doesn't it? The purpose of this chapter is to clarify the place of confession in God's strategy for our forgiveness.

The Greek word we use for *confess* means "to agree with." When we confess our sins to our heavenly Father, we are agreeing with Him. We are agreeing with His attitude about sin; that is, sin is against Him, it is destructive to His purpose for our lives, and it carries with it consequences that will prove painful.

Confession also implies that we are assuming responsibility for our actions. We are not blaming our actions on others. Confession means that we see ourselves in relationship to our deeds of sin just like God does.

1 John 1:9

Undoubtedly, the most often-quoted verse regarding confession is this one: "If we confess our sins, He is faithful and righteous to forgive us our sins and to cleanse us from all unrighteousness" (1 John 1:9). When taken at face value, the verse would seem to indicate that our forgiveness is conditional upon our confession. This raises all kinds of questions: What if we forget to confess a sin? What if we don't realize we have committed a sin? And on and on we could go.

All of a sudden we have lost sight of what Christ has done on the cross, and we are focusing our attention on our memory and our sensitivity to sin. And if eternal life were dependent upon our ability to remember our sins, we would be correct in doing so. But there is a concept that will help us harmonize this verse with verses such as Ephesians 1:7, which says, "In Him we have [present tense] redemption through His blood, the forgiveness of our trespasses, according to the riches of His grace."

According to 1 John 1:9, we would expect Ephesians 1:7 to read, ". . . the forgiveness of our trespasses, according to the confession of our sins." So which is it? Are our sins forgiven based on His grace and the death of Christ two thousand years ago, or our up-to-the-minute confession?

Before I demonstrate how these two apparently conflicting ideas fit together, I want to reemphasize what I have said so far. The basis of our forgiveness is not confession, repentance, or faith, though all three are essential to our experience of forgiveness. The basis of our forgiveness is the sacrificial, substitutionary death of Jesus Christ on the cross. His death as the sinless Son of God paid in full the penalty for all our sins—past, present, and future. We can add nothing to Christ's death that will gain for us any more forgiveness than we already have. That forgiveness becomes a reality in the life of every person who by faith receives Christ as Savior.

After we are saved, the basis of our continuing forgiveness is still none other than the shed blood of Christ at Calvary. Yet many believe that all future forgiveness is conditional upon the proper confession of sins. The basis of this thinking is understandable upon reading 1 John 1:9. The first word in the verse sets up a condition that leads to confusion, "*If* we confess. . . ."

One reason our forgiveness, insofar as our salvation is concerned, cannot be based upon our confession is that we are not always aware of our sins. In a hurried, insensitive moment, with a sharp word we can deeply hurt someone but be unaware of the damage to the person's spirit. In fact only God knows the real depth of our unrighteousness. He has made gracious and adequate provision for such actions. John assures us, "But if we walk in the light as He Himself is in the light, we have fellowship with one another, and the blood of Jesus His Son cleanses us from all sin" (1 John 1:7). Again, our forgiveness is inseparably connected with the blood Christ shed for us.

A Family Affair

The confusion over confession hinges on our tendency to assign certain definitions to words without regard to the context in which they are used. For instance, whenever we read the word *saved* or *save* in the Bible, we immediately think about eternal salvation from the penalty of our sins. And certainly the term *saved* is used that way. But not every time. For instance, when Jesus was hanging on the cross, one of the thieves hanging with Him shouted out, "*Save* Yourself and us!" (Luke 23:39). Clearly this was not a plea for salvation in the eternal sense. He just wanted Jesus to save his physical life. In Act 27:20 Luke describes Paul's shipwreck, "And since neither sun nor stars appeared for many days, and no small storm was assailing us, from then on all hope of our being *saved* was gradually abandoned." Did Luke believe that since the storm was so bad they would all die and go to hell? Certainly not. Once again, *saved* refers to physical deliverance.

When we come to the concept of forgiveness, we must be careful not to assume that the author is always talking about the forgiveness a believer experiences when he or she first puts trust in Christ. Forgiveness in that sense is the door leading to a relationship with God. That type of forgiveness is a one-time-only phenomenon. Once pardoned, always pardoned.

The individual who becomes a child of God, thus establishing an eternal relationship with the heavenly Father, begins to relate to God in a new way. The new believer has new rights as well as new responsibilities. After the individual has become a partaker of eternal life, a new set of guidelines governs the relationship with God. One of these new guidelines has to do with restoring fellowship with the heavenly Father after the believer sins. The believer must receive what one author has termed "familial forgiveness."

Eternal salvation and forgiveness of the debt of sin separating us from God are not the issues here. This is a matter of family business. So John includes himself when he writes, "If *we* confess *our* sins." The parable of the prodigal son is the perfect illustration of this type of confession. The son's fellowship with his father could not have been restored until he first returned home. So it is with us. Until we turn back to God from our sin, fellowship is broken. Notice that God does not withhold fellowship; we, as sinning believers, damage the relationship. The following example may help to clarify this point.

The Case of the Stolen Watch

Suppose that just before I begin to preach I take off my watch and lay it on the pulpit. I forget that it is there and walk off and leave it. Someone from the balcony notices that I left it. He makes his way down to the platform area, and thinking that he is unobserved, he simply walks by the pulpit and slips the watch into his pocket.

However, someone sees him take my watch and the next day informs me as to the identity of the thief. It is someone I know. Naturally, I am surprised and disappointed, but I choose to forgive him. Once I deal with any negative feelings I may have, there is no barrier in my relationship with this man as far as I am concerned. My relationship with him has not changed. Even though he stole my only watch, I have forgiven him for his actions; I have canceled the debt; I have assumed the loss. When I see him sitting in the balcony the following Sunday, I do not say, "Hey, you stole my watch." I have forgiven him, so I must trust the Lord to convict him of his sin.

But suppose the offender discovers that I am aware of his action. By coincidence, we meet in the hallway. There are just the two of us, and I say to him, "How are you? I'm glad to see you." You see, I am free because I have forgiven him. I am not carrying the excess emotional weight of an unforgiving spirit, bitterness, or resentment for his action. But what do you suppose is going on inside him? He feels guilty, embarrassed, ashamed, fearful, regretful, found out.

I give him a warm, friendly handshake; I smile; I even invite him to lunch. But he nervously excuses himself; his eyes are unable to meet mine. He hurries off. He is miserable. His conscience is gnawing at him. His smile and sense of humor are gone.

The only way he is going to be comfortable around me and have fellowship with me again is to clear his conscience by confessing to me that he took my watch and by asking for my forgiveness.

My reply would then be, "You were already forgiven. I forgave you even before I knew who took it."

He did not have to come to me to get forgiveness; he was already forgiven. His confession was necessary for him to clear his conscience and to be restored to his previous fellowship with me.

That is what happens when we come to God confessing our sins. The confession does not persuade God to forgive us. He did that at the Cross. The confession restores us to our previous level of fellowship and intimacy with Him—from our perspective. God did not change. He did not turn away from us because of our sins. His love was not affected. He was not disappointed. He already knows about the sins we are yet to commit, and His response is the same, "Forgiven!"

And the Consequences?

I do not mean to imply that forgiven sins have no consequences. One scriptural principle does not nullify another. We are clearly warned, "Be sure your sin will find you out" (Num. 32:23). Sins may find us out only in our own conscience, or it could be a public discovery. But find us out they will. The apostle Paul warns us, "Do not be deceived, God is not mocked; for whatever a man sows, this he will also reap" (Gal. 6:7). We may not reap it immediately nor in the way we expect, but we will reap.

Does this mean we are not forgiven? No! Then why do we have to suffer if God has forgiven us? There are two reasons. First, sin, by its very nature, is always accompanied by certain painful consequences, and the sin itself determines the nature of the consequences. It does not matter if we are saints or sinners. There are unavoidable consequences. That is the law of life.

For example, imagine a boy who has been instructed by his mother not to go into the street. He disobeys and runs out into the street. A car comes around the corner and hits the little boy. Does the mother forgive her son for disobeying? Absolutely. Even if he never asks for forgiveness. In fact forgiveness is not on her mind as she kneels down and holds his head in her lap. But in his forgiven state, the boy still suffers the pain and possible handicap of disobedience.

A second reason we must suffer the consequences is that God, though forgiving, is committed to conforming us to the image of His Son (Rom. 8:29). The painful consequences of our sins are expressions of God's love, not of His anger. He knows that to allow us to escape would only result in our continued disobedience and our ultimate failure. He reminds us, "For those whom the Lord loves He disciplines" (Heb. 12:6). He further encourages us by reminding us that "all discipline for the moment seems not to be joyful, but sorrowful; yet to those who have been trained by it, afterwards it yields the peaceful fruit of righteousness" (Heb. 12:11).

Confession is essential, not to receive forgiveness, but to experience the forgiveness God has provided through the death of Christ and to have unhindered fellowship with Him. But there is more. In confession we experience release from guilt, tension, pressure, and emotional stress resulting from our sins. Failure to confess our sins ensures the continuation of those unnecessary negative feelings.

The Position of Believers

I have been in small prayer groups where people began to confess their sins aloud. Often I have been tempted to stop them in the midst of their confession so that I can explain the proper way to confess sins to the heavenly Father. They cry out, "Oh, God, forgive me. Please forgive me, Lord. Oh, God, I beg of You to forgive me. I know I don't deserve it. Oh, Lord, what can I do to be forgiven? Oh, Lord, if You will just forgive me this time, I promise I will never do it again. Lord, if You will just give me one more chance, if You will forgive me just one more time." Sometimes it is evident from the increase in volume that they believe that if they pray a little louder. God may be a little more impressed and, therefore respond a little more quickly.

I do not mean to be critical of another Christian's prayer for forgiveness. Heavy conviction by the Holy Spirit will often evoke great emotion and feelings of unworthiness and humiliation before the Lord. Yet demonstrations of emotion, long, loud prayers, and even fasting will not make things any better between the believer and God; only the simple, sincere confession of wrongdoing can do that. The blood of Christ provides for forgiveness, and confession is the avenue by which the believer experiences it.

Failure to understand the purpose and place of confession can result in fear and uncertainty about our salvation; it takes the cutting edge off our joy; it leaves us with a nagging doubt that deprives us of the peace our Lord intends for His children. We must remember that confession does not merit us any more love or forgiveness than we already have. "He who did not spare His own Son, but delivered Him up for us all, how will He not also with Him freely give us all things?" (Rom. 8:32).

If we are not clear about the nature and power of our confession, our service for Him will be hindered. Our ambivalence will short-circuit our motivation to serve God because we will not feel worthy or competent. We will have a nagging sense of guilt: *I wonder what God thinks of me? I wonder if He is pleased with me?* The cloud of doubt will continually hang over us: *Have I confessed everything? Am I sorry enough for my sins? Have I said the right thing?* When we understand our true position in Christ, these thoughts will no longer harass us. We will be able to confess our sins and, on the basis of Christ's shed blood, accept our forgiveness and thank God for His great grace toward us. And if some form of restitution needs to be made toward an offended party, we will do so.

Christ paid our penalty at Calvary. We cannot add to the payment by feeling sorry for our sins or confessing the same sin over and over again. This is not to belittle the awfulness of sin but to magnify the grace of God. Believers are united to Christ by faith. The following verses proclaim our position in Him:

There is therefore now no condemnation for those who are in Christ Jesus.

—Romans 8:1

For He delivered us from the domain of darkness, and transferred us to the kingdom of His beloved Son, in whom we have redemption, the forgiveness of sins.

—Colossians 1:13–14

In Him, you also, after listening to the message of truth, the gospel of your salvation—having also believed, you were sealed in Him with the Holy Spirit of promise, who is given as a pledge of our inheritance, with a view to the redemption of God's own possession, to the praise of His glory.

—Ephesians 1:13–14

Who shall separate us from the love of Christ? . . . I am convinced that neither death, nor life, nor angels, nor principalities, nor things present, nor things to come, nor powers, nor height, nor depth, nor any other created thing, shall be able

to separate us from the love of God, which is in Christ Jesus
our Lord.

—Romans 8:35, 38–39

Hallelujah! We are eternally secure in Christ. Failure to confess our sins does not alter our eternal security, but it interferes
with, and greatly hinders, our fellowship with the Father. That
is indeed a costly mistake.

We've Got to Believe It

A primary reason we have no joy following our confession is
that we do not really believe God has forgiven us. We think, *How
could God forgive me? What I have done is awful*. We remain
under a load of guilt we refuse to lay down because of our unbelief. I saw this principle work its way out in my relationship with
one of my church members.

Alex was one of my best friends. His business was suffering,
and he needed a short-term loan. I loaned him what he needed,
which by the way was all I had and a rather sizable sum. Instead
of investing it in his business, however, he paid off old bills.
Suddenly, I didn't hear from him. He was not in his regular seat
in the worship service He avoided my calls.

Finally, through a mutual friend, I discovered that his business
had folded. Still no contact. I was struggling with my own attitude of disappointment and hurt. Finally, I was able to say to the
Lord, "I forgive him the debt. If he never pays me back, it's all
right. I still love him as a friend."

After a period of time, we met. I told him that he was forgiven
and that I did not expect him to repay me. I tried to communicate to him that he did not owe me anything and that I still
wanted to be his friend.

But Alex could not accept my forgiveness. He became critical
of me to others. Finally, he declared bankruptcy to prevent me
from suing him, which I would never have considered. He ruined

his credit rating, his reputation, his relationship to our church, and his usefulness to the Lord's work—all because he could not accept the full and free forgiveness of a friend who truly loved him. He could not believe that anyone would forgive him for misusing that much money. He is still out of fellowship with God and out of service for God. He carries an unnesssary load of guilt because he would not accept the gift of forgiveness.

So it is with believers if we will not let go of the guilt that always accompanies sin. We put ourselves through unnecessary trauma and pain. Often it affects the relationship with God and relationships with others as well.

But Jesus Said . . .

In the Sermon on the Mount Jesus made a statement about forgiveness that may appear to contradict much or all of what we have discussed in this chapter. He said,

> For if you forgive men for their transgressions, your heavenly Father will also forgive you. But if you do not forgive men, then your Father will not forgive your transgressions.
> —Matthew 6:14–15

Does this mean that my failure to forgive someone who has wronged me will deprive me of the forgiveness God purchased in my behalf through Christ's blood at Calvary?

The answer to this question goes back to understanding what Christ meant by the word *forgive*. He was talking to God-fearing Jews, men and women who were seeking the truth about how they should relate to God. His statement must be interpreted in the context of family.

To forgive means to release others from a debt incurred when they wronged us. The debt may be material or emotional, some form of hurt or embarrassment. When we forgive, we assume the loss. We free others from the bondage of material or emotional indebtedness. If we refuse to forgive, we place ourselves in bondage to an unforgiving spirit, which is accompanied by tension, strife, pressure, irritation, frustration, and anxiety.

Therefore, because it is always the will of the Father for us to be forgiving toward others, refusing to forgive our offenders prevents God from releasing us from the same bondage. In love He cannot simply overlook our un-Christlike spirit; we must deal with it by confessing it and forgiving those who have offended us. Otherwise we bear the pressure of His chastisement, which is His refusal to release us from the natural penalty of an unforgiving spirit.

When Jesus says in this passage, "Then your Father will not forgive your transgressions," He is not implying that our salvation is in jeopardy. Our fellowship with Him is what will suffer. We cannot be right with God and unforgiving toward others. Confession is absolutely essential if we are to walk in fellowship with our heavenly Father whose forgiveness toward us is eternal, whose unconditional love toward us cannot be diminished, and whose grace toward us can never be thwarted.

When you sin, what should you do? Thank Him at that moment for bringing your sin to your attention. Assume responsibility for it, agreeing with Him that you have sinned. Thank Him for His forgiveness purchased at Calvary through the blood of His Son. If the sin is against another person, make things right as soon as possible. Then go on with perfect confidence that things are right between you and your Creator.

Questions for Personal Growth

1. If your sins are already forgiven, why should you confess your sins?

2. What is the basis of continuing forgiveness?

3. How should you treat a person who has wronged you?

   What happens if you refuse to forgive someone who has wronged you?

4. Why is confession essential for believers?

*Let us therefore, draw
near with confidence to
the throne of grace, that
we may receive mercy
and may find grace
to help in time of need.*

Hebrews 4:16

Chapter 7

HANDLING OUR HURTS

As a young man, Jim wanted to be a medical doctor. He studied hard all through elementary school and high school. His hard work paid off, and he graduated with excellent grades. But when the time came for him to go away to college, his father refused to allow him to leave. He forced him to stay on the family farm and work.

At the age of twenty-three, Jim had taken all he could take of farm life. He packed up his belongings, loaded his car, and left. Along with his clothes and a few books, Jim took something else with him as well. He drove away that day with a heart full of bitterness and resentment toward his father.

Everywhere Jim went he had a difficult time getting along with others. As people would try to get close to him, his bitterness would pour out all over them. He seemed unable to make long-lasting friendships, and he was filled with feelings of rejection and isolation. Consequently, he found himself moving from job to job; he was never able to settle down.

Finally, he met a woman who really cared for him. After a short engagement, they were married. She was a widow with one son. Three weeks into the marriage an unexpected outburst of anger

465

marked the beginning of over forty years of hell on earth for his loyal wife. His short temper and vile language drove away the few friends he had, and eventually, his wife's friends could no longer tolerate his behavior. Right up to the last days of his life—nearly blind, senile, and unable to care for himself—the poison of bitterness continued to eat away at Jim's heart. And all because he was unwilling to deal with the rejection and hurt he had experienced as a teenager.

I don't know all the reasons why Jim's father would not let him leave the farm. Maybe he was uneducated and was threatened by Jim's educational pursuits. He may have just been selfish and not wanted to lose Jim as a farmhand. Let's give Jim the benefit of the doubt and say he was justified in feeling hurt because of his father's decision. In spite of being "justified," however, Jim's reaction did not hurt his father half as badly as it hurt Jim. Such is the nature of an unforgiving spirit. It is like a hot coal. The longer and tighter it is held, the deeper the burn. Like a hot coal, bitterness, too, will leave a scar that even time cannot erase.

Developing an Unforgiving Spirit

An unforgiving spirit does not develop overnight. It involves a process of responses and thus takes time to develop. In talking with people through the years I have discovered ten stages an individual is likely to go through. Not everyone will pass through each stage, but almost everyone I have known with an unforgiving spirit could identify several of them.

1. WE GET HURT

The seeds of an unforgiving spirit are planted when we are wronged or hurt in some way. It could be a physical, an emotional, or a verbal hurt. It could be a hurt we experienced in childhood or adulthood. It really makes no difference. Since we live in such a self-centered world, often we experience our first hurt as a child, and unfortunately, this early hurt usually comes from the people we love and respect the most.

As we discussed in chapter 1, all our hurts are really some form of rejection. We may not perceive it as rejection initially, but that is what happens when we are wronged by others. We may feel hurt, pain, abandonment, embarrassment, hatred, or some other negative emotion. But it all relates to rejection.

Feeling rejected then, is the first stage in developing an unforgiving spirit. That being the case, we all have the potential for problems in this area. Therefore, we must always be on our guard to stop the process in its beginning stages.

2. WE BECOME CONFUSED

Often our initial response to hurt, regardless of the form it takes, is confusion. We experience a sense of bewilderment; we are not quite sure how to respond. It is similar to being in a state of shock. In this stage we may think, *This is not really happening*. We may even have a physical reaction, such as a deep feeling of emptiness in the pit of the stomach. Many people have actually gotten sick after experiencing rejection. This stage is usually short-lived, and immediately, we move into the third stage.

3. WE LOOK FOR DETOURS

We all have a desire to avoid pain. Because of that, when we are hurt emotionally, instead of thinking about it we tend to find ways of avoiding those painful thoughts or memories. We take mental detours. We don't allow ourselves to think about certain things. We change the subject when certain topics are brought up. This desire to detour around past hurt motivates many people to drink heavily or to become addicted to both prescription and nonprescription drugs. The fact is, I have never counseled a drug addict or an alcoholic who was not trying to cover up the pain of the past. The root problem was never alcohol or drugs: it was always the inability to cope with rejection.

We also take physical detours. We tend to avoid certain people, places, and things. Anything that reminds us of the hurt becomes off limits. I will never forget one preacher's daughter I counseled. She was full of bitterness toward her father. During our conversation, she made the statement, "I would never marry a preacher." There was certainly no real connection between her father and every prospective preacher in the world. But in her mind there was. Preacher meant "rejection." Therefore, preachers were to be avoided at all costs.

A college student in our church could not stand me, and I did not understand why. Finally, one of his friends explained. His father constantly quoted me, especially when he was disciplining his son. The young man's problem was really between him and his father. But since he had been hurt by his father, he looked with disdain upon anyone or anything associated with his father.

4. WE DIG A HOLE

After we try to "schedule" around our hurt, that is, to arrange our thought patterns and lives in general so as never to come into contact with anything that reminds us of our hurt (an undertaking that is rarely successful), we attempt to forget the whole thing ever occurred. We dig a hole and bury it as deeply as we can.

5. WE DENY IT

The fifth stage is also one of denial. We deny that we were ever hurt or that we are covering up anything. We smile and say, "Oh, I have dealt with that." Or "I forgave him long ago."

This is a tough stage for people to break out of. I have met scores of adults who are carrying around a load of bitterness, as demonstrated through their tempers or other negative behavior, but they see no connection between a turbulent childhood and their problems as adults. One woman's problems were so obviously connected to her relationship with her father that everyone who knew anything about her past tried to get her to see the connection. She flatly denied it.

I know of a lost friend who recommended that a church member get counseling to deal with his bitterness toward his father. The church member, however, just laughed when confronted with the notion that his relationship with his father was in any way connected to his present struggles. "I was just a kid when all that happened," he said, referring to an incident in which he was clearly rejected by his father.

6. WE BECOME DEFEATED

Regardless of how successfully we think we have buried our hurt, it will still work its way out through our behavior. A short temper, oversensitivity, shyness, a critical spirit, jealousy—all of these can be evidence of unresolved rejection. The tragedy is that when we deny that we are harboring hurt, we will look everywhere but the right place for a way to change the resulting undesirable behavior. We can move, change jobs, change friends, rededicate our lives, make New Year's resolutions, memorize Scripture, pray long prayers, fast, or undertake any number of spiritual exercises. But until we deal with the root of the problem, we will ultimately be defeated in our attempts to change.

I see this in marriage counseling all the time. A wife will tell a horror story of how her husband (who is sitting right there) abuses her verbally and sometimes physically. She describes his violent and unpredictable temper in detail. She weeps as she gives account after account of how her husband has made her life and the lives of the kids unbearable.

Surprisingly enough, the husband in this situation often shakes his head in agreement with everything his wife has accused him of. I have seen husbands break down and cry in shame at the things they have done and the pain they have caused. Yet, more times than not, they walk out the door at the end of what seems like a "life-changing" counseling session and repeat the same contemptible behavior. Why? Because even though they may be sorry for their behavior, they have not dealt with the root problem.

On the other hand, I have seen men and women deal with the anger and hurt they have been carrying with them. I have seen men deal once and for all with their tempers. I have seen women lay down forever the unrealistic expectations they had of their husbands. The quick turnarounds always came about after the root of bitterness was discovered, acknowledged, and dealt with. (We will discuss in a later chapter how this is accomplished.)

7. WE BECOME DISCOURAGED

This is the critical stage. It is usually the stage where we either seek professional help or bail out of our present circumstances altogether. After a while it seems as if things will never change or never get any better. Any little bit of progress we may see is always shattered by another incident that just confirms the suspicion that it's hopeless!

This is the stage in which husbands leave their wives either because their wives will not change or because they are unable to rekindle that "loving feeling" they once had. This is the stage in which women begin to depend upon alcohol and prescription drugs to make it through the day.

An unforgiving spirit destroys respect. If allowed to go unchecked, it can dissolve the loyalty and even the sense of duty that are so necessary to hold a marriage together during difficult times. Extramarital affairs become a viable option to people who have publicly spoken out against adultery. Divorce becomes a real option to couples who pledged an unconditional lifetime of commitment. For those who can foresee no better circumstances in this life, they often choose to escape by taking their own lives. Such is the power and the poison of an unforgiving spirit.

8. WE DISCOVER THE TRUTH

For some of us, there is a happy ending. Through someone's help or by God's grace, we discover the root of bitterness. We gain insight into why we act the way we do. We are able to see the connection between the past and the present. The pieces finally fit together.

9. WE TAKE RESPONSIBILITY

The ninth stage is closely associated with the eighth one. In this stage we own up to our responsibility. We decide to quit blaming others. We decide to quit waiting for everybody and everything else around us to change. We open our hearts for God to have His way, regardless of how it might hurt.

10. WE ARE DELIVERED

The final outcome for those of us who are willing to deal with an unforgiving spirit is deliverance. My friend, you can be free of that embarrassing, inappropriate, family-splitting behavior. You say, "But you don't know what has happened to me. You don't know what I have been through." You are right. But I have known people in all kinds of circumstances who have been delivered and restored.

So What Are You Waiting For?

You may be using the excuse that your circumstances are so bad that you could never forgive the person or persons who hurt you. The fact is, however, that you could if you are willing to. If you are not willing to forgive, you will ultimately bring your own life crashing down around you. It will be nobody else's fault but your own.

If you are unwilling to forgive, you have one (or more) of several problems. First, your willingness could be a result of *selfishness*. You have been hurt. Something unfair has happened to you. You did not get your way. Your thoughts have turned inward, and you are concerned only with yourself, your rights, and your feelings. You are waiting for the world to come to you and ask forgiveness before you are willing to forgive. *After all*, you think, *it was that other person's fault.* You live in a prison made of your emotions and expectations. It is selfishness because you have the ability to do something about it if you choose. You just may be too selfish to make the first move.

Perhaps your problem is *pride.* When there is pride in a heart, it is very difficult to be forgiving. Pride steps into the forefront of your thinking and says, "Look what they have done to me. If I forgive them, people will think I am weak and I do not have any backbone."

Pride tells you to somehow get back at those who have hurt you. Harboring anger in your heart makes you feel as if you are getting revenge; in fact, it only destroys you. The real problem is that when you set out to get revenge—even if it is only in your mind—you are assuming a responsibility that has been given to Christ and Christ alone. He is the Judge. At the right time those who have hurt you will pay the penalty for their sin (Rom. 14:10). In the meantime you are to forgive.

A third reason you may not be willing to forgive is that you are struggling with *low self-esteem.* Let me explain how this works. People with low self-esteem feel insignificant to begin with. Often, without really understanding what is taking place, they will attach their significance to the wrong they suffered. I have met people who have lived most of their adult lives in response to a wrong they suffered at the hands of an unfair boss. They are constantly saying things like this: "You know I would not be here if it were not for . . . I could have gone far if I had not lost my job with . . ." The unfair circumstances become a point of reference for everything else in their lives.

When this happens to people, they cannot afford to forgive. To deal with the hurt they suffered would be to take away the thing most essential to their identity. They would no longer get the sympathy from others they have come to rely on. They would have no more sad stories to tell. They would have no more excuses for their lack of diligence and discipline.

Do you have a habit of always bringing up a particular event in your life when you were treated unfairly? To know for sure, ask your closest friends or your spouse. Without knowing it you may have allowed your identity to become intertwined with an event you need to put behind you. Your true and eternal identity is found in your relationship with God through Christ. To experience the joy and freedom available to you in Christ, you must forgive those who have wronged you and move on.

Another reason you may be unwilling to deal with your unforgiving spirit is that *you think you already have*. Sometime in your past you may have acknowledged that you were wronged. You may have admitted that you "needed" to forgive others. You may have even prayed a prayer in which you said the words, "I forgive _____." You may have meant it with all your heart, yet if there is evidence emotionally and verbally that something is still gnawing at you on the inside, if you are still uncomfortable around the people who wronged you or if things that remind you of them still make you become tense on the inside, chances are you have not completely dealt with the situation. In the next chapter we will deal with how to make forgiveness complete.

A fifth reason a person refuses to forgive is that it is *painful*. Being willing to forgive is painful in the sense that thinking about past hurts often brings back the original unpleasant emotions. Forgiveness can be especially painful if the wrong hurt so deeply that the pain suffered was buried and forgotten. The very thought of digging that back up, which is sometimes necessary, causes many people to run.

This is especially true of those who were hurt as children. Cases dealing with child abuse, incest, rape, severe beatings, or catching a parent in an extramarital affair are extremely painful. Sometimes these incidents have all but been erased from memory. Yet they are often the keys to complete healing and freedom. As I have talked to people about their past, looking for a clue to their struggles, often I will touch on a subject that brings immediate tears to their eyes. They say, "I can't talk about that" or "I would rather not go into all that." Usually, the doors they want to walk through least, they need to walk through most.

If you live with events in your past that are painful to even think about, please accept by faith that it is worth the pain in order to be set free. God wants to perform spiritual surgery. He wants to remove the bitterness and the hurt. It will hurt, but it will heal. And whatever scar may be left will be much easier to live with than the open wound you now bear.

There is one last reason: *You don't know how to be forgiving.* Maybe you are at the point of being able to say, "I am ready. Just tell me what to do." I hope so. For a long time I lived with the knowledge that I needed to forgive people in my past, but I did not know exactly what to do. The following chapters will help you understand the process of forgiveness and what you must do to be forgiving.

Where Are You?

Before we go any further, I want you to think back over what I have said in this chapter. Have you been wronged or hurt recently or in your past? Was your tendency to try and forget about it, to move on to something or somebody else? Did you get into the habit of burying the painful emotions that seemed to raise their ugly heads time after time? Do you find yourself staying away from certain people or certain types of people? Are there places and things that cause you to feel the hurt all over again? Are there behavior patterns that you find impossible to change?

Are you wrestling with depression? Are you fighting the urge just to bust loose from your present circumstances because the pressure is too much to bear? Are you tired of hurting the people you love the most? Does the grass look greener somewhere else? Are you beginning to wonder if your family and the world would not be better off without you?

If you answered yes to any of these questions, chances are there are some people you need to forgive. It could very well be that you are harboring an unforgiving spirit. Please don't allow your pride and selfishness to get in the way. Please don't allow your fear of the ensuing pain to stop you. You may be on the verge of a miracle in your life. You may be about to be set free.

Questions for Personal Growth

1. Name and explain the ten stages of an unforgiving spirit.

2. Name six reasons why a person may refuse to forgive others.

3. Give an example of a time when you resisted forgiving another.

How did you feel about God?

Give an example of a time when you freely forgave another.

How did you feel about God?

4. Are there some people you are unwilling to forgive? Think about how an unforgiving spirit has affected you.

Be kind to one another,
tender-hearted,
forgiving each other,
just as God in Christ
also has forgiven you.

Ephesians 4:32

Chapter 8

FORGIVING OTHERS

WHEN I THINK about God's grace and the depth of His healing power, I think about a wonderful woman I met through my son. Never before have I met a woman who has suffered so greatly and yet forgiven so deeply. Her story perfectly illustrates how the principles of forgiveness are applied to the particular circumstances of an individual.

When Jill first showed up at the counseling office, she was a very frightened woman. Sitting in a room with only an empty chair to talk to, she began a process that took her back thirty-one years to when she was twelve years old. (For more information about this process, see Appendix B.) That day, as though her uncle were sitting across from her, she began to talk to him about things that had transpired years ago . . . how he had taken advantage of her innocence and abused her time and time again. She told him of the hurt, the anger, and the hatred that she felt for so many years.

Then the tone of her voice changed . . . the bitterness gave way to understanding and the hate to words of forgiveness. "What you did to me as a child has been a factor in everything that has happened to me since then. How can I forgive you? I'll tell you how.

479

I realized some time ago that I needed to ask someone to forgive me. That someone was God. And when I asked Him for forgiveness, this is what He said, 'Your sins were forgiven when My Son died on the cross. You are already forgiven. Accept it and begin to live your life as a daughter, not as a slave to your sin.' I realized that in the moment when Jesus died on the cross, I was forgiven for everything I would ever do! I just had to accept it. When I realized that God had forgiven me for everything I'd ever done or ever would do, I began to understand that I had no right *not* to forgive you. So today, I'm setting us both free from what happened such a long time ago. I forgive you."

With tears that began to wash away the bitterness, she went through a list of names. With each one, she went through the same process. She spoke of the pain that had consumed her for years. She talked about the rejection, the feeling that it really didn't matter to anyone if she lived or died. When she came to the last name on the list, she stopped. "How can I forgive you? I don't know if I can. Yet, I think if I don't, I won't ever be free." With that, she pictured herself in the chair. She talked about the things she'd done to prove how "bad" she was and to hurt herself. When she had said it all, she said one more time, "If God forgave me for everything I've ever done, what right have I not to forgive you?"

That day as she left the room she had forgiven the people in her past who had hurt her so deeply, and she had forgiven herself, too. Because of that, she walked out a free person—free of the bitterness and hate that had made her a prisoner. It took thirty-one years to forgive the person she had blamed for having "such a miserable life," but it took only a couple of hours to discover the freedom that God has provided when someone learns what it is to forgive.

A Personal Matter

Forgiveness is something that each of us has had to deal with in one way or another. What might take you just a short time to work through might be a process that takes someone else time, prayer, and godly counsel. But it is a process we cannot ignore, not if we want to be free to become the persons God created us to be. If we refuse to deal with the bitterness and resentments that put us in bondage, we cannot have the fellowship with our Father that we are supposed to have.

In my years of being a minister and in counseling with people, I have talked with many people like Jill who have spent years in bondage to someone because they were either unable or unwilling to forgive that person. I have also seen the freedom they come to know when they finally understand and appropriate the idea of forgiveness.

In this chapter we will look at the practical aspects of learning how to forgive. But before we do, we need to get rid of some stumbling blocks to true forgiveness.

Clearing Up Some Confusion

One of the stumbling blocks to actually forgiving others is all the wrong information that has entered into our theology. Some of these ideas have crept in through the repeated use of clichés. Others have just been passed on from generation to generation with no biblical basis whatsoever.

The first idea we need to clear up is this: Is justifying, understanding, or explaining away someone's behavior the same as forgiving him? I can certainly understand that "my brother" was under a lot of stress when he raised his voice to me in front of my customers, but does that mean I have forgiven him? Certainly not. Understanding someone's situation is part of the forgiveness process, but only a part.

Another mistaken idea we have picked up is that time heals all wounds. I think that is one of the most misused (and damaging) clichés I've heard. How could the passage of time or the process of forgetting lead to forgiveness? How many times have we said that to someone, with good intentions? It was thirty-one years later that Jill forgave her uncle. If time was the healing factor, certainly the hurt she experienced would have been taken care of long before she walked into the counseling office. Yet she admitted that time only made things worse.

Here is another misunderstanding that I have already touched on briefly: Is forgiving others *denying* that we have been hurt or pretending that the hurt was no big deal? We may try to convince ourselves (after forgiving others) that what they did really wasn't such a big thing, after all. This form of denial works against the forgiveness process. It's denying that others hurt us in a way that caused us real physical, mental, or emotional pain. It's like denying a real part of ourselves.

Another misconception says that to forgive others, we must go to them personally and confess our forgiveness. Confessing our forgiveness to someone who has not first solicited our forgiveness usually causes more problems than it solves. I will never forget the young man in our church who asked one of the women on our staff to forgive him for lusting after her. She had no idea he had a problem with lust, and his confession caused her to be embarrassed and self-conscious around him from then on.

I rarely counsel people to confess their forgiveness to those who have hurt them if the other persons have not asked for it. Once we begin to understand the nature of forgiveness, it becomes clear why this principle holds true. God forgave us long before we ever asked for it. As we have seen, He has forgiven us of things we will never ask forgiveness for. In the same way, we are free to forgive others of things they will never know about.

I say *rarely* because there are some occasions where confession of this type is appropriate. Keep in mind that there is a difference between telling others you have forgiven them and actually forgiving them Forgiving others should begin at the time you are offended, whereas actually confessing our forgiveness may take place later. We need not wait until a person asks for forgiveness to do so. If that were true, many times we would wait forever.

We should confess our forgiveness if one of two situations occurs. First, we should confess our forgiveness if asked for it. This helps clear the other persons' conscience and assures them that we do not hold anything against them.

Second, we should confess our forgiveness if we feel the Lord would have us confront others about their sin. Their sin may have been directed against us personally or against someone we love. It may be necessary in the course of conversation to assure them that you have forgiven them and are coming more for their sake than your own. When we confront others about their sin, the issue of forgiveness must be settled in our own hearts. We must never confront in order to force another to ask for our forgiveness.

Forgiveness is a much more involved issue than just putting time between us and the event or saying some words in a prayer. It is a process that involves understanding our own forgiveness and how that applies to those who have hurt us.

Forgiving Others

Forgiveness is an act of the will that involves five steps.

1. WE ARE FORGIVEN

First, we must recognize that *we have been totally forgiven*. Most people get hung up on this point. That is the reason I have explained in such detail the foundation for forgiveness. Paul sums it all up beautifully: "For the death that He died, He died to sin, once for all; but the life that He lives, He lives to God" (Rom. 6:10).

Once we understand the depth of our sin and the distance it put between us and God, and once we get a glimpse of the sacrifice God made to restore fellowship with us, we should not hesitate to get involved in the process of forgiveness. To understand what God did for us and then to refuse to forgive those who have wronged us is to be like the wicked, ungrateful slave Jesus described:

> For this reason the kingdom of heaven may be compared to a certain king who wished to settle accounts with his slaves. And when he had begun to settle them, there was brought to him one who owed him ten thousand talents. But since

he did not have the means to repay, his lord commanded him to be sold, along with his wife and children and all that he had, and repayment to be made. The slave therefore falling down, prostrated himself before him, saying, "Have patience with me, and I will repay you everything." And the lord of that slave felt compassion and released him and forgave him the debt.

But that slave went out and found one of his fellow slaves who owed him a hundred denarii; and he seized him and began to choke him, saying. "Pay back what you owe." So his fellow slave fell down and began to entreat him, saying, "Have patience with me and I will repay you." He was unwilling however, but went and threw him in prison until he should pay back what was owed. So when his fellow slaves saw what happened, they were deeply grieved and came and reported to their lord all that had happened.

Then summoning him, his lord said to him, "You wicked slave, I forgave you all that debt because you entreated me. Should you not also have had mercy on your fellow slave, even as I had mercy on you?" And his lord, moved with anger, handed him over to the torturers until he should repay all that was owed him.

—Matthew 18:23–34

We read the parable and think, *How could anyone be so ungrateful?* But the believer who will not forgive another is even more guilty and more ungrateful than that slave. The first step, then, is to realize that we have been totally forgiven of a debt we could never pay and thus have no grounds for refusing to forgive others.

2. FORGIVE THE DEBT

The second step is to *release the person from the debt* we think is owed us for the offense. This must be a mental, an emotional, and sometimes even a physical release. It involves mentally bundling up all our hostile feelings and surrendering them to Christ.

We can accomplish this in one of two ways: either by meeting face to face or, like Jill did, by using a substitute. Both work equally well, but one may be more appropriate than the other. In cases where a person is dead, lives far away, or is totally unapproachable, it will be necessary to use the chair-substitute method.

3. ACCEPT OTHERS

The third step is to *accept others as they are* and release them from any responsibility to meet our needs. I am sure we have all met people who have placed the responsibility for their acceptability on us or someone we know. You may be like that yourself. Certain people can make or break your day depending on the amount of attention they pay you. This is a common trait in people who are unable or unwilling to forgive. But when we decide as an act of the will to forgive, we absolve others of any responsibility to meet our needs.

4. VIEW OTHERS AS TOOLS OF GROWTH

Fourth, we must *view those we have forgiven as tools in our lives* to aid us in our growth in and understanding of the grace of God. Even with all my Bible knowledge and education, I cannot understand and appreciate the grace of God as Jill can. Though she would not go through what she has been through again for a million dollars, neither would she take a million for what she has learned about her heavenly Father.

Joseph certainly understood this principle. After all his brothers did to him, he was able to forgive them. He saw them as the instruments of God to get him to Egypt and to be in such a position of power that he could save his family when the famine destroyed all the crops. So when his brothers fell down before him, fearful of what he might do to them to get even, he said,

Do not be afraid, for am I in God's place? And as for you [speaking of his brothers], you meant evil against me, but God meant it for good in order to bring about this present result, to preserve many people alive. So therefore, do not be afraid; I will provide for you and your little ones.

—Genesis 50:19–21

5. *MAKE RECONCILIATION*

The last thing we must do is to *make reconciliation* with those from whom we have been estranged. This will vary from situation to situation. But if there is a family member, distant relative, former employee, or maybe an ex-friend we have avoided because we had hostility in our hearts against that person, we need to reestablish contact. We may have to begin by apologizing. Regardless of how we go about it, we must do what we can to restore fellowship with those who hurt us. Once our forgiveness is complete, reconciliation will be much easier. In fact, many people I have counseled have rushed back to estranged friends and relatives to reestablish contact. Once the barrier of unforgiveness is removed, all the old pleasant feelings can surface, and there is actually joy in the process of restoration.

After completing the five steps in forgiveness, we should pray this simple prayer:

Lord, I forgive (name of person) for (name the specifics). I take authority over the Enemy, and in the name of Jesus Christ and by the power of His Holy Spirit, I take back the ground I have allowed Satan to gain in my life because of my attitude toward (the person) and give this ground back to my Lord Jesus Christ.

We don't have to pray this prayer word for word, but it is a suggested model to use when dealing with forgiving someone. It *is* essential to name the person and what is being forgiven.

What If It Happens Again?

What if the one we have forgiven hurts us again? What if the very same thing happens again? Will it make what we've done any less real? At first we will no doubt feel hurt, bitter, or angry—or maybe all three. Satan will remind us of our past hurts. We may be tempted to doubt the sincerity of our decision to forgive that person.

If this happens, it is important to remember that forgiveness is an act of the will. The initial decision to forgive the person must be followed by the faith walk of forgiveness. Standing firm on the decision to forgive that person and applying additional forgiveness, if necessary, allow us to replace the hurt and the defeated memories with faith victories. The new offenses can be forgiven as they occur without linking them to past offenses, which have already been forgiven.

It is equally important to remember that forgiveness is for our benefit. The other person's behavior may never change. It is up to God, not us, to change that person. It is our responsibility to be set free from the pressure and weight of an unforgiving attitude.

We Will Know We Have Forgiven When . . .

Several things will occur once the forgiveness process is complete. First, our negative feelings will disappear. We will not feel the way we used to feel when we run into these people on the street or in the office. Harsh feelings may be replaced by feelings of concern, pity, or empathy, but not resentment.

Secondly, we will find it much easier to accept the people who have hurt us without feeling the need to change them; we will be willing to take them just the way they are. We will have a new appreciation for their situation once the blinders of resentment have been removed from our eyes. We will understand more why they acted and continue to act the way they do.

Third, our concern about the needs of the other individuals will outweigh our concerns about what they did to us. We will be able to concentrate on them, not on ourselves or our needs.

Forgiveness is a process that can be painful and at times seem unending. Whatever our pain, whatever our situation, we cannot afford to hold on to an unforgiving spirit another day. We must get involved with the process of forgiving others and find out what it means to be really free. If we will persevere and keep our eyes on the One who forgave us, it will be a liberating force like nothing else we have ever experienced.

Questions for Personal Growth

1. Identify and discuss four common misconceptions about forgiveness.

2. Forgiveness is an act of will that involves five steps. Name and explain these five steps.

3. If people hurt you repeatedly, what should you do?

   Should you try to change their behavior?

   Why or why not?

4. What three things can you expect to happen once the forgiveness process is complete?

   Can you recall experiencing these results?

*Sin shall not be
master over you,
for you are not
under law,
but under grace.*

Romans 6:14

Chapter 9

FORGIVING OURSELVES

FORGIVENESS IS BASED on the atoning work of the Cross, and not on anything we do. God's forgiveness does not depend on our confession, nor does His fellowship. Confession is a means for releasing us from the tension and bondage of a guilty conscience. When we pray, *God, You are right. I've sinned against You. I am guilty of this act. I am guilty of that thought*, we achieve release.

Our fellowship with God is not restored by confession (because it was never broken); rather, our *sense* of fellowship with God is restored. When we sin, we withdraw our fellowship from God; He does not withdraw His fellowship from us. Forgiveness is ours forever as believers. The moment we received Him as Savior, He became our life. But our capacity to enjoy forgiveness—our capacity to enjoy a clean conscience—is based on our willingness to acknowledge and confess that sin.

Let me illustrate. One night when I came home, instead of driving into the garage as is my habit, I pulled in the side parking area. As I was walking toward the back door, I noticed my almost-new Oldsmobile sitting there—with the front end bashed in. My daughter, Becky, had been driving the car. I decided not to mention it. When I entered the house, nothing was said. When we sat down to dinner, nothing was said. After a while, my son Andy said, "Becky, do you have anything you'd like to tell Dad?"

I noticed that Becky was quiet. She hadn't said much that night. She turned to me and said, "Dad, oh, I hate to tell you this." She was having a terrible time. "I want to tell you what happened. This fellow pulled in front of me and he stopped all of a sudden and I ran into him and I bashed up your car." And she started crying.

I didn't say a word until she was finished. Then, "Becky, it's okay. It's all right."

"You mean you're not mad?"

"Why should I be mad? You're not hurt. You can always have the car fixed up again. Even if it were your fault, Becky, it's okay."

Becky is my daughter. If she had totaled the car and we had not had insurance, she would have been just as forgiven. She's my daughter, and as my daughter, she walks in total forgiveness by me—no matter what she does. Even so, Becky had to clear her conscience that night. She had to get it out of her system and tell me about it, or she would have spent a miserable night trying to sleep. And she had to forgive herself.

Isn't this what happens with us and God?

Forgiveness is never complete until, first, we have experienced the forgiveness of God, second, we can forgive others who have wronged us, and third, we are able to forgive ourselves.

People frequently say, "I know that God has forgiven me. And I'm sure that I have forgiven those who wronged me. But I still have no peace in my heart. Something is not quite right." Oftentimes this disquietude can be an unforgiving spirit directed toward ourselves. This unforgiving spirit is not directed toward God for what He has done, nor is it directed toward others for what they have done. There will be no peace in our hearts until we forgive ourselves for the wrongs that we have committed. *But we must be willing to forgive ourselves.*

Not long ago, a young woman, whom I shall call Patsy, came to see me. She was only sixteen, but she had become sexually involved with an eighteen-year-old when she was thirteen. This had continued for two years before he moved to another state.

She called herself "dirty and guilty." Distraught by his departure, overwhelmed by her sense of guilt, and reluctant to talk to her parents, she sought private counseling—only to become emotionally involved with the thirty-year-old counselor on whom she had depended for help.

By the time Patsy came to see me, she was confused and desperate. She had thought about running away from home and had toyed with the idea of suicide. She didn't know what to do or where to turn. She said, "I know that I'm saved, but I'm so full of guilt I don't know what in the world to do. And if, somehow, I don't get an answer, I know I can't keep living."

"Have you asked the Lord Jesus Christ to forgive you?"

"I've asked Him hundreds of times to forgive me."

"Well, has He?" She didn't answer.

"Well, has He forgiven you?"

"I feel so dirty."

"But, did you ask Him to forgive you?"

"Oh, I've asked Him many times."

"How did He respond?"

"I just feel so dirty inside," she repeated.

Because of her testimony, I believe that Patsy was saved. But what she did was so sinful and wicked and vile in her eyes that she could not believe a holy God could forgive her for two years of sexual immorality with one man and almost another year of intimate involvement with another. Patsy said she just couldn't "feel" God's forgiveness.

Patsy's story is a familiar one. But the happy ending is that *being* forgiven has nothing to do with *feeling* forgiven. Being forgiven has to do with what God did for us.

Lest we think that forgiving ourselves is a modern dilemma, consider Peter and Paul, who had to face the problem of forgiving themselves—in a very intense fashion.

After Peter refuted that he even knew Christ, "the Lord turned and looked at Peter. Then Peter remembered" (Luke 22:61 NKJV). How many times did Peter have to deal with that before he was able to forgive himself? He denied his Lord at a moment in His life when, if ever He needed a friend, it was then. This was the same Peter who said in effect, "Lord, all the rest of these may forsake You, but when everybody has forsaken You, You can count on the rock." Ironically, Peter was the very one He couldn't count on. Peter had to learn to forgive himself for that.

Then there was Paul before his conversion. His background, learning, and culture, his intensity and commitment to Jehovah God, and his faithfulness to Judaism all had been committed to removing Christianity—that growing, monstrous philosophy—from the face of this earth. He had been consumed with the task of eradicating from people's minds any remains of that person they called Jesus, and Paul had done everything he could to kill or destroy the Lord's church. Though our scriptural understanding of forgiveness is found most clearly in the writings of the apostle Paul, no doubt he, too, grappled with his own forgiveness.

Many of us are at—or have been at—that place in our lives. We struggle with forgiving ourselves for things we did in the past—some of those mistakes having occurred years and years ago.

. . . Perhaps adults who said cruel things as children or who engaged in sin as teenagers look back and vividly remember how they acted.

. . . Or some women who have had abortions experience a gnawing, haunting feeling of remorse deep down inside. Even though they've asked God and other people to forgive them, somehow they can't seem to forgive themselves.

. . . Or men and women who divorced their spouses realize they were wrong and cannot forgive themselves,

. . . Or parents who ran their children away from home, and their children's lives were wrecked and ruined as a result, can't forgive themselves for being the cause.

Yet, *the ability or capacity to forgive ourselves is absolutely essential* if any peace whatsoever is to be found.

He has not dealt with us according to our sins,
Nor punished us according to our iniquities.
For as the heavens are high above the earth,

So great is His mercy toward those who fear Him;
As far as the east is from the west,
So far has He removed our transgressions from us.
As a father pities his children,
So the LORD pities those who fear Him.
For He knows our frame;
He remembers that we are dust.

—Psalm 103:10–14 NKJV

These verses inspired by the Holy Spirit are a beautiful assurance to us that God is a forgiving Father.

Consequences of Not Forgiving Ourselves

The problem is that some of us are not able to forgive ourselves. We look at whatever we've done and think that we are beyond forgiveness. But what we really feel is disappointment in ourselves—a disappointment that confuses measurement of our sin with merit for our forgiveness.

Sin and self-forgiveness tend to assume inverse proportions in our minds—that is, the greater our sin, the lesser our forgiveness. Similarly, the lesser our sin, the greater our forgiveness. Would we, for instance, withhold forgiveness from ourselves for saying unpleasant things about a friend? pocketing the extra money when a clerk returns the wrong change? putting someone down and pretending it's all in good fun? lying about why we're late coming home? having an abortion? calling a child stupid or dumb? injuring or killing a person while driving intoxicated? fornicating or committing adultery?

We may not think we would be capable of some sins, but not a single one of us fully knows how we would act if we found ourselves in different circumstances. Although some sins bring greater condemnation or chastisement in the life of believers, God's viewpoint is that sin is sin. And just as God's viewpoint of sin covers all sins, so does His viewpoint of forgiveness. But when we choose not to forgive ourselves as God does, we can expect to experience the consequences of a self-directed unforgiving spirit.

SELF-PUNISHMENT

The first consequence of a self-directed unforgiving spirit is that *we punish ourselves on an ongoing basis.* How do we do that? We replay our sins continually. Satan initiates it, and we foolishly follow. We even replay the feelings of guilt. And as we do, we put ourselves in a tortured state that God never intended.

If, for instance, we wake up in the morning under a load of guilt (*Oh, what I have done. I'm so ashamed. God can never forgive me. If my friends find out* . . .), we have put the burden on ourselves, not on God. We are unwilling to forgive ourselves, even though as believers and children of God we are already forgiven. We get up, work, play, go to bed, and sleep in a self-imposed bondage, in a prison we build ourselves.

We spiritually incarcerate ourselves despite the fact that *no* place in the Bible does God say He has forgiven us of all our sins "except. . . ." Jesus paid it all. Jesus bore in His body the price for *all* our sins. No exceptions.

UNCERTAINTY

The second consequence of a self-directed unforgiving spirit is that *we live under a cloud of uncertainty.* We do not accept our forgiveness by God; we exist under an abiding question mark. If we never forgive ourselves, we can never be confident that God has forgiven us—and we bear the weight of this guilt. We are not quite sure of where we stand with God. We are not quite sure what He may do next, because if we are not worthy of His blessing. . . .

Sometimes this cloud of uncertainty is deep and dark. Sometimes it is not so dark, but because our understanding and our acceptance of God's forgiveness are limited by our own guesswork, we are not at all sure how God intends to handle us and our transgressions. And so we pass up the peace that passes all understanding, and we have no contentment.

If we refuse to forgive ourselves—despite the fact that God has *not* dealt with us according to our sins, that God has *not* rewarded us according to our iniquities—we continue to live under that cloud of uncertainty.

SENSE OF UNWORTHINESS

The third consequence of a self-directed unforgiving spirit is that *we develop a sense of unworthiness.* Because we are guilty, we also feel unworthy.

But when we hold ourselves accountable for our sins, we are indulging in a guilt-trip. Satan encourages guilt-trips. He may inject these ideas in our thoughts, *Why should God answer my prayer? He is not going to hear what I am saying. Look what I have done.* Satan punches the button, and we replay the past sin. Satan keeps getting us to replay in our minds what God says he has forgotten—and we guiltily oblige. And each time we replay the past sin by not forgiving ourselves, our faith takes a beating and we feel unworthy. This sense of unworthiness affects our prayer life, our intimate relationship with God, and our service for Him.

To a great degree, we paralyze our usefulness before God when we allow our guilt to cause us to feebly—and always unsuccessfully—attempt payment for our sins when Jesus already paid the debt two thousand years ago for *all* our sins.

EXCESSIVE BEHAVIOR

The fourth consequence of a self-directed unforgiving spirit is that *we attempt to overcome our guilt by compulsive behavior and excesses in our lives.* We try drugs, alcohol, sexual affairs, material possessions.

Whenever we dedicate huge amounts of energy to divert our attention from the real problem (our unwillingness to forgive ourselves), we try to escape from the incessant self-pronouncements of guilt. Some of us invest huge amounts of energy into work—we work harder, faster, longer. But no matter how furiously we work, our guilt cannot be diminished by our frantic pace. Sometimes we take on two, three, or four jobs in the church to prove our dedication. We teach Sunday school, sing in the choir, and visit the shut-ins. What servants of God! And we end up making nervous wrecks of ourselves.

Compulsive behavior of this sort is akin to saying, "God, I want to thank You for Jesus' death on the cross, but it wasn't enough." So because we do not accept God's forgiveness, we double our efforts. (Do we really think that God wasn't able to do it alone? that He needs *our* help?) And we begin a self-feeding, spiritually defeating cycle.

The only real answer to our dilemma is to accept God's forgiveness and to forgive ourselves. We may think, *I can't forgive myself for what I have done.* But God gave us the rebuttal to that type of thinking. When Jesus took our sins upon Himself, it's as if He said, "I have come to liberate you. I have come to free you. I have come to set the captives free." If we do not forgive ourselves because of our unworthiness, we miss the point of Jesus' death on the cross.

FALSE HUMILITY

The fifth consequence of a self-directed unforgiving spirit is that *we develop a false sense of humility when we feel permanently judged guilty and sentenced by God.* We wear but a facade of humility when we declare ourselves so unworthy to serve God. And our "humble face" serves as a mask to keep us from seeing our true face.

Does this sound familiar? We may be complimented. "That was absolutely marvelous!" But then we respond. "I don't deserve your praise. Just give God all the praise and the glory." Sometimes that's a sincere response, but sometimes that's a response motivated by a guilt complex. When we harbor a false sense of humility, it's very difficult to accept a compliment.

Actually, none of us (I no more than you) is worthy of praise. We are worthy solely because of God's truth that "we are His workmanship, created in Christ Jesus for good works" (Eph. 2:10 NKJV). It is amazing how a self-directed unforgiving spirit distorts our viewpoint and perverts our thinking. It makes us harbor and nourish—even covet—our past errors so that we wallow in fake humility. We become focused on our selves and on our unworthiness and on our humility.

Believers need look back only in thanksgiving to the grace of God. Believers can look to the now for what God is doing—and to the future for what God will continue to do.

SELF-DEPRIVATION

The sixth consequence of a self-directed unforgiving spirit is that *we deprive ourselves of things God wants us to enjoy.* Self-deprivation is the opposite of compulsive behavior and excesses. We say things like, "Oh, I couldn't buy myself that. I couldn't go there. I couldn't do that."

Self-deprivation is like an acid that eats away at the truth of Jesus' sacrifice. We do not achieve a state of forgiveness by arbitrarily abstaining from good things in our lives. God does not ask us to deprive ourselves in order to "deserve" forgiveness. Self-deprivation is self-choice, not God's choice. Do we presume to know something about our sin that God does not know? Do we dare think that we have some new information about sin and forgiveness that God does not have? Of course not. If our sovereign, holy, righteous God has seen fit in His omniscience to declare us not guilty and to forgive us our sin, we have no grounds for self-deprivation.

To deny ourselves forgiveness and to put ourselves through unending punishment is to sentence ourselves to hell on earth. Satan is a master at deception, and it is Satan who makes us think that we have to suffer until God says, "Okay, that's enough." At what point do we think we will be free? When will we have suffered enough? It is apparent that this type of thinking is absurd, yet many believers act as if they think that's how God's forgiveness works.

An unforgiving spirit is actually *unbelief*. We fail to exercise faith in God if we fail to forgive ourselves *when Christ says He has paid the penalty*. Why would He pay the penalty if we have yet to pay it? Christ paid the penalty so that we would be pardoned, but that does not mean that our pardon eliminates every problem. The after-effects of sin may linger, and even if we forgive ourselves, we still have to deal with the consequences of our sin.

Satan may try to hinder our understanding of forgiveness by insinuating selfish motives, *I know why you are trying to believe that. You are just trying to get off scot-free*. But we must not allow Satan to twist the truth in our thoughts. We need to repel his influence by remembering that, indeed, there was nothing "free" about the Cross. The ultimate price was exacted and paid.

Talking about grace isn't enough; we must *live* by grace. If we think we can be forgiven by doing anything other than accepting the blood of our Lord, our theology is warped.

Why We Can't Forgive Ourselves

Since we know the negative consequences from not forgiving ourselves, what stands in our way? What hinders our acceptance of God's forgiveness on our own behalf? Our resistance generally can be traced to one of four general problem areas: (1) belief in performance-based forgiveness; (2) disappointment in self; (3) adjustment and surrender to guilt; and (4) expectation of repeated sin.

BELIEF IN PERFORMANCE-BASED FORGIVENESS

Performance-based forgiveness is not biblically based forgiveness. We can't "pay" for God's unlimited forgiveness by working harder or serving more fervently. The Bible says that God accepts us on the basis of what He did, not on the basis of what we try to do. But we tend to rationalize, *I have got to measure up*. Ever since we were children, we have learned that whatever we achieve or receive we do so as a result of our own actions.

"Mom, can I have a cookie?"

"If you are good."

Performance. Our whole lives are based on performance. *If I clean my room, Mom will let me do this. If I take out the trash, Dad will let me do that. If I do well at the tryouts, I may make the team.*

Then, when it comes to the grace of God and the Bible's teachings, what happens? No performance is required. *Hold it*, we may think. *That isn't right*. But it is right—God's idea of forgiveness is in a category all by itself.

As believers, we are forgiven children of God, no matter what we do. This does *not* mean, however, that we can do whatever we like and go merrily on our way. It means that as believers we have already been forgiven of our sins—past, present, and future—whether we confess them or not. We don't have to keep asking for forgiveness and keep working to pay for it.

Our difficulty is not one of being unforgiven; it is one of *feeling* unforgiven. We are separated from God by sin, not by lack of forgiveness. Believers are always forgiven. Grace is an unmerited, undeserved, nonnegotiable gift from God that comes to us prepaid. It can't be purchased, and it is offered freely to all who receive it. And that's what the grace of God is all about.

DISAPPOINTMENT IN SELF

We sometimes have a difficult time accepting the truth about ourselves. I can remember a personal experience where God had done a marvelous work in my life. The Lord was blessing me, and I was just moving right along. Then I acted in a very disappointing way. I knew better, but I blew it horribly. The Lord had lifted me up, and I fell flat on my face. I still remember the feelings of shame and depression.

I wrestled with God's forgiveness for a short period of time before I was able to accept it. At least I thought I accepted it. Because I had sorely disappointed myself, it was difficult for me to forgive myself for not living up to my own expectations.

It is important to realize that we disappoint ourselves; we don't disappoint God. How can we disappoint Someone who already knows what we're going to do? Disappointment is the result of unfulfilled expectations, and God doesn't expect anything of us. God knows that we are going to blow it. And that's what the grace of God is all about.

ADJUSTMENT AND SURRENDER TO GUILT

Emotionally, we may live so long under guilt and self-condemnation that the very idea of being free is threatening. We feel comfortable with what we know, and what we know is guilt. We adjust to our feelings of guilt and surrender the peace we could enjoy if we forgave ourselves.

I have counseled people and clearly outlined what the Bible has to say about their particular problem. After professing understanding, these same people may end up praying the same old prayer they pray all the time, and when they finish praying, they haven't dealt with the issue.

If we want to be released from guilt, we must change our thinking. We need a thorough cleansing of our thought processes. No more thinking, *I know what the Bible says about forgiveness*, but. . . . Every time we include a *but*, we put one more bar in our prison of guilt. We need to get rid of the bars; we need to break out of the prison. We don't have to be there. But we have to want to get out.

EXPECTATION OF REPEATED SIN

I know God could forgive me. And I know He has forgiven me. I guess the reason I don't forgive myself is that I know I am going to repeat that sin. These are the thoughts that cause us so much trouble.

How many sins did we commit before the Cross? We weren't even in existence two thousand years ago. All *our* sins for which Christ died were in the future, including sins that we commit over and over again. God's forgiveness is all-inclusive, regardless of the nature of our sins or the frequency of our indulgence.

This does *not* mean we escape the consequences of our sins simply because we are forgiven. This means that we are assured forever of forgiveness, that we need not withhold forgiveness from ourselves because we may sin again. God forgives us every time for every sin, and so must we.

How We Can Forgive Ourselves

How do we forgive ourselves? Regardless of how long we have been in bondage, we can be free if we follow four biblical steps.

STEP 1. RECOGNIZE THE PROBLEM

We must recognize and acknowledge that we have not forgiven ourselves. We must come to grips with the fact that we still hold ourselves in bondage. *Father, I realize I haven't forgiven myself and am in bondage because of it.*

STEP 2. REPENT OF SIN

We must repent of that sin for which we cannot forgive ourselves. We must tell God that we realize that our unwillingness to forgive ourselves is not in keeping with His Word. And we must thank Him for His forgiveness as we confess our sin to Him. *I thank You, Father, for forgiving me for holding myself in bondage, for keeping myself from You and for limiting Your use of me.*

STEP 3. REAFFIRM TRUST

We must reaffirm our trust in the testimony of Scripture: "As far as the east is from the west, so far has He removed our transgressions from us" (Ps. 103:12 NKJV) *Father, I reaffirm my trust and my faith in the Word of God.*

STEP 4. CONFESS FREEDOM AND CHOOSE TO RECEIVE IT

We must confess our freedom and choose to receive it freely, *Lord Jesus, on the basis of Your Word, by an act of my will, in faith, I here and now forgive myself because You have already forgiven me and I accept my forgiveness and I choose from this moment to be freed of all which I have held against myself. Please confirm my freedom to me by the power and presence of Your Holy Spirit.*

If we are willing to follow these simple steps, not only will we be set free, but the healing process will be initiated.

When we choose by an act of the will to accept what God has said as true, we accept God's acceptance of us. And we can tell Him that we have played back that accusing videotape for the last time. When Satan tries to punch the button again, he will find that he has been short-circuited by Jesus. We are free.

Questions for Personal Growth

1. Name and discuss six consequences of a self-directed unforgiving spirit.

2. What four problem areas usually stand in the way of accepting God's forgiveness?

Why isn't it necessary to measure up to God's forgiveness?

3. Name four biblical steps to forgiveness.

4. Do you understand the point of Jesus' death on the cross?

Put in writing your understanding of Jesus' death on the cross as it relates to your sins—past, present, and future.

*Confess
your sins
to one another,
and pray for one another,
so that you may be healed.*

James 5:16

Chapter 10

BITTERNESS

Bitterness OFTEN LIES beneath our inability to forgive and be forgiven. It is a corrosive culprit that denies our peace and destroys our relationships.

The Bible cautions us about the root of bitterness:

> See to it that no one comes short of the grace of God; that no root of bitterness springing up causes trouble, and by it many be defiled.
>
> —Hebrews 12:15

The Greek word for bitterness (*pikria*) comes from the root word *pik*, which means "to cut," and therefore, "pointed" or "sharp." It refers to what is cutting and sharp. It also implies "bitter taste." Verse 15 refers metaphorically to bitter fruit produced by the root of bitterness.

As I have counseled hurting people over the past three decades, I have helped them discover bitter roots they had been nurturing for weeks, months, and often years. We can be bitter and hide it from the rest of the world by disguising it as various other attitudes. We express bitterness in our lives in a number of ways—

anger, passion, slander, malice. But we cannot hide our bitterness from God, or even from our own bodies.

Bitterness is *never* constructive; bitterness is *always* destructive. It doesn't make any difference what people have done to us or how bad it was or how often they did it. Bitterness as a response to wrongdoing is never acceptable before God. Nothing good ever comes from bitterness.

"See to it. . . ." That is, be diligent. The word *see*, as it is used in verse 15, is derived from the same combination of Greek roots—*epi* ("upon") and *skopeō* ("to look at," "contemplate")—that gives us the word *oversight*. As Christians, we are charged with a duty to fulfill.

"That no one comes short of the grace of God. . . ." We are to care for one another and see to it that we live in grace. We are to respond *in* grace *to* grace. We can't allow ourselves to slip over into our old lifestyles. As Christians, we can no longer respond to hurts, abuse, cheating, criticism, lies, and rejection in any way other than how our Lord responds to us—with forgiveness.

"That no root of bitterness springing up. . . ." The day we received Jesus as our Savior, we forsook all rights to be bitter. We must put all bitterness from us and guard against its taking root in our lives—no matter what happens, no matter how despicably we are treated.

We tend to think, however, that individual, personal circumstances are clearly exceptions. A deliberate smear campaign against us, for instance. Or a husband who walks out on his forty-three-year-old wife and takes up with a twenty-one-year-old. Or a wife who betrays her husband for the fleeting sensation of a weekend affair. Or children who reject their parents' values and play the life of idle degenerates after having been brought up in godly homes. Or women who are held back because they're the wrong sex, or men who are passed over for promotion because they're the wrong color. Or employees who are fired to make room for the boss's friends and family members. Or retirees who are struck with severe disability after having waited years to enjoy the fruits of their labor.

Bitterness can be "justified" so easily. *Well, I have a right to be bitter. He knew I was after that account, and just when I was about to close the deal, he lied about my qualifications. That cost me a bundle, and I'm sure not going to smile and say it's okay. He hurt me, and he's not going to get away with it.* But we must be careful not to allow bitterness to take root in our lives. As a root has fine tentacles that reach out for moisture in order to grow, just so does a root of bitterness have tentacles that reach out. The root of bitterness needs feedback, little evidences of its right for existence, in order to grow. It is fed by our misconceived notions that we have a "right" to feel bitter. But the truth is that believers have no right to respond with bitterness.

I recently read a best-seller, the autobiography of a successful businessman. In the beginning of the book, the author related a tragic event, and in telling the story, he said he would never forgive the person who had wronged him. As I continued to read, however, a cloud hung over all the exciting things that this man accomplished. *For that I will never forgive him.* What that person did was so bad that the author intended to be that person's emotional slave for the rest of his life! Regardless of wealth, fame, or popularity, if we allow bitterness to take root, we relinquish control of our lives. We cannot live with bitterness, because bitterness will eat away at us until we are destroyed.

The Effects of Bitterness

"Causes trouble, and by it many be defiled." We may not even be consciously aware that we are nursing bitter feelings, but the effects of bitterness are subtle and many.

PHYSICAL ILLNESSES

A friend of mine is a fine man and a fine pastor who loves God. His wife had cancer, and they sought the best medical help. I'll call them the Browns. The doctor, who had been studying the relationship between cancer and negative emotions, began to work with Mrs. Brown. He went to see her every day, and every day he would try to get her to talk about her past. Week after week. He tried his best to get her to cry. She wouldn't cry. She couldn't cry. Somehow, there simply was nothing to cry about.

But the doctor and Mrs. Brown kept on talking. And one day, in the midst of their conversation, she began to cry. As the tears gushed out, she confessed bitterness toward her parents for something that had happened years ago. When she got it all out, she was freed, liberated, and forgiven. Today Mrs. Brown stands by her husband's side with love and support for his ministry. It is the doctor's opinion that she would not have recovered had she not rid herself of bitterness.

Though we can't see what is happening on the inside, often we see visible, outer results. Bitterness is like a continually running machine that uses our bodies for its energy source. It runs when we are sleeping, it runs when we are talking with our friends, and it runs when we are simply sitting and being quiet. Because bitterness is a lifestyle and not an isolated occurrence, it never shuts down. It keeps operating and draining energy.

It is impossible to be bitter very long without affecting our bodies. More and more, medical professionals are beginning to see some kind of link between the way our bodies function and the way we think. Bitterness, anger, and other negative emotions have been associated with glandular problems, high blood pressure, cardiac disorders, ulcers, and a host of other physical ailments.

STAINED RELATIONSHIPS

Bitterness causes one person trouble and defiles others. As used in Hebrews 12:15, the Greek word for defile (*miainō*) means "to stain" or "to dye." The bitterness we nourish will stain our relationships. This is one reason why there are so many separations, divorces, and broken homes.

A young couple—John and Linda—got married. Unbeknowing

to either, John came into the marriage with a root of bitterness. Linda tried to love him, but in spite of all her attempts, she couldn't get through to him. She just could not tunnel through John's hardened emotional wall. It had been there for years—ever since he was twelve and his mother had died. Throughout his growing years, John had camouflaged his bitterness. He had been successful in keeping it well hidden until after his marriage. Then when Linda settled into marriage and began to be herself, all of a sudden she was facing a marriage partner whom she loved dearly but could not communicate with. John couldn't let down his defenses. He couldn't be himself.

Linda and John tried to discover their problem. Why did he feel the way he did? Why couldn't he return Linda's love? Even John didn't know why he was unable to love. *Where did it all start? Why can't I love? Why do I have these feelings? Why can't I be myself? Why can't I relax? Why do I have this stress? Why am I critical? Why am I negative about things? What is going on in my life?* John wasn't able to raise the mental blinds and discover the source of his problem—bitterness. He was angry with his mother, and his bitterness toward her was staining his marriage.

Much of the time the cause of such problems is found to be an unforgiving spirit that has taken bitter root As in John and Linda's case, John couldn't forgive his mother for dying and leaving him.

Bitterness can paralyze us. Even when we genuinely want to love another person, we can't. It is not that we don't want to— we simply can't. Parents wonder why they can't love their children. Children wonder why they can't love their parents. Husbands and wives wonder why they can't love their spouses, why they can't break through the barrier. But deep inside, they may find themselves infected by roots of bitterness and resentment, even simmering hatred.

Let me relate another example. Ed and Nancy had a storybook wedding, and they excitedly made plans for their family. They would have a boy and a girl, just as Nancy had dreamed for years. When Nancy got pregnant, they were overjoyed, and when she delivered a firstborn boy, they were ecstatic. About a year-and-a-half later she got pregnant again. But this time there were complications, and the doctor told them this would be their last child. No matter. They had their boy, Michael, and now they would have their girl. Their family would be complete. Except they didn't have a daughter, they had another boy—Jason.

At first Nancy was despondent, but she soon got over her disappointment—she thought. Michael and Jason were both little charmers. As the two boys grew, however, little differences began to emerge. Michael could do no wrong, it seemed, but Jason was forever getting in trouble. Nancy found herself picking at Jason and criticizing him no matter what he did. Ed traveled a great deal in his sales job, and so for a while he didn't notice anything unusual in Nancy's treatment of the boys. When she yelled at Jason, Ed thought she was just tired from running after the boys all day. But when the boys were ages six and four, Ed spent his vacation at home instead of taking the family on their usual vacation rounds. As he puttered around the house, it became evident to him that Nancy adored Michael but could hardly stand Jason. Ed suggested counseling, and Nancy agreed.

During counseling, Nancy confessed that she hated Jason because he had robbed her of the little girl she had always wanted. She could not forgive Jason. Moreover, Nancy felt that Ed couldn't love her if he refused to understand that Jason had ruined her life. Nancy clung to her unforgiving spirit, and the root of bitterness assumed control over her life. She divorced Ed, and he gained custody of the two boys—she didn't even want her beloved Michael around her at that point, because in her mind she thought he, too, would someday turn against her. Nancy felt she had plenty of reason to be bitter. In actuality, her unforgiving spirit fed her bitterness, and the root of bitterness had grown so huge it tainted the lives of her husband and sons.

Bitterness has so many little sprouts to it. Distrust is one of them. Insecurity is another. When the Bible says "see to it that . . . no root of bitterness (springs) up," it is because the consequences are awesome and ongoing.

SPIRITUAL STUMBLING BLOCKS

Bitterness creates a cloak of guilt. We know we shouldn't feel the way we do toward others, and we know God doesn't want us to be full of resentment. And, our reasoning goes, if God isn't pleased with us, how can He accept us? We sense a barrier between God and us and begin to doubt our salvation. How in the world are we going to be secure in our salvation when this turmoil, this civil war, is constantly going on?

Bitterness also hinders our influence for Christ. What kind of a Christian testimony can we have if we are bitter toward God and toward our neighbors? How can we convincingly talk to others about the forgiveness of God when we refuse to forgive those who have wronged us? When we allow bitterness to take over our lives, that bitterness spills over into the lives of those around us.

As I noted earlier, not long ago I sat down with my two children, Andy and Becky, and asked if they had resentful feelings toward me for any wrong I had perpetrated. At the time, they were both in their twenties, and so they felt freer to talk openly and honestly.

Andy was the first to respond. He recalled a time when he was thirteen or fourteen and was practicing one part of a song. Over and over, the same melody. I asked him if that was all he knew. Andy recalled that to his adolescent ears, my words sounded like I was saying, "I don't like you or your music." That damaging impression caused him to decide not to play any music for me again, even though he was a talented musician.

Becky had her memory, too. "When I was five years old, we lived in Miami. One day you put me in my room and you wouldn't let me out. I cried and cried, but you wouldn't let me out."

I asked their forgiveness on both matters, as well as on a few others. What I had quickly said and done and just as quickly forgotten, Andy and Becky had not forgotten. I had gone on for years without knowing that I had hurt them.

How many of us harbor those little things that caused us to

feel rejected? How many of us today are angry adults because we don't feel loved? As we think of those who have hurt us or wronged us, we need to deal with those feelings. Some things may have been said or done long ago, so long ago that we don't think we feel their sting any more, but our thoughts are affected. An unforgiving spirit is a devastating emotion that none of us can afford.

The devastation of bitterness is vividly depicted in the life of King Saul, who began his reign as a respected and favored ruler but who ended his life in defeat, sorrow, and suicide. The ravages of a bitter spirit toward David and toward God were instrumental in his demise.

In 1 Samuel 18:1–7, Saul's seed of bitterness toward David is planted. David had come back from slaying Goliath, and the women played tambourines and lutes. They danced and sang, "Saul has slain his thousands, and David his tens of thousands" (v. 7 NIV). Their song did not set well with Saul. He "was very angry; this refrain galled him" (v. 8). David's fame enraged Saul. "And from that time on Saul kept a jealous eye on David" (v. 9). This is the way bitterness works. We become angry because of some incident. David had saved Saul's reputation in fighting Goliath and defeating him for the cause of Jehovah God. But instead of being indebted to David, Saul became angry, suspicious, and then afraid.

> The next day an evil spirit from God came forcefully upon Saul. He was prophesying in his house, while David was playing the harp, as he usually did. Saul had a spear in his hand and he hurled it, saying to himself, "I'll pin David to the wall." But David eluded him twice.
>
> Saul was afraid of David, because the LORD was with David but had left Saul.
>
> —1 Samuel 18:10–12 NIV

Saul was afraid of David's competition for the kingdom, even though David had made no move toward that end. "So he sent

David away from him and gave him command over a thousand men, and David led the troops in their campaigns" (v. 13). And so Saul separated himself from David. Bitterness drives a hard wedge between even the best of friends.

> Saul said to David, "Here is my older daughter Merab. I will give her to you in marriage; only serve me bravely and fight the battles of the LORD." For Saul said to himself, "I will not raise a hand against him. Let the Philistines do that!"
>
> —1 Samuel 18:18 NIV

Bitterness eventually develops into scheming and plotting. We, like Saul, begin to manipulate events that are harmful to the other party. We arrive at the point where we would like to inflict all the vengeance possible on that person. If we can't, then maybe somebody else can. We just stand back and smile. I have heard of men and women who have divorced their spouses years ago and yet are still scheming to get their vengeance. They are still hoping that circumstances will destroy the former spouses in some form or fashion.

I went fishing one time with a man who had a responsible position in his corporation, but he wanted to be president. He informed me he was going to get that position, even if he had to stomp all over the current president. He did it, too. He destroyed the other man, and he became president. But within eighteen months, he had destroyed himself as well.

When bitterness becomes our master, we act foolishly and irrationally. Saul even tried to cast his javelin straight through his own son's heart when Jonathan questioned Saul's vengeance toward David.

> Saul's anger flared up at Jonathan and he said to him, "You son of a perverse and rebellious woman! Don't I know that you have sided with the son of Jesse to your own shame and to the shame of the mother who bore you? As long as the son of Jesse lives on this earth, neither you nor your king-

dom will be established. Now send and bring him to me, for
he must die!"

"Why should he be put to death? What has he done?"
Jonathan asked his father. But Saul hurled his spear at him
to kill him. Then Jonathan knew that his father intended to
kill David.

—1 Samuel 20:30–33 NIV

Bitter, angry parents often fling verbal javelins at their children,
shattering their children's self-esteem, their sense of belonging,
their sense of competency. Parents, impelled by bitter attitudes,
can destroy their children with bitter attitudes, just as Saul, in a
terrible fit of anger, tried to kill his own son. Saul argued that his
deadly vengeance against David was to protect the kingdom for
Jonathan, but Jonathan's probing question— "What has he done?"
—was more than Saul could handle.

Saul was destroyed by bitterness. What had begun as anger
developed into suspicion, fear, separation, insecurity, and vengeance. Saul's bitterness took control over his life. He seethed
with hatred toward David and sought to plot his murder. He behaved irrationally toward his son Jonathan. Saul's bitterness
spilled over into the lives of many innocent people and caused a
whole town of priests to be destroyed. Because of his bitterness,
Saul could no longer hear from God.

I believe Saul's bitterness began *before* David killed Goliath
and the townswomen taunted him with song. Saul's bitterness
began when Samuel told him that he had lost the kingdom: "the
LORD has torn the kingdom of Israel from you today and has given
it to one of your neighbors—to one better than you" (1 Sam. 15:28
NIV). Saul was bitter toward God, but since it's a little tough to
say so, Saul directed his bitterness toward David.

Saul paid an awful price for his bitterness toward a man God
favored. Every action Saul took against David was turned to
David's advantage. David became Israel's greatest king and most
beloved writer in the Old Testament. We can learn from David's

example. If we are targets of someone's bitterness, we can believe that God will do for us according to His will for our lives. What He did for David, He will do for us if we respond in His will.

Recovery From Bitterness

How can we recover from the effects of bitterness? *Recover* means "to get back" or "to regain." To recover, for example, from an illness means to get back or regain one's health. To recover, then, from bitterness means to get back or regain one's sweet or even temper.

When the root of bitterness has been growing a long time, its removal is not always instantaneous. A husband and wife who decide to get back together after having been separated can honestly confess to each other and repent of their sins, but full restoration comes gradually. The inner healing of the spirit sometimes takes longer than the physical healing of a broken arm or leg, for instance. We may have lived with damaged emotions for years, perhaps since childhood. As children of God, however, we have the capacity to forgive and to root out bitterness from our lives, even when it causes us temporary loss or humiliation. Unless we forgive, we cannot love.

GETTING MOTIVATED TO DEAL WITH BITTERNESS

How can we be motivated to forgive and to root out bitterness? We need to heed the call of our LORD Jesus Christ to forgive others. In the Sermon on the Mount, Jesus said:

> Be merciful, just as your Father also is merciful. Judge not, and you shall not be judged. Condemn not, and you shall not be condemned. Forgive, and you will be forgiven.
>
> —Luke 6:36–37 NKJV

Jesus did not mean that our heavenly Father will not forgive us if we haven't forgiven others. Jesus meant that if we don't emotionally release those who have wronged us, God will keep the pressure on us until we do, because He wants us to be reconciled.

When we fully comprehend God's forgiveness toward us, we simply cannot justify our holding anyone else accountable. Throughout Jesus' ministry, He consistently taught forgiveness. But not only did He proclaim it, He demonstrated it with His words from the cross: "Father, forgive them: for they do not know what they are doing" (Luke 23:34).

Because Christ dwells in us as believers, we have a spiritual nature to forgive. We received this new spiritual nature when we received Christ. Paul put it this way:

> I have been crucified with Christ and I no longer live, but Christ lives in me. The life I live in the body, I live by faith in the Son of God, who loved me and gave himself for me.
> —Galatians 2:20 NIV

The life we live is an expression of the life of Christ. We have the capacity to forgive when we have been deeply hurt because Christ within us is able to release through us forgiveness toward anyone. Just as Jesus forgave those who crucified Him, His life within us makes it possible for us to forgive all kinds of hurt and abuse, even in the most heinous forms. Because we are children of God, it is out of character for us to have unforgiving spirits and allow bitter roots to take hold.

Jesus never withheld forgiveness; so, too, should we never withhold forgiveness. By faith we can allow Christ to express that forgiveness through us toward others.

As we forgive one another, we release ourselves from bitterness. Emotional release enables physical and spiritual healing, and it frees us from bondage to other people. As we forgive one another, we enjoy reconciliation and the joy of healthy, loving relationships.

GETTING RID OF BITTERNESS

Getting rid of bitterness is a step-by-step process that leads toward emotional liberation and spiritual freedom. The steps are simple. As you are reading this, the face of someone toward whom you feel bitter has probably come to mind. Keep that person (or persons) in mind as you continue.

1. Make a list of the ways in which that person has offended you.
2. Make a list of your own faults.
3. Make a list of things you have done and for which God has forgiven you.
4. Ask God to help you view that person who has wronged you as a tool in the hand of God.
5. Ask God to forgive you for your bitterness toward that person.
6. Decide in your heart to assume total responsibility for your attitude
7. If you feel it is appropriate, and will not cause more problems than it solves, go to that person, confess your bitterness and ask for forgiveness. Remember, you are assuming the responsibility for your attitude; you are not trying to solicit repentance.

We have but two choices. We can allow bitterness to destroy us, or we can allow God to develop us into the persons He wants us to be. We must *choose* to view our circumstances and hurts as tools to be used by God to further develop our spiritual lives.

Questions for Personal Growth

1. Explain how bitterness can take control over your life and put you in bondage.

2. Give some examples of how bitterness can affect people physically.

Have you ever made yourself sick because of bitterness?

3. How does bitterness stain relationships?

Has your bitterness ever spilled into other people's lives? Explain.

4. Are you harboring slights or hurts that made you feel rejected, even though they may have occurred long ago?

Name the seven steps you can take to get rid of bitterness.

With one person in mind, then another, begin taking those steps.

Love does
no wrong to a neighbor.

Romans 13:10

Chapter 11

WHEN A BROTHER STUMBLES

I REMEMBER AS a young boy being required to take a battery of fitness tests at the school gym. There were ropes tied to the ceiling I had to climb, mats rolled out for tumbling exercises, parallel bars I had to walk with my hands, and the like.

I distinctly recall the balance beam drill. Remember that one? There was a long, skinny board about a half-inch thick we had to traverse backward and forward. We usually all sat around laughing and waiting for the inevitable slip to happen. Occasionally, some fellows would survive without a bobble, but even they eventually succumbed when boyish pride brought them back for a repeat attempt.

Sometimes I think we set up similar spiritual gymnastics for believers. Once saved, we Christians often unwittingly watch to see if our brothers can walk the straight and narrow way with nary a stumble or miscalculation.

It's an outlandish expectation, of course, since our pilgrimage on earth stretches over decades, and it is fraught at each daily turn with alluring, disorienting distractions and temptations, all capable of throwing us mildly or wildly off balance in our walk with the Savior.

Thus, when a brother stumbles on what Isaiah termed the "Highway of Holiness" (35:8), we should not be overly shocked. But we are. We shake our heads and wonder, *How could such a fine brother in Christ do such a shameful thing?*

Our reaction at this point is pivotal. Will we degenerate into useless gossip, pontificate with self-righteous judgment, stand silently by and see if the victim can somehow extricate himself from his fallen state, or will we extend the redemptive, rescuing arm of forgiveness?

Understanding why a believer falls into sin and grasping God's principles for helping him regain his upright walk will prepare us to be God's agents of reconciliation when a brother in Christ tumbles into transgression. (After all, at some point in time, each of us will be that brother.)

We All Sin

All believers are subject to stumbling. The Word of God gives three very distinct reasons why we are prone to do this.

SIN WITHIN US

First, the Scriptures reveal that the principle of sin is still within us. No matter how committed we are to Christ or how well we understand the dynamics of the Holy Spirit, an active sin principle crouches within our hearts. Paul describes the turmoil it can generate:

> For the good that I wish, I do not do; but I practice the very evil that I do not wish. But if I am doing the very thing I do not wish, I am no longer the one doing it, but sin which dwells in me. I find then the principle that evil is present in me, the one who wishes to do good.
>
> —Romans 7:19–21

Paul is not implying that sin is stronger than the power of the indwelling Spirit; he is making the point that it still exists and exerts a strong downward pull. Believers can resist and overcome the power of sin through the overcoming life of Christ, but there is a battle to be fought. For various reasons, we don't always share in the triumph that is ours through Calvary.

A FORMIDABLE FOE

Second, we stumble because we have an Enemy who seeks to devour, deter, and detour us. He is called by many names—the Prince of this Age, the Prince of the Power of the Air, the Adversary, the Accuser of the Brethren—namely, Satan.

He is always there to harass us, tempt us, put pressure on us, and cause us to fail. He is the Accuser of the Brethren, not of unbelievers. Since he has failed in blinding our eyes to the truth of salvation, he will try to do the next best thing, which is to render us ineffective, frustrated, discouraged, and defeated for fruitful living and service. Luring us into repeated sin and launching ongoing forays into our more vulnerable areas of personality or character are major tactics that work far too often and too effectively.

AN EVIL WORLD SYSTEM

Third, we live in an evil world system, thoroughly permeated by the vile spirit of the Evil One. Books, arts, government, education, business, and recreation are all part and parcel of what Paul referred to as "this present evil age" (Gal. 1:4). This *kosmos*, or fallen worldly system, is masterminded by Satan himself and confronts believers on every front of daily living. We cannot escape it. Though we are not *of* the world, we are certainly *in* it.

This triad of opposition is imposing enough to deal us toppling blows. Anyone who says, "I would never do this or that," is in reality setting the stage for an unflattering fall. This self-conferred standard of righteousness has lowered resistance in that particular area because the individual now rests on personal adequacy as a line of defense against a far superior foe. It's like guarding a fort with a water pistol.

Why We Stumble

The apostle Paul writes the biblical prescription for forgiving a fallen brother,

> Brethren, even if a man is caught in any trespass, you who are spiritual, restore such a one in a spirit of gentleness; each one looking to yourself, lest you too be tempted. Bear one another's burdens, and thus fulfill the law of Christ. For if anyone thinks he is something when he is nothing, he deceives himself. But let each one examine his own work, and then he will have reason for boasting in regard to himself alone, and not in regard to another. For each one shall bear his own load.
>
> —Galatians 6:1–5

Notice Paul's use of the phrase "caught in any trespass." The idea expressed in the original language is one of a surprise, blunder, or fault. In other words, when Christians sin, we do not go out deliberately seeking to transgress. In a moment of weakness or indifference, we yield to or are ensnared by evil. We didn't start the morning by planning to lie, cheat, or lust, but as we walked in harm's way, we were wounded.

Knowing the Bible and God's ways as well as His warnings against sin, why do we still take bites out of the forbidden fruit?

CARELESS LIVING

The first factor that comes to mind is that we become careless in the Christian life. We fail to take the Bible's admonition about living "sensibly, righteously and godly in the present age" (Titus 2:12) as seriously as we should. We become careless in living out the truths we know and forget to take the kinds of precautions we ordinarily should to avoid Satan's snares.

Paul urges us, "Therefore be careful how you walk, not as unwise men, but as wise, making the most of your time, because the days are evil" (Eph. 5:15–16). People who are careless in their work are apt to have accidents that could have been avoided. Christians who develop sloppy prayer and study habits and who do not cultivate disciplined character traits under the tutelage of the Holy Spirit are prime targets for a fiery shaft of the Enemy.

IGNORANCE

A second reason is ignorance. Sometimes we are unaware of sin and how Satan operates. Sometimes we are ignorant of ourselves and how we respond to certain temptations. Many times in the Scriptures, the writers declare, "Be not ignorant." One of the keys to Paul's overcoming life in the midst of such adversity was that he was not ignorant of Satan's schemes (2 Cor. 2:11). Neither should we be.

That is why we are continually challenged by God's Word to "press on toward the goal" (Phil. 3:14). We cannot be satisfied with what we already know. We need to learn so much truth to keep ourselves free from the yoke of sin that ever seeks to keep us in bondage.

DECEPTION

A third reason believers stumble is deception. Satan lures us as an angel of light. He is crafty, cunning, and stealthy. He can cleverly camouflage his murderous traps with appealing enticements. If he could trick Adam and Eve, who enjoyed perfect, wonderful communion with Creator God, why do we think we can outwit him?

PRIDE

A fourth common denominator in tripping us up is pride. When we rely on our self-sufficiency or our self-effort to combat sin, rest assured that our Waterloo is approaching. The "Big I" is no match for the Prince of Darkness. It's like an inflated balloon, just waiting to be deflated.

The Old Testament King Uzziah was a famous king and inventor. He was also a ferocious warrior who enjoyed great success as "long as he sought the Lord" (2 Chron. 26:5). He could have enjoyed a lifetime of victory if he hadn't enthroned the "Big I."

> Hence his fame spread afar, for he was marvelously helped until he was strong. But when he became strong, his heart was so proud that he acted corruptly, and he was unfaithful to the Lord his God, for he entered the temple of the Lord to burn incense on the altar of incense.
>
> —2 Chronicles 26:15–16

Uzziah was struck with leprosy by God for usurping the priests' functions, and his end was tragic. Pride will take us into places we have no business being, and it will not be long before we find ourselves overmatched. Remember Samson?

WEARINESS

A fifth agent in causing believers to sin is weariness. We become physically or emotionally drained and are simply too weak to hold up the shield of faith. Our hands drop to our sides, the shield lies on the ground, and we become stationary targets for the incoming missiles. Elijah was ripe for fear and discouragement when Jezebel threatened him. This was probably because he had just finished running a marathon, beating King Ahab's chariot to Jezreel (1 Kings 18:45–46). His fatigue diluted his resistance.

SATANIC ATTACK

A sixth factor is satanic attack. A satanic attack is a moment or a period of time of intense harassment from Satan, whereby individuals undergo absolutely arduous conflict with the powers of evil. They don't come only when we are close to sin. We can be praying, we can be working, we can be doing almost anything, and Satan can launch a major offensive against us.

Job encountered the blitzkrieg of Satan, losing his family and his possessions in a matter of hours. Though allowed by God, it nevertheless struck like a horde of locusts. That same intensity of persecution, still restrained and limited by almighty God, can swoop down on believers, especially if we are positioned in place of fruitful service in the kingdom.

PRESSURE

A seventh reason is pressure. We buckle under the stress of job, family, and society and look for an emotional release valve that we feel will help meet a particular need at the moment. The strains and burdens become too much, and we struggle to open an escape hatch, not really caring where it may lead so long as it steers us out from under the load.

I think all of us who are honest with one another will have to admit, "Yes, I have failed." We haven't violated just one of the commandments. The truth is, we probably have violated all of them in some fashion or to some degree.

When we look back in the Old Testament, it is interesting to see that God's first three kings were all great men. Saul began his rule as an anointed leader. David was a noble ruler as well as an accomplished musician and poet. Solomon's wisdom has not been equaled.

Despite their success, however, they all stumbled. Saul's kingdom was stripped away because of his pride. David caved in to lust, and Solomon's sagacity was tragically marred by idolatry.

Christians today, no matter how strong, wise, or respected, are subject to some public or private manifestation of the sin principle. Believers who sow to the flesh will reap the same corrupt harvest as nonbelievers do. The flesh lusts against the Spirit and the Spirit against the flesh.

Restoration

Once the believer has blundered into transgression, the body of Christ has a God-given responsibility to restore the offender: "Brethren, even if a man is caught in any trespass, you who are spiritual, restore such a one in a spirit of gentleness" (Gal. 6:1).

The Scripture states it as a command, not a suggestion. It does not say we are to forgive someone who sins after we have examined the situation to discover guilt or innocence or if the person has suffered long enough for the indiscretion. It says we are to be involved in the restoration process, regardless of the nature of the sin.

The Greek word translated "restore" has medical overtones. The word picture is one of a physician who resets the bones of a broken limb. It portrays the setting straight of what was once crooked.

We can readily see the spiritual adaptation of this idea. Forgiving someone who falls is God's method of extending His healing for the wounded soul, helping put back together the joy and intimacy of blessed fellowship with the Father. We are to be the earthly vehicles by which the transgressor's brokenness is mended.

Jesus said, "For God did not send the Son into the world to judge [condemn] the world, but that the world should be saved through Him" (John 3:17). If the righteous Son of God was not to judge, we certainly do not have the right to judge someone caught by the web of sin. We may be discerning and wise, learning all we can for our own protection in such a situation, but we are never justified in condemning a fallen brother.

In fact, it is the specific task of the one who is "spiritual" to initiate the restoration of the one "caught in any trespass." This does not imply someone who has a haughty, superior attitude. It refers to someone who is daily walking under the leadership and influence of the Holy Spirit, someone who has accepted Christ as Savior and longs to see His lordship extended over every area of life.

Such individuals should exhibit the beautiful fruit of the Spirit. We should be caring, loving, forgiving, patient, and compassionate, not judgmental or holier-than-thou. Our actions should always be toward the healing and the recovery of the grieved brother.

Herein, though, is where many of us falter. We do not want to be associated with the sin the brother has been entangled in. We want to keep our distance. But we cannot mend bones from afar, and we cannot restore a shattered life from a prayer closet. If we are acquainted with the one who has sinned, however flagrantly or subtly, and we have a genuine, abiding relationship with the Savior, living as best we can under the dictates of the Spirit, we have a mandate from on high to be a part of helping administer the forgiveness of God.

Often we plead ignorance: "I just don't know how to help restore my friend. I'm afraid if I get involved, I may botch it up and make matters worse." Such sentiment is understandable, but it certainly is not biblical. We have the Holy Spirit. We have the Word of God. We have the love of the Spirit. We have the mind of Christ.

Do we want to see our bruised companion made whole again? If we do, we must ask God how He is going to use us as part of the spiritual rehabilitation. God will forgive the offense, but He may choose us to help bring that pardon through the following process.

Six Principles for Restoration

I believe if we implement the six principles listed below we will be scripturally equipped to assist in the restoration of a brother who has been ambushed or captured by sin.

1. Our first priority is to help the person *recognize the failure and the consequences* of the decision. The problem is not one of a slight miscue or a momentary lapse; it is a sin in the sight of the Lord. No one can deal with sin unless it is first identified as such. More often than not, the individual knows he has sinned, but he still lives in the tentacles of sin because he has not admitted that his behavior was sinful. Like David, the person must be able to confess, "I have sinned, and done what is evil in Thy sight" (Ps 51:4).

2. We must help the person *acknowledge responsibility* for the sin. It is easy to blame sin on somebody else. But even if someone else has been a contributing factor, the individual is still

accountable. Helping a brother assume personal culpability for sinful actions is sometimes a difficult but necessary step. Saul's life was characterized by obvious irresponsibility for his actions. He was always trying to blame someone else. When Samuel confronted Saul over his failure to utterly destroy the Amalekites, Saul responded, "But the people took some of the spoil, sheep and oxen" (1 Sam. 15:21)

3. We need to lead the person to *confess and repent* of the sin. By repentance, I mean a change of mind that will result in a true sense of regret and remorse over the sin as well as a deliberate change of behavior. The inner person will realize the grief of disobedience before God and eternal conduct will be positively affected.

The one who confesses and forsakes sin is the one who will prosper. This is a crucial step in redeeming the person for holy, fruitful living. Forgiveness is abundantly available through the blood of Calvary, but until true repentance occurs, the individual's heart is not ready to receive its cleansing power.

4. The fourth principle is one of *restitution*. Someone who steals something needs to pay it back. Someone who criticizes others in public needs to go to them and ask for forgiveness. Restitution cannot be made for some sins, however. Genuine repentance and confession will have to suffice in those instances. For example, there is no restitution for destroying a person's moral purity. Asking for forgiveness can restore Christlike fellowship, but it can never fully restore what was lost.

5. A fifth concern in reaching out with forgiveness to the fallen brother is helping him receive *God's message* through his failure. Although God does not cause us to fail, He can teach us lessons that will keep us from wandering into similar harmful situations. His reproofs from such errors are invaluable: "He is on the path of life who heeds instruction, but he who forsakes reproof goes astray" (Prov. 10:17).

6. Finally, we need to guide the person who has fallen to *respond to God's chastisement with gratitude*. Granted, this is not easy, but when the person comprehends God's purpose in such

discipline—that he might "share His holiness" (Heb. 12:10)—he can by an act of his will thank the heavenly Father for His loving correction. David said, "It is good for me that I was afflicted, that I might learn Thy statutes. The law of Thy mouth is better to me than thousands of gold and silver pieces" (Ps. 119:71–72). David saw the benefits of God's dealing with him and responded gratefully. Bringing the person to this point protects against the insidious root of bitterness that can spring up in the aftermath of sin.

The Spirit of Restoration

Our success in attempting to restore a fallen brother or sister will be determined to a great degree by the spirit in which we go about it. And what is the spirit in which we are to restore a fellow Christian? The answer to that question is found in our text:

Brethren, even if a man is caught in any trespass, you who are spiritual, restore [let God use you to put back in place, to bring back, to reconcile] such a one in a spirit of gentleness; each one looking to yourself, lest you too be tempted.
—Galatians 6:1

First of all, Paul says we are to approach the guilty one in the *spirit of gentleness*. More than likely the person is already hurting and as fragile as thin glass. Human chastisement, judgment, and condemnation would only worsen the individual's plight. Understanding and acceptance—not agreement, but acceptance—are needed instead.

This does not mean we are ignoring the place of chastisement in the process of restoration. But it is God's responsibility, not ours, to chastise. We are to restore a brother or sister in the spirit of gentleness, not in anger or in a passionate desire to defend the faith.

The spirit of gentleness means we are sensitive to the needs and to the hurt of the fallen one. Often the hurt, the regret, and the personal disappointment are overwhelming.

Second, we are to forgive and restore with the *spirit of humility*, recognizing that what happened to the other person could also happen to us. As fellow believers, we must help the individual recognize the sin, assume responsibility for sinful actions, repent of the sin, make restitution when possible, receive gladly the message God is sending through the failure, and thank Him for His loving chastisement. But if we do it with harshness and arrogance, we will only further damage, rather than restore, the brother or sister. We must be careful about our own lives, examining ourselves, knowing that we, too, are vulnerable to all types of temptation and sin.

When Paul writes to the Galatians, "Bear one another's burdens, and thus fulfill the law of Christ" (6:2), he adds a third dimension to the restoration process—the *spirit of love*. Jesus said, "By this all men will know that you are My disciples, if you have love for one another" (John 13:35). Again He said, "This is My commandment, that you love one another, just as I have loved you" (John 15:12). In the Galatian passage, the word *burden* means a "heavy load." To bear someone's burden means we are willing to get under the load with him. We are willing to share the weight of her hurt as she walks through the valley of suffering or shame. We are willing to vicariously suffer what he is suffering, to some degree feel what she is feeling. And we are to do this with love.

Jesus' encounter with the woman caught in adultery reveals the folly of a condemning, rather than a loving, spirit.

"But Jesus went to the Mount of Olives. And early in the morning He came again into the temple, and all the people were coming to Him; and He sat down and began to teach them. And the scribes and the Pharisees brought a woman caught in adultery, and having set her in the midst, they said to Him, "Teacher, this woman has been caught in adultery, in the very act. Now in the Law Moses commanded us to stone such women; what then do You say?" And they were saying this, testing Him, in order that they might have grounds for accusing Him. But Jesus stooped down, and with His finger wrote on the ground.

—John 8:1–6

What did He write on the ground? Nobody really knows. Some say He wrote the Ten Commandments. Others say He wrote the seventh commandment.

The Scripture continues,

But when they persisted in asking Him, He straightened up, and said to them, "He who is without sin among you, let him be the first to throw a stone at her."

—John 8:7

Jesus did not say the woman was not guilty. He made no attempt to defend her actions before her pious, hypocritical accusers. He simply said, "He who is without sin let him cast the first stone."

They were not prepared to merely throw rocks at the adulteress. The Law said she was to be stoned to death, and they were prepared to do that. But when Jesus challenged anyone present who was not guilty to cast the first stone, one by one they departed from the scene. When confronted with the ugliness of their own sins, their shame and guilt drove them away.

If we are going to restore a brother or sister to Christ, we must come in the spirit of gentleness, humility, and love. The Scripture plainly warns, "For if anyone thinks he is something when he is nothing, he deceives himself" (Gal. 6:3). If we think we are morally or spiritually superior to the fallen brethren, not only are we badly deceived, but we are incapable of adequately restoring others. Restoration can never take place in a cavalier atmosphere.

We still have the indwelling principle of sin within us. We are all vulnerable. That is why each of us is to "examine his own work, and then he will have reason for boasting in regard to himself alone, and not in regard to another" (Gal. 6:4).

When Leaders Stumble

Particularly damaging to the body of Christ is the demise of a spiritual leader, one who has visible influence before the world. When a spiritual leader falls, it is a warning signal to the nation. It is a signal for self-examination; it is a call to personal soul-searching. After all, if a man of such stature can blunder, are we, too, not subject to the same failures?

Tragically, however, the second signal is one of self-deception. When a prominent spiritual figure falls, it relieves pressure from unbelievers living in sin and violating the law of God. They observe what happens and rationalize, "See there, I'm not so bad after all. This man studies the Bible and preaches to others. Look at him. If he can do that, I'm not so bad after all. What I do is no worse, and I don't even claim to be a Christian. If God loves him the way he is living, then He surely must love me, too." So, temporarily, they feel some relief from the guilt or conviction they may have frequently experienced before.

It should be clear from the Scriptures that we have a Christian responsibility to restore a fallen brother or sister. It should also be clear that this sensitive, delicate issue must be handled with great care, lest we greatly damage our witness to the unbelieving world.

Questions for Personal Growth

1. Identify and discuss three reasons the Bible gives for believers stumbling.

2. Despite knowing what the Bible says, believers are vulnerable to stumbling. Name seven factors that contribute to believers taking "bites out of the forbidden fruit."

3. Identify and discuss the six principles for restoration.

4. What is your responsibility toward a fallen brother or sister?

CONCLUSION

FORGIVENESS IS LIBERATING, but it is also sometimes painful. It is liberating because we are freed from the heavy load of guilt, bitterness, and anger we have harbored within. It is painful because it is difficult to have to face ourselves, God, and others with our failures. It seems easier to blame others and go on defending our position of being right, even though we continue to hurt. But the poison of an unforgiving spirit that permeates our entire lives, separating us from God and friends, can never be adequately defended. It is devastating to our spiritual and emotional well-being and to our physical health.

Has there ever been a time in your life when you came to grips with your rebellion against God? acknowledged your need of His forgiveness, and trusted Christ as your personal Savior? Are you keeping short accounts with Him? That is, when you disobey Him, do you confess it immediately and walk on in His Spirit, enjoying your fellowship with Him?

Are you still unable to forgive someone who hurt you deeply and you still bear the scars? How long will you remain a prisoner to your own unforgiving spirit? You have within you the power to forgive, to be healed, and to be set free to live your life to the fullest.

Before you close the cover of this book, forgive the one who has hurt you even as your heavenly Father has forgiven you, and *be really free!*

Appendix A

THE UNPARDONABLE SIN

THROUGH THE YEARS I have talked with many Christians and non-Christians who were afraid they had committed "the unpardonable sin." Just about everyone had a different understanding of exactly what that was. But they all agreed on one thing: They were guilty and felt that theirs was a hopeless situation.

Hundreds of verses in the Bible promise the forgiveness of our sins, but only one passage refers to an unforgivable sin. Let's examine the passage to gain insight into what Jesus meant when He referred to a sin that cannot be forgiven.

Jesus had healed a demon-possessed man who was blind and dumb, "so that the dumb man spoke and saw" (Matt. 12:22). The multitudes following Jesus began to say, "This man cannot be the Son of David, can he?" The implication was that they believed He was the son of David, in other words, the Messiah.

On the other hand, the Pharisees accused Jesus of casting out demons by Beelzebul, the ruler of the demons, Jesus' response to their accusation led Him to conclude,

Therefore I say to you, any sin and blasphemy shall be forgiven men, but blasphemy against the Spirit shall not be forgiven. And whoever shall speak a word against the Son of Man, it shall be forgiven him; but whosoever shall speak against the Holy Spirit, it shall not be forgiven him, either in this age, or in the age to come.

—Matthew 12:31–32

The term *blasphemy* may be defined "defiant irreverence." We would apply the term to such sins as cursing God or willfully degrading things considered holy. In this passage the term refers to the declaration of the Pharisees who had witnessed undeniable evidence that our Lord was performing miracles in the power of the Holy Spirit. Yet they attributed the miracles to Satan. In the face of irrefutable evidence they ascribed the work of the Holy Spirit to that of Satan.

I agree with a host of biblical scholars that this unique circumstance cannot be duplicated today. The Pharisees had seen proof after proof that Christ was who He claimed to be. They could not escape the fact that what He was doing was supernatural in nature. But instead of acknowledging what I believe they knew in their hearts was true, they attributed the supernatural power to that of Satan instead of the Holy Spirit. That, in a sense, was the last straw.

Christ is not in the world as He was then. Although the Holy Spirit is still accomplishing supernatural things through His servants, they are merely representatives of the King. The circumstances of Matthew 12 make it impossible for this sin to take place today. This incident, I might add, is the only one in which a sin is declared unforgivable. The Bible clearly states, "For whoever will call upon the name of the Lord will be saved" (Rom. 10:13). No invitation to salvation carries with it an exception clause, "unless you have committed the unpardonable sin."

No matter how evil our sins, there is pardon for them. God forgave David for his adultery, dishonesty, and murder (2 Sam. 12:13; Ps. 51). He forgave the prodigal for his "loose living." Simon Peter's triple denial of our Lord accompanied by profanity was forgiven (Matt. 26:74–75). The apostle Paul was forgiven of his preconversion merciless persecution of Christians (Acts 9:1).

Although there is no unpardonable sin, there is an unpardonable state—the state of unbelief. There is no pardon for a person who dies in unbelief. The Bible refers to this in terms of having a hard heart. The hardening of the heart is not a one-time act. It is the result of a gradual progression in which sin and the conviction of the Holy Spirit are ignored. Time is a major factor. Grieving the Spirit can progress to resisting the Spirit, which can progress to quenching the Spirit, which (unless there is repentance toward God) can ultimately result in the hardening of the heart against God (Heb. 3:7–8). The hardened heart has no desire for the things of God. Some interpret this to be the unpardonable sin. But if you have any desire in your heart for God, as expressed through concern that you may have committed some sort of unpardonable sin, you do not have a hardened heart.

Appendix B

STEPS TO FORGIVING OTHERS

THE FOLLOWING IS included to facilitate personal application of chapter 8.

1. Understand that forgiveness is not
   - Justifying, understanding, or explaining why the person acted toward you as he or she did.
   - Just forgetting about the offense and trusting time to take care of it.
   - Asking God to forgive the person who hurt you.
   - Asking God to forgive you for being angry or resentful against the person who offended you.
   - Denying that you were really hurt; after all there are others who have suffered more.
2. Understand that it is often unwise to forgive face to face. This tends to make the other person feel "put down" and make you look holier-than-thou.
3. Select a time and place when you can be alone for a season of time.
4. Pray and ask the Holy Spirit to bring to your mind all the people you need to forgive and the events you need to forgive them for.

5. Make a list of everything the Holy Spirit brings to your mind, even if it seems trivial to you. (Do not rush through this step; allow the Holy Spirit all the time He needs to speak to you.)

6. Take two chairs and arrange them facing each other. Seat yourself in one of the chairs.

7. Imagine that the first person on your list is sitting in the other chair. Disclose everything you can remember that the person has done to hurt you. Do not hold back the tears or the emotions that accompany the confessions.

8. *Choose by an act of your will to forgive that person once and for all time.* You may not feel like being forgiving. That's all right. Just do it and the feelings will follow. God will take care of that. Do not doubt what you have done is real and valid.

9. Release the person from the debt you feel is owed you for the offense. Say, "You are free and forgiven."

10. If the person is still a part of your life, now is a good time to accept the individual without wanting to change aspects of personality or behavior.

11. Thank the Lord for using each person as a tool in your life to deepen your insight into His grace and conforming you to the image of His Son.

12. Pray. This is a suggested prayer to pray as you "talk" to each person:

    Because I am forgiven and accepted by Christ, I can now forgive and accept you, _____, unconditionally in Christ. I choose now to forgive you, _____, no matter what you did to me. I release you from the hurts (take time to name the hurts), and you are no longer accountable to me for them. You are free.

13. When you have finished praying through the hurts you have suffered, pray this prayer of faith:

    Lord Jesus, by faith, I receive Your unconditional love and acceptance in the place of this hurt, and I trust You to meet all my needs. I take authority over the Enemy, and in the name of Jesus, I take back the ground I have allowed Satan to gain in my life because of my attitude toward _____ _____. Right now I give this ground back to the Lord Jesus Christ to whom it rightfully belongs.